Drone Law and Policy

DRONE LAW AND POLICY

INTEGRATION INTO THE LEGAL ORDER OF CIVIL AVIATION

RONALD SCHNITKER AND DICK VAN HET KAAR

international publishing

Published, sold and distributed by Eleven International Publishing
P.O. Box 85576
2508 CG The Hague
The Netherlands
Tel.: +31 70 33 070 33
Fax: +31 70 33 070 30
e-mail: sales@elevenpub.nl
www.elevenpub.com

Sold and distributed in USA and Canada
Independent Publishers Group
814 N. Franklin Street
Chicago, IL 60610
USA
Order Placement: (800) 888-4741
Fax: (312) 337-5985
orders@ipgbook.com
www.ipgbook.com

Eleven International Publishing is an imprint of Boom uitgevers Den Haag.

ISBN 978-94-6236-198-0
ISBN 978-90-8974-514-9 (E-book)

© 2021 Ronald Schnitker and Dick van het Kaar | Eleven International Publishing

This publication is protected by international copyright law.
All rights reserved. No part of this publication may be reproduced, stored in a retrieval system, or transmitted in any form or by any means, electronic, mechanical, photocopying, recording or otherwise, without the prior permission of the publisher.

TABLE OF CONTENTS

Acronyms and Abbreviations	vii
Introduction	xi

Chapter 1 The Development of Drones — 1
- 1.1 History of Drones — 1
- 1.2 Terminology — 10
- 1.3 Applications — 16

Chapter 2 Legal Basis for Drone Operations — 33
- 2.1 Introduction — 33
- 2.2 Outline of ICAO UAS Regulatory Framework — 37
- 2.3 EASA Rule-Making Process on Drones — 50
- 2.4 FAA Drone Rules and Access to the National Airspace System — 96
- 2.5 Future Considerations — 125

Chapter 3 Commercial, Private and Sports Use — 133
- 3.1 Commercial Drone Utilization — 133
- 3.2 Private Drone Use — 141
- 3.3 Drones in Sports — 148

Chapter 4 Integration into Airspace — 155
- 4.1 Access to Airspace — 155
- 4.2 Safe Integration of Drones into the Single European Sky — 163
- 4.3 RPAS Integration Alongside Manned Aviation — 170
- 4.4 U-Space — 185
- 4.5 Preserving Airspace Access — 219

Chapter 5 Safety Requirements in UAS Operations — 229
- 5.1 Introduction — 229
- 5.2 Remote Pilot Requirements — 230
- 5.3 UAS Operator Requirements — 237
- 5.4 Technical Requirements — 244
- 5.5 Operational Use — 254

Chapter 6 Privacy, Data Protection and Security — 269
- 6.1 Privacy and Data Protection — 269

Table of Contents

    6.2   Privacy and Security   305

Summary   319

About the Authors   353

Index   355

Acronyms and Abbreviations

ACAS	Airborne Collision Avoidance System
ADS-B	Automatic Dependent Surveillance-Broadcast
AFIS	Aerodrome Flight Information Service
AFMU	Airspace Flow Management Unit
AFUA	Advanced Flexible Use of Airspace
AGL	Above Ground Level
AIM	Aeronautical Information Management
AIMP	Aeronautical Information Management Provider
AIS	Aeronautical Information Service
AMC	Airspace Management Cell
ANS	Air Navigation Service
ANSP	Air Navigation Service Provider
APIS	Autonomous Pollination & Imaging System
ASBU	Aviation System Block Upgrade
ASD	Aerospace and Defence Industries Association of Europe
ATC	Air Traffic Control
ATM	Air Traffic Management
ATPL	Air Transport Pilot Licence
ATZ	Aerodrome Traffic Zone
BDL	Bundesverband der Deutschen Luftverkehrswirtschaft
BMVI	Bundesministerium für Verkehr und digitale Infrastruktur
BRLOS	Beyond Radio Line of Sight
BVLOS	Beyond Visual Line of Sight
C2	Command and Control Link
CAA	Civil Aviation (Aeronautics) Authority
CAV	Cargo Air Vehicle
CBARS	Carrier-Based Aerial-Refueling System
CE Marking	Conformité Européenne marking
CFMU	Central Flow Management Unit
CFR	Code of Federal Regulations
CIA	Central Intelligence Agency
CLASS	Clear Air Situation for UAS
CNS	Communications, Navigation, Surveillance
CofA	Certificate of Airworthiness
COM	Communications Technology
CONOPS	Concept of Operations
CRM	Crew Resource Management
CS	Certification Specification
CTR	Control Zone
CU	Control Unit
D&A/DAA	Detect and Avoid
DLR	Deutsches Zentrum für Luft- und Raumfahrt e.V.
DPD	Data Protection Directive
DPIA	Data Protection Impact Assessment
DTM	Drone Traffic Management

Acronyms and Abbreviations

EAS	European Air Sports
EASA	European Union Aviation Safety Agency
EC	European Commission
ECA	European Cockpit Association
ECAC	European Civil Aviation Conference
ECHR	European Convention on Human Rights
EDA	European Defence Agency
EDPB	European Data Protection Board
EDPS	European Data Protection Supervisor
EEZ	Exclusive Economic Zone
EIP-SCC	European Innovation Partnership on Smart Cities and Communities
EREA	European Research Establishments in Aeronautics
ERSG	European RPAS Steering Group
ESA	European Space Agency
EU	European Union
EUROCAE	European Organization for Civil Aviation Equipment
EVLOS	Extended Visual Line of Sight
FAA	Federal Aviation Administration
FAI	Fédération Aéronautique Internationale
FAR	Federal Aviation Regulations
FIMS	Flight Information Management System
FIS	Flight Information Service
FL	Flight Level
FLARM	Flight Alarm
FPV	First-Person View
FRN	Federal Register Notice
FUA	Flexible Use of Airspace
GA	General Aviation
GANP	Global Air Navigation Plan
GCS	Ground Control Station
GDPR	General Data Protection Regulation
GIS	Geographic Information System
GUTMA	Global UTM Association
HALE	High-Altitude Long Endurance
HAPS	High-Altitude Pseudo Satellite
IASTA	International Air Services Transit Agreement
IATA	International Air Transport Agreement
ICAO	International Civil Aviation Organization
IFR	Instrument Flight Rules
IMC	Instrument Meteorological Conditions
ITU	International Telecommunication Union
JARUS	Joint Authorities on Rulemaking for Unmanned Systems
LAANC	Low Altitude Authorization and Notification Capability
LAPL	Light Aircraft Pilot Licence
LBA	Luftfahrt Bundesamt
LDZ	Limited-Drone Zone
LTE	Long-Term Evolution
MAA	Military Aviation Authority
MALE	Medium-Altitude Long Endurance
MASPS	Minimum Aviation System Performance Standards
MAV	Micro Air Vehicle

MTOM	Maximum Take-off Mass
NAC	National Aero Club
NAMC	National Airspace Management Cell
NASA	National Aeronautics and Space Administration
NDZ	No-Drone Zone
NOAA	National Oceanic and Atmospheric Administration
NOTAM	Notice to Airmen
OA	Operation Authorization
PANS	Procedures for Air Navigation Services
PBN	Performance-Based Navigation
PDRA	Predefined Risk Assessment
PIA	Privacy Impact Assessment
QE	Qualified Entity
RAE	Royal Aircraft Establishment
RAF	Royal Air Force
RATO	Rocket-Assisted Take-off
RCC	Rescue Coordination Centre
RLOS	Radio Line of Sight
RNP	Required Navigation Performance
ROC	RPAS Operator Certificate
RPA	Remotely Piloted Aircraft
RPA-L	Remotely Piloted Aircraft Light
RPAS	Remotely Piloted Aircraft System
RPS	Remote Pilot Station
SARPs	Standards and Recommended Practices
SERA	Standardized European Rules of the Air
SESAR	Single European Sky ATM Research
SID	Standard Instrument Departure
SIM	Subscriber Identification Module
SJU	SESAR Joint Undertaking
SORA	Specific Operations Risk Assessment
SRA	Strategic Risk Assessment
STAR	Standard Terminal Arrival Route
STM	Space Traffic Management
sUAS	Small Unmanned Aircraft System
SVS	Synthetic Vision System
SWIM	System Wide Information Management
TEC	Treaty establishing the European Community
TFEU	Treaty on the Functioning of the European Union
TMA	Terminal Control Area/Terminal Manoeuvring Area
TMZ	Transponder Mandatory Zone
TORUS	Targeted Observation by Radars and UAS Supercells
TSA	Transportation Security Administration
UA	Unmanned Aircraft
UAM	Urban Air Mobility
UAS	Unmanned Aircraft System
UASSG	Unmanned Aircraft Systems Study Group
UAV	Unmanned Aerial Vehicle
UDHR	Universal Declaration on Human Rights
UPP	UTM Pilot Program
USAAF	United States Army Air Force

Acronyms and Abbreviations

USAF	United States Air Force
USFM	UAS Facility Map
USS	UAS Service Suppliers
USSP	U-space Service Provider
UTM	UAS Traffic Management
UTMS	UAS Traffic Management System
UVR	UAS Volume Reservation
UVSI	Unmanned Vehicle Systems International
VARM	Visual Air Risk Mitigation
VFR	Visual Flight Rules
VHL	Very High Level
VLL	Very Low Level
VLOS	Visual Line of Sight
VMC	Visual Meteorological Conditions
WRC	World Radiocommunication Conference

Introduction

The history of manned flight is rather short, but the idea that man can bridge distances, like birds, through the air, is as old as mankind itself. In fact, not very long ago, on 17 December 1903, at Kill Devil Hills, south of Kitty Hawk, North Carolina, the Wright brothers, ordinary men but with an extraordinary dream, managed to take the Wright Flyer into the air and successfully completed the first engine-powered, heavier-than-air controlled flight. This was unmistakably a magnificent and memorable achievement.

Since then, aviation has advanced more rapidly than almost any other means of transportation. There is no other means of transport than the aircraft, where speed has increased so incredibly in such a short period. While traffic moving on the Earth's surface, such as trains and ships, took decades to double their highest possible speed, aircraft were able to achieve a seventeen-fold increase on their speeds in less than thirty years. On 12 November 1906, the Brazilian Alberto Santos-Dumont, resident in France and famous for his experiments with small airships and balloons, made the first observed flight, longer than 25 m, in European airspace at Paris with a speed of approximately 41 km per hour. Actually, that was the first official world speed record.[1] In October 1934, an Italian, Francesco Agello, achieved a speed average of over 709 km per hour with a Macchi-Castoldi M.C.72 experimental piston-powered seaplane.[2]

The advent of the aircraft added a new dimension to transport, which could no longer be contained within strictly national confines. Civil air traffic became a more international business. Random cross-border flying increased correspondingly. In fact, international flight demonstrations and aerial record breaking became everyday practice.

Pioneering flights, proliferation of aeronautical competitions and increasingly rapid technological advances, all confirmed the spectacular beginning of the modern aviation era. Owing to the increased speed and extended range of aircraft, civil air travel changed social life. Driven by constantly improving aviation technology, especially during World War I and the aviation's Golden Age (1918-1939), further boosted by the tremendous increase in aircraft development and production during and in the wake of World War II, air transport became a major global industry. Today, civil air transport is globally recognized as one of the most convenient, fastest and safest modes of travel. Aviation has evolved from executive to mass transport and makes it possible for mankind to

---

1   www.fai.org/news/12-november-1906-first-flight-santos-dumont.
2   The Macchi M.C.72, with its nine-and-a-half-metrewingspan and three tonnes of weight, built by the Italian aircraft company Macchi Aeronautica, had its moment of glory in 1934, when it set the world speed record at 709,209 km/h, which still stands today in the propeller-driven seaplane category (www.italianways.com/the-macchi-castoldi-m-c-72/).

consider travelling across the world in a new way, in terms of time rather than great distances.

However, since the post-war modernization and globalization of civil aviation, the entire aerospace industry is currently at a major technological tipping point represented by unmanned aircraft. The development of remotely piloted aircraft (RPA), also known as unmanned aircraft (UA) or unmanned aerial vehicles (UAVs), or colloquially known as drones, and their associated systems, although there is some nuanced difference, has opened a promising new chapter in the history of aerospace, albeit combined airspace use with manned aircraft will face significant challenges.

Drones create opportunities beyond traditional markets, provide ground-breaking solutions and simplify everyday processes. Actually, drones may be the ultimate in disruptive technology. Drone technology, a modern section within the aerospace environment, could apply in almost all societal sectors. However, drones are difficult to control because applicable regulations are lagging behind technological progress and volume growth. Therefore, as both traditional manned aviation and unmanned air mobility inevitably continue to expand, tremendous efforts are required to keep air transportation, of any modality, safe and sustainable.

Initiated by the military to adopt and use these systems, the civil and commercial sector of aviation soon has come to the conclusion that the use of drones would become limitless. Drones, a catch-all term representing a vast variety of remotely controlled UA, and having a military connotation, come in many sizes and shapes, some of which are extremely small like the size of an insect, while others are nearly as big as a standard commercial aircraft.

The societal impact of drones can be found not only in many different industries but also in the domestic garages of hobbyists. The great importance of drone operations lies in the provision of assistance regarding a wide spectrum of utility, where manned flight poses a considerable risk. Moreover, they can perform important tasks better, faster, cheaper and with less risk than other transportation systems.

Exploitation of drones in private, military and public domains, has not only grown considerably in recent years, and repeatedly demonstrated major potential for diverse applications, but has also increased the demand for access to non-segregated airspace. Drones have one thing in common: they all are unmanned, implying not controlled by a person on board the aerial vehicle. Since these UAVs are generally qualified as aircraft, they plainly do fall under the scope of (international) air law, regulating the safe operation of these vehicles.

INTRODUCTION

To guide the use of ubiquitous drones in the right direction, adequate and harmonized international regulation is a prerequisite. To make this relatively novel activity work in a safe and efficient way, air law ought to modify or accommodate existing rules or establish new coordinated rules.[3] The safe and efficient co-existence of traditional manned aircraft and UA in the airspace is one of the major challenges in global aviation for the next decades.

While during the past years a number of Civil Aviation Authorities (CAAs) have implemented various domestic regulations on UA to safely integrate into national airspace, the absence of a common set of international rules applicable to UA, apart from the existing international regulation represented by Article 8 of the 1944 Convention on International Civil Aviation (hereinafter referred to as the Chicago Convention), was emphatically felt.

Article 8 of the Chicago Convention, 1944:

> Pilotless aircraft.
> No aircraft capable of being flown without a pilot shall be flown without a pilot over the territory of a contracting State without special authorization by that State and in accordance with the terms of such authorization. Each contracting State undertakes to insure that the flight of such aircraft without a pilot in regions open to civil aircraft shall be so controlled as to obviate danger to civil aircraft.

ICAO states that all UA, whether remotely piloted, fully autonomous or a combination of both, are subject to Article 8 on pilotless aircraft of the Chicago Convention (Doc 7300).[4]

Actually, the legal description of pilotless aircraft has been established at an earlier stage. Because of the Protocol of 15 June 1929 to amend the Convention Relating to the Regulation of Aerial Navigation (Paris Convention of 13 October 1919), pilotless aircraft were considered part of the legal framework for international civil aviation.

Article 15, 1919 Paris Convention:

> Every aircraft of a contracting State has the right to cross the air space of another State without landing. In this case it shall follow the route fixed by the State over which the flight takes place. However, for reasons of general security it will be obliged to land if ordered to do so by means of the signals provided in Annex D.

---

3 Scott, B.I. (Ed.), *The Law of Unmanned Aircraft Systems: An Introduction to the Current and Future Regulation under National, Regional and International Law*, Aviation Law and Policy Series, Alphen aan den Rijn: Kluwer Law International, 2016, with a Foreword by Pablo Mendes de Leon, Director of the International Institute of Air and Space Law, Leiden University.
4 ICAO Manual on Remotely Piloted Aircraft Systems (RPAS) Doc 10019 AN/507, First Edition 2015, 1.1.

INTRODUCTION

The Protocol modified Article 15 of the 1919 Paris Convention, in pertinent part as follows:

> No aircraft of a contracting State capable of being flown without a pilot shall, except by special authorization, fly without a pilot over the territory of another contracting State.[5]

When the Chicago Convention superseded the 1919 Paris Convention and the 1928 Havana Convention (Pan-American or Inter-American Convention on Commercial Aviation) in 1944, Article 8 of the Chicago Convention also replaced the modified Article 15.[6]

The original text of Annex 7 to the Chicago Convention defined 'aircraft' as "any machine that can derive support in the atmosphere from the reactions of the air". This definition was adapted from the French language text of the definition of 'aircraft' in the 1919 Paris Convention: *"Le mot aéronef désigne tout appareil pouvant se soutenir dans l'atmosphere grâce aux reactions de l'air."*[7]

In 1967, amendments to Annex 7 included a new, contemporary definition of 'aircraft' as "any machine that can derive support in the atmosphere from the reactions of the air other than the reactions of the air against the Earth's surface", to exclude hovercraft from its scope. Today, Annex 7 (International Standards 2. Classification of aircraft) makes it clear that RPA systems are simply one type of unmanned aircraft systems (UAS) and that all unmanned (pilotless) aircraft, whether remotely piloted, fully or semi-autonomous, or combinations thereof, are subject to the provisions of Article 8 of the Chicago Convention.[8]

ICAO RPAS Concept of Operations (CONOPS), Introduction:

> Any aircraft intended to be flown without a pilot on board is referred to in the Chicago Convention and amended by the ICAO Assembly as 'pilotless aircraft'. Today we call these aircraft 'unmanned' rather than 'pilotless'. Unmanned aircraft include a broad spectrum from meteorological balloons that fly free to highly complex aircraft piloted from remote locations by licensed aviation professionals. The latter are part of the category referred to as 'remotely piloted aircraft' that operate as part of a system, a remotely piloted aircraft system (RPAS).

---

5 'Convention Relating to the Regulation of Aerial Navigation', *Journal of Air Law and Commerce* 94, 1930.
6 Chicago Convention Art. 80 Paris and Habana Conventions.
7 *See* Diederiks-Verschoor, I.H.Ph., Butler, M.A. (Legal adviser), *An Introduction to Air Law*, Eighth Revised Edition, Alphen aan den Rijn: Kluwer Law International, 2006, p. 5.
8 Descriptions and definitions of unmanned aircraft systems are included in Chapter 1 of this book under 1.2 Terminology. *See also* Bestaoui Sebbane, Y., *Intelligent Autonomy of UAVs: Advanced Missions and Future Use*, Boca Raton: CRC Press Taylor & Francis Group, 2018, p. 3.

Thus, although RPA are aircraft, as a consequence of the special authorization requirement stated in Article 8 of the Chicago Convention, their operation is not considered within the scope of the special permission or other authorization for scheduled international air services under Article 6 of the Chicago Convention, which typically takes the form of a reciprocal exchange of air traffic rights between states by means of a bilateral air transport agreement. The special authorization required for overflight of the territory of another state by pilotless aircraft under Article 8 is essentially analogous to the authorization by special agreement or otherwise required for overflight of or landing in the territory of another state by so-called state aircraft under Article 3 of the Chicago Convention.

The Chicago Convention provides an overarching as well as underpinning legal framework to international civil aviation, in particular to manned aircraft operations. In fact, it is the world's civil aviation constitution. Thus, civil UAS, to the extent that they are qualified as aircraft, may fall under the scope of the Chicago Convention as long as they meet the international criterion, that is, where its provisions refer to the international air navigation regime.

However, the requirement for a comprehensive regulatory framework at an international level, including technical and performance specifications and standards, certification, licensing, third-party liability and insurance, to develop the market of UAS on a global scale, was to be considered as highly needed.

With respect to UAS technical and performance specifications and standards, it was determined, during an exploratory meeting of ICAO on 23 and 24 May 2006 at Montreal, that only a portion was needed to become ICAO Standards and Recommended Practices (SARPs) and at the same time that ICAO was considered not to be the most appropriate organization to undertake the effort to establish such specifications. The objective of the meeting was to determine the potential role of ICAO in UAS regulatory development work.

ICAO should coordinate the development of a strategic guidance document to be used as the basis for development of regulations by the various Member States and organizations. In supporting the harmonization of terms, strategies and principles regarding the UAS regulatory framework, the ICAO Unmanned Aircraft Systems Study Group (UASSG) has been active since its establishment in January 2007, in Florida.

As the high-level focal point for interoperability within ICAO, the UASSG serves to develop a regulatory concept and coordinate the development of UAS SARPs with supporting Procedures for Air Navigation Services (PANS) and guidance material (GM) contained in the Manual on Remotely Piloted Aircraft Systems (RPAS), published in March 2015. The purpose of this document is to provide guidance on technical and operational issues applicable to the integration of UA into non-segregated airspace and aerodromes throughout the world, which, however, will be a lengthy process to accomplish.

ICAO differentiates UA and RPA as follows: UA include free flying balloons, fully automatic and/or autonomous aircraft and drones, while RPA are subject to airspace/aerodrome integration and require control, which means control in real time, provided by a licensed remote pilot. In terms of the ICAO terminology, an RPA or RPAS cannot, by definition, include fully autonomous systems, whereas UA or UAS may include or exclude them.

Although the common term drone or UA is used throughout this book as it is recognized on a worldwide scale, the terminology in the different domains of UA has been followed. This means that the terms drone and UA are used as well as abbreviations of derived types and associated systems. For the purpose of uniformity and to reflect the terminology used by ICAO, this book refers to UA systems as UAS, to include all types of unmanned systems, such as RPAS, however, excluding model aircraft used for hobby or recreational purposes. In spite of that, recreational drone operations often fall under national model flying regulations or codes of conduct.

ICAO contributes to the development of technical specifications and to identify communication requirements for UAS operations so that they can be integrated in non-segregated airspace and at aerodromes alongside traditional manned aircraft operations in a safe, harmonized and seamless way. To inform states on future integration of UAS in non-segregated airspace and aerodromes as well as to consider the fundamental differences between manned and UA in these operating areas, ICAO published in 2011 Circular 328 AN/190.

As far as the European Union Aviation Safety Agency (EASA) is concerned, common rules on drones have been published or are in the process of being published to ensure drone operations across Europe are safe, secure and sustainable. These rules will, among others, assist in protecting the safety and the privacy of EU citizens while enabling the free circulation of drones as well as a level playing field within the European Union.

In its Opinion No. 01/2018, entitled 'Introduction of a regulatory framework for the operation of UA systems operations in the Open and Specific categories', EASA states that in accordance with the proposed new Basic Regulation (Regulation (EU) 2018/1139),[9] for which a political agreement between the Council, the European Commission and the European Parliament was reached on 22 December 2017, the competence of the European Union, since UA also operate in the airspace alongside

---

9   Regulation (EU) 2018/1139 of the European Parliament and of the Council of 4 July 2018 on common rules in the field of civil aviation and establishing a European Union Aviation Agency, and amending Regulations (EC) No. 2111/2005, (EC) No. 1008/2008, (EU) No. 996/2010, (EU) No. 376/2014 and Directives 2014/30/EU and 2014/53/EU of the European Parliament and of the Council, and repealing Regulations (EC) No. 552/2004 and (EC) No. 216/2008 of the European Parliament and of the Council and Council Regulation (EEC) No. 3922/91, OJ L 212/1, 22 August 2018.

traditional manned aircraft, has been extended to cover the regulation of all civil UAS, regardless of their respective maximum take-off mass (MTOM).

The objective of EASA Opinion No. 01/2018 is to create a new regulatory framework that defines measures to mitigate the risk of operations in the Open category, by means of a combination of limitations, operational rules, requirements for the competency of the remote pilot and technical requirements for UAS, such that the UAS operator may conduct the operation without prior authorization by the competent authority, or without submitting a declaration; risk mitigation with respect to the Specific category, through a system that includes a risk assessment being conducted by the UAS operator before starting an operation, or an operator complying with a standard scenario, or an operator holding a certificate with privileges.[10]

The proposed regulations will provide flexibility to EU Member States, mainly by allowing them to create zones within their territories where the use of UAS would be prohibited, limited or, in contrast, facilitated.

On 11 June 2019, common European rules on drones, Commission Delegated Regulation (EU) 2019/945 and Commission Implementing Regulation (EU) No. 2019/947 (EU UAS Regulation), have been adopted to set the framework for the safe operation of drones in European skies, which means the airspace of EU and EASA Member States.

By adopting a risk-based approach, and as such, without distinguishing between recreational and commercial drone activities, these two new EU Regulations build the basic structure of the total EU regulatory regime on UA operations, including various applicable rules in different legal documents referred to in these EU Regulations, together with the pending (2021) EU Regulation on a high-level regulatory framework for the U-space.

The rules will, among others, help to protect the safety and privacy of EU citizens while enabling the free circulation of drones and a level playing field within the European Union. Taking into consideration the specific characteristics of UAS operations, they should be as safe as those in manned aviation. A uniform implementation of and compliance with rules and procedures should apply to operators, including remote pilots, of UA and UAS, as well as for the operations of such UA and UAS.

The rules and procedures applicable to UAS operations should be proportionate to the nature and risk of the operation or activity and adapted to the operational characteristics of the UA concerned, and the characteristics of the environment of operations, such as the population density, surface features and the presence of buildings.

---

10 ICAO Circular 328 AN/190: Operator. A person, organization or enterprise engaged in or offering to engage in an aircraft operation. *See also* Commission Delegated Regulation (EU) 2019/945 of 12 March 2019 on unmanned aircraft systems and on third-country operators of unmanned aircraft systems, *OJ* L152/1, 11 June 2019, Definitions (4): 'unmanned aircraft system operator' ('UAS operator') means any legal or natural person operating or intending to operate one or more UAS.

Introduction

> Europe will be the first region in the world to have a comprehensive set of rules ensuring safe, secure and sustainable operations of drones both, for commercial and recreational activities. Common rules will help foster investment, innovation and growth in this promising sector. (Patrick Ky, Executive Director EASA, June 2019)

The new rules include technical as well as operational requirements for drones. On the one hand, they define the capabilities a drone must have to be flown safely. For instance, new drones will have to be individually identifiable, allowing the authorities to trace a particular drone if necessary. This will help to prevent perilous events like the 2018 suspected infringements by drones concerning the Gatwick and Heathrow airports. On the other hand, rules cover each type of operation, from those not requiring prior authorization to those involving certified aircraft and operators, as well as minimum remote pilot training requirements. The new rules are replacing existing national rules in EU Member States.

This book is about the disruptive technology called drone, an emerging innovative phenomenon in the world of aviation. Not very long ago, civil aviation was based on the notion of a pilot operating the aircraft from within the aircraft itself and, more often than not, with passengers on board. Removing the pilot from the aircraft raises significant technical, operational and legislative issues. However, drones are a promising source for delivering innovative and exceptional services. Yet these emerging technologies also present a challenge.

The significant rise in the number of drone operations, with seemingly unlimited applications, poses safety, security and airspace integration issues on a global scale. In view of the foreseen increase in manned air traffic in the upcoming years, even after a temporary economic setback, and the proliferation of drones, with both types of aircraft sharing non-segregated airspace, hazards to air traffic, persons and property will correspondingly increase.

The establishment of the U-space airspace, the enabler to manage complex and longer-distance operations but also urban air mobility (UAM), and the provisions for U-space services, especially in low-level airspace, at least for the time being, are considered essential to respond to such growth of drone operations. As drone operations are generally conducted close to the ground, privacy and personal data protection are aspects that must be taken into account from a legal perspective.

U-space should eventually lead to the prevention of collisions between manned and UA and mitigate the air and ground risks. Therefore, there is a worldwide need to complement advanced and existing regulations on drone operations with an international regulatory framework that together enable a harmonized implementation of U-space as well as to integrate drones safely into the existing air traffic management environment.

Chapter 1 sets out the history of UA, or drones, as these aircraft have conveniently come to be known as; the terminology, descriptions and definitions of various drone types; and the increasing number of civilian applications. Chapter 2 covers the legal basis for drone operations. Chapter 3 provides insight into the use of drones in different areas. Chapter 4 explains the issue of integrating drones into non-segregated airspace and operations in U-space. Chapter 5 sets out various safety requirements for drone operations. Chapter 6 deals with privacy, security and personal data protection related to private and government drone use. A summary completes the book.

Chapter 1 The Development of Drones

1.1 History of Drones

Public, commercial, scientific and recreational drones actually grew out of the battlefield. In other words, the predecessors of the present types of unmanned aircraft were originally built for military purposes. Unmanned aircraft can be divided into three categories: 1. autonomous aircraft, which fly without any intervention from an operator, 2. model aircraft, which are small unmanned devices used for a variety of purposes and 3. remotely piloted aircraft.

The earliest recorded use of such unmanned aircraft, or drones, for aerial warfare, in particular aerial bombardment, occurred in 1849 during the siege and fall of the city of Venice as part of the First Italian War of Independence, from 23 March 1848 to 22 August 1849. These revolutionary years were all about Italian unification (*Risorgimento*, which eventually led to *Italia irredenta*).

In the final phase of the Italian, in principle liberal, pan-nationalist war, on 12 July, the Austrian imperial forces launched, on the basis of a novel plan devised by Austrian artillery lieutenant Franz Freiherr von Uchatius, pilotless hot-air balloon bombs against the city of Venice located in the Lombardo-Venetian Kingdom, constituent state of the Austrian Empire. The city of Venice, in the proclaimed Republic of San Marco, was the last stronghold of the Italian revolts on the peninsula. This novel bombing was prompted by the fact that the shallow lagoons prevented the artillery from getting in range of the city. However, the attempt failed. A sudden change in wind direction blew them in such a way that none of them hit their targets. On the contrary, some balloons unfortunately drifted back towards the launch site to explode over the Austrian imperial forces.

On 22 August, the Austrians, who controlled much of Italy at the time, launched, in a second attempt, 200 balloons, each carrying approximately 33 lbs of explosives and armed with half-hour time fuses, from a frigate in the Venetian lagoon. It has been said that the incendiary bombs were to be ignited by means of electromagnetism, using a long copper wire connected to a large galvanic battery installed on the launch site. Partly because of unpredictable weather, especially wind shift, only a small number hit their proposed targets, causing only little damage. Notwithstanding the direct psychological effect, Venice did not surrender to the Austrian Empire until 27 August 1849. However, this aerial attack signalled the arrival of a new dimension to warfare.[1]

---

1   See www.historytoday.com/archive/bombs-over-venice. See also The first air raid – by balloons! (https://dbpedia.org/page/Franz_von_Uchatius).

During the American Civil War, also known as the War between the States (1861-1865), manned balloons were used for aerial reconnaissance and battlefield mapping. The Union Army Balloon Corps, a branch of the Union Army, employed a group of prominent American civilian aeronauts and seven especially built, gas-filled balloons; a number of field gas generators; and a flat-topped, converted coal barge, an aircraft carrier *avant la lettre*, to perform combat aerial reconnaissance on the Confederate States Army. Because of the effectiveness of the Union Army Balloon Corps actions, the Confederates felt compelled to incorporate reconnaissance balloons as well.[2]

However, the hot-air balloon also acquired a different function in the conflict. In February 1863, two years after the beginning of the Civil War, Charles Perley, an inventor from New York City, registered a patent for an unmanned aerial bomber. Perley was one of the many inventors who all flocked to the White House and the War Department to plead, offer and try to peddle their ideas for a government at war. He designed an unmanned hot-air balloon that could carry a basket laden with explosives attached to a specific timing device. Before starting a bombing attack, Perley recommended to send up a trial balloon to gauge the wind direction. Both Union and Confederate forces are said to have launched Perley's balloons during the war, though with limited success due to inaccuracy.[3]

Around the turn of the century, scientists such as Samuel Pierpont Langley, an American astronomer, physicist, inventor and Secretary of the Smithsonian Institution, began experimenting with rubber-band power aircraft models and gliders following Alphonse Pénaud, a French aviation pioneer, who was the originator of the use of twisted rubber to power model aircraft in the 1880s. Langley even attempted to construct a working piloted heavier-than-air aircraft. Larger unpiloted models, powered by miniature steam engines, launched from a boat on the Potomac River, made successful flights. To beat the Wright brothers, he designed and built a series of full-scale aircraft, all with the name Aerodrome. After several failed attempts, Langley gave up this project.[4]

World War I was responsible for the tremendous growth of both manned and unmanned aircraft, the latter category, however, in smaller numbers. The most important reason for limited production at the start of the war was insufficient technology. During *The War That Will End War* (by H.G. Wells), technology advanced, and many eccentric weapons were developed on all sides of the conflict. One of the amazing examples was a pilotless aircraft, called Ruston Proctor Aerial Target, which operated with the help of revolutionary radio-controlled techniques, representing the cutting edge of drone technology in 1916. It was used by the British forces in kamikaze-style, ramming strikes against German Zeppelins.

---

2   Newell, C.R., Shrader, C.R., *Of Duty Well and Faithfully Done: A History of the Regular Army in the Civil War*, Lincoln: University of Nebraska Press, 2011, pp. 298-300.
3   Civil War Ballooning (www.battlefield.org/learn/articles/civil-war-ballooning).
4   Baxter, W.E., 'Samuel P. Langley: Aviation Pioneer' (Part I), *Smithsonian Libraries*.

Elementary knowledge of electronic range finding, based on the principles of radar, developed by Professor Archibald Low, was used in parallel designing and developing this radio-guided pilotless aircraft by the Sopwith Company, well known for its fighter aircraft, and the Ruston Proctor & Co. Ltd. The Sopwith AT (Aerial Target) was fitted with a 35 horsepower (hp) engine of A.B.C. Motors Ltd, a so-called throwaway engine specifically for use in a remotely controlled pilotless aircraft.[5]

In the United States, inventors like Nikola Tesla, Peter Cooper Hewitt and Elmer Ambrose Sperry as well as Glenn Hammond Curtiss (Curtiss-Sperry Aerial Torpedo) were obsessed with remotely controlled unmanned aircraft. Nikola Tesla, a mechanical and electrical engineer, best known for his contributions to the design of the modern alternating current electricity supply system, was a pioneer in radio remote control. Sperry, at times alongside his aviator son Lawrence Burst Sperry, who had been perfecting gyroscopes for naval use since 1896, became in 1911 intrigued with the concept of applying radio control to aeroplanes. He realized that automatic stabilization was essential for effective radio control and adapted naval gyro-stabilizers into a gyro-based autopilot to test and evaluate to control a navy flying boat.[6]

The Hewitt-Sperry Automatic Airplane was a project undertaken during World War I to develop an aerial torpedo, a pilotless aircraft capable of carrying explosives to its target, preferably an enemy warship. A year later, in 1918, a more sophisticated unmanned aircraft than the Hewitt-Sperry project, a properly functioning unmanned aerial vehicle, a forerunner of present-day cruise missiles, which eventually came to be known as the Kettering Bug, formally called the Kettering Aerial Torpedo, was developed under the management of Charles Franklin Kettering, an electrical engineer and founder of the Dayton Engineering Laboratories Company. Kettering and Sperry worked together to create a control system for this aerial torpedo. The Kettering Bug was an autopilot-controlled unmanned aircraft that was computerized to drop a bomb on a pre-selected target.

This self-flying aerial torpedo, regarded as the first practical example of an unmanned aircraft, was considered to be a notable success, but the war ended before it could be deployed. Kettering believed that his Bugs, built in collaboration with legendary aviation pioneer Orville Wright by the Dayton-Wright Airplane Company, could make precision attacks within a range of 120 km, which was much greater than could be reached by any current artillery system.[7]

The technology for this autonomous aircraft was rather simple: after determining wind speed, direction and desired distance, operators calculated the number of required

---

5   The 'Aerial Target' and 'Aerial Torpedo' in Britain (https://en.wikipedia.org/wiki/Sopwith_Aviation_Company).
6   Keefe, P., Elmer A., 'Sperry: Pioneer of Modern Naval Tech', *MarineLink*, 16 May 2014.
7   Stamp, J., 'World War I: 100 Years Later – Unmanned Drones have been around since World War I', *Smithsonian.com*, 2013. They have recently been the subject of considerable scrutiny, but the American military first began developing similar aerial vehicles during World War I.

engine revolutions to take the Bug to its predetermined target (practically the same method applied during World War II on the German V-1 flying bomb), and after the proper number of revolutions, a cam dropped into place that shut off the engine and released the wings from the payload-carrying fuselage, which made a ballistic trajectory towards the target to detonate at impact. Modern cruise missiles are a variant of the Kettering Bug.

During the *Interbellum,* conventional aircraft were converted into drones, mainly for target practice. Starting in 1917, but mainly during the early 1920s, test flights with radio-controlled unmanned aircraft such as the RAF Aerial Target (AT) and the Royal Aircraft Establishment (RAE) 1921 Target Aircraft were not encouraging, at least not until the introduction, in 1925, of the second generation of unmanned aerial vehicle design, called Larynx (Long-Range Gun with Lynx engine), an aircraft intended to fly to a target, autopilot-guided, controlled by radio, and detonate on impact, making it an early cross between a cruise missile and a drone.

It produced some positive results, but the programme was eventually cancelled owing to high costs and inaccuracy. The autopilot principles were developed by Professor Archibald Montgomery Low, scientist and inventor, who had already designed the autopilot apparatus for the AT. In the 1920s, pilotless aircraft would be further developed in accordance with Low's principles, but it would be years before the Nazis used the technology in a war setting.[8]

A special radio-controlled pilotless target aircraft, the Queen Bee, actually a De Havilland-built Tiger Moth biplane (DH.82B) from 1933, was successfully tested. Around 420 units of this radio-controlled unmanned aircraft were built. Although initially made as an aerial target for target practice, the Queen Bees were even used for a short time in World War II for coastal reconnaissance. It has been said that the name Queen Bee is considered to have introduced the term drone into general use, in the 1930s, specifically referring to radio-controlled aerial targets.[9]

Just before World War II, unmanned aircraft could be controlled by radio signals, usually from another aircraft. In the United States, the first large-scale production of radio-controlled aircraft was established by Reginald Denny (born Reginald Leigh Dugmore), inventor, aviator, actor and UAV pioneer. The Radioplane OQ-2, to operate within visual sight of the ground operator, was the first mass-produced UAV or drone in the United States and was intended for U.S. Army combat operations. The follow-up version, the OQ-3, became the most widely used target drone in U.S. service. At the

---

8 Desmond, K., *Electric Airplanes and Drones: A History,* Jefferson: McFarland & Company, Inc. Publishers, 2018, p. 173.
9 *See* www.dehavillandmuseum.co.uk/aircraft/de-havilland-dh82b-queen-bee/.

same time, Edward Martin Sorensen invented a radio-controlled aircraft that could fly beyond visual perception.[10]

During the late 1930s, the U.S. Navy developed the Curtiss N2C-2, an unmanned aerial vehicle that was remotely controlled from another aircraft. This revolutionary concept was also adopted by the U.S. Army Air Force (USAAF), which subsequently started improving it.[11]

During World War II, Germany focused on developing missiles instead. While unmanned aircraft are intended to be recovered after a mission, a cruise missile completes its mission once it hits its target. Cruise missiles are faster, normally have a longer range and are much more accurate, not to mention more difficult to shoot out of the sky than other types of unmanned autonomous aerial vehicles.

The emergence of the secret Fi 103 V-1 weapon, a winged pilotless fuel-propelled flying bomb, manufactured by Fieseler, which actively participated in the development, was the first genuine military application of unmanned autonomous aircraft. The flying bomb was the result of technical and technological know-how new for that time and was part of a comprehensive missile programme, the first of which was started in the 1930s. Its first flight was performed on 10 December 1942.

During the last years of the war, the German armed forces used the V-1 (Vergeltungswaffe 1) as a retaliatory weapon on an astonishingly large scale from the Western European German-occupied territories to destroy vital targets in Great Britain, including terror attacks on London. In the fall of 1943, the first dispersed launch sites were being discovered after repeated photo reconnaissance sorties flown over an extensive coastal area near Abbeville, France.[12]

The V-1, actually the world's first jet-powered unmanned aircraft, was initially launched to target London on 13 June 1944, just after the Normandy invasion. Out of 6,725 V-1s, also known as 'buzz bombs' or 'doodlebugs', that were launched at Great Britain, 2,340 hit London and rural areas surrounding the city until March 1945, leaving almost 6,000 dead and approximately 17,000 injured. Another major target was the strategic port of Antwerp, Belgium, during the Allied advance in 1944. The Allied forces captured Antwerp from the Germans in their effort to liberate the Low Countries and to be able to use the port facilities for the military supply line to the battlefield.

---

10 The Radioplane OQ-2 aerial target drone was the first quantitative UAV purchased for the United States. Approximately 15,000 units were built (www.MilitaryFactory.com).
11 Hodgekinson, D.I., Johnston, R., *Aviation Law and Drones: Unmanned Aircraft and the Future of Aviation*, Milton Park, Abingdon, Oxon: Routledge, 2018, p. 9. *See* History of Drone: The Wonderful Story You Never Heard (www.Dronesquery.com). *See also* The early Days of Drones-Unmanned Aircraft from World War I and World War II (www.historyonline.com/military-vehicle-news/short-history-drones-part-1-m.html).
12 Stanley II, R. M. (Colonel Ret.), *V-Weapons Hunt: Defeating German Secret Weapons*, Barnsley, South Yorkshire: Pen & Sword Military, 2010, pp. 252-257.

However, German V-1 attacks killed around 3,000 persons in the city and the area of greater Antwerp.[13]

The V-1, designed by Robert Lusser, was perhaps the most infamous unmanned aircraft but, above all, a terrifying German revenge weapon. It was certainly the most widely used guided missile of World War II and the world's first 'successful' cruise missile-type unmanned aircraft. In fact, it was the only production aircraft to use a pulse-jet as a power source, manufactured by Argus Motors Berlin. The V-1 was developed at Peenemünde Army Research Center by the Nazi German Luftwaffe in 1939 and became operational during the war after some modifications. It was capable of carrying 1,000 kg of explosives over a distance of approximately 500 km. Because of the rather limited range, thousands of V-1s, targeted at Great Britain, were fired from launch facilities along or behind the French and Low Countries' coastal areas. Owing to the characteristics of the pulse-jet and the very high stall speed, it had to be launched by means of a ground steam catapult system or air-launched from a modified bomber aircraft such as the Heinkel He 111.

The V-1 guidance system used a fairly simple autopilot unit to regulate altitude and airspeed. A weighted pendulum system provided for-and-aft attitude measurement to control pitch, damped by a gyrocompass. Operating power for the instruments was provided by two large built-in spherical compressed air tanks that also pressurized the single fuel tank with a capacity of approximately 640 litres of kerosene. Through a sophisticated interaction between yaw, roll and sensors, rudder control was sufficient for steering, and thus no banking control was needed.

Propulsion is simple: fuel is injected in a combustion chamber, where it is mixed with air, in one direction allowed through an effective shutter system, and then ignited at the launch site. When the compressed air-fuel mixture detonates, the shutter system will close automatically, forcing the resulting jet exhaust through an exhaust tube. The power unit is a simple blowpipe and a pure jet or reaction propulsion engine without compressor or turbine sections.

In take-off, the launch cycle and the remainder of the powered flight, the combustion cycle could be sufficiently self-sustaining since secondary shock waves returning to the combustion chamber could be used to ignite consecutive pulses. During flight, the airflow turned a small propeller, a vane anemometer, on the nose. Before launch, the number of rotations of a tachometer, connected to the propeller, was fixed according to the distance of the target and the atmospheric conditions, in principle the prevailing winds. Every 30 propeller-revolutions counted down one rotation of the preset value on the tachometer, which also triggered the arming of the warhead a couple of minutes after take-off.

At point zero, certain actions occurred. Two detonating bolts were fired. Two spoilers on the elevator were released, the linkage between the elevator and the servo was jammed

---

13 Smith, D., 'Seventy Years On, Antwerp Remembers the V-bomb', *Flanders Today*, 27 September 2019. *See also* www.nationalarchives.gov.uk.

and control hoses to the rudder servo were instantly cut off, setting the rudder in a neutral position. All actions resulted in a steep, straight power dive. However, in most dives the engine stopped owing to fuel starvation, which caused a sudden silence but also an alert signal to ground forces. The last V-1s were modified and hit their targets with power on. This weapon was accurate enough for area bombing. By the end of the war, accuracy had been improved to about 7 miles.[14]

In the years following World War II, drones were used mainly for military practices, such as the Ryan Aeronautical Company-developed jet-propelled target drones, which in turn were adapted to perform reconnaissance missions over South East Asia during the 1960s. The Ryan Firebee drone series was developed in 1951. It could be air-launched from a specially modified launch aircraft or ground-launched with a single rocket-assisted take-off (RATO) booster.

Owing to advanced technologies at the time, the series was further developed. These so-called second generation drones consisted of different models, upgraded power plants, stealth technology and versatile capabilities.

During the Cold War, the two superpowers of the world, the United States and the USSR, used unmanned aerial vehicles to spy on each other, although traditional manned aircraft, like the Lockheed U-2, were preferred at the time. In 1964, the U.S. Strategic Air Command began flying drones called 'Lightning Bugs' for surveillance across Cold War battle spaces such as North Vietnam, China and Cuba, contributing to thousands of successful surveillance missions.

Another reconnaissance drone, the Israelian Tadiran Mastiff, was one of the most advanced military large-scale UAVs with a unique design. It flew for the first time in 1973 and had advanced electronic equipment that enabled the transmission of high-quality video. The Israeli Defence Forces (IDF) learned vital lessons about UAVs during the Yom Kippur War, also known as the 1973 Arab-Israeli War. The Firebee 1241, an Israeli-modified version of the U.S. Ryan AQM-34, played an important role, both as reconnaissance vehicles and also as decoys.

In essence, modern drone warfare started in 1982, when the Israel Defense Forces used drones for reconnaissance regarding enemy positions during the Israeli-Lebanese conflict for the purpose of wiping out Palestine Liberation Organization (PLO) positions in southern Lebanon. In addition, drones were used to jam communications and to act as decoys that would prevent capture by the enemy of possibly downed Israeli military pilots. After this conflict, Israel developed pilotless surveillance vehicles such as the RQ 2 Pioneer, a medium-sized reconnaissance drone. Israel was making drone operations more and more successful, and international interest increased considerably.[15]

---

14 Kikuchi, I., 'The Terrifying German "Revenge Weapons" of the Second World War', *Imperial War Museum* (GB), 18 July 2018. *See also* www.zensa.se/vw.
15 Combat experience in the 1970s drove the Israeli Defense Force/Air Force to develop such measures as the Tadiran Mastiff Unmanned Aerial Vehicle, *Military Factory*, 2019.

In 1995, The U.S. Air Force (USAF) and the CIA (Central Intelligence Agency) started to use the General Atomics MQ-1 Predator, an unmanned remotely controlled drone for reconnaissance and combat tasks, with a range of more than 1,000 km and capable of carrying and firing missiles. General Atomics was the prime contractor supported by various subcontractors in the field of electronics, synthetic aperture radar, optical reconnaissance, intelligence workstation, satellite communication link, mission planning and laser-guided missile systems. In the aftermath of the 9/11 attacks on New York City and Washington D.C., the CIA began flying armed drones over Afghanistan as part of the war against the Taliban in late 2001.[16]

Years later, the CIA expanded its operations in Afghanistan and offensively used heavier and more powerful military drones such as the MQ-9 Reaper, also known as Predator B, to hunt and kill Taliban militants and bomb makers, day and night. The Reaper, a further development of the Predator, is a high-altitude long-endurance (operational ceiling of 50,000 ft) UAV, referred to as RPV/RPA (remotely controlled), capable of carrying four anti-armour missiles, two laser-guided bombs and 500 lbs of joint direct attack munition (JDAM). Lightweight military reconnaissance drones are the AeroVironment RQ-11 Raven, a small hand-launched remote-controlled unmanned aerial vehicle (sUAV), and the Boeing Insitu ScanEagle, a small, long-endurance, low-altitude unmanned aerial vehicle, launched by a pneumatic catapult launcher.[17]

A striking example of the versatile applications with regard to robotic warfare, in a series of game-changing products for military use, was the recent introduction of the Boeing MQ-25 Stingray, an autonomous refuelling drone that resulted from the 2016 Carrier-Based Aerial-Refueling System (CBARS) programme. This first carrier-launched autonomous unmanned stealth-type aircraft performed its maiden flight on 19 September 2019, entirely remotely controlled by Boeing pilots from a ground control station (GCS). The new system is capable of refuelling conventional U.S. Navy carrier aircraft like Boeing F/A Super Hornets, Boeing EA-18G Growlers and Lockheed Martin F-35C fighters, resulting in significantly extended combat ranges.[18]

On the other hand, in Russia or the Russian Federation, Sukhoi developed the S-70, a military stealth-type autonomous unmanned aircraft, equipped with photoelectric sensors, onboard reconnaissance and laser devices for detecting and tracking targets. It has the shape of a flying wing with a wingspan of 19 m and a range of 3,500 km.

---

16 www.af.mil/About-Us/Fact-Sheets/Display/Aricle/104469/mq-1b-predator/.
17 *See also* Kreuzer, M.P., *Drones and the Future of Warfare: The Evolution of Remotely Piloted Aircraft*, CASS Military Studies, Milton Park, Abingdon, Oxon: Routledge, 2016, Tactical and Networked RPAS.
18 www.boeing.com/defense/mq25/.

The plans on the horizon, the next of which is the Loyal Wingman, which will utilize the latest technologies, will certainly make drone development pushing the boundary of autonomous force unprecedented.[19] With respect to recoverable hypersonic drones for intelligence, surveillance and reconnaissance, to be operating through the atmosphere below about 90 km at speeds above Mach 5, the launch of these NextGen vehicles is not expected to be possible until the 2040s.[20]

The history of non-military drones and their versatile use started only just after the beginning of the third millennium. The fact that the same technological improvements in the military sector could be used in the civil sector was a major reason for the immense production and proliferation of commercial and recreational drones.

By issuing the first commercial drone permits in 2006, lifting some of the limitations placed on consumer drones flown for recreational purposes, the U.S. Federal Aviation Administration (FAA), the former Federal Aviation Agency, recognized the potential of non-military drone applications. Within a few years, ready-to-fly or pick-up-and-play drones became a great success. Companies also saw the benefits of drone use. From 2010, the drone-based delivery system concept, autonomous vehicles used to transport packages, food or other goods by air, was about to be launched, in particular by e-commerce providers such as Amazon and the Alibaba Group. However, all these initiatives were hampered or even blocked by strict regulation. Nevertheless, new legislation will allow package deliveries by drones, albeit under certain conditions. There is, however, also a bad side to package deliveries, which is illegal, criminal shipping. Transport of drugs, in the upcoming jumble of drone traffic, could take place almost unnoticed.

Without any doubt, both military and commercial drones have immensely affected world society, both positively and negatively. The positive effect has been seen in life-saving operations, such as delivery of medical supply to remote areas or first response to mass casualty incidents, accidents and disasters, while the negative effect has been seen in breaches on privacy and personal data.

The popularity of drones is on the rise. They have quickly become one of the most popular devices for recreational, commercial and government uses. Unmistakable recent data shows that the market for commercial and private (recreational) drones may grow at a compound annual rate of 19% by 2021. *A fortiori*, the rather turbulent growth, technological progress and expansion of drone application areas are expected to continue into the future.

---

19 The Boeing Airpower Teaming System (BATS), also known as the Boeing Loyal Wingman project, is a stealth UCAV (unmanned combat aerial vehicle) being developed by Boeing Australia to perform autonomous missions using artificial intelligence (AI) (2020).
20 Osborn, K., 'Airforce Plans Recoverable Hypersonic Drones by 2040', *Defence Systems*, 23 March 2017.

Nanotech, algorithms, computing power and programming are only just now starting to catch up with drone capabilities, presenting such exciting opportunities as artificial intelligence (AI) drone operations, high-end imagery, extreme durability, new materials and innovative power sources.

1.2 Terminology

There are many appellations for unmanned aircraft. The different terms do not always have exactly the same scope, and different stakeholders have divergent preferences for the term to be used. Today, the drone, usually depicted as being fully autonomous, is the most popular name for a variety of unmanned military, civil utility and recreational aircraft. The term drone was originally used for military applications and still has a military connotation for many people, though depending on the application concerned. This rather negative connotation seems to be slowly changing, with the result that drones are increasingly associated with civilian applications, not least by the significant global increase in the number of civil drones. However, both the rapidly developing drone technology and the continuously expanding unmanned aircraft industry make it difficult to use a single descriptive term to serve as a consistent basic principle for an elaborated regulatory framework on drones.

In 1929 and 1944, the term pilotless aircraft emerged in legal instruments, although, essentially, it turned out to be a rather incomplete designation. In the 1960s, the term remotely piloted vehicle (RPV) was used, to be replaced in the 1980s by unmanned aerial vehicle, all terms of military origin, later to be adopted as unmanned aircraft or as unmanned aircraft system, although this term is literally quite extensive. More recently, remotely piloted aircraft system has been introduced, eliminating the somewhat controversial designation of unmanned.

The designation remotely piloted aircraft, rather than unmanned aircraft, provides more clarity, in accordance with the remote element. RPA is used to indicate the flying part, also known as the platform, with or without payload, while RPAS includes the associated remote pilot station(s) (RPS) or ground control station(s), which has one or more pilots operating the RPA, the required command and control (C2) data link and other system elements as may be required at any point during flight operations, according to the International Civil Aviation Organization (ICAO) explanation.

These more descriptive terms are used mainly in the United States and other English-speaking regions, but also in many different countries as an alternative to the term drone. In official (legal) instruments, including international treaties, protocols, documents and national legislation, the terms UAV(s), UAS and RPAS, indicated in this book as the singular or plural forms, are mainly used. However, there are some differences in designation and definitions of civil unmanned aircraft and their associated systems among supranational bodies, governmental entities and non-governmental international aviation organizations and associations.

EASA widely uses both the terms 'drone' and 'unmanned aircraft'. The Agency considered several terms such as 'UAS' and 'RPAS', the latter being considered a subcategory of UAS, but eventually followed the general usage of the term drone. The Agency uses the following definition of the term drone:

> Drone shall mean an aircraft without a human pilot on board, whose flight is controlled either autonomously or under the remote control of a pilot on the ground or in another vehicle.

This definition has significant consequences. It encompasses the two main groups of command and control systems, thus addressing the fast-growing development of drones that are operating autonomously. Flexibility is provided through separation by defining only the drone, allowing to regulatory-wise treat the drone apart from, for example, the command and control station.[21]

An unmanned aircraft system, according to the description proposed by EASA, is composed of the drone (the flying component), a command and control station, a data link and any other components necessary for operations (e.g. take-off ramp). There are two groups of drones: those that are remotely piloted and those that are autonomous. An autonomous drone does not allow pilot intervention in the management of the flight. A UAS operator means any legal or natural person operating or intending to operate one or more UAS.[22]

The European Union uses the term 'unmanned aircraft' and 'unmanned aircraft system' in a number of EU legal documents such as Commission Delegated Regulation (EU) 2019/945, Commission Implementing Regulation (EU) 2019/247 and Regulation (EU) 2018/1139.[23]

The regulatory definition of a drone, according to the European Union, is:

---

21 ICAO Ann. 2 Definitions: Command and control (C2) link. The data link between the remotely piloted aircraft and the RPS for the purpose of managing the flight.
22 *See* Advance Notice of Proposed Amendment (A-NPA 2015-10) Introduction of a Regulatory Framework for the Operation of Drones, 31 July 2015, 2.1.
23 Commission Delegated Regulation (EU) 2019/945 of 12 March 2019 on unmanned aircraft systems and on third-country operators of unmanned aircraft systems. Commission Implementing Regulation (EU) 2019/247 of 24 May 2019 on the rules and procedures for the operation of unmanned aircraft, *OJ* L 152/45, 11 June 2019. New Basic Regulation: Regulation (EU) 2018/1139 of the European Parliament and of the Council of 4 July 2018.

> An unmanned aircraft which means any aircraft operating or designed to operate autonomously or to be piloted remotely without a pilot on board.[24]

A fully autonomous aircraft, other than a RPA, is an unmanned aircraft, the flight of which is, however, "programmed in advance and does not allow pilot intervention in the management of the flight". These aircraft are often equipped with autopilot and navigation technology allowing them to fly autonomously without manipulation by the remote pilot at all times. Therefore, if the remote pilot can take control over the aircraft at any time, such aircraft cannot be classified as fully autonomous.

Remote pilot means a natural person responsible for safely conducting the flight of an unmanned aircraft by operating its flight controls, either manually or, when the unmanned aircraft flies automatically, by monitoring its course and remaining able to intervene and change the course at any time.

In 2003, ICAO started discussions on unmanned aircraft systems, followed by meetings to determine the potential role of ICAO in unmanned aircraft systems' regulatory framework as well as technical specifications and special SARPs. In 2011, ICAO issued Circular 328 AN/190 to provide guidance material to develop a fundamental international regulatory framework provided with terms officially or not recognized by ICAO.

ICAO's (non-binding) Circular 328 AN/190 provides an explanation of terms related to unmanned aircraft:

> Aircraft: any machine that can derive support in the atmosphere from the reactions of the air other than the reactions of the air against the Earth's surface.
> Unmanned aircraft: an aircraft which is intended to operate with no pilot on board.
> Unmanned aircraft system: an aircraft and its associated elements which are operated with no pilot on board.
> Autonomous aircraft: an unmanned aircraft that does not allow pilot intervention in the management of the flight.
> Autonomous operation: an operation during which a remotely-piloted aircraft is operating without pilot intervention in the management of the flight.
> Remotely-piloted aircraft is an aircraft where the flying pilot is not on board the aircraft.

---

24 Commission Delegated Regulation (EU) 2019/945, Art. 3 Definitions.

Detect and avoid (DAA): the capability to see, sense or detect conflicting traffic or other hazards and take the appropriate action to comply with the applicable rules of flight.
Segregated airspace: airspace of specified dimensions allocated for exclusive use to a specific user(s).

An RPA is an aircraft, a subset of unmanned aircraft, piloted by a licensed remote pilot situated at an RPS located external to the aircraft, which could mean on the ground, at sea, in another aircraft or in space, who monitors the aircraft at all times and can respond to instructions issued by the air traffic control (ATC) unit, communicates via voice or data link, as appropriate to the airspace or operation, and has direct responsibility for the safe conduct of the aircraft throughout the flight. An RPA may possess various types of auto-flight management technology, but the remote pilot can intervene at any time in the management of the flight. This equates to the ability of the pilot of a manned aircraft being flown by its auto-flight system to take over prompt control of the aircraft.[25]

The roles of RPA continue to expand as technologies and performance characteristics become better understood. Extended flights, long flight durations, covert operational capabilities and reduced operational costs will serve as natural benefits to many communities, such as long-range air transport, law enforcement, agriculture and environmental analysis. Currently, regulators are focusing mainly on the regulation of RPA because only RPA so far have the potential to be integrated into non-segregated airspace and at aerodromes operating alongside manned aircraft.[26]

RPA operations may involve the pilot and all associated responsibilities being handed over while the aircraft is in flight. The remote pilots may be co-located or situated thousands of kilometres apart, for instance, for an oceanic flight of a long-range RPA, handover of RPA flight operation responsibilities to a remote pilot situated in Asia from a remote pilot in North America or between an en-route pilot and a local (terminal) remote pilot.

Handover may also occur as a result of routine shift work of the remote pilots. Changes will be required to address the handover of such responsibilities between different remote pilots. Adding to the complexity of this scenario is the possibility that the remote pilots and their ground control stations may be located in different states.

In accordance with Article 12 of the Chicago Convention and Annex 2, both dealing with the rules of the air, the pilot in command is responsible for the operation of the aircraft in compliance with those rules of the air. This also extends to having final

---

25 ICAO Circular 328 AN/190 Unmanned Aircraft Systems (UAS), Chapter 3 Overview of UAS, General Concept of Operations, Para. 3.2.
26 ICAO Manual on Remotely Piloted Aircraft Systems (RPAS) Doc 10019 AN/507 First Edition 2015, Para. 1.2.14. *See also* ICAO Ann. 1 and 2 Definitions.

authority as to disposition of the aircraft while in command. This is true whether the pilot is on board the aircraft or located remotely.[27]

Article 12 of the Chicago Convention, 1944:

> Rules of the air.
> Each contracting State undertakes to adopt measures to insure that every aircraft flying over or maneuvering within its territory and that every aircraft carrying its nationality mark, wherever such aircraft may be, shall comply with the rules and regulations, relating to the flight and maneuver of aircraft there in force. Each contracting State undertakes to keep its own regulations in these respects uniform, to the greatest possible extent, with those established from time to time under this Convention. Over the high seas, the rules in force shall be those established under this Convention. Each contracting State undertakes to insure the prosecution of all persons violating the regulations applicable.

Regarding RPAS, the opinion of the European Civil Aviation Conference (ECAC), with its 44 Member States, is that these systems are considered to have become a strategic sector with transversal implications affecting a number of industries. ECAC is well aware that the civil RPAS sector has experienced significant and exponential growth, with a strong impact on traditional aviation systems and topics. In this context, ECAC Member States are being challenged with the safe, secure and efficient integration of RPAS into environments shared by a highly regulated and established manned aircraft industry.

The FAA, one of the world's leading governmental bodies with powers to regulate all aspects of civil aviation, has adopted the name unmanned aircraft to describe aircraft systems without a flight crew on board. The full definition is as follows:

> Unmanned aircraft means an aircraft operated without the possibility of direct human intervention from within or on the aircraft.[28]

The U.S. Department of Defense (DoD) provides the following definitions in its Joint Publication 1-02):

> Unmanned aircraft: An aircraft that does not carry a human operator, and is capable of flight with or without human remote control. Also called UA. (JP 3-30).

---

27 ICAO Circular 328 AN/190, Chapter 4 Legal Matters, Paras. 4.7 and 4.9.
28 Electronic Code of Federal Regulations (e-CFR): Title 14. Aeronautics and Space, Chapter I – Federal Aviation Administration, Department of Transportation, Subchapter A – Definitions and Requirements, Part I – Definitions and Abbreviations, Section 1.1 General definitions.

Unmanned aircraft system: That system whose components include the necessary equipment, network and personnel to control an unmanned aircraft. Also called UAS. (JP 3-30).[29]

Remotely piloted aircraft: An unmanned aircraft controlled by a trained pilot; this is a term primarily used by the USAF to denote unmanned aircraft.

Drone, according to the military, is a common term used to refer to UAS but can refer to any form of automated robot or machinery.

Unambiguous terminology regarding the concept of unmanned aircraft, considered internationally, is still a long way from completion. In the future, another aspect emerges, namely, the description of the flying vehicle called urban air taxi, an element of the urban air mobility services concept. This compact unmanned aerial vehicle is essentially not unmanned, as it has the potential to transport human passengers. Be it autonomous or remotely piloted, there are persons on board, assuring a perfectly safe journey in any environment.

Safety is universally acknowledged to be a fundamental requirement, especially in civil aviation, although the feeling of safety in novel automated air taxis and similar crafts is determined more by intuitive aspects, based on non-empirical information. Apart from the societal constituent of fear for human safety, technologically the concept of autonomous or remotely piloted aircraft systems is undoubtedly feasible and safe.

However, for novel (semi-)autonomous human passenger aerial transport systems, the definition should be adapted to:

A passenger aircraft, vehicle or drone which is intended to operate without a pilot on board, or a passenger transport aircraft system, including the associated elements for an operation without a pilot on board, or a remotely piloted passenger transport aircraft system, including all the elements as may be required for all phases of flight operation, where the pilot is not on board the aircraft, such as an urban air mobility aircraft. In case the flight operation of this drone type of highly automated passenger aircraft is fully autonomous, no pilot intervention in the management of the flight is to be considered. In other words, the ancient description of (autonomous) pilotless aircraft suffices.

The future uses of drones are only limited by our imagination. By 2050, we will have full integration of airspace at low and high altitudes, including a variety of

---

29 Joint Publication 1-02 Department of Defense Dictionary of Military and Associated Terms, 8 November 2010 (As Amended Through 15 February 2016), App. A-1.

vehicles of all sizes, passenger drones, traditional aircraft, and even vehicles we have yet to imagine.[30]

Throughout this book, drone, as a generally well-known concept, will be used as an all-encompassing term that covers all types of aircraft that are operated with no pilot on board. It will be used most often, although the other descriptions and abbreviations of unmanned aircraft (systems) are to be stated when required by the context of treatises and documents, etc. in the book in the interest of explanation and clarity.

1.3   Applications

Drones are a rapidly emerging technology that has gained considerable popularity over the past few years. Ever since drones have been developed and researched, they have expanded their horizons to different sectors. Although drones have a military background, it has just recently become clear that there are many other areas where they might be useful. Today, drones already offer a wide range of possibilities for the benefit of global society, from environmental control to civil security, as well as a fascinating variety of commercial services, which stand for a large number of applications. A reluctant but also extremely interesting aspect of these unmanned aircraft is that their virtually unlimited use so far is unimaginable. They are able to perform air operations that traditional manned aircraft in all forms struggle with. Moreover, the use of drones clearly results in economic savings and environmental benefits while reducing the risk to human life.

In the future, drones will use global airspace in significantly large numbers simultaneously. This will require a completely different airspace infrastructure to cope with the new situation. This sounds incredible in the light of the relatively few drones that are currently operational. In the foreseeable future, drones will become more and more disruptive, in the sense that this innovative force will create a strong new aviation market in the medium term.

Because the possibilities and applications of drones are immense, the predictable disruptive effect on relevant existing markets will be significant. To name just a few, the need for agricultural machinery will become superfluous; the same will definitely apply to manpower during inspections and applications where drones will replace land vehicles, conventional fixed-wing aircraft and helicopters.

---

30   Statement of Diana Marina Cooper, Head of U.S. Policy at Hyundai Air Mobility, and former Senior Vice-President Strategic, Policy and Legal Affairs at PrecisionHawk. *See also* Cureton, P., *Drone Futures: UAS in Landscape and Urban Design*, Milton Park, Abingdon, Oxon: Routledge, 2020, pp. 38-39.

A remarkable application is virus control by drones. At the end of 2019, the outbreak of the new infectious coronavirus disease (Covid-19, scientifically known as SARS-Coronavirus-2) in Wuhan in the province of Hubei (People's Republic of China) was the first major epidemic, which even turned into a pandemic, causing a severe global economic recession.

The extensive network of data collection systems that the Chinese government had built up in record time over the past years contains information concerning the whereabouts of citizens. Real-time searches by smart drones equipped with special digital sensors, cameras and scanners were even able to deduce who suffered from symptoms related to the new coronavirus. In this case, any existing privacy concerns were supposed to be subordinate to the state of emergency, within China and other locations. Incidentally, from the initially reported outbreak, the coronavirus spread quickly throughout the world.

In many infected countries around the world, robots and drones have been used to support humans in battling the coronavirus. Owing to the contagiousness of the virus, it was safer to drastically minimize human-to-human contact in order to be able to control the infection rate. Since robots and drones are immune to infection, these semi-autonomous vehicles proved to be quite valuable in fighting the incredibly persistent coronavirus.

Quarantine measures forced people to have essential resources delivered contactless, including medicines and food but also beverages, mainly purchased online. Home delivery of meals by drones to quarantined people, aimed to reduce cross-infection, significantly scaled up. In some cities, drones were deployed that could patrol areas in order to observe crowds and traffic more efficiently. Monitoring social distancing in crowded places such as parks and beaches was one of the key tasks carried out by police surveillance drones.

The drone technology proved to be effective in potentially containing the outbreak of infection, limiting the risk of contamination, and spread of the virus. Digital virus control methods, based on direct body temperature measurements, face recognition, not even hindered by mouth masks, all accomplished by drone sensors, and the use of combined data, augmented reality, 5G-Internet and algorithms as well as artificial intelligence, are able to accurately predict disease spread models.

Additional drone applications during virus outbreaks are spraying of disinfectant to constrain virus-related diseases, detecting people who practically invisibly violate mandatory quarantine measures, broadcasting information to a larger area than traditional loudspeakers can, airlifting medical supplies without exposing any personnel to infection and preventing health workers from entering contaminated areas. In a pandemic, such as Covid-19, drones could become an increasingly essential human support device to contain such an outbreak, under any circumstances.[31]

In practice, the functioning of a drone is a combination of the platform and payload. In addition to the flying drone, the possible payloads are just as important to distinguish between the applications and the method of deployment. The number of different payloads that can be attached to drones is virtually endless, subject only to weight and volume.

Applicable payloads range from cameras; microphones; biological, chemical and meteorological sensors; medical assistance supplies such as defibrillators and medicines; Wi-Fi hotspots; and various goods to deliver to urban mobility passenger transportation.

With the exception of military applications, there are two other sectors in which the application of drones is commonplace. The two sectors are the public and private sector. It must be stated that the distinction between public and private application of drones is not always very clear. Many public applications are often performed by private institutions, on a semi-commercial or scientific basis. Applications include both the opportunities and the threats associated with the use of drones. From a coherent point of view, opportunities and threats regarding applications are close together in particular situations.

We now turn to an examination of a variety of applications:

A random view of the use of drones in the public sector.

Through the years, new technologies have turned drones into vital tools to save lives, provide disaster relief and emergency supplies, fight against fires of any nature whatsoever, for works at heights, for safety and security in society and for humans in harsh and hostile environments. Even the sky is no limit, since drones are also used in space.

Drones are widely used for specific safety purposes, for example in the field of civil aviation safety, drone technology is used to investigate aircraft accidents. Any aircraft accident that occurs needs to be investigated thoroughly and accurately. The paramount consideration in an aviation accident or incident investigation should be the determination of the most likely cause and possible contributing factors in order to prevent future recurrences.

The main benefits of using drones over manned aeroplanes or helicopters for aviation accident site imagery are as follows:

Significantly lower cost compared with hourly costs of conventional aircraft. Immediate deployment of drones on arrival at site. The images and videos from a drone can be viewed and preliminarily interpreted live on the ground, while the

---

31 Marr, B., 'Robots and Drones are Now Used to Fight COVID-19', *Forbes,* 18 March 2020.

engineering investigator has full control over the images and videos that are taken. A drone can easily be launched to take additional footage. A drone can be flown close to trees and other obstacles as well as the wreckage to obtain close-up images without the disturbance caused by helicopter-rotor downwash.

A drone can easily be programmed to take a series of geo-tagged and overlapping overhead shots for photogrammetry purposes. It has been determined that the use of drones at accident sites is extremely important in regard to the wreckage and site survey, search for debris, tree/obstacle height estimations, site safety assessment and flight path reconstruction/visualization. Another advantage of drone operation at the accident site is that a drone can operate in low-visibility and low-cloud conditions that would prevent conventional fixed-wing aircraft or helicopters being operated.[32]

Within the public safety domain, the use of drones as observation and surveillance instruments, equipped with cameras and sensors, can generally provide background information about certain situations, such as the presence of people, exploration of terrain and the development and lay-out of a certain urban area. This information can contribute to situational awareness should it become necessary in the event of a serious incident. Furthermore, drones can proactively be deployed to either consolidate or enhance safety levels in a variety of sectors.

Mainly in the public sphere, but also in the private domain, drones are used in agriculture, particularly precision farming and smart agriculture. They are also used for soil and field analysis, planting, crop spraying and monitoring, irrigation and plant health assessment, conducting topographic surveys to support agriculture, application rate of seeds and fertilizers and pesticides, to mention a few. Benefits are less time required to gather data, reduction of operation expenses and a more environmentally friendly operation.

A rather specific application in agriculture, pollination by drones, has been researched by a group of aerospace students at the Dutch Delft University of Technology. Pollination, the process whereby the pollen is transferred from the anther (male part) to the stigma (female part) of a flower, is the most important step in the production of seeds. In other words, it is the process of reproduction in plants, which allows plants to bear fruits and vegetables.

The ever growing problem of the shrinking bee population necessitated the search for alternatives to the natural process of pollination by bees, especially in greenhouses restricting the mobility of bees. It is absolutely certain that pollination work on a large scale by human hands proves to be a hopeless endeavour. In this case, the replacement of immense human effort, involving time-consuming and expensive manual pollination, by the use of aerial vehicles, in particular micro air vehicles (MAVs), to pollinate flowers, is undoubtedly an efficient option. Thanks to the relatively small size, agility and the ability

---

32 ECACNews # 61 Spring 2017, Hawkins, S., 'The Benefits of Using Drones at Aircraft Accident Sites', Senior Inspector of Air Accidents, United Kingdom Air Accident Investigation Branch (AAIB), pp. 12-15.

to operate completely autonomously, these drones could keep the need for human intervention down to the bare minimum.[33]

With regard to the environmental domain, drones can be equipped with sensors, so-called sniffers to detect chemical particles in order to determine the intensity of emissions of certain substances. Measuring high concentrations of chemical substances and particulates is important in connection with pollution of surface water, soil and contamination through particulate matter.

High concentrations could imply a decrease in biodiversity, desiccation as well as health risks. If there are potential health risks, the population should be alerted at all times. Drones are also able to monitor illegal dumping of drugs-related waste.

Drones are useful in industrial infrastructure, especially in carrying out inspections and maintenance of existing infrastructural buildings. It may involve traffic infrastructure and waterworks such as highways, roads, bridges, overpasses, railways and tunnels, dams and dikes, and energy infrastructure such as wind farms, solar parks and oil rigs.

It often concerns bottlenecks and weak spots as a result of erosion and wear that can cause danger. Patrolling of pipelines and electric power lines, in particular, in order to detect physical abnormal activity like encroachment or intrusion is crucial to sustain the economy and society.

Monitoring the use of infrastructure by observing traffic flows in shipping, road and air traffic may be important for analyses and remedies. Drone monitoring can be done on other infrastructural works such as natural gas and water pipe systems for leaks, power lines and Internet coverage for disruptions or optimal performance.

Another area where drones are used is in law enforcement. Equipped with cameras and sensors, they can play a role in criminal and administrative enforcement and investigation of illegal practices. In more and more states, police departments are making use of drone technology in creative and life-saving ways. Collecting aerial data while surveying disaster sites can assist in directing resources to places where they are needed most. Optical, zoom and/or thermal cameras allow law enforcement agents to have a better vantage point in chaotic situations where deploying ground personnel is too risky. Drones can assist in crowd control, tracing and arresting suspects, identifying witnesses and in search and recovery missions for missing or lost persons. They are widely used in accident and traffic control and traffic collision reconstruction.

Drones can deal with explosives and other hazardous materials, can assist in forensic examination of crime scenes, and are able to produce aerial data to help police officers better understand specific situations on the scenes or locate stolen goods and vehicles. Border patrol and seaport security become easier with the help of drones.[34]

Drones are used in firefighting as they are able to quickly reach a vantage point not conveniently accessible by humans. Firefighter drones are sent to fire locations as scouts,

---

33   APIS Autonomous Pollination & Imaging System, DSE Team S9, Delft University of Technology.
34   *See* Police Drone Infographic (www.dronefly.com/police-drone-infographic).

using cameras with thermal imaging technology to be able to see in low light to dark conditions in order to assist first responders in their rescue efforts, to detect irregularities in various kinds of infrastructure such as solar panels and insulation on buildings and even check for hotspots in burning premises. From wildland firefighting to burning buildings, thermal drones can see through smoke and darkness to detect the hotspots and monitor and direct the crew. Transferring real-time data from fire and emergency scenes to firefighter and police forces on the ground in order to assess danger and locate persons at risk can be decisive. It is this type of leverage that can really make a difference to more property damage and greater loss of life. Firefighter drones can help in reducing firefighter injuries and deaths by providing a complete picture, including 360-degree views, of a fire and structure before firefighters enter the scene.[35]

Drones are increasingly being used in search and rescue operations. Preparing for, and responding to, disasters is a major logistical challenge. A number of governmental, non-governmental and intergovernmental organizations are considering the use of drones in search and rescue operations in the toolkit of the disaster responder. Traditionally, search and rescue operations that involve dangerous tasks are performed by rescuers using conventional equipment and rescue dogs.

Drone advancements in recent years have resulted in an increased capacity for these unmanned rescue vehicles to undertake effective early-stage search actions so that lives can be saved. Drones are especially able to reduce exposure to high risk, rescue from otherwise inaccessible places and gain valuable time. The same is true of drones that deliver emergency medical supplies such as medicines and defibrillators for cardiac arrest.

Drones are playing a role in wildlife conservation. Cost-effectiveness and higher performance of new technology make relatively small low-noise drones more useful for conservation applications, over terrain as well as over the high seas. So-called ecodrones or conservation drones are used for wildlife surveying, monitoring of protected areas, mapping land and marine ecosystems, supporting anti-poaching and anti-wildlife trafficking efforts as well as collecting wildlife data in remote areas while minimizing disturbance.

Drones are used in collecting and monitoring (extreme) weather data. Unmanned technologies, such as drones and tethered weather balloons, can cost-effectively collect weather data in severe or remote environments such as the Arctic regions. These easily deployable platforms, mostly quite small, are proving that they are capable of capturing data that are unobtainable by other means. Capturing data is performed especially over tundra, ice and open water masses, which is important to improving the accuracy of

---

35 *See* PowerDMS. Fire Department Drone Policies. Developing a policy that makes sense for your department, 20 March 2019. NFPA 2400 – Standard for Small Unmanned Aircraft Systems (sUAS) Used for Public Safety Operations (https://www.powerdms.com/blog/fire-department-drone-policies/).

forecasts of high-impact weather events, according to recent research done by the U.S. National Oceanic and Atmospheric Administration (NOAA).[36]

Drones are useful for providing more real-time information in parts of the sky that are hardly monitored by observation satellites (satellite coverage gap). The U.S. National Aeronautics and Space Administration (NASA) contributes to storm watching by ex-military drones capable of flying at high altitudes into a cyclone. In this particular situation, drones monitor the progression of storms by storm tracking, such as a tropical storm developing into a hurricane. Forecasting of these phenomena is of utmost importance.

Analysing storms, assessing storm features such as intensity and expanse, will significantly improve warning signals to aid in the preparation of better evacuation plans, limit damage to properties and infrastructure and reduce risk to life. To understand how tornadoes are formed, so-called parent storms or supercells must be observed, according to the U.S. National Science Foundation (NSF), which, together with the NOAA, will financially support the so-called Targeted Observation by Radars and UAS of Supercells (TORUS), a drone-based investigation of severe storms, launched by a group of tech institutions.[37]

Drones are used for public and private security. Enhanced surveillance is one of the main benefits of drone deployment as far as public or private security is concerned. Drones, equipped with cameras and sensors, including uninterrupted view, thermal imaging and night vision lenses, provide extensive coverage, even in remote areas to check on crucial and valuable objects. They are able to monitor large areas of estates, government facilities, private and commercial properties, any other sites where security is needed. In addition, they can autonomously provide real-time alerts to security and law enforcement in the event of suspicious or unlawful activity.

However, it is important to distinguish between protection of privacy and that of personal data. Processing of personal data and privacy-sensitive recordings without prior permission could pose a legal issue, inasmuch as privacy has always been a fundamental public concern.[38] Drones, considered as flying platforms *pur sang*, are unable to collect and process personal data, but equipped with high-tech instrumentation, such as cameras, sensors for interception of telecommunication, microphones, radars, GPS and Wi-Fi routers, may give rise to diverse commercial, professional, law enforcement surveillance, intelligence and private uses.

---

36   *See* NOAA Unmanned Aircraft Systems Program (https://uas.noaa.gov/).
37   TORUS is launched by the University of Nebraska-Lincoln, Texas Tech University, the University of Colorado Boulder and the NOAA.
38   Universal Declaration of Human Rights (UDHR), proclaimed by the General Assembly of the United Nations on 10 December 1948, Art. 12 Right to privacy. European Convention on Human Rights (ECHR) or the Convention for the Protection of Human Rights and Fundamental Freedoms (Rome, 4 November 1950), Section 1 Rights and Freedoms, Art. 8 Right to respect for private and family life. Charter of Fundamental Rights of the European Union, Art. 7.

When using all these applications, especially with instruments like cameras and sensors, it is possible that people come into 'the picture' or objects that can be linked to specific people. This may compromise the privacy of those involved, although the probability is somewhat greater in one application than in another. For example, using drones for investigative purposes puts privacy at stake. The government may not infringe on the right to privacy except to the extent provided for by law and what is necessary in a democratic society.

> ECHR, Article 8 Right to respect for private and family life:
> 1. Everyone has the right to respect for his private and family life, his home and his correspondence.
> 2. There shall be no interference by a public authority with the exercise of this right except such as is in accordance with the law and is necessary in a democratic society in the interests of national security, public safety or the economic well-being of the country, for the prevention of disorder or crime, for the protection of health or morals, or for the protection of the rights and freedoms of others.

There is no such thing as private airspace, but there is a far-reaching right to human privacy. With regard to airspace, only the state has complete and exclusive sovereignty over the airspace above its territory.[39] That means, a state has a sovereign right over every person and foreign powers when it comes to the use of its airspace. Likewise, the state has sole competence over the design, management and regulation of its national airspace. Nevertheless, each ICAO contracting state undertakes to collaborate in securing the highest, practicable degree of uniformity in regulations, standards, procedures and organization in relation to aircraft, personnel, airways and auxiliary services in all matters in which such uniformity will facilitate and improve air navigation. (Chicago Convention, Art. 37).

Private and Commercial (Industrial) Sector

Drones are increasingly being used for civilian purposes. They are simply another use of flying robots. Where normally a manned aircraft was to be used for certain private or business activities, today a drone could possibly be a more attractive and less costly tool in surveying a construction worksite; flying over a real estate property; delivering packages or food to customers and consumers; conducting business promotion, marketing and

---

39 Chicago Convention, Art. 1.

advertising; inspecting infrastructure; or just using this incredible invention in the drone racing sport.

Drones are used in construction, where they act mainly as workforce multipliers. They are having a huge impact in construction, which means considerable changes within the global construction industry. They are used for land and building surveillance methods, enabling the capture of necessary data in a short time. Drones are cost-cutting tools that will shorten construction time by rapidly gathering and reporting data and maintaining constant contact at worksites. They are able to perform difficult on-site inspections and security and safety surveillance to reduce theft of materials and machinery and to keep workers safe. Efficient transportation of goods, communication and management of workflow and construction processes are accomplished by on-site drones. As safety is a key factor in the construction industry, drones can be usefully deployed to reduce the risk to both the workforce and the general public.[40]

Local surveying drones are likely to be used in the real estate industry to capture aerial views of properties for sale or promotional purposes. Drone and camera technology, capable of capturing still and map images, video and 360-degree panoramas, is one of the most important innovations in real estate marketing and listing. It gives visual insight on previously inaccessible vantage points by taking awesome aerial pictures that provide a unique perspective when it comes to featuring property.

However, the use for promotional purposes and visualization will be affected by high competition between real estate agencies, as evidenced by luxury real estate companies providing clients with virtual reality tours of properties. Although these real estate drones are today still basic units, they will in the near future, as technology becomes more robust be likely to complete indoor modelling for agencies as an additional value. Overall, these aerial images are of most value with larger, more luxurious properties.

Drones are used in the insurance sector. They have the opportunity to increase safety in performing claim assessments in tandem with making the process more efficient overall. External damage or roof assessments often require an inspector to be in time-consuming but, above all, hazardous environments, whereas drones can capture these images more timely and without exposing an inspector to such risk. In addition, insurance companies could map the state of properties on contract signature, which could be used as reference to record damages in case of adverse events.

Drones are used in the mining industry for maintenance, mapping and monitoring as well as pre- and post-blast data collection. Mineral surveillance drones can help to build 3D maps of mine sites to constantly monitor the progress and safety of the mines. They can also help in identifying minerals for potential extraction by looking at mineral patterns or in delivering samples from sites, and even in preserving cultural heritage

---

40 Burger, R., '6 Ways Drones are Affecting the Construction Industry', *The Balance Small Business*, 15 August 2019 (www.thebalancesmb.com/drones-affecting-construction-industry-845293).

and nature close to the mine sites, since drones are generally environmentally and nature friendly.

Furthermore, drones are useful in maintaining safety and enhancing security in mining, which is among the most unsafe industries for workers, especially those performing deep underground activities in an environment associated with rock falls, extremely humid conditions, gas leaks, dust explosions and floods. Drones are also able to monitor and inspect deep shafts, saving approximately 90% of the traditional cost per hour.[41]

Drones are used in maintenance and inspection work. They are ideal devices to inspect all kinds of otherwise time-consuming and difficult to approach objects and are confirmed as a safe, cost-effective and efficient approach in the infrastructure inspection industry. Constructions such as buildings and infrastructure must be inspected for preventive or periodical maintenance, and power line inspections are carried out in areas that are difficult to access, e.g. confined areas or areas such as nuclear power plants, oil and gas infrastructure, cooling towers, solar farms and wind farms, where access poses health, safety and environmental risk to humans. The telecom industry uses drones in the category of High-Altitude Long Endurance (HALE) and/or High-Altitude Pseudo Satellite (HAPS) capable of providing communication services.[42]

There are even specific drones for inspection of large-sized commercial aircraft. These drones, individually or in a group, examine aircraft for hailstone damage, lightning strike burn marks or holes, flaws in paint quality and foreign object damage, to name some defects. Inspections are carried out during maintenance checks of the hull and high-rise sections of an aircraft, such as vertical stabilizers or tail fins or any other essential parts. A drone can make images of every square inch of an aircraft in equal detail and releases human inspectors from risky and laborious duties. It reduces cost and the unscheduled on ground time and the administrative process through real-time detection and digital processing.[43]

Drones are conveniently used for movie production and media activities, such as news coverage and entertainment. The media and film industry are already a driving force behind the use of drones, particularly in broadcasting sport events and producing movies and documentaries. As drones provide a cost-effective alternative to helicopter

---

41 See Brightmore, D., 'How Drone Technology is Influencing the Mining Industry', *MiningGlobal*, 13 November 2019 (www.miningglobal.com).
42 A HALE is an unmanned aircraft that flies at altitudes of over 60,000 ft and can remain airborne for extremely lengthy periods. It can be used for various applications such as extensive surveillance, image-collection operations and communications (https://dronecenter.bard.edu/high-altitude-drones/). *See also* Aurora Flight Sciences (A Boeing Company) Odysseus High-Altitude Pseudo Satellite solar-powered autonomous aircraft powered by the sun (www.aurora.aero/odysseus-high-altitude-pseudo-satellite-haps/). Moreover, UAVOS Inc. developed in 2020 the Saker-1C, an autonomous Medium-Altitude Long Endurance (MALE) drone for SAR missions.
43 Exploring the Potential of Drone Inspection for Aircraft Maintenance Checks (https://eleks.com/blog/drone-inspection-for-aircraft-maintenance-checks/).

flights for aerial views, and offer new opportunities to capture unique vantage points or specific data in assessing weather conditions, wide adoption across the media landscape is expected. They are being used mainly as a single recording device or in a composite system to film movies, television serials and documentaries in order to provide real-life experience to the viewers, to cover news footage, to produce digital video journalism, to record events and functions and for aerial photography.

Aerial views of action sequences in movies can now be taken smoothly, and journalists and photographers can now cover news and pictures in areas where human entry could be dangerous or prohibited or places in nature that may otherwise be inaccessible (so-called drone journalism). Broadcasting of sports events and entertainment are expected to be the greatest users, and other nationwide and regional news and programming attract relatively high numbers of users.

In Europe alone, approximately 30,000 drones may potentially be demanded, most of them being stationary imaging multicopters with exceptions for beyond visual line of sight (BVLOS) drones that replace some helicopter-based imaging.[44] Multi-drone systems can provide novel visual effects and enhanced forms of viewer engagement and interactivity to future media production. Drones can also be used for advertisement or can be equipped with projectors to display live images on high-rise buildings or walls.

Drones are being used in applied sciences to support research and education, for a variety of tasks varying from wildlife behaviour to pollution monitoring or geological studies. These tasks might include a mix of drones for localized surveying where researchers are present in the immediate vicinity and for more complex BVLOS systems that provide access to new environments, including hazardous settings. Drones are able to collect data for the benefit of various sciences in inaccessible places while minimizing disturbance. As a result, new scientific insight can be obtained in the field of archaeology and geology such as tracing, locating and exploring of mineral resources by means of 3D maps or watching volcano lava flows.

Biology is using drones to track sea mammals and to count animal populations and migrations, where ecology uses them to investigate forestry and to monitor vegetation communities, species and habitats such as plants and the environment in which they exist or try to survive, for example how invasive plants are pushing out native plants, especially in wildland areas and the European Nature 2000 protected natural areas network. In the domain of geography, the ease of sampling by drones means that drones can repeatedly visit areas to acquire new physical data to measure change of relatively fixed objects in the landscape or to determine such change as erosion in valleys. Thousands of such drones are used in larger universities in assisting an increasing number of applicable areas of research.

---

44 SESAR (Single European Sky ATM Research) European Drones Outlook Study: Unlocking the Value for Europe, November 2016, pp. 69-70.

There is a relentless flow of new developments and advancements related to drones themselves. Innovation requires testing facilities, ranging from an indoor closed environment to an outdoor research, testing, developing and training site for unmanned systems on land, in the air and/or water. University-based drone laboratories, often in collaboration with pure technological research institutions, are allowing for rapid innovation prototyping as well as testing and deploying of new technologies.

Drones are used in sports in a passive (assisting, broadcasting) and active (action) way. There is increasing potential for drones in the broadcasting of sport events, where they offer a multitude of angles and heights that conventional cameras cannot. They are also assisting coaches to monitor training or the progress of the game from different perspectives in order to develop new tactics, strategies and better techniques. They provide usable coaching data and sport-wide applications, such as guidance of blind athletes. Widespread use will only increase in the years to come and help advance the science of coaching. But there are also active drone performances like very popular (indoor) drone racing, where drone pilots have the opportunity to show off their skills in tournaments. Today, drone racing, generally seen as a private sporting activity, is a global activity.[45]

The growing interest of users in drone technology has resulted in new areas of application for this state-of-the-art device, such as pocket-sized quadcopters equipped with HD cameras to make stunning selfies. Advancing technology will lead to more complex dedicated applications such as urban air mobility. New small aircraft designs linked to autonomous flight technology, on the one hand, and increasing two-dimensional capacity unable to ease existing congested traffic situations in urban areas on the other, are ingredients for a new time-efficient mode of travel along urban air mobility routes. This mode, a new era in air travel, may serve as air taxis, airport shuttles and intercity flight services, and in air cargo configuration for delivery of goods in urban and rural areas.[46]

It is only a matter of time before automated cargo air vehicles (CAVs) begin to transport time-sensitive and high-value goods from air cargo logistics centres to end users or, in a larger context, take delivery from producers and manufacturers to distribution centres. To ensure safe flight operations, a CAV will always fly within

---

45 FAI World Air Sports Federation (www.fai.org/world-cups/drone-racing-2019).
46 U.S. FAA has granted a CFR Part 135-Air Operator Certificate (AOC) to United Parcel Service (UPS) for a drone airline called UPS Flight Forward. The airline intends to operate commercial drone flights, BVLOS during the day and night under certain restrictions. UPS starts delivering medicines to hospitals. UPS cooperates with the North Carolina Department of Transportation (NCDOT) on the Unmanned Aircraft Systems Integration Pilot Program.

designated airspace and is equipped with automated safety features that can command the vehicle to land.

In the context of the European Innovation Partnership on Smart Cities and Communities (EIP-SCC), a European study on mobility drones is targeting the non-urgent transport of patients. In a city like Geneva, 30,000 patients are transported each year between the University Hospitals of Geneva (HUG) and the geriatric hospital of Trois-Chênes via busy roads. These special air taxicab drones need favourable conditions, put in place by the local government, within the regulatory framework in order to be able to operate with the objective of unclogging roads and saving time.[47]

However, there is a malicious, criminal and frightening side to the use of drones as well, namely to commit or hatch a conspiracy to commit serious crimes, including terrorist offences. Following the al-Qaida organization attacks on 11 September 2001 within the United States, Yoshihiro Francis Fukuyama described this new threat environment thus:

> The possibility that a relatively small and weak non-State organization could inflict catastrophic damage is something genuinely new in international relations, and it poses an unprecedented security challenge.

In most earlier historical periods the ability to inflict serious damage to a society lay only within the purview of States: the entire edifice of international relations theory is built around the presumption that States are the only significant players in world politics. If catastrophic destruction can be inflicted by non-State actors, then many of the concepts that informed security policy over the past two centuries – balance of power, deterrence, containment, and the like – lose their relevance.[48]

Drone technology could be deployed by criminal minds seeking to attack cities and citizens around the world. Drones are becoming even more powerful and smarter, making them increasingly attractive for legitimate use, but also for subversive hostile acts, according to Sir Julian King, European Commissioner for the Security Union (September 2016). The European Commission warns against the use of drones for terrorist purposes and wants to support the EU Member States on relevant defensive measures in the coming years, to build networks for sharing information, increasing

---

[47] The EIP-SCC, launched in 2013, seeks to establish strategic partnerships between industries and European cities to develop and roll out the urban systems and infrastructures of tomorrow. It aims to boost the development of smart technologies in cities by pooling research resources from energy, transport and ICT and concentrating them on a few demonstration projects that will be implemented in partnership with cities (https://ec.europa.eu/info/eu-regional-and-urban-development/topics/cities-and-urban-development/city-initiatives/smart-cities_en).

[48] Fukuyama, F., *After the Neocons: America at the Crossroads*, London: Profile Books, 2006, pp. 67-68.

international engagement, and to provide funding for projects to counter the threat of drones.[49]

With a view to enhancing security, the EU is funding projects to develop autonomous drone swarms, possessing artificial intelligence, to patrol its borders.

Despite divergent conclusions from previous studies on the possible use of drones by terrorists, there are two important factors that will contribute to the use of drones by terrorists. The first is communication or messaging, as a tactical objective of terrorist violence, while the second is the effects of commercial expansion of drones on the costs and accessibility of drones.

Terrorist groups will be interested in acquiring lethal autonomous weapon systems in the form of drones, preferably provided with artificial intelligence, for three reasons: cost, traceability and effectiveness. It is conceivable that terrorist groups or individual terrorists will utilize these tools for destabilizing activities or acts of retaliation. These kinds of reprehensible actions can have huge implications for future security, global economy and international relations. Therefore, the terrorist threat from drones is a very serious concern to authorities around the world. The terrorist drone threat might include deadly attacks such as spreading of biological agents over football stadiums and other such crowded spaces or other extremely significant soft targets. Terrorists could also create swarms of autonomous drone weapon systems, killer robots, each capable of engaging its own target, to execute rapid and coordinated horrifying attacks, while the attackers will stay far away from their targets.[50]

The success of potential attacks is based on three primary tactical outcomes:
1. targeted individuals are injured or killed;
2. property is damaged or destroyed; or
3. an activity in or by the target state is disrupted.

The employment of drones by terrorists is not to be dismissed as a distant threat. Drone manufacturers and technology providers will endeavour to make this technology more accessible. Unfortunately, commercial development will make drone technology more attractive and accessible to terrorists as well. Terrorists seek to acquire small drones because of their significant potential benefits.

One of the key components of terrorism is communication. Terrorists engage in violence to send a message to a target audience. The primary audience will be those who witness and observe the violence and destruction and engage in discourse about what they have seen. Thus, the message is not the violence or destruction itself; rather, the message is either embedded within the violence or follows from it in subsequent messaging. Therefore, the tactical output of a terrorist action may not be the people

---

49 Schilz, C.B., 'Terrorgefahr: EU warnt vor "feindseligen Akten⊠ durch Drohnen⊠, *Welt am Sonntag*, 03 August 2019.
50 Ware, J., 'Terrorist Groups, Artificial Intelligence, and Killer Drones', *War on the Rocks*, 24 September 2019.

killed or the damaged property but rather the message it sends to a target audience that is separate from those targeted in the attack. The more attention the action will yield, through sheer destruction or because of the targets' high value, the more lucrative a particular target becomes. The assumption that terrorists will attack soft targets rather than protected ones because of the additional operational complexity amounts to oversimplifying the issue.

Human supervisory control is one of the biggest advantages of drone technology, allowing individuals with minimal training to control these aircraft. Instead of having to understand aeronautical principles and the complex controls of an aircraft, as a pilot must, drone operators are simply performing human supervisory control, a higher-level function where the operator encourages the aircraft to do whatever he or she wants. Drone technology allows operators to move away from traditional command and control systems that require them to micromanage the behaviour of the aerial vehicle and to concentrate instead on the more mission-relevant part of command and control, which appeals to terrorists. Additionally, the relatively low cost of small and medium-sized drones will make them a viable delivery mechanism for terrorists.[51]

Drones are also used by smugglers and traffickers for contraband transport, including drugs and weapons. Recent evidence shows that criminal organizations now use drones to scope out exploitable security gaps before a robbery, for instance memorizing the movements of security guards from the air. Improved artificial intelligence has made drones valuable for more high-profile crimes, such as spying on police departments to collect information about who might be collaborating with the police, to be able to intimidate witnesses and, in no uncertain terms, to discourage snitching.

Another major drawback of using drones is infringement on privacy with potentially far-reaching consequences.

Regarding all these unlawful activities, comprehensive drone regulation must be established and applied to prevent the use of felonious actions. Other restrictions are to use drones only within the operator's visual line of sight (VLOS) and to make identification mandatory.[52] In the most extreme case, governments could choose to employ drone-jamming equipment around security-sensitive areas and buildings, although this method might pose an interference problem with traditional civil aircraft.

Better prevention methods are to set up (temporary) no-fly zones, for example, by making use of geofencing systems, such as the Geospatial Environment Online (GEO)

---

51 Card, B.A., 'Terror from Above: How the Commercial UAV Revolution Threatens the US Threshold', *Air and Space Power Journal*, Vol. 32, no. 1, Spring 2018, pp. 81-93.
52 VLOS means a type of operation in which the remote pilot maintains continuous unobstructed and unaided visual contact with the UA, allowing the remote pilot to monitor the flight path of the UA in relation to other aircraft, persons and obstacles, for the purpose of keeping them separate and avoiding collisions

2.0-system, especially developed to prevent drones from airspace infringements, in particular with regard to European aerodrome control zones (CTRs).[53]

---

53 Drone Watch, 12 February 2019.

Chapter 2 Legal Basis for Drone Operations

2.1 Introduction

In the International Civil Aviation Organization regulatory scheme, no distinction is made between manned and unmanned aircraft, probably because the earlier regulatory structure under ICAO was inadequate to address the unique characteristics of unmanned aircraft. The Chicago Convention and its Annexes do not provide a clear definition of an unmanned aircraft. On the other hand, a number of ICAO Annexes, including Annex 2, do provide a definition of an aircraft: "any machine that can derive support in the atmosphere from the reactions of the air other than the reactions of the air against the Earth's surface", which clearly establishes a connection with aerodynamic capabilities.

Annex 2 defines an aeroplane as "a power-driven heavier-than-air aircraft, deriving its lift in flight chiefly from aerodynamic reactions to surfaces which remain fixed under given conditions of flight". There are, however, two definitions where the term unmanned is displayed, namely remotely piloted aircraft, which is defined as "an unmanned aircraft which is piloted from a remote pilot station", and unmanned free balloon, defined as "a non-power-driven, unmanned, lighter-than-air aircraft in free flight".[1]

Both first definitions in Annex 2 do not describe the term unmanned, while they do not exclude an unmanned version either. These definitions provide the first point of analysis in answering the key question of whether unmanned aircraft are governed by ICAO rules. Almost any aircraft, manned or unmanned, meets each element of both definitions without even naming the unmanned version. Only Article 8 of the Chicago Convention, and amended by the ICAO Assembly (Doc 7300), provides some guidance:

> Pilotless aircraft.
> No aircraft capable of being flown without a pilot shall be flown without a pilot over the territory of a contracting State without special authorization by that State and in accordance with the terms of such authorization. Each contracting State and in accordance with the terms of flight of such aircraft without a pilot in regions open to civil aircraft shall be so controlled as to obviate danger to civil aircraft.

---

1 In 1948, the ICAO Council noted that the provisions of Ann. 2, including the definitions of aircraft and aeroplane, were written to facilitate incorporation into national legislation without major textual changes (ICAO website, Introduction).

The Chicago delegates, who actually drafted in 1944 three agreements – the Chicago Convention, the International Air Services Transit Agreement (IASTA) and the International Air Transport Agreement (IATA) – presumably recognized through Article 8 the danger to persons and property on the surface and to other airspace users, which could possibly result in unilaterally inflicted damage. Undeniably, this behaviour still has an enormous impact on the sharing of airspace.

Discussions about Article 8 led to the release of ICAO Circular 328 AN/190 in 2011, determining that all unmanned aircraft fall under Article 8, including fully autonomous systems, and that existing SARPs are predominantly applicable. Model aircraft are regulated nationally.

To safely merge unmanned aircraft into non-segregated airspace, for operations equal to traditional manned aviation, is considered quite a challenging objective. Such a seamless, efficient and safe integration into airspace will be achieved only through the application of innovative technologies and pioneering research as well as the careful development and implementation of a tight and solid regulatory framework, preferably internationally.

In this time frame of exponential growth of innovations, modern aerospace technology is capable, with the use of a variety of novel high-performance techniques and materials, of developing and manufacturing very specific civil unmanned aircraft systems or UAS, demonstrating a high level of safety, acceptable to the aviation oversight authorities and the public.

It is the unmanned aircraft or drone technology that is developing at such an exponential rate that it outpaces the capacity of regulators in most states in the world, and certainly of international aviation organizations, to react timely with adequate, coordinated and harmonized rules to ensure the safety of drone operations, both commercial and recreational, to a level equivalent to manned aviation.

Especially, before (international) commercial UAS activities may be commenced, full compliance is required with a complete, uniform international regulatory framework, based on appropriate principles and guidelines. The principal objective of such a comprehensive regulatory framework is the safety of any other airspace user and the safety of persons and property on the surface. While elements of the regulatory framework for UAS certainly exist inasmuch as UAS are considered aircraft, and as such major portions of the international regulatory framework for manned aviation are directly applicable, the development may be a prolonged exercise, probably lasting years.

As safety is the predominant requirement in any mode of air transportation, the safety of UAS operations is equally important to that of traditional manned aircraft operations. Automation and new technologies will continue to revolutionize current safety standards that will give reliability an incredible boost. In the foreseeable future with respect to air traffic control, Regional Flow Management Units (RFMU) will be capable of and responsible for managing the flow of total air traffic, including unmanned aircraft, through the airspace in their particular regions by an Aviation System Block Upgrade (ASBU) to the air traffic management (ATM) performance as a stepping stone to the future Single Global Sky.[2]

The separation of aircraft in flight will be managed by a network of computers. New flight levels at higher altitudes are introduced for NextGen aircraft, creating space for specific slower UAS operations, such as unmanned all-cargo transport. However, there will still be serious objections concerning some or all modes of UAS operations. In particular, owing to lack of public confidence, despite the ultra-high level of automation and computerized decision-making, passenger-carrying aircraft will continue to have pilot(s) on board, at least in the medium term and most probably for a considerable time thereafter.

The pilot is still the pilot, whether he or she is at the remote console of the RPAS or on the actual flight deck. The skills must be the same. With the potential of unmanned aircraft, the standards for pilot training need to be set high to ensure that those on the surface and other airspace users are not put in jeopardy. A rather paradigmatic, though professional, statement comes from the side of International Federation of Air Line Pilots' Associations (IFALPA) concerning UAS. A couple of years ago this international organization was of the opinion that UAS technology would not be capable of replacing human capacities, particularly in complex and safety-critical situations. Therefore, IFALPA strongly opposed the use of UAS to supplant the role of pilots in any type of air transport system.[3]

Contrary to this, the European Commission High Level Group (HLG) on aviation and aeronautics research consistently proclaimed in its report on future aviation of 2011:

> The European air transport system operates seamlessly through fully interoperable and networked systems allowing manned and unmanned air vehicles to safely operate in the same airspace.[4]

As non-segregated airspace users, UAS have to comply with not only the minimum international personnel licensing and airworthiness standards established by ICAO

---

2   ICAO 12th Air Navigation Conference, Montreal, on 19 November 2012. The ASBU framework is ICAO's systems engineering approach to achieve global ATM interoperability and harmonization. The Block Upgrades are the product of inclusive and prolonged collaboration between ICAO, Air Navigation Service Providers (ANSPs), Member States and industry stakeholders from around the world.
3   International Federation of Air Line Pilot's Associations (IFALPA) statement on UAS, 13POS04, 12 October 2012.
4   Flightpath 2050 Europe's Vision for Aviation, Maintaining Global Leadership & Serving Society's Needs, Report of the High Level Group on Aviation Research, Luxembourg: Publications Office of the European Union, 2011, p. 17.

Annexes 1 and 8, but, additionally, with critical rules of the air as laid down in ICAO Annex 2.[5]

With respect to rules of the air for unmanned aviation, but also to other essential issues such as flight operations, maintenance and licensing, the intention is to stay as close to existing rules as possible. However, a prerequisite for UAS integration in non-segregated airspace is to possibly amend ICAO Annexes on these three essential domains, if specific characteristics and safety give reason to do so.

As traditional manned aviation developed in the early 20th century to become an international activity, so too did the principles and regulations governing it. In these particular regulations, a distinction is made between commercial flights and non-commercial activities. In other words, this kind of regulation is based on the nature of the particular operation. Stricter rules apply to the more uninvolved persons being air transported. This is particularly evident in pilot licensing, ranging from a rather modest but adequate light aircraft pilot licence (LAPL), allowing the pilot to fly small aircraft in Europe, to a professional air transport pilot licence (ATPL), required to be able to fly a large commercial airliner worldwide.

Regarding the existing EU regulations on drones, so far a distinction has also been made on the basis of the nature or characteristics of the drone operation, commercial or non-commercial. With the upcoming new EU regulations on drones, this distinction ceases to exist.

Which rules will apply will soon be determined on the basis of a risk profile. This risk profile also determines which of the three main categories the drone operations will fall into: open, specific or certified. The latter category relates to manned aviation, because this concerns, for instance, large drones that transport cargo. An unmanned Airbus A330 is conceivable and feasible in this setting.

Naturally, manned aviation regulations are also risk based, but in manned aviation the starting point is the risk for aircraft occupants, namely passengers and crew as well as livestock (e.g. racing horses and equestrian horses).

Because today an unmanned aircraft does not carry a flight crew as well as any passengers (yet), regulations for this category are focused mainly on the risk of people and property on the surface and to avoid collisions with manned aircraft. Precisely for manned aviation transporting passengers and/or cargo, stricter rules apply to aircraft and

---

5 See also Art. 31 Certificates of airworthiness, Art. 32 Licenses of personnel, Art. 33 Recognition of certificates and licences and Art. 38 Departures from international standards and procedures, of the Chicago Convention, 1944. In the European Union, Standardized European Rules of the Air (SERA) have been laid down by Commission Implementing Regulation (EU) No. 923/2012 of 26 September 2012 laying down the common rules of the air and operational provisions regarding services and procedures in air navigation and amending Implementing Regulation (EU) No. 103/2011 and Regulations (EC) No. 1265/2007, (EC) No. 1794/2006, (RC) No. 730/2006, (EC) No. 1033/2006 and (EU) No. 255/2010, OJ L 281/1, 13 October 2012.

flight crew than to non-commercial, recreational flights. Basically, unmanned aviation does not make this difference.

In manned aviation, the requirements in terms of safety measures are meticulously established. Detailed, for example, are operation-related requirements for the flight crew, such as mandatory proficiency checks, type recurrent training, medical examinations and crew resource management (CRM), all under state authority oversight. Under the new unmanned aircraft regulation, it is left to the operator to determine, on the basis of the nature of the flight, which associated risks are involved and, if necessary, to provide additional training.

The conclusion might imply that these divergent regulations (rule based and risk based), and the way different stakeholders work with these rules, will differ greatly. This can lead to conflicting regulations and requirements for manned and unmanned aviation that, remarkably enough, are intended to operate safely together in the same airspace – a huge challenge in the short term and certainly in the long term when the forecast on drone traffic growth in the specific and certified categories becomes reality.

2.2 Outline of ICAO UAS Regulatory Framework

ICAO recognizes a variety of aircraft categories, among them balloons, gliders, engine-powered fixed-wing and rotary-wing aircraft. Aircraft can be land based, sea based or amphibious. Whether the aircraft is manned or unmanned does not affect its status as an aircraft. Each category of aircraft will potentially have unmanned versions, now and in the future. This position is central to all further issues pertaining to unmanned aircraft, and provides the foundation for addressing airworthiness, personnel licensing, rules of the air, airspace use, etc.

In the early days of remotely piloted aircraft, no standards had been developed on how to approve an RPAS, assess the airworthiness of the RPA or evaluate the remote pilot qualifications. This was because this new area required new classifications and licensing not only for aircraft but for pilots and other crew members as well.

Moreover, it must be evident that these new rules consider RPAS as a specific aviation product and likewise a total aircraft system. In this respect, the aircraft is no longer the system, but the system comprises the aircraft. This position has also been taken by the Joint Aviation Authorities (JAA), EUROCONTROL and EASA.[6] Therefore, discussions are under way on the perspective of whether the total system applies not only to the certification or approval of the various elements that contribute to aviation safety, but also how to approach the airworthiness certificates in case these individual elements would control multiple vehicles or different types of vehicles.

---

6   EUROCONTROL, European Organization for the Safety of Air Navigation.

Any aircraft intended to be flown without a pilot on board is referred to in the Chicago Convention and amended by the ICAO Assembly, as a pilotless aircraft. Today, these aircraft are commonly known as unmanned aircraft rather than pilotless aircraft. Remotely piloted aircraft (RPA) are one type of unmanned aircraft, whether remotely piloted, fully autonomous or a combination thereof. They are all subject to the provisions of Article 8 of the Chicago Convention.

Unmanned aircraft include a broad spectrum, from meteorological free flying balloons to highly complex aircraft piloted from remote stations by fully licensed aviation professionals. These complicated aircraft are part of the category of RPA that operate as part of a system, *in casu*, a remotely piloted aircraft system (RPAS). In addition to RPA, a range of new aviation activities has recently gained momentum. These include small unmanned aircraft (sUAS) with a future perspective, referred to as delivery service drones able to transport a variety of goods and persons (air taxis) that will operate alongside existing airspace users. However, in the foreseeable future, it is plausible that only RPAS will be able to integrate into the international civil aviation system.

RPAS are creating a new industry with significant economic potential. They offer a vast range of capabilities and sophistication. The operation of RPAS has been identified as having the potential for significant economic, societal and environmental benefits. Associated technologies, designs and operating concepts of RPAS are evolving rapidly. It is within this context that states, and organizations such as ICAO, are being challenged with the safe and efficient integration of RPAS into environments shared by a highly regulated and well-established manned aviation industry.

ICAO initiated a comprehensive RPAS full regulatory approach, including RPAS workshops. These workshops offer a unique opportunity for rule-making authorities, air navigation service providers (ANSPs), industry partners, international organizations and other stakeholders to share knowledge and experiences.

To facilitate the expansion of ICAO's work programme, which means activities to support and accelerate the development of regulatory frameworks for RPAS, an innovative and flexible approach should be adopted, taking into account ongoing development at the national, regional and international levels. Obviously, there is a need to increase the rate of regularity development to support the safe and socially responsible operation of unmanned aircraft.

Until recently, ICAO had not established specific SARPs on drones. Standards have been established only when there was an agreement between contracting states. In this light, every effort should be made among contracting states to collect data in a coordinated manner and share it plainly to expedite the development of international civil aviation standards on drone operations.

In 2003, the first discussions in ICAO began about this issue, which was increasingly becoming popular. During the first meeting of the 169th Session of the Air Navigation Commission (ANC), on 12 April 2005, ICAO's Secretary General was requested to

CHAPTER 2   LEGAL BASIS FOR DRONE OPERATIONS

consult selected states and international organizations about present and future international activities in civil airspace of unmanned aircraft and procedures to prevent danger to civil aircraft posed by unmanned aircraft operated as state aircraft, together with states' procedures that might be in place for the issuance of special operating authorizations for international civil unmanned aircraft operations.[7]

From 23 to 24 May 2006, at ICAO's headquarters in Montreal, ICAO held its first exploratory meeting on unmanned aircraft (ICAO-UAV SD 24/05/06). The meeting was attended by 37 delegates from 15 states and seven international organizations. Its primary objective was to explore the current state of affairs in regard to the development of regulatory material related to unmanned aircraft and to determine the potential role of ICAO in the regulatory process. The Secretariat would use the results of the meeting as the basis for developing a report to the ICAO ANC along with recommendations on an ICAO work programme.

ICAO initiated work on unmanned aircraft systems as early as 2007 when the ANC decided, during its 174th Session in April 2007, to establish a study group on UAS (UASSG). This study group served as the ICAO focal point for all UAS-related issues until it was superseded by the RPAS panel (RPASP) at the 196th Session in May 2014. This panel is composed of six working groups with experts in the fields of airworthiness, telecommunication for the command and control link and air traffic control, detect and avoid, personnel licensing, RPAS operations and air traffic management. Other panels of the ANC are involved in RPAS/UAS topics such as aircraft accident investigation, communications, flight recorders, frequency spectrum, aerial surveillance and safety management.[8]

The intention is that 18 of the 19 Annexes (Annex 5 – Units of Measurement to be used in Air and Ground Operations was not affected) will be amended to accommodate RPAS/UAS requirements.

Considerations, based on replies and reviews, were put forward by the Secretariat to assist in the discussions as follows: that Assembly Resolution A35-14, Appendix A – Formulation of Standards and Recommended Practices and Procedures for Air Navigation Services –, resolving clause no. 4 states:

> In the development of SARPs, procedures and guidance material, ICAO should utilize, to the maximum extent appropriate and subject to the adequacy of a verification and validation process, the work of other recognized standards-making organizations. Where deemed appropriate by the Council, material

---

7   ICAO Circular 328 AN/190, Chapter 1 Introduction, 1.2.
8   ICAO UAS Study Group (UASSG) ToRs: "to assist the Secretariat in coordinating the development of ICAO SARPs, Procedures and guidance material for civil unmanned aircraft systems (UAS), to support a safe, secure and efficient integration of UAS into non-segregated airspace and aerodromes".

developed by these other standards-making organizations should be referenced in ICAO documentation.

In addition to the intended amendments to the Annexes, it was considered that ICAO's concern is with international civil unmanned aircraft operations and the applicable standards that affect such operations and, furthermore, that ICAO should place increasing emphasis on the development of performance-based standards and less on technical standards and detailed specifications. It was the 35th Session of the ICAO Assembly that endorsed the understanding of unmanned aerial vehicles as stated by the Global Air Traffic Management Operational Concept (Doc 9854), First Edition – 2005, presenting the ICAO vision of an integrated, harmonized and globally interoperable ATM system:

> An unmanned aerial vehicle is a pilotless aircraft, in the sense of Article 8 of the Chicago Convention, which is flown without a pilot-in-command on board and is either remotely and fully controlled from another place (ground, another aircraft, space) or programmed and fully autonomous.

ATM considers the trajectory of a manned or unmanned vehicle during all phases of flight and manages the interaction of that trajectory with other trajectories or hazards to achieve the optimum system outcome, with minimal deviation from the user-requested flight trajectory, whenever possible.

The airspace will be organized and managed in a manner that will accommodate all current and potential new users of airspace, inter alia, unmanned aerial vehicles. Thus, both manned and unmanned aerial vehicles will form part of the ATM system. The ATM system will accommodate the limited ability of some vehicles to dynamically change trajectory. The regulatory framework under development by ICAO is being shaped within the context of the above statement.[9]

The exploratory meeting agreed that, although there would eventually be a wide range of technical and performance specifications and standards, only a portion of those would need to become ICAO SARPs. It was also determined that ICAO was not the most suitable body to lead the effort to develop such specifications. However, it was agreed that there was a need for harmonization of terms, strategies and principles with respect to the regulatory framework and that ICAO should act as a focal point.

The ICAO Secretariat has conducted the research among 43 states and nine international organizations, actively involved in unmanned aircraft activities or work

---

9   Global Air Traffic Management Operational Concept, First Edition 2005 (Doc 9854 AN/458), Chapter 1 General and Chapter 2 ATM Operational Concept Components.

efforts. The discussions identified the following critical issues related to unmanned aircraft operations that had to be addressed and resolved:
- Certification
    o Airframes
    o Air operations
    o Continuing airworthiness
    o Training institutions
    o Maintenance organizations
    o Manufacturers
    o Air navigation service providers with respect to unmanned aircraft operations
- Licensing
    o Operator qualifications
    o Medical fitness
    o Mutual recognition
- Regulations
    o Safety oversight
    o Terminology
    o Common standards to serve as the basis for national regulations
    o Operating permits
    o Air traffic services requirements
    o Accident investigation
    o Carriage of dangerous goods
- Technical issues
    o Frequency spectrum
    o Common approach to the concept of detect (or sense) and avoid
    o Data link issues for communication and surveillance
    o Separation minima
- Human factors issues
- Public acceptance
- Environment
- Security

The meeting was presented with the work of European Organization for the Safety of Air Navigation (EUROCONTROL), European Organization for Civil Aviation

Equipment (EUROCAE) and Radio Technical Commission for Aeronautics (RTCA). At the second informal ICAO meeting, which took place in Palm Coast, Florida, in January 2007, it was concluded that progress was made on technical specifications for UAS operations by working groups of both RTCA and EUROCAE.[10]

For the purpose of uniformity and to reflect the terminology used by ICAO, all texts refer to drones as UAS (the umbrella term for any aircraft intended to be flown without a pilot on board), in line with RTCA and EUROCAE agreements, to include all types of unmanned aircraft, which in most cases can be operated only as part of a system, and hence the term UAS, excluding model aircraft used for hobby or recreational purposes.[11] As a consequence, the main issue for ICAO was to coordinate the development of a strategic guidance document that would guide the regulatory evolution to be used as the foundation for the development of regulations by the various states and organizations. This document would serve as the basic principle for achieving consensus in the later coordinated development of SARPs. However, it was agreed that there was no specific need for new ICAO SARPs at that early stage.

To assist in the harmonization of terms, strategies and principles with respect to the regulatory framework, the ICAO UASSG has been active. The first meeting of UASSG was held in Montreal from 7 to 10 April 2008 at the ICAO headquarters. Ms. Nancy J. Graham, Director of the ICAO ANC, provided the participants with a brief synopsis of the expectations being placed on the UASSG in regard to the work to be done to review, develop and recommend amendments to ICAO SARPs and associated PANS necessary to accommodate civil UAS into non-segregated airspace.

As the high-level focal point for global interoperability within ICAO, the UASSG, predecessor of the RPASP, served to develop a regulatory concept and coordinate the development of RPAS SARPs, to develop a UAS regulatory concept and associated GM to support and guide the regulatory process, review ICAO SARPs, propose amendments and coordinate the development of UAS SARPs with other ICAO bodies, and to contribute to the development of technical specifications by other bodies and identifying communication requirements for RPAS so that they can be integrated in a safe, secure and most efficient way alongside traditional manned aircraft into non-segregated airspace and at aerodromes, without posing an undue hazard to other airspace users.

---

10 European Organization for Civil Aviation Equipment (EUROCAE), a non-profit organization established in 1963 in Switzerland, at Lucerne, and formally recognized in 1966 by the European Civil Aviation Conference (ECAC). The organization deals exclusively with aviation standardization for both airborne and ground systems and equipment (source: www.eurocae.net/). The Radio Technical Commission for Aeronautics, Inc. (RTCA), founded in 1935, is a US volunteer organization that develops technical guidance for use by government regulatory authorities and by industry (source: www.rtca.org/). EUROCAE and RTCA established a partnership in 1963.

11 De Florio, F., *Airworthiness: An Introduction to Aircraft Certification and Operations*, Third Edition, Kidlington, Oxford: Butterworth-Heinemann, 2016, pp. 476-477.

The ICAO RPASP, coordinating their work with the various groups of experts responsible for relevant ICAO Annexes and disciplines, initiated the continuation of the work of the UASSG with the following objectives and scope:
- to serve as the focal point and coordinator of all ICAO RPAS-related work, with the aim of ensuring global interoperability and harmonization;
- to develop SARPs, procedures and GM to facilitate safe, secure and efficient integration of RPA into non-segregated airspace and aerodromes;
- to review ICAO SARPs, propose amendments and coordinate the development of RPAS-related SARPs with other ICAO expert groups;
- to assess the impacts of proposed provisions on existing manned aviation, maintain the existing level of safety for manned aviation, prioritize instrument flight rules (IFR) operations in controlled airspace; and
- to coordinate as needed and support the development of a common position on bandwidth and frequency spectrum requirements for C2 link of RPAS for negotiations with the International Telecommunication Union (ITU) and its subsidiary World Radiocommunication Conference (WRC).

The increased use of UAS for civilian applications has presented many states with regulatory challenges. Such challenges include the need to ensure that UAS are operated safely, without jeopardizing people and national security, and in a way that would protect areas of national, historical and natural significance. A variety of states are requiring a comprehensive international regulatory framework to underpin routine operations of UAS throughout the world in a safe, harmonized and seamless manner comparable to that of manned aviation operations.

In 2011, ICAO issued Circular 328 AN/190 on UAS operations. Its purpose was, inter alia, to inform states of the emerging ICAO perspective on the integration of UAS into non-segregated airspace and aerodromes and to consider the fundamental differences from manned aviation that such an integration will involve, as well as to encourage states to assist with the development of ICAO policy on UAS by providing information on their own experiences associated with these particular aircraft.[12]

Circular 328 calls on states to provide comments, in particular with respect to its application and usefulness, in an effort to proceed with the development of the fundamental international regulatory framework through SARPs, with supporting PANS and GM. Furthermore, it iterated that unmanned aircraft are indeed aircraft and that, therefore, existing SARPs shall apply to a very great extent. The complete integration of UAS at aerodromes and in the various airspace classes will, however, necessitate the development of UAS customized SARPs to supplement those already existing.

---

12 An ICAO Circular consists of technical information of interest to states.

Progress of amendments to the Annexes. Amendments, including specific SARPs, are made in Annex 2 – Rules of the Air – , Annex 7 – Aircraft Nationality and Registration Marks –, and Annex 13 – Aircraft Accident and Incident Investigation – . Annex 1 – Personnel Licensing – is amended and in the phase of further amendments. Annex 6 – Operation of Aircraft – will contain a new Part IV, International Operations Remotely-Piloted Aircraft Systems. Annex 8 – Airworthiness of Aircraft – will be expanded to cover RPA and C2 link for control and management. Annex 10 – Aeronautical Telecommunications – will contain provisions for C2 link, frequency spectrum and detect and avoid capability. Annex 17 – Security – will include security measures for RPA and RPAS. Annex 18 – Dangerous Goods – will include requirements for RPA operations, and Annex 19 – Safety Management – will include RPAS industry safety requirements.

Circular 328 notified, as regards the integration of UAS into non-segregated airspace and at non-segregated aerodromes, that there shall be a pilot responsible for the UAS operation. In relation herewith, the term RPA was introduced to reflect the status of such aircraft monitored at all times by a remote pilot station, staffed by at least one qualified remote pilot, with the constant possibility of intervention.

Instigated by ICAO's cooperation with the European Union, during the Twelfth Air Navigation Conference of ICAO, held in Montreal from 19 to 30 November 2012, a Working Paper (AN-Conf/12-WP/48, of 4 October 2012), titled the Integration of Remotely Piloted Aircraft Systems in Civil Aviation in Europe, was presented by the presidency of the European Union on behalf of the European Union and its Member States, by the other Member States of ECAC, and by the Member States of EUROCONTROL, taking into account some overlap in the number of Member States concerned. The working paper provided an overview of the integration of RPAS in the civil aviation system in Europe, including the approach to ATM.

The general consensus is that RPAS should:

a. first be 'safe to fly', that means, the RPA needs an individual and valid certificate of airworthiness (CofA), while all the other elements of the system also need appropriate certification, as, for example, the remote pilot station and/or be under proper safety oversight, intended for service providers of satellite communications for C2 link;
b. be safely flown by properly competent and licensed pilots and other personnel; and
c. be under the legal and managerial responsibility of a certified RPAS operator, for both commercial and corporate operations, since the risk to society is identical.

Since 2012, ICAO is actively involved in facilitating the development of a regulatory framework for unmanned aviation and in leading the discussion on RPAS and UAS through the organization of global symposia. These consecutive symposia provide opportunities to states, international organizations and stakeholders to get a more detailed comprehension of the functioning and responsibilities of RPAS operators, airspace management, training options, licensing authorities and relevant requirements, regulators and the aerospace industry towards ensuring safe and secure operations.

Furthermore, these symposia provide the way in which entities can get information in regard to the transitioning from airspace segregation to integration and concerning the ability to assess the status of established regulations currently used in various parts of the world. Discussions during these symposia focus on complex issues to be resolved, such as finding solutions for domestic UAS operations, for a common global UAS traffic management (UTM) framework for low-altitude airspace use and, in particular, necessary registration, communication, geofencing or geofencing-like systems to prevent UAS operations in sensitive security areas and restricted and danger areas, and categorization for RPAS operations.[13]

As aviation safety rules have been developed to protect paying passengers and crews on board and other airspace users with respect to the risk of ground and mid-air collisions as well as third parties and property on the surface, the need to protect persons on board RPAS does not exist. Protection of people and property on the surface could, where appropriate, be mitigated by specific measures consisting of parachutes or any other system to reduce kinetic energy at impact, and prohibition to overfly densely populated areas, or fly into volcanic and other dangerous or contaminated clouds. Another important mitigating condition is that certain RPAS are designed and operated in specific airspace volumes, *in casu* very low-level (VLL) airspace, where almost no manned aircraft traffic will be present, with the exception of take-off and landing.

Moreover, the integration into non-segregated airspace must be such that UAS, including RPAS, should be accommodated within the current and the future modernized ATM system. The largest obstacle perceived for integration in non-segregated controlled and even uncontrolled airspace is the capacity of UAS to replicate the ability of humans to see and be seen (see, detect or sense and avoid). The main principle towards integration into non-segregated airspace is that UAS will have to fit into the ATM system and not the other way around, that the ATM system needs to adapt to enable UAS to integrate safely.

The current time is undoubtedly the optimal moment to succeed in this integration. Especially in this time frame, the technological advancements and resulting upgrades that the ATM systems are experiencing globally, in particular through the various continuous initiatives in Europe (Single European Sky ATM Research), the United States (US nationwide NextGen air transport system), Japan and other states, make this optimal

---

13 Unmanned aircraft system traffic management (UTM). A specific aspect of air traffic management that manages UAS operations safely, economically and efficiently through the provision of facilities and a seamless set of services in collaboration with all parties and involving airborne and ground-based functions. The UTM system is a system that provides UAS traffic management through the collaborative integration of humans, information, technology, facilities and services, supported by air, ground or space-based communications, navigation and surveillance (source: ICAO Unmanned Aircraft Systems Traffic management (UTM) – A Common Framework with Core Principles for Global Harmonization, p. 3).

moment a unique opportunity to have a favourable parallel evolution of UAS and ATM domains.

On 7 March 2012, at the fifth meeting of its 195th Session, the ICAO Council adopted new amendments for RPAS. Amendment 43 applies to the international Standards of Rules of the Air (Annex 2 to the Chicago Convention), and Amendment 6 to the international SARPs of Aircraft Nationality and Registration Marks (Annex 7 to the Chicago Convention). ICAO took Article 8 of the Chicago Convention as a starting point for the new amendments.

Firstly, Amendment 6 to Annex 7 acknowledges an RPA as a classification of aircraft, defining a remotely piloted aircraft as an unmanned aircraft that is piloted from a remote station (see Annex 7, 6th edition July 2012 under: International Standards).

Annex 7 – Aircraft Nationality and Registration Marks.
1. Definitions: A remotely piloted aircraft is an unmanned aircraft that is piloted from a remote pilot station.
2. Classification of aircraft.
2.1 aircraft shall be classified in accordance with Table 1.
2.2 an aircraft that is intended to be operated with no pilot on board shall be further classified as unmanned.
2.3 unmanned aircraft shall include unmanned free balloons and remotely piloted aircraft.

Secondly, Amendment 43 to Annex 2 provides the important safety-related details concerning the scope and content of the special authorizations governing RPA operations over a state's territory. This includes standards mandating approval of the RPAS, a certificate of airworthiness for the RPA, an operator certificate, remote pilot licences and licences of other members of the remote crew. These certificates and licences should be in accordance with national standards and consistent with the respective Annexes (Annex 8, 6 and 1).

Ability to act like any other aircraft.
    Issues to be considered:
– Certification: RPA, operator, remote pilot.
– Approval: RPAS as a complete system.
– Collision and hazard avoidance.
– Security: data links, RPA, remote pilot station.
– C2/C3 failure.

Annex 7 – Aircraft Nationality and Registration Marks.
    Applicable 15 November 2012:

CHAPTER 2   LEGAL BASIS FOR DRONE OPERATIONS

- An aircraft intended to be operated with no pilot on board shall be classified as unmanned.
- RPA: an unmanned aircraft which is piloted from a remote pilot station.
- Nationality, common and registration marks.
- Identification plate.

Annex 2 – Rules of the Air.
  Applicable 15 November 2012:
- RPA "shall be operated in such a manner as to minimize hazards to persons, property or other aircraft and in accordance with the conditions specified in Appendix 4":
  o Authorization of State of departure.
  o Special authorization from all States affected.
  o Coordination with ANSPs of high seas airspace.
  o Operated in accordance with conditions specified by the State of Registry, the State of the Operator and States overflown.
- RPAS shall be approved as a system, additionally:
  o The RPA shall have a Certificate of Airworthiness; and
  o associated RPAS components specified in type design shall be certificated and maintained.
- Operator shall have an RPAS Operator Certificate (ROC).
- Remote pilots shall be licensed or have their licences rendered valid.

Certificate of Airworthiness.
- Issued to RPA
  o RPA must be registered.
  o Certificate of Airworthiness considers entire system.
  o State of Design of RPA identifies on Type Certificate Data Sheet remote pilot station type(s) which can be utilized + all associated required components.
  o Continuous airworthiness of RPA per norm.
  o State oversight of remote pilot station essential.
  o ROC details specificities.
  o Quality of Service/Required Communication Performance (QoS/RCP) for C2/C3.

ICAO RPAS CONOPS for International IFR Operations, March 2017, Page 2-3:

> The existing SARPs and PANS must be revised, amended or enhanced to define the manner in which RPAS will have to comply. Where RPAS can comply in a manner similar to manned aircraft, they should do so. RPA are not yet considered to be able to meet the intent of 'see and avoid' comparable to a pilot on board, but will eventually be equipped with the capability to 'detect

and avoid' other aircraft and hazards. Thus, some alternate means of compliance for RPAS must be included, where necessary, in future iterations of these documents.

By 2030, a large number of RPA will share the airspace with manned aviation, some will be flying IFR. While some RPAS operations will be conducted in accordance with IFR for a portion of their flight, others will operate only under visual flight rules (VFR). Similarly, RPA will operate in and transit through national and international airspace as well as controlled and uncontrolled airspace. These RPA may depart from less congested aerodromes and arrive at similar destination aerodromes, while others may use congested aerodromes. All RPA will be expected to comply with the applicable procedures and airspace requirements defined by the State, including emergency and contingency procedures, which should be established and coordinated with the respective ANSPs. These types of operations mean that RPA will need to fly in national and international airspace.

Other RPA will only operate at low altitudes, where manned aviation activities are limited. For example, activities such as border protection, environmental uses, and wildfire and utility inspections, these could still mean transiting international airspace.

As airspace is scarce and sought after resource, States need to take a balanced approach that harmonizes and meets the needs of users. This CONOPS highlights aspects needed for integration of RPAS, the newest entrant into the civil aviation system.

The ability to pilot an aircraft remotely offers vast potential for new types of aircraft and their operation that are not constrained by the need to accommodate human beings on board. This impacts the design of aircraft, e.g. mass, size, performance, endurance, where and how they can operate and how they can be assimilated into the airspace and its air traffic management system. There are also implications for the safety assurance processes, as the focus can move from protecting the persons on board an aircraft to those potentially affected by undesirable events, such as mid-air collisions or injury to people and damage to property on the surface.

The general consensus within ICAO is that RPAS should be under the legal and managerial responsibility of a certified RPAS operator. Legal responsibility of the RPAS operator will automatically imply liability for damage caused by the operation of RPAS. This is in line with the European regulations for the operation of air services in the Community that provide for insurance requirements to cover liability, among other things, with respect to third parties in the event of an air calamity.

Regulation (EC) No. 1008/2008, on insurance requirements for air carriers and aircraft operators, requires that air carriers contract insurance to cover liability with respect to passengers, baggage, cargo and third parties in the event of an air disaster. The basic EU position is now enshrined in Article 4(h) and Article 11 of this Regulation, which replaced Council Regulation (EEC) No. 2407/92, requiring compliance with the requirements of Regulation (EC) No. 785/2004.[14]

At the time of adoption of Regulation (EC) No. 785/2004, the use of UAS, such as RPAS for civil purposes, was non-existent and probably not considered. Nonetheless, operating RPAS may pose a real risk regarding damage to third parties, including people and property on the surface.

One of the highlights of the Drone Enable/2 event, ICAO's UAS Industry Symposium in Chengdu, China (13-14 September 2018) was the presentation of ICAO's Global Aviation Trust Framework (IATF): A Unified Approach for a Single Sky by Mr. William R. Voss, Special Adviser to the Director, ICAO ANC:

> Implementation of the IATF to help enable innovation and interoperability. Providing a possible solution for integration of unmanned aircraft into non-segregated airspace and enabling the provision of a digital identity capability, with the potential of such information to be globally transferable. The presentation will discuss how previous experience in establishing trust in the aviation community can be applied in a modern context to solve today's demands for the interoperability, security, and innovation required to enable UAS operations.

The aim of the framework is to provide a high-level architecture that can assist in tackling two of the main challenges faced by aviation today. First, the industry must manage the growth in air traffic caused by increased traditional civil aviation activities and by new entrants, such as drone operators. Second, as a corollary to the digitalization of aviation, protecting communication links between UTM and ATM systems from cybersecurity, in other words, a collective answer to cybersecurity threats, is required in order to avoid a lack of interoperability between different airspace users. There is a growing realization

---

14 Regulation (EC) No. 1008/2008 of the European Parliament and of the Council of 24 September 2008 on common rules for the operation of air services in the Community, *OJ* L293/3, 31 October 2008. Art. 4 Conditions for granting an operating licence. An undertaking shall be granted an operating licence by the competent licensing authority of a Member State provided that: h) it complies with the insurance requirements specified in Art. 11 and in Regulation (EC) No. 785/2004. Art. 11 Insurance requirements. Notwithstanding Regulation (EC) No. 785/2004, an air carrier shall be insured to cover liability in case of accidents with respect to mail. *See also* Regulation (EC) No. 785/2004 of the European Parliament and of the Council of 21 April 2004 on insurance requirements for air carriers and aircraft operators, *OJ* L138/1, 30 April 2004 and Council Regulation (EEC) No. 2407/92 of 23 July 1992 on licensing of air carriers, *OJ* L 240/1, 24 August 1992.

across the industry that such an aviation trust framework could be a vital enabler to meet these challenges. A summary of actions being considered by ICAO on behalf of global system users:
– Develop a Trust Framework for mutual recognition of digital certificates.
– Procure a global Top-Level Domain dedicated to aviation to limit threat surface.
– Obtain a private block of IPv6 (Internet Protocol version 6) addresses that allows for increased shielding of safety-focused communication from public attacks.
– Enable global interoperability and a single digital sky.

2.3 EASA RULE-MAKING PROCESS ON DRONES

EASA provides opinions and formulates technical rules relating to the construction, design and operational aspects of aircraft, including drones, and is also responsible for assisting the European Commission by providing technical, administrative and scientific support.[15]

Unmanned aircraft regulatory segmentation, which means regulatory differences among EU Member States, in particular with regard to RPAS, recently had to be addressed without delay for various reasons. Fragmentation of applicable rules could become a burden on the development of the comprehensive unmanned aviation sector. Furthermore, the regulatory and technological landscape of this sector is subject to constant change.

National regulations on drones became incomparable and unmanageable by new developments. Obviously, drones need to be treated as new types of aircraft with proportionate international rules based on the risk of each operation. Technologies and standards need to be developed for the full integration of drones in European airspace. An adequate European regulatory framework on drones is a prerequisite to achieve harmonization and modernization and to engage the challenges of large-scale deployment of these types of aircraft. The proposed regulatory framework should set a level of safety and of environmental protection acceptable to society and offer enough flexibility for the new industry to evolve, innovate and mature. Therefore, the implementing exercise is not simply transposing the system put in place for traditional manned aviation but creating one that is proportionate, progressive and risk based. The new system must express objectives that will be complemented by industry standards.[16]

Defined common rules for design, classification, certification, licensing, types of operation as well as demonstrating and validating the feasibility of technological drone

---

15 *See also* Regulation of Drones, April 2016, p. 124, The Law Library of Congress, Global Legal Research Center.
16 EASA Concept of Operations for Drones: A risk based approach to regulation of unmanned aircraft, pp. 3-4.

services, are all key elements of rule-making enabling full and safe integration, with substantial functional and economic benefits predicted. The operation of drones should be regulated in proportion to the risk of the specific operation.

Since not all key technologies required for RPA to fly in non-segregated airspace are mature and standardized yet, all aeronautical experts in the world agree that integration of RPA in airspace will be gradual, well substantiated and evolutionary. The progress of technology, regulation and societal acceptance will be a significant and decisive factor.

While currently RPAS operations are in the developing process to be carried out locally and at very low altitudes, these aircraft and their systems are certainly also able to perform operations at high altitude covering large distances from their operational bases, intended to engage in activities in the field of transporting persons and goods. This future image, technically feasible, has not been resolved yet when it comes to integration into non-segregated airspace and aerodromes. This is because this new area requires new classifications and licensing not only for aircraft but for (remote) pilots and observers as well.[17]

Moreover, it is evident that new rules for airworthiness assessment and qualifications consider RPAS as a total aviation system, in which the aircraft is no longer the system but in which the total system comprises the aircraft. This position has also been taken by EASA, EUROCONTROL and the (former) JAA. Therefore, rule-making must be accomplished on the perspective of the total system, not only applied to the certification of approval of the various elements that contribute to aviation safety, but also in what manner to approach the airworthiness certificates in case these individual elements would control multiple vehicles or different types of vehicles.

In addition to the licenses for the (remote) pilot and the certificate for the civil RPAS operator, the new adopted rules establish that the associated RPAS components, specified in the type design, shall be covered by appropriate approval certificates. However, only the RPA, the flying part or the so-called platform of the system, needs, according to Article 31 of the Chicago Convention, an individual certificate of airworthiness as well as registration.

Article 31 of the Chicago Convention, 1944:

Certificate of airworthiness.

---

17 Roadmap for the Integration of Civil Remotely-Piloted Aircraft Systems into the European Aviation System. Final Report from the European RPAS Steering Group, June 2013, Chapter 2. Essential requirements considered for RPAS operations. Specific annexes to this Roadmap are: Ann. 1 provides a Regulatory Work Plan identifying the improvements to the existing regulatory framework considered necessary to allow RPAS operating outside segregated airspace; Ann. 2 presents a Strategic R&D Plan identifying the technology enablers and the research activities necessary to achieve a safe integration of RPAS; Ann. 3 analyses aspects of the societal impact of RPAS.

Every aircraft engaged in international navigation shall be provided with a certificate of airworthiness issued or rendered valid by the State in which it is registered.

In 2005, EASA launched a public consultation on the certification of UAV weighing more than 150 kg as a first step towards a more comprehensive UAS regulation. At that time, EASA used the term UAV. Although from 2003 onwards, EASA was responsible for aviation safety in the European Union, the then prevailing Regulation (EC) No 216/2008 (the Basic Regulation until 4 July 2018 when it was repealed by Regulation (EU) 2018/1139, the new Basic Regulation) covered only UAV weighing more than 150 kg.[18]

The regulation of UAV weighing less than 150 kg remained the responsibility of the national Civil Aviation Authorities of the EU Member States. However, there was a need for a first step towards a more comprehensive UAV regulation, especially a European policy for the certification of UAV. When preparing its rule-making decision, EASA is required to follow a structured process, which may include a preliminary consultation. The purpose of the consultation process of the A-NPA 16-2005 (Advance Notice of Proposed Amendment) was to propose a policy for the certification of UAV. Remarkably, the weight limit in the EU Basic Regulation was merely a legal limit, and technically there appeared to be no reason to treat a UAV of 140 kg differently from a 160 kg UAV.[19]

NPA 2012-10 considered the alignment of the Standardized European Rules of the Air (SERA) with Amendment 43 to Annex 2 to the Chicago Convention, in line with Article 2.2(d) of the Basic Regulation and the implementing essential requirement 1(a) of Annex Vb – Essential requirements for ATM/ANS and air traffic controllers – thereto.[20]

---

18 Regulation (EC) No. 216/2008 of the European Parliament and of the Council of 20 February 2008 on common rules in the field of civil aviation and establishing a European Aviation Safety Agency, and repealing Council Directive 91/670/EEC, Regulation (EC) No. 1592/2002 and Directive 2004/36/EC, OJ L 79/1, 19 March 2008. Regulation (EC) No. 216/2008, the Basic Regulation, has been repealed by Regulation (EU) 2018/1139 of the European Parliament and of the Council of 4 July 2018, the new or EASA Basic Regulation.

19 A-NPA 16-2005. Policy for Unmanned Aerial Vehicle (UAV) certification. The purpose of the A-NPA is to propose a policy for the certification of UAV systems and is a first step towards more comprehensive UAV regulation.

20 NPA 2012-10. Transposition of Amendment 43 to Ann. 2 to the Chicago Convention on RPAS into common rules of the air. Amendment 43 to the International Standards, Rules of the Air (ICAO Ann. 2) was adopted by the Council at the fifth meeting of its 195th Session on 7 March 2012. Amendment 43 became applicable on 15 November 2012. Regulation (EC) No. 216/2008 of the European Parliament and of the Council of 20 February 2008 on common rules in the field of civil aviation and establishing a European Aviation Safety Agency, and repealing Council Directive 91/670/EEC, Regulation (EC) No. 1592/2002 and Directive 2004/36/EC, OJ L 79/1, 19 March 2008. Regulation (EC) No. 216/2008 is repealed by Regulation (EU) 2018/1139 of the European Parliament and of the Council of 4 July 2018, OJ L 212/1, 22 August 2018.

NPA 2012-10 included five major aspects:
- the certification of the RPAS, including the airworthiness of the RPA;
- the certification of RPAS operators involved in commercial air transport (CAT) and/or specialized operations (SPO);
- the licensing of remote pilots;
- provisions to facilitate the so-called special authorization mandated by Article 8 of the Chicago Convention for international RPAS operations;
- improvement of air traffic control planning in oceanic and remote airspace through more accurate position reporting and estimating by flight crews of manned aircraft.

Basic Regulation Article 2.2(d): Additional objectives are, in the fields covered by this Regulation, as follows: to assist Member States in fulfilling their obligations under the Chicago Convention, by providing a formal basis for a common interpretation and uniform implementation of its provisions, and by ensuring that its provisions are duly taken into account in this Regulation and in the rules drawn up for its implementation.

Basic Regulation (Consolidated version) Annex Vb – Essential requirements for ATM/ANS and air traffic controllers – 1(a): All aircraft, excluding those engaged in the activities referred to in Article 1(2)(a), in all phases of flight or on the movement area of an aerodrome, shall be operated in accordance with common general operating rules and any applicable procedure specified for use of the airspace.[21]

NPA 2012-10 also provided for alignment with ICAO regulations with respect to ICAO SARPs and harmonization of the ICAO airspace classification to ensure the seamless provision of safe and efficient air traffic services within the Single European Sky (SES), while covering commercial air transport as well as specialized operations. It proposed no threshold limit at 150 kg, while model aircraft were to be excluded.

With respect to access to non-segregated airspace, special authorization should be necessary for national as well as international flights, based on the following requirements: the RPA must have a certificate of airworthiness; the components, such as the remote pilot stations, both on the ground and airborne, must have specific certificates; the operators must have an operator certificate, and the remote pilots must

---

21 Basic Regulation Art. 1.2 This Regulation shall not apply to (a): products, parts, appliances, personnel and organizations referred to in Para. 1(a) and (b) while carrying out military, customs, police, search and rescue, firefighting, coastguard or similar activities or services. The Member States shall undertake to ensure that such activities or services have due regard as far as practicable to the objectives of this Regulation.

have licences. The NPA had to deal with comments, many of which were submitted by UVS International (UVSI), which have led to proposed modifications on a number of the following issues:[22]

- Amendment 43 to Annex 2 to the Chicago Convention, which will apply to EASA, as well as non-EASA regulated aircraft (requiring national regulations), was not intended to apply to RPAS operations within the borders of the signatory states. Nevertheless, the text of the NPA makes its provisions applicable to all RPAS operations within Europe, apparently including operations within the boundaries of the EU Member States. Even though ICAO rules may be adopted by various countries for national operations, such adoption should not be mandated in Europe.
- NPA 2012-10 refers to certificates of airworthiness, remote pilot licences and operator licences, as well as other regulatory guidance documents, which currently do not exist and for which there are no agreed procedures or requirements or timelines established by ICAO or EASA. The implication could be that a European state could issue a certificate or a licence based on criteria not agreed on at the EU level and that the other European states would have to accept it (also allow the relevant approved RPAS or pilot or operator to operate in their country, even though such a certificate or licence does not meet their national requirements). SERA rules should not apply to domestic operations. As long as certificates of airworthiness, remote pilot licences, as well as other regulatory guidance of documents in the field of RPAS did not exist yet, it seemed premature at that time to introduce such requirements at the EU level.
- Furthermore, to make a clear distinction between RPAS and model aircraft, the definition of RPA(S) should be modified to read: "Remotely piloted aircraft means an unmanned aircraft which is piloted from a remote pilot station for the purpose of commercial air transport or specialized operations."

NPA 2014-09 revised NPA 2012-10 on the same subject: Transposition of Amendment 43 to Annex 2 to the Chicago Convention on RPAS into common rules of the air. But before that, the Comment-response Document 2012-10 (CRD) contained a summary of the comments on NPA 2012-10 of 21 August 2012. More than 200 adverse comments were received. Hence, EASA organized a subsequent 'focused consultation' and its conclusions thereto. The outcome was a significantly revised resulting text of the proposed rules and, therefore, the need to withdraw NPA 2012-10 and to publish instead the second NPA on the same issue: NPA 2014-09 of 3 April 2014.

Stakeholders were informed on this line to be taken through the 2012 CRD of 18 November 2013 and did not react adversely.

---

22 UVSI is a non-profit association, founded in 1995 as EURO-UVS (European Unmanned Vehicle Systems Association) by Peter van Blyenburgh (President of UVS International), focusing on the promotion of the use of remotely piloted systems (air, ground, naval and space) of all types, sizes and classes, and their relevant subsystems. *See also* https://uvs-international.org.

The purpose of NPA 2014-09 on the subject was still to propose the alignment of the SERA with Amendment 43 to Annex 2 to the Chicago Convention, in relation to RPAS and in line with Article 2.2(d) of Regulation (EC) No. 216/2008. NPA 2014-09 also implemented Article 4(a) and 4(b) of Regulation (EC) No. 551/2004 on the organization and use of the airspace in the Single European Sky.[23] In other words, the proposed rules have a double basis and propose:

- Rules of the air applicable to RPAS of any mass, when flown under General Air Traffic (GAT) rules;
- Nothing related to airworthiness, licensing of remote pilots and operations of RPAS outside the scope of Regulation (EC) No. 216/2008 (for example, below MTOM 150 kg).

The specific objectives of this proposal are to:

a. amend SERA to cover also RPAS flight operations under GAT rules, including military or governmental non-military or other public flights when they elect to fly GAT, as well as any civil RPAS flight, regardless of the mass of the aircraft;[24]
b. establish the basic principle that EU Member States shall authorize RPAS operators for the intended operations within their respective sovereign airspace;[25]
c. transpose Amendment 43 to ICAO Annex 2, as mentioned in Regulatory Improvement 01 in the EU RPAS Roadmap for cross-border flights inside the European Union, without prejudice to future adoption of common EU rules on mutually recognized certifications; and
d. establish a clear demarcation between RPAS, on the one hand, and model aircraft and toy aircraft, on the other.

In 2015, EASA was tasked by the European Commission, following the Riga Conference and its associated Riga Declaration on RPA, whose principles would be reflected in a new A-NPA, to develop a regulatory framework for drone operations as well as concrete proposals for the regulation of low-risk drone operations.[26] The intended objective is to ensure a safe, secure and environment-friendly development and to respect the citizens' legitimate concerns for privacy and data protection.

---

23 Regulation (EC) No. 551/2004 of the European Parliament and of the Council of 10 March 2004 on the organization and use of the airspace in the single European sky, *OJ* L 96/20, 31 March 2004.
24 The term 'public flights' is not used in current EU legislation but is used in the United States to include, e.g., flights with prototypes built by universities, which have a public interest, but which are not strictly state flights.
25 This so-called operation-centric approach is already applicable in many EU Member States and many other states around the world.
26 Riga Declaration: 'Framing the Future of Aviation'. Conference on remotely piloted aircraft systems (drones), Riga 6 March 2015. This document uses both the terms RPAS and drones.

The objective of A-NPA 2015-10 (Introduction of a regulatory framework for the operation of drones) comprises the preparation of EU regulations on drone operations and, additionally, to consult stakeholders on the proposed Concept of Operations (CONOPS) for drones, and on key elements of the future Implementation Rules (IR), especially for low-risk drone operations. Following the publication of A-NPA 2015-10, EASA adopted a Technical Opinion in December 2015. This Technical Opinion is the result of the consultation performed with A-NPA 2015-10. It has been developed in parallel to the draft modifications to the Basic Regulation, included in the 'Aviation Strategy to Enhance the Competitiveness of the EU Aviation Sector'.[27]

It includes 27 concrete proposals for a regulatory framework and for low-risk operations of all unmanned aircraft irrespective of their MTOM. This regulatory framework is operation-centric, proportionate, risk- and performance-based and establishes three categories of unmanned aircraft operations as follows: Open, Specific and Certified, with different safety requirements and proportionate to the risk. The three preliminary categories are briefly described as follows:

- Open category (low risk): There is no pre-approval of the design of the unmanned aircraft, of the operator or of the pilot. Safety is ensured through compliance with operational limitations, mass limitations as a proxy of energy, product safety requirements and a minimum set of operational rules.
- Specific category (medium risk): Authorization by a national civil aviation authority (CAA), possibly assisted by a Qualified Entity (QE), following a risk assessment performed by the operator. A manual of operations lists the risk mitigation measures.
- Certified category (higher risk): Requirements comparable to those of manned aviation. Oversight by the national CAA (issue of licences and approval of maintenance, operations, training, air traffic management/air navigation services (ATM/ANS) and aerodrome organizations) and by EASA (design and approval of foreign organizations).

The Technical Opinion did not include new draft legal text beyond the one that has been proposed by the aviation strategy. Its purpose has been to lay the foundation for future work, illustrate the content of the draft changes to the Basic Regulation and serve as guidance for EU Member States to develop or modify their regulations on unmanned aircraft.

While the rules for manned aircraft are usually driven by an aircraft-centric approach, in the European Union there was a significant change in the regulation approach policy,

---

27 The Aviation Strategy for Europe, which the European Commission published in 2017, sets out a range of policy proposals to support an open and connected aviation market within and outside the European Union. *See also* COM(2015) 598 Final. Communication from the Commission to the European Parliament, the Council, the European Economic and Social Committee and the Committee of the Regions: An Aviation Strategy for Europe, Brussels, 7 December 2015.

moving away from the traditional aircraft-centric approach (starting with factors associated with the aircraft itself such as airworthiness certification), usually in combination with a pure purpose-centric approach, towards a more comprehensive approach, the operation-centric approach, initially focusing on risks as recognized by society and imposing certain restrictions regarding drone operations.[28]

The choice of operation-centric approach is justified by the fact that there is no one on board unmanned aircraft as yet. Therefore, the consequences of a loss of control of an unmanned aircraft is highly dependent on the operational environment. The less hazardous operations, RPA flights over non-populated areas and away from aerodromes or flight routes, are subject to lighter legal regulations than the flights where damages can be caused on the surface or in the air.

The operation-centric approach involves rules for operations that are dependent on the risks associated with these operations. The stringency and scrutiny of the operation rules will increase in the same measure as the operational risks. In fact, the operation-centric approach should be risk based as well as proportionate.

Reasonably, a legislation based only on risk assessment could work but would lead to a significant burden for drone operators and competent authorities when it comes to assessment of production and approval. Under the operation-centric approach, the properties of the drones, such as the weight, and purposes of the flight will still affect the result.

In addition, a variety of other common factors will also be taken into account to determine the appropriate rules imposed on the operations. This type of approach, the most proper choice compared with the other approaches, has been adopted by the European Union and will be codified into the new EU Regulation on unmanned aircraft operations.[29]

The operation-centric approach, the risk-based approach, different from the aircraft-centric and purpose-centric approach, deals with the risks associated with the operations as the starting point of regulation. Additional factors are anticipated to assess the risks concerned. The regulation shall be proportionate, progressive and risk-based, and the rules must express objectives that will be complemented by industry standards. Only this way, the challenges posed by the wide variety of drones and their specific operations will be addressed. Further experience is needed to learn and progress from simple operations to higher risk operations.

In Europe, the CONOPS proposed by EASA reflects the consensus among the EU Member States: "the operation of drones should be regulated in a manner

---

28 Masutti, A., Tomasello, F., *International Regulation of Non-Military Drones*, Cheltenham: Edward Elgar Publishing, 2018, 6.4 Proportionality in Europe.
29 *See* EASA Prototype Commission Regulation on Unmanned Aircraft Operations of 22 August 2016, Art. 1 Subject matter and scope, Art. 3 Categories of UA operations.

proportionate to the risk of the specific operation." This concept focuses on safety risks but recognizes the importance of risks to privacy and security.[30]

For extremely complex operations conducted with complicated unmanned aircraft, there could be beneficial reasons to adopt a certification approach as it would avoid repeating compliance demonstration and as it would give societal acceptance. The balance between these considerations has led to the creation of the three categories.

The low-risk Open category does not require any pre-approval as safety is assured, especially by a combination of measures including requirements and limitations on the operation, the UAS and the involved personnel and organizations. These general measures are complemented by conditions with respect to access to airspace determined by the EU Member States.

The medium risk Specific category requires operators to obtain an authorization given by the competent authority based on a risk assessment performed by the operator. As this could be burdensome for authorities and operators, a concept of standard scenarios covering certain types of flight operations has been developed. As operations with different risk levels are envisaged, the standard scenario will identify the cases where instead of the authorization, a simple declaration by the operator will be sufficient to start the operation. These standard scenarios will be included in certification specifications (CSs) applicable to specific operational topics.[31]

EU Member States agreed that the Dutch Presidency, the European Commission and EASA would develop a road map to provide more clarity on what the plans are to roll out the operation-centric concept, applicable only in the SES airspace. The road map includes information on rule-making tasks, development of standards, research, cooperation with international organizations and the FAA. The road map was developed during three workshops with EU Member States in March, April and May 2016 and presented to the industry at a workshop in the following month.

EASA was in favour of producing a road map to deliver plans for the operation-centric concept for UAS operations. However, this road map did not clarify all issues to be covered. Instead, the Agency decided to produce a prototype regulation, called the Prototype Commission Regulation on Unmanned Aircraft Operations, concerning the licensing and operational requirements for UAS operations in the Open and Specific categories to accomplish clarity on relevant unmanned aircraft operation issues. The

---

30 EASA Concept of Operations for Drones, A risk based approach to regulation of unmanned aircraft. Publication type: EASA Brochure, published on 01 May 2015.
31 CSs are non-binding technical standards adopted by EASA to meet essential requirements of the Basic Regulation and are used for establishing the certification basis for applications made after the date of entry into force of a CS, including any amendments. There are CSs in the field of airworthiness, aerodromes, air operations, air crew aeroplane/helicopter flight simulation training devices and ATM/ANS interoperability.

term prototype in this context is used to reflect the fact that it should assist in preparing the upcoming formal rule-making process by gathering reactions to be used to develop the necessary NPAs covering all issues in the formal consultation process, later in 2016.

The Prototype Regulation is focusing on the Open and Specific categories because these are the areas where the activities are developing at a quite rapid pace. The Certified category will be developed in parallel; however, the requirements for this particular category will be included as amendments to existing manned aircraft regulations and not as part of a stand-alone regulation. Unlike the Technical Opinion, the Prototype Regulation is written in the form of a draft regulation, which is an indicative blueprint for the future formal regulation.

The Prototype Regulation does not bind either EASA or the European Commission in any way. This document is showing the vision of the European Union regarding UAS legislation. Its sole purpose has been to inform and consult stakeholders in view of the ongoing negotiations with the Parliament and the Council on the review of Regulation (EC) No. 216/2008 and in view of giving indications on the possible direction that EASA will take on its implementation, after appropriate consultation, in an NPA planned for the end of 2016. It represented the views of EASA at the time. However, it did not constitute any formal commitment on behalf of either EASA or the European Commission.

Yet informal comments on the Prototype Regulation did make sense on matters such as general operational requirements and registration. The main body of the Prototype Regulation established the three categories for UAS operations that have been familiar since the launch of the CONOPS for drones in 2015. On 22 August 2016, EASA provided an explanatory note, known as the Explanatory Note on Prototype Commission Regulation on Unmanned Aircraft Operations, to support the understanding of the Prototype Regulation.

The balance of the Prototype Regulation concentrated only on the Open and Specific categories, but the Explanatory Note confirmed that existing manned aircraft regulations should be amended to incorporate requirements for the Certified category of unmanned aircraft, rather than creating stand-alone CSs for unmanned aircraft. The relevant regulations amendment programme and a timetable for publication of a subsequent NPA (NPA 2017-05) and decisions on the subject were envisaged to run until 2019.

The operation-centric approach is not applicable to indoor operations, such as indoor drone racing events or, for example, drone inspections inside a tank, simply because the concept is applicable only in the Single European Sky airspace. Another important issue in civil aviation is insurance, which, however, falls outside the scope of EASA's competencies.

Nevertheless, Regulation (EC) No. 785/2004 already established minimum insurance requirements for air carriers and aircraft operators concerning passengers, baggage, cargo and third parties. This Regulation shall not apply to model aircraft with an MTOM of less than 20 kg, which means that its insurance obligations are therefore applicable to unmanned aircraft not qualified as model aircraft. Furthermore, insurance may also be required by national legislation.[32]

Some of the provisions of the Prototype Regulation, as laid down in the 2016 text, will contribute to the application of other pieces of legislation such as security, privacy, data protection and environment, in this case, for example, applicable requirements for geofencing together with the possibility for EU Member States to define zones where the activities of drones are prohibited or restricted in order to contribute to security and privacy.[33]

The Prototype Regulation, considered as a non-binding document, will not directly address issues such as security, privacy, data protection and environment simply because they are regulated at the European or national level. They will, however, contribute to implementing them as follows:

- Operators must register unless they operate only unmanned aircraft of the simpler subcategories;
- the EU Member State may define zones or airspace areas where unmanned aircraft operations are prohibited or restricted; these zones or airspace areas can be created, for instance, for security reasons;
- obligation for the operator, defined as a natural or legal person that operates the unmanned aircraft, to comply with security requirements;
- the pilot of an unmanned aircraft must not fly close to emergency response efforts;
- the learning objectives for the pilot involved in flying the most complex subcategories of the Open category envisage the knowledge of flight restrictions (e.g. security) and the understanding of ethical airmanship. The same applies for the competence of a pilot for the Specific category;
- the risk assessment of the Specific category must take into account areas with special limitations, for instance for security or privacy reasons;
- geofencing and electronic identification will be required in the standards of subcategories A2 and A3 in the Open category.

The Prototype rules are organized as follows:

---

32 Regulation (EC) No. 785/2004 of the European Parliament and of the Council of 21 April 2004 on insurance requirements for air carriers and aircraft operators, OJ L138/1, 30 April 2004, Art. 2.2.(b).
33 Geofencing: an automatic function to limit the access of the unmanned aircraft to airspace areas or volumes provided as geographical limitations based on the unmanned aircraft position and navigation data, or, in other words, geofencing is a virtual barrier created using a combination of the Global Positioning System (GPS) network and Local Radio Frequency Identifier (LRFID) connections such as Wi-Fi or Bluetooth beacons. This boundary is dictated by a combination of hardware and software, which dictates the parameters of the geofence, i.e., a drone app and an unmanned aircraft. See EASA 'Prototype' Commission Regulation on Unmanned Aircraft Operations, Explanatory Note of 22 August 2016.

- A cover regulation that introduces clearly and logically the operation-centric concept of operation.
- Two annexes, supporting this cover regulation:
  o Annex I (Part-UAS), containing the rules for Open and Specific categories and the requirements to be complied with to obtain a Light UAS Operator Certificate (LUC). This certificate is not mandatory for an operator in the Specific category, but it provides useful privileges.
  o Annex II, containing the framework for the product legislation: obligations of manufacturers and other economic operators; conformity assessment procedures; notifying authorities; requirements related to notified bodies; obligations and powers of EU Member States.

Annex I introduces, in particular, the subcategories of operations for the Open category. The broad limitations for the subcategories are provided in Part-UAS and the associated essential requirements in the sense of Regulation (EC) No. 768/2008, together with examples of conformity assessment, which are included in several appendices for Part-UAS.[34]

The Prototype Regulation regulates the operation of all unmanned aircraft in the Open and Specific categories within the SES airspace. It does not regulate so-called state operations (e.g. police, customs, military, coastguard, firefighting), because such operations with whatever type of aircraft are not regulated by the new Basic Regulation. However, the new Basic Regulation has introduced an opt-in provision that could be used by EU Member States to put such operations under EU rules. In line with a risk approach, the Prototype Regulation applies to commercial and non-commercial activities. This decision would have had a significant impact on existing model aircraft activities if transition provisions had not been introduced.

The Prototype Regulation does not introduce changes to the SERA. There will be a need in the short term to review SERA and identify provisions that could hinder operations in the Open and Specific categories. For the longer term, it will be necessary to modify such rules to introduce a concept of traffic management system for unmanned aircraft. To fully take into account the range of unmanned aircraft operations, such a concept should address VLL below 150 m, the integration into non-segregated airspace (above 150 m up to FL 600) and very high altitude operations (above FL 600). The

---

34 Regulation (EC) No. 768/2008 of the European Parliament and of the Council of 9 July 2008 on a common framework for the marketing of products, and repealing Council Decision 93/465/EC, OJ L 218/82, 13 August 2008.

concept should address the interface between these three domains. This approach, developed by JARUS, is more encompassing than the UTM system, which is usually limited to VLL.[35]

The safety element of the Open category relies in particular on a set of limitations: unmanned aircraft MTOM must be below 25 kg as a proxy to a limitation in energy. Flights are limited to heights below 150 m above ground level (AGL), and the unmanned aircraft must be in VLOS of the remote pilot in order to reduce the risk of collision with other unmanned aircraft.

The 25-kg limit has been chosen because it is quite frequently the limit for model aircraft to fly without an approval of its design. It is also the limit adopted by the EU bilateral partners: the FAA, Agência Nacional de Aviação Civil (ANAC) Brazil and Transport Canada. Obviously, with such an MTOM, there is a need to have subcategories in order to have rules proportionate to the risk. The limitations to 150 m height and VLOS are very important to mitigate the risk of collision with other aircraft.

EASA strives for consistency in regard to international activities. EASA is participating in the ICAO RPAS panel. ICAO has released a draft concept of operations whose scope for the future is defined as follows: the magnitude is limited to certified RPAS operating internationally under IFR conditions in non-segregated airspace and at aerodromes in 2030. The RPAS panel focuses on international IFR operations, close to the Certified category. Therefore, the risk of inconsistencies is limited at this stage.

EASA is involved in JARUS and intends to make full use of JARUS products. All deliveries provided by JARUS have been and will be taken into account in the EASA regulation. This is certainly the case with the Specific Operations Risk Assessment (SORA) methodology considered as an Acceptable Means of Compliance (AMC), for the risk assessment developed by JARUS.[36]

The FAA and EASA keep each other informed about their regulatory activities. Part 107 is the adopted regulation for sUAS below 25 kg (55 lbs). It will create a process that will replace their present exemption process. It corresponds broadly to the EU Open category.

– Some common points: MTOM 25 kg, operation VLOS, maximum altitude 400 ft (EU proposal is 500 ft); competence requirements for the remote pilot.
– Some differences: it does not apply to model aircraft, where the Prototype Regulation does; in principle, it does not require geofencing or identification; no subcategories; no essential requirements for design.

---

35 JARUS (Joint Authorities for Rulemaking on Unmanned Systems) is a voluntary membership body comprising experts of national Civil Aviation Authorities from EU and non-EU countries and regional aviation organizations. Its purpose is to recommend a single set of technical, safety and operational requirements for the certification and safe integration of UAS into airspace and at aerodromes. Around 61 states, EASA and EUROCONTROL are contributing to the development of JARUS.
36 *See* Executive Director Decision 2019/021/R of 9 October 2019 Issuing Acceptable Means of Compliance and Guidance Material to Commission Implementing Regulation (EU) 2019/947, p. 2.

Before the new Basic Regulation, *in casu* Regulation (EU) 2018/1139, was formally adopted, the regulation of UAS with an MTOM of less than 150 kg was a subject within the competence of the EU Member States, according to Regulation (EC) No. 216/2008, until it was repealed with effect from 11 September 2018. This disharmony has led to a fragmented regulatory system hampering the development of a single EU market for UAS and cross-border UAS operations. The aim was to solve this issue by extending the competence of the European Union to regulate all UAS regardless of their MTOM.

This impediment could be eliminated by establishing a new Basic Regulation, laying down, among other things, harmonized and essential requirements for unmanned aircraft regarding the design, production, maintenance and operation for these particular aircraft and their engines, propellers, parts, non-installed equipment and equipment to control these aircraft remotely, as well as the personnel, including remote pilots, and organizations involved in those activities.

The draft Regulation (EU) 2018/1139 has envisaged the use of product legislation as one of the tools to set up the regulatory framework for unmanned aircraft. This is valid mostly for small unmanned aircraft where manufacturers are indeed small organizations that are quite familiar with product legislation. Some of these small unmanned aircraft can be considered as toys, which are regulated by the product legislation. As a consequence, the Prototype Regulation integrated aviation safety rules and product legislation.

On 11 September 2018, the European Parliament adopted updated aviation safety rules for Europe, including a new mandate for EASA that redefined the Agency's competences. Regulation (EU) 2018/1139, adopted on 4 July 2018, empowers EASA to propose to the European Commission the technical expertise to regulate unmanned aircraft of all sizes, including the small ones.

In order to ensure the uniform implementation of and compliance with the essential requirements for the operation of unmanned aircraft, as well as for personnel, including remote pilots and the involved organizations, the European Commission shall adopt implementing acts laying down detailed provisions concerning specific rules and procedures with regard to the following: operation of unmanned aircraft, including personnel and organizations, as well as the rules and procedures for issuing, maintaining, limiting, suspending or revoking of appropriate certificates and the privileges and responsibilities of the holders of certificates, the registration and marking of unmanned aircraft, the establishment of digital, interoperable, harmonized, national registration systems and conversion of national certificates into certificates required under Article 56(1) of the new Basic Regulation.

Article 56(1) Compliance of unmanned aircraft:

Taking into account the objectives and the principles set out in Articles 1 and 4, and, in particular, the nature and risk of the activity concerned, the operational characteristics of the unmanned aircraft concerned and the characteristics of area of operation, a certificate may be required for the design, production, maintenance and operation of unmanned aircraft and their engines, propellers, parts, non-installed equipment and equipment to control them remotely, as well as for the personnel, including remote pilots, and organizations involved in those activities, in accordance with the delegated acts referred to in Article 58 and the implementing acts referred to in Article 57.

Instead of simply transposing the existing traditional manned aviation regime for the operation of unmanned aircraft, EASA has created a completely new regime including rules that enable the accommodation of a variety of unmanned aircraft, from very small size to RPA with the size and weight of a contemporary cargo aircraft to be used in international air services, operating in non-segregated airspace any suitable time in the future.[37]

Furthermore, the European Commission is empowered to adopt delegated acts with regard to specific conditions such as compliance with the essential requirements referred to in Article 55 (Essential requirements for unmanned aircraft), which may include the conditions under which unmanned aircraft are required to be equipped with necessary features and functionalities related, in particular, to maximum operating distance and altitude limitations, position communication, geographical zones entry restriction, collision avoidance, flight stabilization and automated landing. Conditions for the treatment and conversion of certificates and declarations, privileges and responsibilities are subject to these delegated acts. The European Commission is also empowered to adopt delegated acts to amend certain annexes to the new Basic Regulation.[38]

Whereas the new Basic Regulation provides for essential requirements for unmanned aircraft, in particular breakthrough issues, the need for a comprehensive regulatory framework on unmanned aircraft in all its facets, as demonstrated in the non-binding Prototype Regulation, has significantly increased. This new European regulatory framework on unmanned aircraft can be accomplished by the assignment of appropriate implementation and delegation competences in this particular area to the European Commission, as laid down in provisions of the new Basic Regulation.

---

37 Guo, Y., 'Regulation of Drones from a Safety Perspective: With Special Focus on the EU Drone Regime', *Leiden University, Institute of Air and Space Law*, 26 August 2019, p. 17.
38 *See* Regulation (EU) 2018/1139 of the European Parliament and of the Council of 4 July 2018, Section VII Unmanned aircraft, and Ann. IX Essential requirements for unmanned aircraft.

On the request of the European Commission, EU Member States and other stakeholders, EASA anticipatively developed a proposal for an elaborated regulation to cope with the expected risks involved of the rapidly developing sector of all unmanned aircraft types. This particular activity should be developed in a safe, secure and environmentally friendly manner that respects the concerns of citizens concerning privacy and protection of personal data. Following the publication of A-NPA 2015-10 and the adoption of the 2015 Technical Opinion, NPA 2017-05 evolved from the Prototype Regulation.[39]

At an earlier stage, associated with the review of Regulation (EC) 216/2008, EASA has given an indication of the possible direction that the Agency should take on the implementation of the regulation on unmanned aircraft operations, after appropriate consultation, in an NPA that was planned for the end of 2016 or early 2017 (NPA 2017-05).

A preceding workshop took place on 20 June 2016 when EASA announced the completion of the Prototype Regulation for the Open and Specific categories. This Prototype Regulation was published on 22 August 2016, providing a first draft of the UAS regulation. The purpose of the workshop was to identify, on the basis of the comments received, the most important issues and to discuss possible resolutions of these issues. The workshop assisted in the preparation of the formal NPA for the Open and Specific categories.

This rule-making activity is included in the 5-year Rulemaking Program under rulemaking task (RMT).0230. EASA set up two task forces dedicated to assess the risk of collision between drones and aircraft and to study and develop recommendations regarding drone geo-limitations.[40]

NPA 2017-05, divided into A and B, covers all the regulatory elements for operations in the Open and Specific categories and provides for a meaningful Open category in order to set the balance between technical requirements, remote pilot competency and operational limitations. The NPA integrates both aviation and product legislation; covers commercial and hobby; includes model aircraft; clarifies the role of and flexibility for EU Member States; includes the foundation of U-space; and contributes to security, privacy and data protection and environmental protection.

The specific objectives of NPA 2017-05 related to UAS, as defined in the impact assessment (IA), are:

---

39 NPA 2017-05 Introduction of a regulatory framework for the operation of drones – Unmanned aircraft system operations in the Open and Specific category, consists of sub-NPA 2017-05 (A) containing the explanatory note and the proposed draft rules, and sub-NPA 2017-05 (B) containing the full impact assessment (IA) for this rule-making task (RMT).
40 See also Safe Operations of Drones in Europe: Update on EASA's Activities. EASA has recently published the first formal Opinion on safe operations for small drones in Europe. These first-ever EU-wide rules for civil drones will allow RPA to fly safely in European airspace and bring legal certainty to this rapidly expanding industry.

- to ensure an operation-centric, proportionate, risk- and performance-based regulatory framework for all UAS operations conducted in the Open and Specific categories;
- to ensure a high and uniform level of safety for UAS;
- to foster the development of the UAS market; and
- to contribute to enhancing privacy, data protection and security.

This NPA proposes to create a new regulation that is likely to be adopted in 2020. This regulation, part of the EU regulatory regime on unmanned aircraft operations, defines the measures to mitigate the risk of operations in:
- the Open category through a combination of limitations, operational rules, requirements for the competence of the remote pilot, as well as technical requirements for the UAS; and
- the Specific category through a system including a risk assessment conducted by the operator before starting an operation, or the operator complying with a standard scenario or the operator holding a certificate with privileges.

Ahead of the extension of competence of the European Union, under the new Basic Regulation, to cover the regulation of all UAS, EASA decided, in February 2018, to issue the proposal for a new UAS regulation by means of Opinion No. 01/2018 to the European Commission, inasmuch as EASA is bound to follow a structured rule-making process as required by Article 115(1) of the new Basic Regulation. Such a rule-making process has been adopted by the EASA Management Board and is referred to as the 'rulemaking procedure'.[41]

EASA has been working on the draft of the proposed UAS regulation for the past two years, taking into account both the expertise gained by EU Member States and all the developments in the international arena, such as work done within ICAO, JARUS, FAA and thousands of comments received from private citizens, the aviation industry and operations during a four-month public consultation process. Opinion 01/2018 formally states that in accordance with the proposed new Basic Regulation, for which a political agreement between the Council, the European Commission and the European Parliament was reached on 22 December 2017, the competence of the European Union has been extended to cover the regulation of all UAS, regardless of their MTOMs.

Quite important are the requirements related to operation and registration (Implementing Act) as well as requirements related to the CE (Conformité Européene) marking, technical requirements and third-country operators (Delegated Act).

---

41 Art. 115 Procedures for the development of opinions, certification specifications and other detailed specifications, acceptable means of compliance and guidance material (AMC/GM). EASA Opinion No. 01/2018 Unmanned aircraft system (UAS) operations in the Open and Specific categories, 6 February 2018. See also www.easa.europa.eu/the-agency/management-board/decisions/easa-mb-decision-18-2015-rulemaking-procedure.

The two acts must remain fully consistent in the future as they together implement the operation-centric concept. The objective of Opinion 01/2018 is quite similar to the preceding NPA 2017-05, *viz.* to create a new regulatory framework that defines measures to mitigate the risk of operations:

- Open category, through a combination of limitations, operational rules, requirements for the competency of the remote pilot, as well as technical requirements for UAS, in a way that the UAS operator may conduct the operation without prior authorization by the competent authority, or without submitting a declaration; and
- Specific category, through a system that includes a risk assessment being conducted by the UAS operator before starting an operation, or an operator complying with a standard scenario, or an operator holding a certificate with privileges.

Given the immense preparatory process, the new UAS regulation has the following structure:

- The regulatory scope, definitions of significant and relevant terms and acronyms, the timeline required for the transition period until the full implementation, high-level requirements for UAS operations in the Open and Specific categories (e.g. requirements for registration, geofencing and electronic identification, competent authorities, the concept of drone zones and model aircraft).
- Annex I (Part-UAS) with detailed aviation requirements for UAS operations in the Open and Specific categories; and
- Annex II (Part-MRK) containing the conditions for making UAS in the Open category available on the market.

Opinion 01/2018 is also intended to propose the implementation of all requirements, subject to approval, specified in the objective of NPA 2017-05. On 28 February 2019, the EASA Committee on Future Drone Operation Rules has given its positive vote to the proposal of the European Commission for an Implementing Act regulating the operations of unmanned UAS in the Open and Specific categories, which means harmonized drone rules to ensure safe, secure and sustainable operations of drones in Europe. These new European drone rules came into force as of 31 December 2020. The proposal is based mainly on Opinion 01/2018. During the adoption phases, EASA has continuously provided technical support on the issues to the European Commission.[42]

The proposed regulation will harmonize operation regulations in Europe and create a common EU market for drones. It will allow everyone to buy and operate a drone ensuring:

---

42 *See also* One step closer to harmonized rules for safe drones operation in Europe: EASA welcomes positive vote in the EASA Committee on Future Drone Operation Rules, 1 March 2019.

- safety, by keeping drones away from manned aircraft, which could otherwise pose a real hazard, protecting people and critical and sensitive infrastructure;
- security, by keeping drones at an appropriate distance from extremely crucial objects such as nuclear reactors, military bases or oil pipelines;
- privacy, by means of a proper separation from residential areas; and
- environmental protection, by reducing the noise level.[43]

The main aspects of the proposed regulation are as follows:
- It provides a framework to safely operate drones while allowing the drone industry to remain agile, to innovate and to continue to grow. The risk posed to people on the surface and to other aircraft as well as privacy, security and data protection issues created by such drones are also taken into account.
- It defines the technical and operational requirements for drones. Technical requirements refer, for example, to the remote identification of drones. Operational requirements refer, among others, to geo-awareness, a system that informs the remote pilot when a drone is entering a prohibited zone. The proposal also addresses the pilots' qualifications. Furthermore, drone operators will have to register themselves, except when they operate drones lighter than 25 g and without a camera.
- It breaks new ground by combining product legislation and aviation legislation. Indeed, design requirements for small drones will be implemented by using the legislation relative to making products available on the market (the well-known CE marking). The standard CE mark will be accompanied by the identification of the class of the drone (from C0 to C4) and by a do's and don'ts consumer information that will be found in all drone boxes. Based on the drone class, an operator will know in which area he can operate and what competence is required.
- It allows a high degree of flexibility for EASA Member States; they will be able to define zones in their territory where either drone operations are prohibited or restricted, for example, to protect sensitive areas, or certain requirements are alleviated. For operations posing higher risks, an operational risk assessment will define the requirements that the operator needs to comply with before flying the drone.

The proposal also provides special alleviations for people flying model aircraft (also considered as drones) to recognize the good safety records in aeromodelling by identifying three options:
- EU Member States may issue a special authorization to model clubs and associations defining deviations from the UAS regulation;
- operations can be conducted in specific zones designated by EU Member States; or

---

43 EASA Newsletter On Air, issue 20, 28 September 2018: Safe Operations of Drones in Europe.

– operations can be conducted in the Open category according to the operational limitations defined for one of the subcategories (A3).

The first EU-wide regulations for civil drones are based on an innovative way of regulating, where the rules are kept as simple as possible with a strong focus on the particular risks of the operations; flying the same drone over a city centre or over the sea entails a completely different risk. It takes into account the expertise of many international players in the drone domain. They will allow remotely piloted aircraft to fly safely in European airspace and bring legal certainty for this rapidly expanding industry.[44]

Safety, as defined by ICAO, is the state in which the possibility of harm to persons or property damage will be reduced to, and maintained at or below, an acceptable level through a continuing process of hazard identification and risk management. Safety risks associated with unmanned aircraft operations can be grouped according to third parties subject to damage or (fatal) injury. This includes people on the ground and water surface, respectively, other airspace users and critical infrastructure.[45]

To ensure the free circulation of drones and a level playing field within the European Union, EASA has developed common European rules. The overall regulatory intention is that the highest safety standards achieved in manned aviation have to apply to drones as well. The rules are based on an assessment of the risk of operation and to find a balance between the obligations of drone manufacturers and operators in terms of safety, respect for privacy, environmental issues, noise protection and security.

The new rules ensure that drone operators, whether recreational or professional, will have a clear understanding of the do's and don'ts. The rules cover the entire spectrum, which means each operation type from those not requiring prior permission to those involving certified aircraft and operators, including minimum training requirements for remote pilots.

On 11 June 2019, since no objections were raised by the European Parliament or by the Council, common European rules on drones, Regulation (EU) 2019/945 and Regulation (EU) 2019/947, were adopted and published to ensure drone operations across Europe are safe and secure. The rules will, among other things, help to protect the safety and privacy of European citizens while enabling the free circulation of drones and a level playing field within the European Union. Owing to the Covid-19 crisis, the

---

44 Regulation of Drones, April 2016. *See also* Regulation (EU) 2018/1139 of 4 July 2018 (new Basic Regulation), pp. 4-6, Recitals (25) to (35).
45 ICAO Safety Management Manual Doc 9859 AN/474, Fourth Edition 2017, Part I, Chapter 2 Safety Management Fundamentals, 2.1.1.1.. *See also in this respect* ICAO Handbook for CAAs on the Management of Aviation Safety Risks related to COVID-19, 1st Edition, May 2020 (Doc 10144).

applicability dates of Regulation (EU) 2019/945 and Regulation (EU) 2019/947 have been delayed from 1 July 2020 to 31 December 2020.[46]

Regulation (EU) 2019/945 lays down the requirements for the design and manufacture of UAS, intended to be operational under the rules and conditions defined in Regulation (EU) and of remote identification add-ons. Regulation (EU) 2019/945 also defines the type of UAS whose design, production and maintenance shall be subject to certification. This Regulation also establishes rules on making UAS intended for use in the Open category and remote identification add-ons available on the market and on their free movement in the European Union. Regulation (EU) 2019/945 also lays down rules for third-country UAS operators, when they conduct a UAS operation pursuant to Regulation (EU) 2019/947 within the Single European Sky airspace.[47]

The common rules will help drone operators, whether professional or recreational, to have a clear understanding of what is allowed or not. At the same time, it enables them to operate across international borders. Once drone operators have received an authorization from the State of Registration, they are allowed to circulate freely in the European Union. This means that they can operate their drones seamlessly when travelling right through the European Union or, in the case of developing a business involving drones, around Europe.

The new rules include technical as well as operational requirements for drones. On the one hand, they define the capabilities a drone must have to be flown safely. For instance, new drones will have to be individually identifiable, allowing the national authorities to trace a particular drone if necessary. This will help to better prevent events similar to those that happened in 2018 at Gatwick and Heathrow airports, and at Madrid Barajas

---

46 Owing to new insights (two new UAS classes and standard scenarios), Commission Delegated Regulation (EU) 2019/945 of 12 March 2019 and Commission Implementing Regulation (EU) 2019/947 of 24 May 2019 have been amended in 2020 by Commission Delegated Regulation (EU) 2020/1058 of 27 April 2020 amending Delegated Regulation (EU) 2019/945 as regards the introduction of two new unmanned aircraft systems classes, *OJ* L 232/1, 20 July 2020, and Commission Implementing Regulation (EU) 2020/639 of 12 May 2020 amending Implementing Regulation (EU) 2019/947 as regards standard scenarios for operations executed in or beyond the visual line of sight, *OJ* L 150/1, 13 May 2020, respectively.

47 Single European sky airspace means airspace above the territory to which the EU treaties apply, as well as any other airspace where EU Member States apply Regulation (EC) No. 551/2004 of the European Parliament and of the Council of 10 March 2004 on the organization and use of the airspace in the single European sky, in accordance with Para. 3 of Art. 1 of that Regulation. Art. 1, Para. 3: Without prejudice to Art. 10, this Regulation shall apply to airspace within the ICAO EUR and AFI regions where EU Member States are responsible for the provision of air traffic services in accordance with the service provision Regulation. EU Member States may also apply this Regulation to airspace under their responsibility within other ICAO regions, on condition that they inform the Commission and the other EU Member States thereof.

airport in 2020.[48] On the other hand, the rules cover each operating type, from those not requiring prior authorization to those involving certified unmanned aircraft and operators, as well as minimum remote pilot training requirements. The new rules will replace existing national rules in EU Member States.

> With large parts of the economy looking at ways to use drones to streamline their operations, it is essential that we have strong rules in place to ensure that there is no danger to people or property from drone usage, and that noise levels are acceptable. It is our job to ensure that Europe's citizens are kept safe as drone use increases.
> (Patrick Ky, Executive Director of EASA, July 2020).

The safety of drone operations is still a major concern to commercial aviation around the world. At first glance, innocent drone operations can easily disrupt the international community. In December 2018, hundreds of flights were cancelled at Gatwick Airport, located south of London, following reports of drone sightings close to the runway and its extended centre line. As early as 2015, in the midst of the tremendous increase in commercial and recreational drones, the European Cockpit Association (ECA) issued a paper describing the position of Europe's professional pilots on the standards and rules necessary for the safe use of drones in EASA's Open category.

ECA states that EASA foresees that the Open category is established for the very low-risk-level drone operations and thus would not require any authorization by aviation authorities. Operators and drone pilots in this group, whether commercial or not, would thereby only be subject to a minimal aviation regulatory system. ECA is particularly concerned that in the Open category group, the airspace users operating drones may in many cases not be familiar with aviation rules and falsely assume that their operation would not affect the safety of manned aviation.

Acknowledging the potential the drone technology has for innovation and benefit to society, it is absolutely critical that this technology is introduced safely, in particular with regard to existing manned aviation. A future aviation accident involving drones in which people are seriously harmed or property damaged will be far more detrimental to the industry's development than carefully thought out, consistent, effective and efficient regulation.

It must always be the case that real people, whether in the air or on the ground, have their safety prioritized over the ability or right to operate a drone. It must be borne in

---

48 Israel Aerospace Industries (IAI) and its subsidiary ELTA Systems have developed the Drone Guard Counter-Drone System, a sophisticated system, equipped with 3-Dimensional (3D) radars, an Electro-Optical (EO) sensor and a Communication Intelligence system (COMINT) for tracking, detection, identification and jamming to disrupt and even neutralize drone flights, both civilian and military, for example, suitable to protect the CTR of a civil airport.

mind that most drones in the Open category will be mass market consumer products but may have significantly different capabilities in a few years' time, and that as a consequence, any regulation needs to deal with this. This cannot happen without proper risk assessment, especially with regard to mid-air collision risk.[49]

A major milestone in the regulation of operations of UAS in Europe was achieved on 10 October 2019 with the publication of the AMC and GM for the regulation on UAS operations in the Open and Specific category.[50] EASA will support UAS operators and EU Member States in complying with the adopted EU regulation. The document includes a revised version of the draft AMC and GM that were published together with Opinion 01/2018, the description of a risk assessment methodology to better evaluate the possible danger of a UAS operation and to identify mitigation measures to make the operation safe.

The rising number of UAS operations in the European airspace poses a safety issue: how to ensure safe drone traffic management and how to integrate drones safely into the existing air traffic environment. The airspace integration of such an untold number of UAS constitutes a major challenge and another milestone in the regulation of drones, not only in Europe but globally.

A high-level conference on UAS was held in Helsinki on 21 and 22 November 2017 on the need to ensure that safe and effective use of airspace would be achieved by the delivery of cost-effective U-space services and that the investment in demonstrators would systematically help to open the UAS services market. The development of a detailed safety regulation for U-space, linked to the ongoing rule-making process for a regulation on UAS in the Open and Specific categories, would be a tremendous challenge owing to the lack of experience in this field and the lack of a commonly agreed CONOPS. The conclusions of the Drone Helsinki Declaration were as follows:

Called for clear and simple rules that keep the burden for citizens, operators and authorities as light as possible, and that lower the threshold for entering the EU drone services and U-space markets; confirmed the commitment of all stakeholders present to open the EU drone services market by 2019 by working in parallel and with maximum cooperation on three pillars:
1. The legal requirements for drones and drone operators, for the safe and effective use of the airspace, and for the delivery of cost-effective U-space services;

---

49 ECA Position Paper of 23 July 2015. The RPAS Open Category in EASA's Concept of Operations for Drones, p. 1.
50 Publication of Guidance Material (GM), Acceptable Means of Compliance (AMC) and First Pre-Defined Risk Assessments by EASA. Guidance Material means non-binding material developed by EASA that helps to illustrate the meaning of a requirement or specification and is used to support the interpretation of the (new) Basic Regulation, its Commission acts, Certification Specifications and Acceptable Means of Compliance.

2. Further investment in demonstrators that systematically help to open the drone services market, as well as in longer term R&D projects that prepare for more autonomous vehicles and more dense traffic; and
3. An effective standard setting process that is adapted to fast evolving digital technologies from all sectors, and uses and adapts existing standards where available.

Stressed the need for protection of citizens based on safety, security, privacy and the environment.

During the development of NPA 2017-05, it was considered that the fundamental pillars of U-space should be included in it: registration, e-identification and geo-awareness. Several comments on this issue were received during the NPA commenting period and during discussion in the expert group. The following two options were proposed:
- wait for a better definition of the U-space requirements and avoid including in the new regulation on UAS operations in the Open and Specific category any requirements that may potentially need to be adapted in the future;
- define in this regulation a minimum set of requirements on registration, e-identification and geo-awareness.

The impact of the two approaches has been extensively discussed in dedicated meetings with industry, UAS operators and security authorities. EU Member States clearly stated that registration and e-identification requirements are already essential elements in their national regulations. Without these elements, enforcement authorities would not have tools, making it necessary to impose some limitations on UAS operations, or for specific additional requirements to be added by some EU Member States. However, apart from registration and e-identification, more data is necessary to be able to develop safety performance requirements, especially but not limited to U-space operations.

The high-level conference on drones on 28 December 2018, in Amsterdam, concluded that the European Commission and EASA would be urged to, in close cooperation with the EU Member States and stakeholders, develop an institutional framework for a competitive U-space service market and examine how drones need to be operated in the Single European Sky. U-space is the term adopted by the European Commission for a set of services supporting low-level drone operations (below 120 m). In particular, U-space will provide BVLOS operations and will be the fundamental basis for dense operations in urban areas. Urban airspace is known as U-space, the label used by the European Union to refer to unmanned aircraft traffic management.

As an immediate follow-up of the 2018 conference, EASA, together with the European Commission, has developed a preliminary draft regulatory framework containing high-level safety requirements on the establishment of U-space to enable competent authorities to set performance requirements, including environmental objectives, needed to satisfy traffic density and complexity of operations, setting high-level requirements for the U-space services and service provider certification, and that will lay the foundation for innovative U-space services. Thereby, a fully automated infrastructure will provide the drone pilots with all information needed to conduct a safe operation, including air traffic management, and will ensure that drones do not enter any restricted zones.

About a year later, during the high-level conference on drones in Amsterdam, held on 5 and 6 December 2019, policymakers, experts and leading companies in the UAS industry from all over the world, focusing on the subject 'Scaling Drone Operations in European Airspace', discussed the development of a common European market for drones and to share the latest developments on operations in the urban U-space.

The operation of drones, the implementation of U-space/UTM and operations in complex urban environment will be possible only with high levels of automation and use of disruptive technologies like artificial intelligence or blockchain. The implementation of U-space solutions to cope with a significant numbers of drones will not be possible using traditional approaches.[51] Early implementation of solutions of supercomputing-powered machine learning (ML), a form of AI, is a must for operations of small automated drones with different performance, performing very fast and unscheduled trajectories in a congested environment, such as the urban environment. ML is, in fact, an application of AI that provides systems with the ability to automatically learn and improve from experience without being explicitly programmed.[52]

The development of detect and avoid solutions is also expected to require the support of ML solutions, in particular for analysing images from radar or camera-based systems. AI/ML could also support contingency management, for instance, in the case of C2 link loss. Moreover, autonomous localization/navigation solutions, without GPS, are anticipated to reap benefits from AI/ML techniques, for instance, by improving and simplifying current positioning sensors, data aggregation and the overall performance of the functions.

AI has evolved along with technology and is defined in the EASA Artificial Intelligence Roadmap as any technology that appears to emulate the performance of a human. AI is a fast-emerging technology and is being adopted widely, including in the aviation domain, although it still raises major ethical issues. While the concept of AI has been in existence

---

[51] Bensoussan, A., Gazagne, D., *Droit des Systèmes Autonomes: Véhicules Intelligents, Drones, Seabots*, Bruylant Éditions Juridiques, Bruxelles: Lefebvre Sarrut Belgium S.A., 2019, 1.2 Le Vecteur Aérien: Le Marché Européen du Drone.

[52] *See* Mohanty, S., Vyas, S., *How to Compete in the Age of Artificial Intelligence: Implementing a Collaborative Human-Machine Strategy for Your Business*, New York City: Apress, 2018, pp. 35-37.

since the 1950s, its development has significantly accelerated in the last decade owing to three concurrent factors:
- Capacity to collect and store massive amount of data;
- Increase in computer power; and
- Development of increasingly powerful algorithms and architectures.

AI systems are already integrated in everyday technologies such as smartphones and personal assistants, and it has been observed that the civil and military aviation system has begun to be affected by this technological revolution. At the same time, AI is probably the most disruptive, giving rise to many questions that must be answered:
- How to establish the public trust in AI-based systems
- How to integrate the ethical dimension of AI in safety certification processes, including key elements as transparency, non-discrimination and fairness
- How to prepare the certification of AI systems
- What standards, protocols and methods do we need to develop to ensure that AI will further improve the current level of safety in air transport, including unmanned aviation?[53]

In regard to the aviation sector, AI will not only affect the products and services provided by the industry, but will also trigger the rise of new business models. The current breakthrough is linked with ML, which is the use of data to train algorithms to improve their performance. Deep learning (DL) is a subset of ML that emerged through the use of deeper neural networks (NNs) that bring the learning capacity a bit closer to the function of a human brain.

It enables applications like computer vision and natural language processing (NLP) that were out of reach before the emergence of deep learning. Data-driven learning techniques are disruptive in essence and, by opposition to software development techniques, cannot be assessed by means of traditional approaches. Thus, they raise the need for developing novel approaches. AI is a strategic technology that can improve a variety of public services, ranging from healthcare, all modes of transport, resources to finance or justice.

Most probably more than any technological fundamental evolutions so far, AI raises major ethical questions. A European ethical approach to AI is central to strengthen citizens' trust in the digital development and aims to build a competitive advantage for European companies. Only if AI is developed and used in a way that respects widely shared ethical values, it should be considered trustworthy. Therefore, there is a need for ethical guidelines that build on the existing regulatory framework.

---

53 EASA Artificial Intelligence Roadmap: A human-centric approach to AI in aviation, Version 1.0, February 2020, pp. 2-4.

Multiple domains in the aviation sector will be impacted by the emerging technology of ML. The civil air transport system is facing new challenges: increase in traffic volumes, more stringent environmental standards, growing complexity of systems, greater focus on competitiveness, for which AI could provide opportunities. Generally speaking, in the aircraft design domain, the current implementing rules (Part 21 and Certification Specifications) are already creating an open framework for the introduction of AI/ML solutions.[54]

AI, and more specifically the ML field of AI, is bringing enormous potential for developing applications that would not have been possible with the development techniques that have been used so far. The current breakthrough of DL brings about a wide range of applications that could benefit aviation, in particular, computer vision and natural language processing. In aviation, these types of application could open the door to solutions such as high-resolution camera-based traffic detection or visual assistance to the pilot.[55]

The most discussed application of ML is autonomous flight. The drone market has paved the way, and we can now see the emergence of new business models striving for the creation of air taxi systems to respond to the demand for urban air mobility. Autonomous aircraft will inevitably have to rely on systems to enable complex decisions, for example, to ensure the safe flight and landing or to manage the separation between aircraft with reduced distances compared with current ATM practices. This is where AI will come into play: to enable full autonomy, very powerful algorithms will be necessary to cope with the huge amount of data generated by the embedded sensors and by the machine-to-machine communications.[56]

AI and ML could be used in nearly any application that implies mathematical optimization problems, removing the need for analysis of all possible combinations of associated parameter values and logical conditions. Typical applications of ML could be flight control computational laws (flight control modes) optimization, sensor calibration, fuel tank quantity evaluation, icing detection and many more to come. Moreover, such techniques could also be used for improving the design processes. AI/ML can provide a solution for the modelling of physical phenomena. It could also be used for optimization of qualification processes that rely on physical phenomenon demonstration.

---

54 EASA Part 21 Airworthiness and Environmental Certification. Part 21 covers certification, design organizations and production organizations. *See also* Commission Regulation (EU) No. 748/2012 of 3 August 2012 laying down implementing rules for the airworthiness and environmental certification of aircraft and related products, parts and appliances, as well as for the certification of design and production organizations, *OJ* L 224/1, 21 August 2012.

55 AI in the cockpit: why is the pilot of your plane on the ground? AI in the future will provide pilots with the keys to managing complexity, which means assuring safety (André Cléroux, Thales Avionic Functions Product Line Director).

56 Source: EASA Artificial Intelligence Roadmap, pp. 7-12.

Production and maintenance, including component logistics, are domains where digitalization is likely to affect processes and business models significantly. The unmanned aviation domain is a forerunner of automation. In the quest for autonomous flights, most of the drone industrial actors are envisaging flights with human (remote) supervision and, ultimately, through a rapid transition, fully autonomous flights.

From 2019, U-space will be gradually deployed by setting up the foundation elements such as drone registration, e-identification and geo-awareness system. Additional functionalities will be progressively deployed until U-space is operational, according to plan in 2025, allowing fully autonomous operations. The latest technology will be used to enforce the regulation and protect citizens' rights.

The U-space regulatory framework workshop, held in Cologne on 14-15 May 2019, produced some interesting conclusions on the subject:

- U-space is characterized by its high degree of automation and digital connectivity, while U-space operations must remain safe, secure, green and respect privacy. Furthermore, there is a need to take into account the way cities can take a leading role in U-space.
- There is a need for a separate U-space regulation to reflect the innovative character and the paradigm shift, distinct from yet building on other aviation safety regulations, for example, ATM present regulatory framework. There is also a regulatory need to define flight rules and airspace where U-space services will apply, and roles and responsibilities of the actors, what applies and who are to be affected.
- EU Member States have sovereign powers to designate the volumes of airspace where U-space services will be available and/or provided. They have to decide where those services will be provided on the basis of traffic complexity and who will act as authority at the national, regional or local level, while cities do have a complementary role to address societal concerns.
- The same flight rules should apply in the same airspace for all airspace users, unless a segregation-like approach is applied.
- The draft regulation needs to be technology neutral, and open standards must be applied. Furthermore, it should, ideally, contain an airspace classification for U-space, while the ICAO framework and SERA should not be ignored when establishing U-space regulatory framework.
- ATM and U-space are distinct but complementary frameworks. The traditional human-centric ATM/ANS is not always suitable for data-driven drone operations. The existence of clear rules on the interaction between U-space and ATM is imperative.
- There is a regulatory need for a list of basic services, in order to make clear what is being regulated, whereas the minimum list of services, which are needed, depends on

traffic complexity in that airspace and its environment. However, a short list would be sufficient as it can always be extended later on, leaving flexibility to the authorities. Evidently, identification, airspace authorization and geo-awareness are considered as crucial services.
- Organizations to become U-space service providers (USSPs) are the ones that are meeting the requirements to qualify for these U-space services and that can provide U-space services across the European Union. The USSPs' certificates will be mutually recognized, which is one of the major benefits of the future U-space regulation. In addition, there is a need to establish service-level agreements, in particular to non-regulated services to meet the required performance level for the UAS operations.
- U-space flight rules should be built on SERA, which, however, are not suitable for UAS operations in the U-space; thus the flight rules need to be adapted to drone operations. A more ideal starting point is the development of flight rules specific for UAS operations in the U-space, but this requires considerable time for demonstrations.
- There is an agreement on the user-pays principle, but effective competition will reduce the costs, and there is a need to develop the EU market to scale operations.

To enable efficient drone operations in the U-space, which covers the ecosystem of services and specific procedures necessary for these kinds of operations, safety will be strengthened in order to support the development of these operations. Restricted airspace such as urban airspace will be opened up to drone operations according to UAS airworthiness, societal acceptance and strict risk assessment.

The methodology for conducting a risk assessment of the operations in the Specific category, called SORA, offers an in-depth structured approach to evaluate all aspects and identify mitigations and safety objectives.

In addition, the first predefined risk assessment (PDRA) will assist operators when applying for an authorization in the Specific category for special UAS operations, such as the ones conducted over sparsely populated areas, in uncontrolled airspace, at very low level, beyond visual line of sight with visual air risk mitigation (VARM), using unmanned aircraft with a characteristic size of up to 3 m. Additional PDRA will be developed in the near future together with the national CAAs and UAS operators to cover the most common operations conducted in Europe.

As part of its rule-making process, EASA published, on 7 November 2019, Opinion 05/2019 on standard scenarios for UAS operations in the Specific category. Opinion 05/2019 concerns drones that pose a low risk and fall within this category. The objective of the Opinion is to provide cost-efficient rules for low-risk UAS operations in the Specific category. EASA has developed this Opinion in line with Regulation (EU) 2018/1139.

The Opinion proposes the addition of two standard scenarios (STSs) in Appendix 1 to the Annex to Regulation (EU) 2019/947, defining the conditions when UAS operators can start an operation after having submitted a declaration to the competent authority.

Moreover, the Opinion proposes the introduction of two new Parts in the Annex to Regulation (EU) 2019/945, including the technical requirements that UAS need to meet in order to be operated in the STSs, and establishing two new UAS classes, entitled 'class C5 and class C6'. These classes would then eliminate the need for a certificate of airworthiness.

The relevant drone operators will be allowed to just send a declaration to the authority concerned instead of applying and waiting for an authorization. The two STSs include urban VLOS operations and rural BVLOS operations above a controlled ground area, defined as the ground area where the UAS is operated and within which the UAS operator can ensure that only involved persons are present.

Opinion 05/2019 contains the proposed amendments to both Commission Regulations on unmanned aircraft operations. The conditions to conduct the STSs are based on the in-service experience of some EU Member States, and they have been validated through the application of SORA. The proposed changes are expected to increase the cost-effectiveness for UAS operators, manufacturers and competent authorities and to improve the harmonization of UAS operations in the EU Member States.

Following the discussion process by a special EASA Committee in December 2019, Opinion 05/2019 is expected to be transformed in a legislative act in February 2020 by the EU Commission and adopted after positive voting by the EU Member States.[57]

Starting from June 2020, all drone operators shall register themselves before using a drone:
- in the Open category, with a weight:
- more than 250 g or
- less than 250 g when it is considered not to be a toy and it is equipped with a sensor able to capture personal data.
- in the Specific category.

All certified drones, operated in high-risk operations, shall be registered as well. The registration number needs to be displayed on the drone. Operations in the Specific category may be conducted after the authorization given by the national CAA, based on:
- The risk assessment and procedures defined by the appropriate EU regulation.
- Predefined risk assessment published by EASA as an AMC.

---

57 EASA Opinion 05/2019 Standard scenarios for UAS operations in the Specific category, rule-making task (RMT).0729. The rule-making activity is included in the European Plan for Aviation Safety (EPAS) 2019-2023 under this rule-making task number.

Notice: the above mentioned timeline has been delayed due to the COVID-19 pandemic, whereas measures introduced to contain this pandemic severely hamper the ability of EU Member States and the aviation industry to prepare for the application of a number of recently adopted Implementing Regulations in the field of aviation safety. A delay in executing the different tasks required for the proper and timely implementation of Regulation (EU) 2019/947, notably the establishment of registration systems that are digital and interoperable, as well as the adoption of authorizations, declarations and certifications issued on the basis of national law, is unavoidable as a consequence of the COVID-19 pandemic. All UAS types should thus be allowed to operate under the existing conditions for an additional 6 months. Therefore, the dates of application of Regulation (EU) 2019/947 should be postponed accordingly in order to allow UAS operators to be able to use UAS not complying with Regulation (EU) 2019/945 for an additional 6 months period. The transition year has been postponed accordingly.[58]

STSs will be developed only for UAS operations in the Specific category with low risk, for example, with Specific Assurance and Integrity Levels (SAIL) as defined in SORA. The risk-based approach in the Specific category is demonstrated by laying down the requirement for a risk assessment to be conducted by the operator before starting an operation.

For these UAS operations, UAS operators will be allowed to start the operation as soon as they have submitted a declaration of registration to their respective national CAA, and have received the receipt of confirmation and completeness.

The two STSs included in this Opinion have been derived from the in-service experience gained in many EU Member States where large numbers of UAS operations have been conducted and thousands of flight hours have been accomplished without any accident being recorded. In some of these EU Member States, such UAS operations are subjected to an operational declaration, as defined by relevant national regulations, or are even conducted without the need for a declaration. The two STSs are related to the following UAS operations:

- STS-01: VLOS operations at a maximum height of 120 m, at a ground speed of less than 5 m/s in the case of untethered UA, over controlled ground areas that can be in populated (e.g. urban) environments, using UA with MTOMs of up to 25 kg. STS-01 may be considered as an extension of the UAS operations in the Open subcategory (A2), since it allows UAS operations in VLOS, in urban environments, below 120 m, with UA having an MTOM of less than 25 kg.[59] Therefore, several of the

---

58 Commission Implementing Regulation (EU) 2020/746 of 4 June 2020 amending Implementing Regulation (EU) 2019/947 as regards postponing dates of application of certain measures in the context of COVID-19 pandemic, *OJ* L 176/13, 5 June 2020.

requirements defined in STS-01 are similar to those for the Open subcategory (A2); and
- STS-02: BVLOS operations with the UA not more than 2 km from the remote pilot, if visual observers are used, at a maximum height of 120 m, over controlled ground areas in sparsely populated environments, using UA with MTOMs of up to 25 kg.

The UAS operator is required to define the volume within which the UAS can operate, the so-called flight geography. The maximum vertical limit that the UAS operator can define for the flight geography for UAS operations under STS-01 is 120 m (from the closest point on the surface of the Earth). From an air risk point of view, STS-01 is considered equivalent to subcategories A2 and A3 of the Open category. Therefore, the operational limitations and the technical requirements imposed on the UAS are consistent (e.g. VLOS and a maximum height of 120 m, except when overflying an artificial obstacle). The limitation is a little more conservative than the in-service experience of some EU Member States where UAS operations similar to STS-01 are allowed up to a height of 150 m (500 ft). In STS-01, a 30 m margin above the maximum height has been considered for usage in abnormal situations. As in the Open category, the possibility to operate the UAS close to or above an artificial obstacle taller than 105 m (e.g. for building or infrastructure inspections) under the same condition was preserved.

Drone users can start operating in the limited Open category, between June 2020 and June 2022 (which means postponement by at least 6 months compared with the original timeline):
- Drones with a weight of less than 500 g may be operated in an area where it is reasonably expected that no uninvolved person is overflown.
- Drones with a weight of up to 2 kg may be operated at 150 m horizontal distance of residential, recreational and industrial areas, in a range where it is reasonably expected that no uninvolved person is overflown during the entire time of the operation.

By mid-2022, EU Member States need to complete the definition of geographical zones where drones are forbidden or where special authorization is needed. One year later, all model clubs and associations should receive an authorization by the national CAA, which means that an EU Member State may provide model clubs and the umbrella associations allowing their members to deviate from all requirements of the EU regulation.

---

59 VLOS operations at a maximum height of 120 m, in an urban environment, using UA with MTOMs of up to 4 kg.

Parallel to the rule-making process towards the adoption and implementation of a new Regulation for UAS operations in the Open and Specific categories, in order to address the fragmentation of drone regulations in the European Union, EASA, by proposing the U-space regulatory framework in line with Regulation (EU) 2018/1139, will create and harmonize the necessary conditions for manned and unmanned aircraft to operate safely in the U-space airspace to prevent collision between aircraft and to mitigate the air and ground risks.

In October 2019, EASA issued an advisory body consultation about the planned Opinion 'High level regulatory framework for the U-space' (RMT.0230).[60] Comprehensive responses, including comments, were received from, for example, the European Air Sports (EAS) organization and its members.

Under the topic of the 2019 EASA High Level Conference on Drones, scaling drone operations, a number of presentations, discussions and workshops on a variety of subjects were held, the highlights being as follows: the interface with the current ATM environment in the U-space, the roles and responsibilities of the U-space actors, the types of services, addressing societal concerns, the future of urban mobility, integrated and digital airspace, U-space challenges and operational chances and the adoption and implementation of a new EU Regulation for UAS operations in the Open and Specific categories.

The conclusion of the conference was that the vision of a world where drones are to be used for emergency services, urban (automated) transportation or parcel delivery in cities around the world can become a reality only if safety standards are met and solutions found to issues such as privacy and noise. Feedback from countries around the world where there are regular drone operations indicates that the concern of the population is not so much about privacy as about noise nuisance, which is a much bigger environmental issue. Aviation safety regulation on drones will go well beyond normal safety. The future comprehensive regulatory framework tries to give answers to the questions as to how to deal with issues in relation to security, privacy and data protection as well as to noise and emissions.

In response to a question of a member of the European Parliament to whether Europe is lagging behind the rest of the world in making plans for unmanned aircraft operations in civil airspace, EASA Executive Director Patrick Ky told the experts audience:

> The only country that I know is ahead of us for commercial use of drones for delivery in urban environments is Australia, where the city of Canberra has been operating a Google Wing project for the delivery of parcels for the last two years. My Australian counterpart told me that based on the feedback

---

60   EASA Opinion 01/2020 of 13 March 2020.

> received from the citizens of Canberra that by far the main concern is not the fear of something flying over their heads. It is the noise.
> [...] We have had feedback from other countries around the world where there are regular drone operations. The concern of the populations dealing with these drone flights is not that much about privacy, not much about safety, but much more about noise. It is therefore important, that since we are putting together the regulatory framework for drone operations in urban or populated areas, we set the right societal targets in terms of safety, risk exposure and environmental impact.

Societal concerns about these drone operations, a rather recurring theme during the conference, were a common subject of interest among manufacturers, politicians, societal experts, providers and regulators seeking their resolution, as they would otherwise present a considerable barrier to the successful introduction of drone services.

EASA is working at an unprecedented pace to issue rules and guidelines on drone activities to meet the demands from industry for the basic rules concerning drone operations. Requirements for mandatory registration of all drones will pass into law at the end of December 2020.

The Opinion 01/2020, entitled 'High-level regulatory framework for the U-space', has been sent as a proposal to the European Commission in 2020. The rule-making activity is included in the European Plan for Aviation Safety (EPAS) 2020-2024, under rule-making task RMT.0230.[61] This Opinion will focus on urban airspace or U-space, referring in particular to unmanned aircraft traffic management. It will lay down the principles that will allow multiple types of drone traffic to interact safely within an urban airspace, taking account also of other airborne and ground traffic, and people, at the same location. Undeniably, there is a need to develop a robust regulatory framework. Therefore, the U-space regulatory framework, supported by clear and simple rules, should permit safe aircraft operations in all areas and for all types of unmanned operations.

Opinion 01/2020 proposes an effective and enforceable regulatory framework to support and enable operational, technical and business developments and provide fair access to all airspace users so that the market can drive the delivery of the U-space services to cater to airspace users' needs. Only a manifest EU regulatory framework can establish a competitive European U-space services market in order to attract the necessary business investments in both the UAS and U-space services markets. The draft Commission Implementing Regulation, on a high-level regulatory framework for the U-space, would initially target densely populated urban areas or locations close to an aerodrome and would not attempt to cover the entire airspace. The objectives of this draft

---

61 European Plan for Aviation Safety (EPAS), EASA, 13 November 2019. *See also* EASA 2020-2024 EPAS Strategic Priorities and Key Actions: New developments in the area of UAS and U-space are included. Ensure the safe operation of UAS.

Regulation are to:
- support safe, secure and environmentally friendly operations of aircraft in the U-space airspace while respecting the privacy of European citizens;
- maintain the current safety levels for manned aviation;
- create the conditions for an internal market for U-space services; and
- ensure fair, affordable and efficient access to the U-space airspace to all airspace users.

The draft Regulation has been submitted to the European Commission, which will use it as a technical basis for the final phase. The draft Regulation will first be discussed with EU Member State experts in 2020. Two or three additional meetings with EU Member States are foreseen before a vote on the Regulation will take place, probably in 2022.[62]

The Opinion is, therefore, a first regulatory step to allow immediate implementation of the U-space after the entry into force of the future Commission Implementing Regulation and to let the UAS and U-space technologies evolve. The expert assumption is that U-space at the initial stage is not active everywhere. It will depend mainly on the maturity of services and solutions.

Eventually, U-space must ensure the orderly handling of all unmanned air traffic, for instance, because drone flights should be monitored or authorized via a central control system. However, the foundation under U-space is still far from established, let alone the start-up of its roll-out. That process is expected to take years to come.

One of the biggest challenges of the safe integration of drones into the airspace is that of ensuring sound traffic management practices that take into account safety risks related to manned aircraft, unmanned aircraft and people and property on the surface. Unlike ATC in manned aviation, UTM does not depend on radio communications and radar detection. It performs its functions autonomously, relying on software and sensors, with no human involvement in the loop, which means a risk-based and performance-driven approach to regulation. As it will rely heavily on software, the existing regulatory framework for certification and safety assurance of software operating in ATM will likely have to be continuously updated to reflect the highly automated operations of U-space and the safe and secure development of interfaces between the two.

The exponentially developing drone technology, which is not harmonious with existing regulatory regimes, will be as disruptive for businesses as it will be challenging for regulators. The types of operations that need to be regulated do not exclusively cover traditional commercial air traffic. Effective regulations related to drone functions, operations and administration are still lagging behind.

---

62 *See also* Appendix to Opinion 01/2020 Comment-response document (CRD) to draft Opinion. Draft Regulation Table of Contents, pp. 10-33.

CHAPTER 2   LEGAL BASIS FOR DRONE OPERATIONS

The required regulatory framework regarding drones must well protect the safety, security, privacy and environment of people, as drones, capable of flying much closer to people and buildings, are performing their operations in a manner that in a sense was, and still is, simply not possible with manned aircraft. On the other hand, the drone technology is expected to evolve significantly in the foreseeable future, but it is impossible to anticipate right now what this technological innovation will bring far into the future. Hence, the need to shift from the current prescriptive aircraft-focused approach to a distinct performance-based and operation-centric approach.

The starting point of this novel approach is the focus on the specific risk of a particular operation. Rules and procedures should be kept proportionate with the identified risk. The rules and procedures must be made more flexible because the range of possible drone operations goes from harmless, *in casu*, with no meaningful risk at all or generally accepted as risk-free operations, to more traditional operations with risks equivalent to manned aviation.

In addition, technological evolution should be promoted at all times. Therefore, rules should only define the required performance of functional requirements. Thereafter, industry standards could be developed to provide the means to satisfy these requirements, while leaving scope for alternative technological solutions.

In total, the operation-centric approach could be organized in three layers. The first layer concerns the principles of the approach. More specifically, the building blocks of the operation-centric approach are given in the review of Regulation (EC) No. 216/2008 on the EU aviation safety rules. The proposals, laid down in the context of the Proposal included in the COM(2015) 613 final – 2015/0277 (COD),[63] to establish common EU rules for all UAS, irrespective of their MTOM, provided at an early stage the principles and the building blocks for an operation-centric approach:
–   The principle is laid down in Article 4 of the new Basic Regulation.[64]
–   The wording of the new Basic Regulation reflects the necessary flexibility.
–   Use of lighter rules: the new Basic Regulation contains the building blocks; the detailed rules will become Commission Regulations; extensive use of industry standards will be made.
–   The rules will be drafted in terms of performance objectives, leaving it to the industry to establish the standards that comply with the requirements.

---

63   COM(2015) 613 final, Proposal for a regulation of the European Parliament and of the Council on common rules in the field of civil aviation and establishing a European Union Aviation Safety Agency, and repealing Regulation (EC) No. 216/2008 of the European Parliament and of the Council.
64   Regulation (EU) 2018/1139, Art. 4 Principles for measures under this Regulation. Para. 2. The measures taken under this Regulation shall correspond and be proportionate to the nature and risk of each particular activity to which they relate. *See also* Proposal for a Regulation of the European Parliament and of the Council on common rules in the field of civil aviation and establishing a European Aviation Safety Agency, and repealing Regulation (EC) No. 216/2008, Brussels 7 December 2015 COM(2015) 613 final, 2015/0277 (COD), p. 4, Arts. 45-47. These articles create the legal basis for providing for more detailed rules on unmanned aircraft, in view of the extended scope of the proposed Regulation (EASA Basic Regulation).

- The standard procedures for certification and licensing to demonstrate that requirements are complied with are complemented by lighter procedures to deal with lower risk operations: declarations, market surveillance mechanisms in the meaning of Regulation (EC) No. 765/2008.[65]
- Qualified entities are given a clear institutional role in the oversight process so as to complete the tasks of authorities and provide more flexibility.

Unmanned aircraft manufacturing has a cross-border dimension since many unmanned aircraft are purchased online, are imported or at least have imported parts. Mutual recognition in the internal market is difficult to achieve in the presence of detailed and diverging national standards and rules. Likewise, with regard to unmanned aircraft services, many operators are developing cross-border activities. For instance, infrastructure inspections, from oil rigs to rail tracks, are being organized at an international level. Even if operations have a limited scope, operators should be in a position to use the same unmanned aircraft and the same operating requirements with the same pilot at different places in the European Union to develop their business, especially if they operate in niche markets. Large delivery enterprises have expressed their intentions to organize their services at the European level, which requires common operational rules.

Subsidiarity applies at the level of the implementation of the common operational rules, e.g. EU Member State authorities will carry out local risk assessments and decide which airspace shall be open or closed to unmanned aircraft operations, and under what conditions. Most of the light unmanned aircraft operations have a local dimension, and it should be for the local authorities to assess the level of risk and authorize the specific type of operation.

Eventually, the new Basic Regulation has superseded Regulation (EC) No. 216/2008, as an elaboration of the Proposal included in the COM(2015) 613 final. It generally states that a high and uniform level of protection of the European citizen should at all times be ensured in civil aviation, by the adoption of common rules and by measures ensuring that products, persons and organizations in the Community comply with such rules and with those adopted to protect the environment. This should contribute to facilitating the free movement of goods, persons and organizations in the internal market.

The new Basic Regulation further describes with regard to operations with unmanned aircraft, that:
- Since unmanned aircraft also operate within the airspace alongside manned aircraft, this Regulation should cover unmanned aircraft, regardless of their operating mass. Technologies for unmanned aircraft now make possible a wide range of operations,

---

65 Regulation (EC) No. 765/2008 of the European Parliament and of the Council of 9 July 2008 setting out requirements for accreditation and market surveillance relating to the marketing of products and repealing Regulation (EEC) No. 339/93, *OJ* L 218/30, 13 August 2008.

and those operations should be subject to rules that are proportionate to the risk of the particular operation.
- In order to implement a risk-based approach and the principle of proportionality, a degree of flexibility should be provided for EU Member States in regard to unmanned aircraft operations, taking into account various local characteristics within individual EU Member States, such as population density, while ensuring an adequate level of safety.
- The rules regarding unmanned aircraft should contribute to achieving compliance with relevant rights guaranteed under EU law and, in particular, the right to respect for private and family life, set out in Article 7 of the Charter of Fundamental Rights of the European Union, and with the right to protection of personal data, set out in Article 8 of that Charter and in Article 16 Treaty on the Functioning of the European Union (TFEU), and regulated by Regulation (EU) 2016/679 of the European Parliament and of the Council (General Data Protection Regulation, GDPR).[66]
- The essential requirements applicable to unmanned aircraft and their engines, propellers, parts and non-installed equipment should also cover matters relating to electromagnetic compatibility and the radio spectrum, in order to ensure that they do not cause harmful interference, that they use the radio spectrum effectively and that they support the efficient use of the radio spectrum. However, many types of aviation equipment are not necessarily intended specifically for use in either unmanned aircraft or in manned aircraft but could rather be used in both. Therefore, those requirements relating to electromagnetic compatibility and the radio spectrum should apply only from the moment that, and in as far as, the design of the unmanned aircraft and their engines, propellers, parts and non-installed equipment are subject to certification in accordance with this Regulation. The reason for this is to ensure that the regime applicable to such aviation equipment is aligned with the regime applicable to other aircraft and their engines, propellers, parts and non-installed equipment in respect of which such certification is also required under this Regulation. In terms of content, in order to ensure consistency, those requirements should be equivalent to those in Directive 2014/30/EU and Directive 2014/53/EU, both of the European Parliament and of the Council.[67]

---

66 Regulation (EU) 2016/679 of the European Parliament and of the Council of 27 April 2016 on the protection of natural persons with regard to the processing of personal data and on the free movement of such data, and repealing Directive 95/46/EC, OJ L 119, 4 May 2016.

- For some types of unmanned aircraft, the application of the provisions of this Regulation related to registration, certification, identification, oversight and enforcement, as well as of the provisions regarding the Agency, is not necessary in order to reach adequate levels of safety. Market surveillance mechanisms provided by EU product harmonization legislation should be made applicable to those cases.
- In view of the risk that unmanned aircraft can present for safety, privacy, protection of personal data, security or the environment, requirements should be laid down concerning the registration of unmanned aircraft and of operators of unmanned aircraft. It is also necessary to establish digital, harmonized and interoperable national registration systems in which information, including the same basic data, about unmanned aircraft and operators of unmanned aircraft, registered in accordance with this Regulation and the implementing acts adopted on the basis thereof, should be stored. Those national registration systems should comply with the applicable EU and national law on privacy and processing of personal data, and the information stored in those registration systems should be easily accessible.

The conditions, rules and procedures for situations in which the design, production, maintenance and operation of unmanned aircraft, as well as the personnel and organizations involved in those activities, should be subject to certification, should take into account the nature and risk of the type of operation concerned. Those conditions, rules and procedures should, in particular, take into account the type, scale and complexity of the operation, including, where relevant, the size and type of the traffic handled by the responsible organization or person; whether the operation is open to members of the public; the extent to which other air traffic or persons and property on the surface could be endangered by the operation; the purpose of the flight and type of airspace used; and the complexity and performance of the unmanned aircraft involved.

- It should be possible to prohibit, limit or make subject to certain conditions the activities referred to in Chapter III of this Regulation where necessary in the interest of civil aviation safety. That possibility should be exercised in accordance with the delegated and implementing acts adopted by the European Commission for that purpose. EU Member States have the possibility to take measures, in accordance with EU law, falling outside the scope of this Regulation, for reasons including public security and the protection of the right to privacy and protection of personal data.

---

67 Directive 2014/30/EU of the European Parliament and of the Council of 26 February 2014 on the harmonization of the laws of the Member States relating to electromagnetic compliance, OJ L 96/79, 29 March 2014. Directive 2014/53/EU of the European Parliament and of the Council of 16 April 2014 on the harmonization of the laws of the Member States relating to the making available on the market of radio equipment and repealing Directive 1999/5/EC, OJ L 153/62, 22 May 2014.

- Model aircraft are considered to be unmanned aircraft for the purposes of this Regulation and are used primarily for hobby/leisure activities. Delegated and implementing acts concerning unmanned aircraft, adopted on the basis of this Regulation, should take into account that such model aircraft have so far had a good safety record, especially those operated by members of model aircraft associations or clubs that have developed specific codes of conduct for such activities. In addition, when adopting those delegated and implementing acts, the European Commission should take account of the need for a seamless transition from the different national systems to the new EU regulatory framework so that model aircraft can continue to operate as they do today, as well as take into account existing best practices in the EU Member States.[68]

The three Articles and the related Annex on drones laid down in the Proposal (Art. 45-47 and the specific Annex IX), integrally included in the new Basic Regulation under Section VII Unmanned Aircraft, Article 55 Essential requirements for unmanned aircraft, Article 56 Compliance of unmanned aircraft, Article 57 Implementing acts as regards unmanned aircraft, and Article 58 Delegated powers, as well as Annex IX Essential requirements for unmanned aircraft, to view the EU safety rules, must be read in this broader context as before and should be conceived as the keys to unlock and steer the operation-centric, performance-based approach for these three categories.

The core of the operation-centric approach is the specific risk of a specific type of operation. The operation-centric approach is based on the following principles:
- Proportionality: is the key objective of the regulatory framework. The requirements associated with each drone operation should remain proportionate to the risk of each operation.
- Operation-centric: instead of focusing on the aircraft (aircraft-centric approach), the focus shifts to the particular risk of a particular drone operation.
- Risk-based: the level of risk depends on a range of factors, such as the energy, the size and complexity of the drone, the population density of the overflown area, the design of the airspace, the density of traffic and the services provided therein. As the risk may also come from whatever the purpose of the operation, the regulatory framework applies to both commercial and non-commercial operations.
- Performance-based regulation: is a regulatory approach that focuses on desired, measurable outcomes instead of the method or the technical solution. It can be objective based, process based or performance standard based. A key element is the development of non-binding documents such as industry standards, certification,

---

68 Regulation (EU) 2018/1139, Section VII Unmanned aircraft, Arts. 55-58 and Ann. IX Essential requirements for unmanned aircraft.

specification and AMC or GM; in addition, a proposed methodology for independent auditing may be required.
- Progressive: the three categories of operations were established with the idea that the regulatory complexity is proportionate to the operational complexity, so that operators are able to move seamlessly from one type of operation to another, without having to make big leaps or that the rules become a hurdle to advance in operational complexity.
- Smooth: the introduction of drones in the aviation system should not create an undue burden for other aviation stakeholders.

The technical rules will be developed by EASA, to the extent possible, on the basis of international consensus reached in JARUS. The detailed rules will take the form of a Commission Regulation and should precisely describe the required performance levels for drone operations. In addition, the essential unmanned aircraft industry may support the development of standard ways to satisfy the regulatory performance targets.

Standards are not mandatory as such but will facilitate compliance with the rules. Industry-driven standards are deemed the most flexible tools to support technological innovation as well as to boost business opportunities.

As of 31 December 2020, the national rules on drones in Europe are replaced by a common EU Commission Regulation. By means of Commission Implementing Regulation (EU) 2020/746 of 4 June 2020, the European Commission has confirmed that the new European regulatory framework on unmanned aircraft operations will take effect on the aforementioned date, due to a six-month delay. In the preceding years, the majority of unmanned aircraft operations within the European Union did not fit within the scope of the new Basic Regulation and, as a consequence, were still regulated by national regulations. While in principle safety was addressed by those national regulations, the levels of safety provided therein were most likely not harmonized among EU Member States.

From 31 December 2020, drone operators are required to register and, in most cases, to receive training. National permits and exemptions remain valid for another year, the so-called transition year, until 1 January 2022.[69]

The European regulatory framework will cover all types of existing and future drone operations, fostering the development of innovative applications and the creation of a European market for unmanned aircraft services. While aiming primarily at ensuring safe operations of drones, the European regulatory framework will also facilitate the enforcement of EU citizens' rights and contribute towards addressing security issues and environmental concerns for the benefit of EU citizens.

---

69 *See* Commission Implementing Regulation (EU) 2019/947 of 24 May 2019, Art. 21 Adaption of authorizations, declarations and certificates, Art. 22 Transitional provisions and Art. 23 Entry into force and application.

In addition, The European Commission is developing an institutional, regulatory, architectural framework (Commission Implementing Regulation on a high-level regulatory framework for the U-space) for the provision of U-space services, which aims to enable complex drone operations with a high degree of automation, operating in low-level airspace, under BVLOS and in congested areas, as well as the deployment of UTM. This U-space regulatory framework should determine the main principles concerning the role and responsibilities of the organizations involved in the U-space, the necessary services that need to be provided and the requirements for unmanned aircraft in order to operate in the U-space airspace.

The new European regulatory framework on unmanned aircraft operations, postponed by the European Commission, will be based on the following principles:
- A risk-based and proportionate approach: the new regulatory framework will introduce three categories of operation: Open (low risk), Specific (medium risk) and Certified (high risk); appointed by JARUS as A, B and C categories according to the levels of risk involved.
- A sharing of responsibilities between the European Union and its Member States: to bring the necessary flexibility. EU Member States will be able to define so-called zones to restrict the access of certain portions of their airspace or, contrariwise, to relax the conditions there (zones for drones). Thereby, national specificities will be addressed at the most appropriate level. Registration and authorizations will also be implemented at the national level on the basis of applicable common rules.[70]

A participation process is part of the EU policy to designate drone zones, which are low-level airspace portions where national rules are to be applied, deviating from current European rules as of 1 January 2021. In EU Member States, feedback has been given about potential drone zones and requirements. Information from Dutch participants, including airspace experts and drone operators, produced the following suggestions applicable for drone zones in the Netherlands:
- A distinction must be made between drone zones for the Open and Specific category.
- There is a need for a dynamic zone chart. Incidentally, such a chart is required under European regulations. It has been agreed that there will be a uniform chart for all EU Member States. The following items should be included: real-time information about, for example, open-air events, seasonal restrictions on flying over the Natura 2000 network of protected areas and advanced messaging to be able to plan drone operations within two weeks. If no events are published, the European prohibition for the Open Category to fly over crowds remains valid.

---

70   *See also* EASA Terms of Reference for rule-making task RMT.0230, Regulatory framework to accommodate unmanned aircraft systems in the European aviation system, Issue 2, 4 June 2018, pp. 2-3.

- The possibility of a layered chart and the chart in the form of a web app, the GoDrone NL app, developed by LVNL, Luchtverkeersleiding Nederland (Air traffic control agency of the Netherlands) and British Altitude Angel, for all drone operators flying in Dutch airspace, providing information about areas safe to fly and drone no-fly zones, which may include airports and airfields, city centres or big events, apart from other restricted or prohibited areas, such as hospitals. The drone zone chart also provides information about drone test and experimental flying zones.[71]

Privacy, sustainability and environment are criteria on the basis of which the European Union prescribes the way to create a drone zone. In order to create a zone, at least a careful consideration should be made. Law enforcement of flights within a drone zone must be properly regulated, especially in view of the existence of illegal drones, unregistered operators and import of drones without CE marking. Police forces are responsible for this task, while national CAAs conduct oversight in advance on the Specific category through the granting of permits mitigating the risks involved.

The operation of drones should be regulated in a way proportionate to the risk of the specific operation. Only unmanned aircraft operations that pose an acceptable level of risk to people on the surface, other airspace users and critical infrastructure should be allowed by regulation. This acceptable risk should not be misunderstood to be no risk.

The effects of the involvement of the regulating authority, as determined by the unmanned aircraft operational category, in combination with other mitigations, such as airworthiness, identification, operational limitations and approvals, operator confidence, design approvals and design functionality features, should ensure that the unmitigated safety risk of the operation is brought down to an acceptable level. Considering the broad range of operations and types of drones and the logical development around the world within the international JARUS group of drone regulatory bodies, EASA has proposed, just as JARUS, to establish three risk-based categories for drone operations and their associated regulatory regime:[72]

o Category A (Open). This category identifies those unmanned aircraft operations that present low unmitigated risk. The risk for the people on the surface is mitigated by establishing minimum distances to neighbouring people, and through the use of low-energy aircraft, designed to allow simple operations. Flights above crowds are prohibited, but flights above people not related to the operation within cities or

---

71 The GoDrone app, criticized by drone operators because of confusing and slow information, is intended as a source of information about Dutch airspace, tailored to the needs of drone operators. The idea is that the app indicates where you can and cannot fly. The app, subject of updating by feedback, is a first step towards a much wider range of services, such as air traffic control service for drones in U-space.
72 EASA Concept of Operations for Drones: A risk based approach to regulation of unmanned aircraft, Concept of Operation, pp. 3-6. *See also* JARUS UAS Operational Categorization, Document Identifier JAR-DEL-WG7-UASOC-D.04, pp. 16-17.

populated areas are allowed provided that these drones are compliant with acceptable industry standards. This category should not require a prior authorization by a national CAA for the flight. This does not mean that there are no rules. This group of operations would only be submitted to a minimal aviation regulatory system.

Self-certification or adoption of industry standards may apply, but there are no mandatory airworthiness requirements. Risk mitigation is applied through the adoption of operational limitations, for example, limited to specific geographical locations and in VLOS. It merely means that the operational envelope is well described and limited to particular low-risk operations, taking place within defined boundaries where there is no or very limited risk of interfering with other air traffic. There will be no mitigation applied through approvals issued by an aviation authority. The risk for other airspace users is mitigated through separation with manned aircraft, which means that drones must be flown:
– Under direct VLOS: 500 m.
– At an altitude not exceeding 120 m above the surface, including ground and water.
– Outside of specified reserved areas (airport, environmental, security).
– MTOM of less than 25 kg.

Category A is subdivided into three subcategories:
– A1: flights over people (but not over open-air assemblies of people) intended for hobby users flying unmanned aircraft under 900 g (or 80 J), class C0 or C1 (see below);
– A2: flights close to people, but at a safe distance from them for the heavier class C2, require passing a recognized theory test;
– A3: flights far from people – generally intended for model aircraft clubs – classes C3 and C4.

Additionally, EASA has prepared draft regulations on making unmanned aircraft intended for use in the Open category available on the market. These regulations specify five classes of unmanned aircraft that, among other things, have the following characteristics: C0 – MTOM: 250 g, maximum speed: 19 m/s, C1 – MTOM: 900 g, maximum speed: 19 m/s, maximum noise: 60 db(A), C2 – MTOM: 4 kg, maximum noise: 60 db(A), C3 and C4 – MTOM 25 kg. Classes C0, C1, C2 and C3 have a maximum height of 120 m, while classes C1, C2 and C3 must have an eID, lights, GEO-aware and a serial number.

Categories C0, C1 and C2 must have no sharp edges and safe propellers.

In fact, no airworthiness approval is required, or approvals or licences for operators and pilots. The operator is indeed responsible for safe operations. Open operations do not require the operator to complete a SORA. This saving in effort and time is of interest to

some professional users in the Open category.
- o Category B (Specific). This category is a bridge between categories A and C. As soon as an unmanned aircraft operation starts posing more significant aviation risks to persons overflown or involves sharing the airspace, the operation would be placed in a Specific category. When an operation goes beyond the operational limitations of category A and safety is not, at least fully, assured by relying on a certificated design as foreseen in category C, the operation will need to be independently assessed under this category. An acceptable level of risk is ensured by a risk assessment, which should follow the JARUS SORA, regarding the operation that identifies the applicable mitigations, which can contain requirements addressing the design, operational limitations and qualifications of the operator or of the remote pilot. Varying levels of oversight will be needed in this category. The aviation authority will need to decide what level of oversight is required and to issue an operational approval.

In other words, this Specific category is intended for medium-risk operations where the risk of the particular operation would need to be assessed in view of the type of operation, the territory overflown, the particular drone or the quality of the operator. Based on the safety risk assessment, before the operation can be started, each specific aviation risk would be analysed, and mitigation would be agreed by the national CAA, which will issue an Operation Authorization (OA) with specific limitations adapted to the operation.

The safety risk assessment would not be necessary if the operator is approved and has the privilege to perform and approve its own safety risk assessment. In case of operations in non-segregated airspace, the operator can only approve its own safety risk assessment when it has received the agreement of the ANSP concerned.

The issuance of the OA could possibly be supported for technical tasks by Qualified Entities (QEs) as defined in the new Basic Regulation, or by a specially approved body. The OA should clearly specify the specific conditions and limitations for the intended operation and can be issued to authorize a single event or a series of operations under specified conditions. The safety risk assessment has to address airworthiness, operating procedures and environment, competence of involved personnel and organizations as well as airspace issues and could be based on the one being defined by JARUS WG-7 (CONOPS) or equivalent processes acceptable to EASA either as industry standards or AMC.

The minimum level of safety for airworthiness will be based on the results of the safety risk assessment. It may be acceptable to compensate certain airworthiness risk factors by operational risk mitigation factors. The airworthiness assessment is closely linked to the operational environment and procedures, for example, the operation close to crowds could be acceptable when the unmanned aircraft has some additional functionality such as automatic loss of link procedures and impact energy limiting devices as well as adequate operating procedures.

The required competence of involved personnel will also be established on the basis of safety risk assessment, such as specific training up to an EASA licence. An operation manual will be required to define the operating procedures, required airworthiness level, required competence of involved staff members and the type of airspace considering the results of the safety risk assessment.

On 17 December 2020, EASA published the full regulatory framework setting parameters for drone services such as parcel delivery in urban areas, railway and power lines inspection or delivery of essential supplies into crisis zones. The framework enables UAS operations in urban environment categorized as medium risk in the Specific category. It comprises ED Decision 2020/022/R (Regular update of AMC and GM to Regulation (EU) 2019/947), amending the risk assessment methodology with regard to flight over populated areas and assemblies of people, and the Airworthiness Standards known as Special Condition Light UAS Medium Risk.[73]

Standards for the operations characterized by a high risk in the Specific category are scheduled to be published in 2021 by EASA.

o Category C (Certified). When the aviation risks rise to a level akin to traditional manned aviation, the operation would be positioned in the category of certified operations. This Certified category for high-risk operations, including the aircraft involved therein, would be treated in the classic aviation manner. That means full regulatory oversight will apply in this category similar to that of traditional manned aviation. EASA will be the competent authority for the approval of unmanned aircraft system designs involving high-risk operations only and will issue type certificates and design organization approvals for those systems in the same way as it currently does for manned aircraft. Operation of large unmanned aircraft (MTOM above 150 kg) is already within the scope of the new Basic Regulation. EU Member States will remain the competent authorities for the other domains, such as UAS operations and remote pilot licences.

For UAS operations, EASA will develop certain amendments to the existing regulations applicable to manned aircraft. Specific elements of the high-risk UAS operations are as follows:
– the certification and continuing airworthiness of UAS and related products, parts and appliances;
– the approval of design, production and maintenance organizations;
– operation of UAS; and
– licenses of personnel.

---

73 *See* Ann. II to ED Decision 2020/022/R – AMC and GM to the Annex (Part-UAS) to Regulation (EU) 2019/947 – Issue 1, Amendment 1.

Generally, the UAS in the Certified category will be highly complex systems operating in intricate environments with the potential to carry medium to high levels of unmitigated risks, which cannot be mitigated solely through operational limitations. A level of risk mitigation will be applied through regulatory oversight. The most stringent example may be illustrated by an unmanned aircraft, within the system, of the size of a Boeing B-747 performing international cargo-only flights between two major hubs, where the aviation safety regulator likely issues a Type Design approval (Type Certification), a certificate of airworthiness, aircraft operating manuals (AOM), directives for continued airworthiness, production approvals and other associated certificates used in traditional manned aviation.

A Type Certification will be required for operations with a higher associated risk due to the category of operation or might be requested on a voluntary basis by organizations providing services such as remote piloting or equipment such as detect and avoid. The proposed regulatory framework will be quite comparable to what is done for traditional manned aircraft. The competent authorities will be the same as for manned aviation.

The need for this category could be debated because one could imagine that Category B (Specific) would not have a real upper limit. However, this may be challenged for several reasons: a fully regulated approach may be necessary for political reasons or convenient for practical reasons. It would be difficult for the (travelling) public to accept a drone of the size of an Airbus A-320 or a Boeing B-737 which is not certified. Another reason is that the regulated approach could limit the number of safety risk assessments to be performed. The future rules shall provide all the requirements to allow UAS operations with comparable procedures applied today to manned aircraft without increasing the level of risk to third parties on the surface and in the air.

2.4 FAA Drone Rules and Access to the National Airspace System

In recent years, the United States, like the rest of the world, has experienced a tremendous growth in UAS. While the introduction of UAS in the national airspace system (NAS) has opened up numerous possibilities, it has also brought operational challenges, including safe integration into the system. The fact is that incidents involving unauthorized and unsafe use of small, remotely controlled aircraft have risen dramatically. The mass proliferation and adoption of private and commercial UAS turned out to be a major problem. Despite the small size of most UAS, they are considered aircraft and, unfortunately, can disturb air traffic, interfering with traditional fixed and rotary-wing aircraft.[74]

To ensure safety of flight, and safety of people and property on the surface, UAS are subject to regulation by the FAA. However, since the emergence of civil UAS, states and local jurisdictions were increasingly exploring regulation of UAS operations or were actually in the process of enacting regulation related to these operations. This situation was an important reason why the FAA has clashed in the past with local governments over best practices to control UAS operations.

Various local restrictions on these operations were rather confusing and incompatible with federal air traffic rules, resulting in the fact that the FAA has taken action to maintain strict oversight over local laws to ensure consistency across the NAS. Hence, the FAA's Unmanned Aircraft Systems (UAS) Integration Office cautioned state and local government legislators against creating an unwanted patchwork of rules and regulations relating to the operation of UAS, generating great safety concern.

Ordinances, enacted by local authorities, regulating UAS in the navigable airspace could result in fractionalized airspace control. This patchwork of different restrictions could severely limit the flexibility of the FAA in controlling the airspace and flight patterns, and ensuring safety and an efficient air traffic flow throughout the NAS. Furthermore, a navigable airspace free from inconsistent state and local restrictions is an essential prerequisite in maintaining a safe and sound air transportation system.

To clarify this, the FAA intended to provide basic information about the federal regulatory framework for use by states and localities when considering laws affecting UAS. State and local restrictions affecting UAS operations should be consistent with the extensive federal statutory and regulatory framework pertaining to control of the airspace, flight management and efficiency, air traffic control, aviation safety, air navigation facilities and the regulation of aircraft noise at its source.[75]

The background of these different political policies and rule-making is that there are 50 states, over 3,000 counties and county equivalents and approximately 20,000 incorporated cities, towns and villages (as of 2018) in the United States. Most of these geographical and political entities have local governments, including the State Legislature (House of Representatives and Senate), as well as city councils that take jurisdictional issues, such as UAS legislation, very seriously.[76]

---

74 Helicopter or rotary wing aircraft. A heavier-than-air aircraft supported in flight chiefly by the reactions of the air on one or more power-driven rotors on substantially vertical axes. Some states use the term 'rotorcraft' as an alternative to 'helicopter'. ICAO Ann. 6 Operation of Aircraft, Part III – International Operations – Helicopters, Ninth Edition, July 2018, Chapter 1 Definitions.
75 *See* Docket No.: FAA-2015-0150, Operation and Certification of Small Unmanned Aircraft Systems, A Proposed Rule by the FAA, Pub. L. 23 February 2015.

Some of these entities have an independent political mindset, and are not willing to accept federal interference in their local affairs. For various reasons, locally approved UAS regulations were placing severe restrictions on the use of UAS over populated areas.

The FAA, as a federal agency, had to approach authorities of local governments to clarify that what matters in the airspace over states, counties and cities is the sole responsibility of the FAA. This is contrary to the situation in the European Union, being a regional organization with its unique and specified supranational powers and decision-making procedures.

While the European Commission, supported on rule-making by EASA, establishes harmonizing aviation rules and legislation that are mandatory for all EU Member States, these independent states still have sovereign rights regarding their respective airspaces, both civilian and military, despite the efforts to establish the Single European Sky under a legislative package adopted in 2004, which consisted of four principal regulations, followed by legislation concerning the SES technological element.[77]

In 2017, laws regulating the drone industry existed in 32 US states, and five states adopted resolutions regarding drones. At least 38 State Legislatures considered legislation to regulate the drone industry, and 17 states passed 31 pieces of legislation. Many local governments proposed ordinances impacting the drone industry at the local level. Drone pilots would face the challenge of understanding which state and local law apply to each commercial operation and whether any of these laws may be pre-empted by federal law.

An example of how drones can be a potential hazard to traditional civil aviation shows the near miss with a drone that was reportedly operating in an area near Prospect Park in Brooklyn, New York, in 2015. While on the way to LaGuardia Airport, a passenger airliner had to take evasive action to avoid hitting the drone, according to a statement of the FAA, which would investigate the near collision (near miss). The drone was

---

77 A fundamentally new aspect of the EU is that Member States (27 in total by February 2020, post Brexit) have renounced parts of their sovereignty and have transferred them to the EU, whereby the EU has been granted autonomous powers independent of the Member States. In the exercise of these powers, the EU can adopt sovereign decisions at the European level that have the same effect as those of its Member States. The SES

77 A fundamentally new aspect of the EU is that Member States (27 in total by February 2020, post Brexit) have renounced parts of their sovereignty and have transferred them to the EU, whereby the EU has been granted autonomous powers independent of the Member States. In the exercise of these powers, the EU can adopt sovereign decisions at the European level that have the same effect as those of its Member States. The SES initiative was launched in 2000 by the European Commission following the severe delays, additional associated costs and environmental impact experienced in Europe in 1999. Regulation (EC) No. 549/2004 of the European Parliament and of the Council of 10 March 2004 laying down the framework for the creation of the single European sky (the framework Regulation), *OJ* L 96/1, 31 March 2004. *See also* Regulation (EC) No. 550/2004 (the service provision Regulation), Regulation (EC) No. 551/2004 (the airspace Regulation), Regulation (EC) No. 552/2004 (the interoperability Regulation) and Council Regulation (EC) No. 219/2007 of 27 February 2007 on the establishment of a joint undertaking to develop the new-generation European air traffic management system (Single European Sky ATM Research, SESAR), *OJ* L 64/1, 2 March 2007.

spotted at an altitude of 2,700 ft. The FAA was at that time in the process of drafting rules to regulate how drones can operate in public airspace.[78]

Another example: high winds caused a fire to spread rapidly near Interstate 15, a main artery between Los Angeles and Las Vegas, but heavy aviation response awaiting deployment had to stand down because a drone violated flight restrictions, normally imposed by the FAA over fire areas. It was concluded that without that critical 20-minute delay, the fire could have been contained within a 100-acre area through the immediate support of aerial firefighting, according to the FAA. Instead, it continued to spread rapidly, taking out 18 vehicles and two trucks. In July 2016, the U.S. Congress passed the FAA Extension, Safety, and Security Act of 2016, which criminalized unmanned aircraft flights near wildfires.[79]

In the same year, the FAA published a memorandum titled Educational Use of Unmanned Aircraft Systems. The rationale was uncertainty in the model aircraft community about when an unmanned aircraft is a model aircraft operated for hobby or recreational purposes or is an operation requiring FAA authorization. The FAA has received many inquiries from students and educational institutions offering coursework in the design, construction and operation of small unmanned aircraft with respect to the types of activities in which students and faculty may lawfully engage pursuant to the existing legal framework.

One of the answers was that a person may operate an unmanned aircraft as a hobby or recreation in accordance with Section 336 of the FAA Modernization and Reform Act (Pub. L.112-95), enacted by the U.S. Congress in 2012, at educational institutions and community-sponsored events provided that the person is not compensated or that any compensation received is neither directly nor incidentally related to that person's operation of the aircraft at such events.

Despite these tough challenges, the UAS sector holds enormous promise. The sector includes sUAS for private and recreational flying as well as commercial UAS experimenting with package and medical supply delivery, support for search and rescue missions and urban air mobility.

The FAA has produced several areas of UAS forecasting, based on the use of trends and insights from the industry. Forecasts are driven primarily by the assumption of continuing evolution of the regulatory environment, the commercial ingenuity of manufacturers and operators and underlying demand, including business models. The FAA will continue to enable the thriving UAS industry with safe integration into the NAS.

---

78 Luckerson, V., 'Passenger Plane Barely Dodges Drone Above New York', *Time*, 29 May 2015.
79 Analysis: Drone Registration One of Many Regulations Needed for $9 Billion Industry (2016), Drone Interference Increasing Concerns over Airspace Integration (http://onforb.es/1OuBn4s).

In the 1990s, strong conditions were applied to the issuing of flight permits and operation of civil drones. In fact in those years, commercial drone operations were heavily restricted. In 2012, the FAA Modernization and Reform Act demanded that the FAA should make the certificates of waiver or authorization (COAs) issuing process faster for government non-military drone use such as border patrol and law enforcement and search and rescue and establish a number of operational test sites where UAS could be integrated into normal (non-segregated) airspace under certain conditions such as weight (less than 2 kg) and altitude (below 400 ft) restrictions, within VLOS, daylight only (30 minutes before official sunrise to 30 minutes after official sunset, subject to local time) or in twilight with appropriate anti-collision lighting, and away from sensitive airspace such as populated areas and aerodromes (at least 5 miles).

Tests consist of System Safety & Data Gathering, Aircraft Certification, Command & Control Link Issues, Control Station Layout & Certification, Ground and Airborne Sense & Avoid and Environmental Impacts. However, with respect to the test sites, delays were encountered most probably because of the impact on US citizens' rights to privacy under the Fourth Amendment.

The FAA initially established six test sites.[80] These six test applications achieved cross-country geographic and climate diversity and also considered the location of ground infrastructure and research needs. The test-range programme addressed and accounted for

- Manned – unmanned operations,
- Certification standards and air traffic requirements,
- Coordinating and leveraging of NASA and the U.S. Department of Defense (DoD) resources,
- Civil and public UAS, and
- Coordination with NextGen.

In September 2013, the U.S. Department of Transportation's UAS Comprehensive Plan, developed by the FAA Joint Planning and Development Office (JPDO), was presented to the Senate and the House Committees, as required by Section 332(a) of the FAA Modernization and Reform Act of 2012.[81] The UAS Comprehensive Plan details work that has been accomplished, along with future efforts needed to achieve safe integration of UAS into the NAS. The continued safe integration and increased NAS access for UAS will be driven by incremental advances in R&D, including test ranges; rule-making,

---

[80] FAA Selects Six Sites for Unmanned Aircraft Research, 30 December 2013 (FAA News and Updates). In 2020 the total number of approved UAS test sites was seven (https://www.faa.gov/uas/programs_partnerships/test_sites).

[81] The UAS Comprehensive Plan: A Report on the Nation's UAS Path Forward was presented to the Chairman and Ranking Members of the Senate Committee on Commerce, Science and Transportation and the Chairman of the House Committee on Transportation and Infrastructure.

including operational approval and airworthiness standards; and the development of UAS technologies. Safe integration will lead the unmanned aviation community from today's need for accommodation of UAS through individual approvals to a time when standardized/routine integration into the NextGen environment is well defined.

Six high-level strategic goals – specific, measureable, attainable, realistic and timely – were developed to reflect the principal objective of safe UAS integration into the NAS. The overarching approach for the goals was to allow public integration to lay the framework for civil integration. The first two goals applied to sUAS (under 55 lbs) within VLOS, assuming the public realm would be accomplished first and civil would follow; the third and fourth goals applied to the other UAS, with the same process: the public would occur first and civil would follow; goal five was established to plan and manage growing automation capabilities through research; and goal six provided the opportunity for the United States to remain leaders in the international forum. The sum of these goals showed a phased-in approach for UAS integration into the NAS.

In November 2013, the FAA published the first edition of its integrating road map describing the integration procedure in terms of three overlapping perspectives.[82] The first perspective, which is called accommodation, is the shortest-term perspective, referring to granting UAS limited access to the airspace on a case-by-case basis. The second perspective, called integration, addresses medium-term goals such as enabling routine, regulated airspace access without the need for special authorization. The third and most long-term perspective, called evolution, focuses on adaption to emerging needs and capabilities.

The need to respect citizens' privacy rights has been discussed, referring to the use of dialogic approaches at the time to inform regulations. The purpose of this road map is to outline, within a broad timeline, the tasks and considerations needed to enable UAS integration into the NAS for the planning purposes of the broader UAS community. The five-year road map, aligning FAA actions with the Congressional mandate in the FAA Modernization and Reform Act of 2012, is intended to guide aviation stakeholders in understanding operational goals and aviation safety and air traffic challenges when considering future investments.

The drone test sites became operational in 2014, the same year the FAA announced that it would establish a Center of Excellence for UAS in a university consortium focusing on several aspects of the integration of civil drones into American airspace, including the training and certification of pilots. As for commercial drone operation permits, the FAA was still reluctant, not least because of integration into the NAS.[83]

The purpose of the FAA-approved UAS test sites is expressed as follows:

---

82 FAA Integration of Unmanned Aircraft Systems (UAS) in the National Airspace System (NAS) Roadmap, First Edition 2013, Perspective 1: Accommodation, p. 22, Perspective 2: Integration, p. 32, Perspective 3: Evolution, p. 38.

- The research of UAS test site data collection and Analyses will collect and analyse UAS test site data and make recommendations to improve data quality and consistency.
- The data requires analysis to determine technical and operational trends to derive conclusions that support critical safety decisions required to integrate UAS into the NAS.

The FAA-designated (now seven) UAS test sites from 2014 onwards are as follows:
- North Dakota Department of Commerce. North Dakota's Northern Plains UAS test site. The Northern Plains Unmanned Systems Authority assists in advancing North Dakota's UAS opportunities and in providing oversight of the test site. It launched its first research flight in early May 2014. The Northern Plains UAS Test Site, the first FAA test site to conduct flights, is headquartered in Grand Forks, ND.
- State of Nevada. Nevada Institute for Autonomous Systems (NIAS). NIAS is a state-sanctioned 501(c)3 non-profit organization leading the FAA-designated UAS test site on behalf of the State of Nevada. It leads the growth of the Nevada Autonomous Aerial Vehicle Industry through business teaming relationships, collaborating with primary research institutions and helping enhance the UAS industry knowledge base in order to attract new and permanent business to and within the State of Nevada. Its mission is to coach, teach and mentor public and commercial UAS companies and their staff to develop advanced and innovative UAS applications, procedures, technologies and techniques to facilitate safe integration into the NAS.
- New Mexico State University. NMSU's Physical Science Laboratory Flight Test Center assisted in a number of successful Long-Endurance Unmanned Aircraft flights and is performing research with NewFields Aviation & Robotic Services to develop procedures enabling UAS to collect and provide high-resolution remote sensing data to enhance the safe and efficient operation within the extractive industry sector. The NMSU UAS Test Site operates under a certificate of authorization (CoA) that permits UAS flights in over 15,000 square miles of coordinated airspace in southwestern New Mexico.

The airspace, which extends from the surface to 18,000 ft mean sea level (MSL), the US transition altitude, normally features a very low volume of aviation traffic and overlies mostly undeveloped government-owned land. Flexible scheduling practices, low costs and vast airspace allow the UAS test site to accommodate a wide range of UAS operations.
- University of Alaska. Alaska Center for UAS Integration (ACUASI). The centre operates a variety of UAS, ranging from small racing drones used in Science,

---

83 The FAA Center of Excellence (COE) for Unmanned Aircraft Systems (UAS) collaborates with the nation's academic community and its affiliates by fostering cooperative research and developing intellectual capabilities of primary interest to the FAA and UAS community. U.S. Congress mandated that the FAA should establish the COE under the Consolidated Appropriations Act of 2014.

Technology, Engineering and Mathematics (STEM) outreach to the large 300 lbs or greater class of research platform aircraft. The centre also possesses the vehicles, ground control stations, communication equipment, generators and other accessories needed to transport and deploy the aircraft around the world, as well as a variety of payloads for UAS operations, including ground-based and airborne detect and avoid systems, anti-GPS jamming systems, electro-optical/infrared (EO/IR) cameras, lidars, methane detectors, aerosol samplers, etc

The ACUASI supports research and test activities related to public operations, civil/commercial operations, mixed manned and unmanned operations, high-altitude long endurance and high-altitude balloon operations.

Its mission is to maintain a world-class research centre for UAS, providing integration of unique payloads and supporting pathfinder missions within government and science communities, with a special emphasis on the Arctic and sub-Arctic regions. The ACUASI oversees the Pan Pacific UAS Test Range Complex (PPUTRC) test-range facilities in Alaska, Oregon, Hawaii, Kansas and Mississippi, and one international test facility in Iceland.

- Texas A&M University Corpus Christi. Its UAS test site is managed and operated by the Lone Star UAS Center of Excellence & Innovation (LSUASC). The research facility is a Texas-wide partnership for research, development, testing and evaluation of UAS technologies led by the Texas A&M University – Corpus Christi, Texas Engineering Experiment Station (TEES) and Huntington Ingalls Industries, the lead systems integrator that established a UAS facility in the city of Hampton, Virginia, bringing UAS to America's skies. Its mission is to operate for the benefit of advancement and use of unmanned technologies, specifically UAS technics across state agency interests, and to provide an economic stimulus to attract industry to Texas, while being compliant with the Texas Privacy Act.

Furthermore, it will provide the FAA with UAS research, development and operational data to assist in the development of procedures, standards and regulations to facilitate UAS civil operations into the NAS. Research and focus areas are UTM, BVLOS, autonomous behaviour, detect and avoid technology, cybersecurity, test and evaluation of UAS standards, processes and procedures as well as protocols and procedures for airworthiness testing.

- Virginia Polytechnic Institute & State University has as its slogan 'Research-driven solutions to critical challenges in the UAS industry'. The Virginia Tech Mid-Atlantic Aviation Partnership (MAAP), managing the FAA-designated Virginia Test Site for UAS, has, since 2013, been focusing on progressively overcoming obstacles to move the UAS industry forward at an accelerated pace. MAAP combines risk management, operations, research and testing expertise with the intellectual resources of a top-50 research university to tackle the most daunting technical challenges facing UAS integration.

- MAAP has pioneered and validated a rigorous safety-case process that has quickly become an exemplar in the industry. Their method for systematically evaluating operational objectives against potential risks and mitigations has supported robust waiver applications and ultimately enabled new real-world use cases. MAAP partners closely with faculty members in the Virginia Tech College of Engineering and across the university – tapping the extensive experience and capabilities of many world-class faculty. It connects industry challenges with solutions driven by world-class research in the field of operations over people, airworthiness certification, BVLOS and UAS communications and is working closely with regulating authorities and industry partners on groundbreaking studies that inform evidence-based policies and standards. To implement NextGen technology in a safe way, there is a need to combine operational expertise and innovative thinking in a secure environment that facilitates efficient prototyping. MAAP provides support with safety-case development, operational approvals, strategic partnerships, safety cases and test and evaluation of almost any type of unmanned system.
- Griffiss International Airport, New York State UAS Test Site, a Part-139 certified airport with Class D airspace, consists of a highly instrumented UAS test ecosystem with functionalities that include tracking of cooperating and non-cooperating targets, United Support Services (USS) support, simulation capabilities, secure data collection and detect and avoid systems.

The Test Site is operated by the Griffiss International Airport Commissioner and managed by the Northeast UAS Airspace Integration Research Alliance (NUAIR). NUAIR is a New York-based non-profit organization that provides unsurpassed expertise in UAS operations, aeronautical research, safety management and consulting services, situated and operational at Griffiss International Airport, Rome, NY. NUAIR, with its non-profit status, is responsible for the continued development and advancement of New York's 50-mile UTM corridor between Syracuse and Rome, facilitating BVLOS testing, commercial operations in Central New York and the safe integration of UAS into the NAS.

The effective Griffiss International Airport-NUAIR public/private team builds on collaboration between New York State, Oneida County and the Central New York and Mohawk Valley regions and includes experienced and dedicated aviation and safety professionals.

In 2015, the FAA proposed regulations for the use of small drones. While there was speculation among commercial drone users that the allegedly promising regulations were considered to be unnecessarily restrictive, the officially revealed FAA proposal at that time indicated this to be largely unfounded. The proposed regulations, only for drones under 55 lbs, covered straightforward aspects of drone operation such as requiring the operator to avoid populated areas and crowds and determining the degree of risk associated with the operation in any given location, assuming a drone crash.

Other requirements were that the operator should also be able to see the drone at all times when operating, which means remaining within VLOS of the aircraft, and should at any time manoeuvre away from any manned aircraft that might fly nearby. Furthermore, drone operators should not exceed 100 mph, should maintain an altitude not exceeding 500 ft and should stay outside restricted areas and away from aerodrome arrival and departure routes. According to regulations, a drone operator must be at least 17 years of age and must pass an 'aeronautical knowledge test', to get an FAA UAS operator certificate.

The FAA also requires that to stay certified, such test should be passed again once every 24 months. From 2016, the drone operator must be at least 16 years of age to qualify for a remote pilot certificate or be in the possession of a remote pilot certificate or be under the direct supervision of someone who has one. An applicant can obtain a (temporary) remote pilot certificate in two ways: pass an initial aeronautical knowledge test at an FAA-approved knowledge testing centre or, if already in possession of a Part 61 pilot certificate, complete a flight review in the previous 24 months and fulfil an sUAS online training course provided by the FAA.

Section 107.12 Requirement for a remote pilot certificate with a sUAS rating.[84]
- Except as provided in Paragraph (c) of this Section, no person may manipulate the flight controls of a sUAS, unless:
- That person has a remote pilot certificate with a sUAS rating issued pursuant to Subpart C of this Part and satisfies the requirements of Section 107.65, or:
- That person is under the direct supervision of a remote pilot in command and the remote pilot in command has the ability to immediately take direct control of the flight of the small unmanned aircraft.
- Except as provided in Paragraph (c) of this Section, no person may act as a remote pilot in command unless that person has a remote pilot certificate with a sUAS rating issued pursuant to Subpart C of this Part and satisfies the requirement of Section 107.65.
- The Administrator may, consistent with international standards, authorize an airman to operate a civil foreign-registered small unmanned aircraft without an FAA-issued remote pilot certificate with an sUAS rating.

On 14 December 2015, the FAA announced a streamlined and user-friendly web-based aircraft registration process for owners of sUAS weighing more than 0.55 lbs and less

---

84 Electronic Code of Federal Regulations (e-CFR) > Title 14 Aeronautics and Space > Chapter I FAA, DOT > Subchapter F. Air Traffic and General Operating Rules > Part 107. Small UAS > Subpart B. Operating rules > Section 107.12. Requirements for a remote pilot certificate with a small UAS rating.

than 55 lbs, including payloads such as onboard cameras. Registration is a statutory requirement that applies to all aircraft. Under this rule, any owner of an sUAS who has previously operated an unmanned aircraft exclusively as a model aircraft prior to 21 December 2015 must register no later than 19 February 2016.

In the United States, the legal system, based on a system of federalism or decentralization, is a common law jurisdiction, largely based on jurisprudence. Consequently, the UAS regulations in the United States follow the case-by-case, bottom-up approach. The rules of the FAA for small unmanned aircraft operations other than model aircraft (FAA Part 107 Regulations) cover a wide spectrum of commercial and government uses for drones weighing less than 55 lbs.[85]

A significant point is that the FAA Reauthorization Act of 2017 enacted the Drone Operator Safety Act. This bill amends the Federal Criminal Code to make it a crime to knowingly or recklessly operate an unmanned aircraft that interferes with or disrupts an aircraft or airborne vehicle carrying at least one occupant in US airspace. It imposes criminal penalties: a fine, prison term or both on a violator. The prohibition includes the unauthorized operation of an unmanned aircraft within an airport's runway exclusion zone, which is a defined area of controlled airspace around an active runway, unless the operation is the result of an unforeseeable circumstance, such as a malfunction (S.1755 – Drone Operator Safety Act of 2017).

According to a federal law passed on 3 January 2018, a recreational drone user must register the drone with the FAA, mark the outside of the drone with the registration number and carry proof of registration when actually flying, which means flying only for recreational purposes.

According to Section 107.13 Registration, a person operating a civil sUAS for the purposes of flight must comply with the provisions of Section 91.203(a)(2) Civil Aircraft: Certification required:

> Except as provided in Section 91.715, no person may operate a civil aircraft unless it has within it the following:
> [...] (2) An effective U.S. registration certificate issued to its owner or, for operation in the United States, the second copy of the Aircraft registration Application as provided in Section 47.31(c), a Certificate of Aircraft

---

[85] On 5 October 2018, the President signed the FAA Reauthorization Act of 2018. Section 349 of that Act repealed the Special Rule for Model Aircraft (Section 336 of Pub. L. 112-95; 14 February 2012) and repealed it (84 FR 22553) with new conditions to operate recreational small unmanned aircraft without requirements for FAA certification or operating authority. The Exception for Limited Recreational Operations of Unmanned Aircraft established by Section 349 is codified at 49 U.S.C. 44809. Operators of small unmanned aircraft (also referred to as drones) for recreational purposes must follow the rules in 14 CFR Part 107 for FAA certification and operating authority unless they follow the conditions of the Exception for Limited Recreational Operations of Unmanned Aircraft. The FAA refers to individuals operating under that statutory exception as 'recreational flyers'.

registration as provided in Part 48, or a registration certification issued under the laws of a foreign country.

The FAA rules for sUAS other than model aircraft cover a broad spectrum of commercial and government uses for drones, as is shown by Part 107, which was released on 21 June 2016. The rules apply to recreational and commercial unmanned aircraft with a weight less than 55 lbs. Part 107 does not apply to model aircraft that satisfy all the criteria specified in Section 336 of Public Law 112-95.[86]

According to Part 107 rules, a drone operator must avoid manned aircraft at any time and never operate carelessly or recklessly. Yet there are drone pilots who stubbornly violate the rules.[87] Normal operation requires VLOS, or, alternatively, if the drone operator uses First-Person View (FPV) or similar technology, the operator must have a visual observer to always keep the drone within unaided sight, which means, for example, no binoculars. Neither the operator nor the observer can be responsible for more than one drone operation at a time. If a drone operator follows Part 107 rules, there is no need for a waiver. However, if an operator wants to operate a drone contrary to the rules in Part 107 under the waivable operations, a waiver is mandatory for the following:

- Flying an UAS from a moving aircraft or a vehicle in populated areas, as directed in Section 107.25 Operation from a Moving Vehicle or Aircraft.
- Flying a UAS at night, as directed in Section 107.29 Daylight Operations.
- Flying a UAS beyond the operator's ability to clearly determine its orientation with unaided vision, as directed in Section 107.31 Visual Line of Sight Aircraft Operation.
- Using a visual observer without following all visual observer requirements, as directed in Section 107.33 Visual Observer.
- Flying multiple UAS with only 1 remote pilot, as directed in Section 107.35 Operation of Multiple sUAS.
- Flying a UAS without having to give way to other aircraft, as directed in Section 107.37(a) Yielding Right of Way.
- Flying a UAS over a person/people, as directed in Section 107.39 Operation over People.
- Flying a UAS:

---

86 *See* Special Rule for model aircraft (FAA Section 336) in FAA Advisory Circular AC 91-57A Model Aircraft Operating Standards – Including Change 1 (Cancelled) 6. Model Aircraft Operations, and AC 91-57B Exception for Limited Recreational Operations of Unmanned Aircraft.

87 Niles, R., 'Drone Pilot Facing $ 182,000 In Fines', *AVweb*, 3 January 2021. The FAA is proposing a total of $182,000 in fines to an unlicensed drone pilot who was warned three times to stop making illegal flights around Philadelphia. After a warning letter was sent in October of 2019, the FAA contacted him two more times in November of 2019 to explain the ways in which he was violating fundamental rules governing drone flights. At last, the FAA tallied 26 violations of Part 107 regulations, ranging from flying without a special use authorization for the airspace being used to flying at night, in poor visibility and too close to buildings.

- o over 100 miles per hour ground speed.
- o over 400 ft AGL.
- o With less than 3 statute miles of visibility.
- o Within 500 ft vertically or 2000 ft horizontally from clouds.
- o As directed in Section 107.51 Operating Limitations for Small Unmanned Aircraft.[88]

Responding to natural disasters or other emergency situations by individuals or organizations makes their specified operations eligible for expedited approval through a Special Governmental Interest (SGI) process. Operations that may be considered include firefighting, search and rescue, law enforcement, utility or other critical infrastructure restoration, incident awareness and analysis, damage assessment supporting disaster recovery-related insurance claims and media coverage providing crucial information to the public.[89]

On 14 January 2019, U.S. DOT Secretary Elaine L. Chao announced proposed new rules as well as a pilot project to allow UAS, by the American people, more commonly known as drones, to fly overnight over people without waivers under certain conditions and to further integrate drones safely into the NAS as stated in a draft Notice of Proposed Rulemaking (NPRM) of 13 February 2019. These proposed changes to Part 107 would attempt to balance the need to mitigate safety risks without inhibiting technological and operational advances.[90]

The issue of safe integration is dealt with in another Advance NPRM of 13 February 2019 titled Safe and Secure Operation of Small Unmanned Aircraft Systems.

On 17 May 2019, the FAA started implementing Section 349 and 350 of the FAA Reauthorization Act of 2018, establishing new conditions for recreational use of drones and repealing the special rule for model aircraft.[91] On 31 May 2019, the FAA published Advisory Circular (AC) 91-57B Exception for Limited Recreational Operations of

---

88 A waiver is an official document issued by the FAA that approves certain operations of aircraft outside the limitations of a regulation. These (on request) waivers allow drone pilots to deviate from certain rules under Part 107 by demonstrating they can still fly safely using alternative methods. *See also* Part 107 Subpart D – Waivers, Section 107.200 Waiver policy and requirements and Section 107.205 List of regulations subject to waiver. For the purposes of this Section: flight visibility means the average slant distance from the control station at which prominent unlighted objects may be seen and identified by day and prominent lighted objects may be seen and identified by night (if night flying is authorized).
89 *See* JO 7200.23A – Unmanned Aircraft Systems (UAS) Document information.
90 *See* draft NPRM – Operation of Small Unmanned Aircraft Systems over People. *See also* Electronic Code of Federal Regulations (e-CFR), current from 16 January 2020, Title 14 Aeronautics and Space, Chapter I FAA, DOT, Subchapter F – Air Traffic and General Operating Rules, Part 107 Small Unmanned Aircraft Systems, Subpart A-General, Subpart B-Operating Rules, Subpart C-Remote Pilot Certification, and Subpart D-Waivers.

Unmanned Aircraft, which repealed AC 91-57A, intended to bring all relevant rules up to date. AC 91-57B provides interim safety guidance to individuals operating unmanned aircraft, often referred to as drones, for recreational purposes under the statutory exception for limited recreational operations of unmanned aircraft (Title 49 of the United States Code (49 U.S.C.) Section 44809). Guidance and current policies for recreational use of drones must be followed because the Reauthorization Act could not be fully implemented immediately.

Therefore, The FAA has to evaluate the impacts of the change in the law and the way in which the implementation should proceed. The new Advisory Circular restates the statutory conditions to operate under the exception and provides additional guidance on adhering to those conditions. Per 49 U.S.C. Section 44809, recreational flyers may operate under the statutory exception only if they adhere to all of the conditions listed in the statute.[92]

AC 91-57 of 9 June 1981 was the earliest document the FAA published concerning model aircraft flying, encouraging voluntary compliance with safety standards for non-commercial model aircraft operators. AC 91-57 was updated to AC 91-57A on 2 September 2015, which created more restrictions and also a prohibition on drone flying in special flight rule areas, one of which was the Washington D.C. Special Flight Rules Area (Washington National Capital Region Flight Restricted Zone), which was, however, challenged by one of the three *Taylor v. FAA* lawsuits.[93]

Section 349 and 350 created Title 49 U.S.C. Section 44809, The New Recreational Drone Laws.

---

92 See Title 49 – Transportation, Subtitle VII – Aviation Programs, Part A – Air Commerce and Safety, subpart iii-safety, Chapter 448 Unmanned Aircraft Systems. §§ under Chapter 448 are: 44801 Definitions, 44802 Integration of civil unmanned aircraft systems into national airspace system, 44803 Unmanned aircraft test
93 *Taylor v. Huerta* (FAA)-Drone Registration Class Action Lawsuit. On 12 December 2017. John A. Taylor (drone hobbyist) as Petitioner and Michael P. Huerta, as Administrator FAA and as Respondent. On 14 March 2017, the U.S. Court of Appeals for the District of Columbia Circuit argued the challenge to the registration process established by the FAA to model aircraft hobbyists. The case No. 15-1495 (856 F.3d 1089, D.C. Cir. 2017) was decided on 19 May 2017. The court pushed back on the FAA's attempts to exceed its statutory powers.
In brief concerning this lawsuit: Congress has charged the FAA with maintaining the safety of the NAS and the control of its air traffic. As small unmanned aircraft or drones (up to 55 lbs) became more popular, the

Modification regarding the Recreational Drone Laws:
- Section 336 repealed. In October 2018, Congress passed the FAA Reauthorization Act of 2018, establishing new conditions for recreational use of drones, which ceased Section 336, and added many more restrictions to model aircraft pilots.
- Part 101 Subpart E's regulations (Special Rule for Model Aircraft), which were basically a copy of Section 336, no longer valid.
- The recreational drone operator must pass a test and keep proof of passing the test to show to the FAA or law enforcement. The test will cover the recreational drone laws.

---

93 *Taylor v. Huerta* (FAA)-Drone Registration Class Action Lawsuit. On 12 December 2017. John A. Taylor (drone hobbyist) as Petitioner and Michael P. Huerta, as Administrator FAA and as Respondent. On 14 March 2017, the U.S. Court of Appeals for the District of Columbia Circuit argued the challenge to the registration process established by the FAA to model aircraft hobbyists. The case No. 15-1495 (856 F.3d 1089, D.C. Cir. 2017) was decided on 19 May 2017. The court pushed back on the FAA's attempts to exceed its statutory powers.
In brief concerning this lawsuit: Congress has charged the FAA with maintaining the safety of the NAS and the control of its air traffic. As small unmanned aircraft or drones (up to 55 lbs) became more popular, the number of drone-related incidents increased, and the FAA enacted the Registration Rule, without notice and comment period, which required anyone operating drones to register their drone with the FAA and to pay a fee. Unmanned aircraft operated for recreational purposes are known as model aircraft. Taylor argued that the FAA had no statutory authority to issue the Registration Rule, and the Court agreed with him. For both, it all comes back to the 2012 FAA Modernization and Reform Act Section 336(a), which states that the FAA 'may not promulgate any rule or regulation regarding a model aircraft'. The Court (Circuit Judge Kavanaugh) concluded that the FAA Registration Rule of 2015, which applied to model aircraft, directly violates that clear statutory prohibition, to grant Taylor's petition and vacate the Registration Rule to the extent it applies to model aircraft. The ruling applies only to those flying their aircraft in accordance with Section 336.
Noteworthy regarding this case: the National Defense Authorization Act (NDAA) of 2017 was passed. Under Section 1092(d) Restoration of Rules for Registration and Marking of Unmanned Aircraft; it was stated: The rules adopted by the Administrator of the FAA in the matter of registration and marking requirements for small unmanned aircraft (FAA-2015-7396, published on 16 December 2015) that were vacated by the U.S. Court of Appeals for the District of Columbia Circuit in *Taylor v. Huerta* shall be restored to effect on the date of enactment of this act. The Registration Rule for model aircraft was put back into effect.
In 2018, in the following Drone Registration Lawsuit, Case No. 16-1302 (D.C. Cir. 2018), on Petition for Review of an Order of the FAA, the court rejected Taylor's arguments, who last year (2017) had successfully overturned the FAA's system for registration of unmanned aircraft. His brother, Robert C. Taylor (also drone hobbyist), filed the Second Drone Registration Class Action Lawsuit against the FAA (Four count class action lawsuit involving 800,000-plus members (Case No. 18-cv-00035 APM, 2018) regarding that the FAA violated the previous Taylor decision by collecting money and personal information under Part 48, that the FAA violated the class's constitutional and privacy rights by unlawfully promulgating and enforcing the Registration Rule, that the FAA did not delete the private and personal information of model aircraft owners and did not refund their registration fees, that the FAA unlawfully maintained the class's private and personal information even after the court held that the FAA was prohibited from doing so, that the FAA violated in this case the Little Tucker Act and the Privacy Act and the Constitution. The conclusion of the Court: for the foregoing reasons, the Court grants Defendants' Motion (FAA, *et al*) to Dismiss, ECF No. 36, for lack of standing and for failure to state a claim.
See also Wallace, R.J., Loffi, J.M., 'Evolution of UAS Policy in the Wake of Taylor v. Huerta', *International Journal of Aviation, Aeronautics, and Aerospace* 4(3), 2017.

CHAPTER 2 LEGAL BASIS FOR DRONE OPERATIONS

- The recreational drone operator must obtain authorization prior to flying in Class B, C, D or E at the surface associated with an airport airspace and comply with all airspace restrictions and prohibitions. The authorization and restrictions for recreational drone operators will be a National Authorization for fixed sites in controlled airspace as detailed below:
    o Recreational drone operators will be authorized to fly in controlled airspace at fixed sites that will be listed via multiple venues from Federal Register Notice (FRN), Advisory Circular (AC) and FAA Office of Communications public releases.
    o Approximately 350 Academy of Model Aeronautics (AMA) fixed sites are located in controlled airspace, but less than 200 are listed for recreational drone use.
    o These sites will be more than 2 miles from a runway surface and be required to operate in accordance with altitudes that are specified in Unmanned Aircraft Systems Facility Maps (UASFM).
    o The authorizations will be in the form of a National Authorization with national restrictions that have been approved by law, U.S. DOT and FAA HQ. Therefore, air traffic controller personnel or support staff should not make any phone calls or authorizations. In summertime, Low Altitude Authorization Notification Capability (LAANC) will accept and authorize recreational requests in UASFM values but will not accept or authorize anything for altitudes higher than 400 ft or outside the UASFM. In November 2017, LAANC was deployed by the FAA for drone operators at several air traffic facilities in an evaluation to see how well the prototype system functions and to address issues that will arise during testing. Further deployment started in April 2018 followed by the final deployment phase from13 September 2018.

LAANC automates the application and approval process for airspace authorizations. Through applications developed by FAA-approved UAS Service Suppliers (USS) of LAANC, drone pilots can request an airspace authorization to fly in controlled airspace around airports. When a drone pilot submits a request through a LAANC USS, the request is checked against multiple airspace data sources in the FAA UAS Data Exchange. If approved, pilots receive their authorization in near-real time. LAANC also provides FAA's air traffic visibility into where and when planned drone operations will take place. LAANC is available at nearly 400 air traffic facilities, covering approximately 600 airports.
- Recreational aircraft have to be registered and marked, and their pilots have to show registration to the FAA or police if asked.
- Drone operation is strictly for recreational purposes.

- The aircraft is operated in accordance with or within the programming of a community-based organization's set of safety guidelines that are developed in coordination with the FAA.
- The aircraft is flown within VLOS of the person operating the aircraft or a visual observer co-located and in direct communication with the operator.
- The aircraft does not interfere with and gives way to any manned aircraft.
- In Class G airspace, which is uncontrolled airspace in which the FAA does not provide air traffic services:
  o The aircraft is flown from the surface to not more than 400 ft AGL in uncontrolled airspace and requires approval for any operation in controlled airspace.
  o Complies with all airspace restrictions and prohibitions. This would include the thousands of listed security flight restrictions all over the United States. Security flight restrictions can be punished with prison time.
  o Unmanned aircraft, which includes model aircraft, cannot interfere with wildfire suppression efforts, law enforcement or emergency response efforts (49 U.S.C. Section 46320 and 18 U.S.C. 40A).
  o It is a crime to fly in runway exclusion zones without authorization (49 U.S.C. 39B).
  o It is also a crime to fly knowingly or recklessly interfere with, or disrupt the operation of, a manned aircraft in a manner that poses an imminent safety hazard to the occupant(s) (49 U.S.C. 39B).

Many drone operations can be conducted under the Small UAS Rule (14 CFR Part 107), namely as a recreational drone operator or as part of a modeller community-based organization.[94] However, more complex drone operations may need additional certification or approval. To fly an unmanned aircraft that weighs 55 lbs or more, operators need to apply for an exemption under the Special Authority for Certain Unmanned Systems (49 U.S.C. Section 44807). This authority replaces Section 333 of the 2012 FAA Modernization and Reform Act, which was repealed by the 2018 FAA Reauthorization Act.

The Special Authority for Certain Unmanned Systems grants the Secretary of Transportation the authority to use a risk-based approach to determine whether an airworthiness certificate is required for a drone to operate safely in the NAS. Under this authority, the Secretary may grant exemptions to the applicable operating rules, aircraft requirements and pilot requirements for a specific operation on a case-by-case basis, although this method does not compromise a safe and legal entry in the NAS.

---

94 14 CFR (Code of Federal Regulations) Part 107 – Small Unmanned Aircraft Systems: Subpart A General, Subpart B Operating Rules, Subpart C Remote Pilot Certification, Subpart D Waivers.

Whatever be the type of aircraft operation, whether for recreational or commercial use, the FAA's top priority remains safety. The FAA requires that with both manned and unmanned aircraft, all operators follow specific guidelines for the operation they request.

In the commercial field, the FAA is encouraging innovation through the UAS Integration Pilot Program (IPP) by working with industry, state, local and tribal government to realize the benefits of drones, while informing future rules and regulations. Part 135 air carrier certification is the only path for small drones to carry the property of another, such as the package delivery concept, for compensation BVLOS. At a Drone Advisory Committee meeting in Santa Clara, California, the FAA announced that UAS package delivery operations would need an AOC issued under 14 CFR Part 11, as required by 14 CFR 135. That certification also requires 'economic authority' from the U.S. Department of Transportation (U.S. DOT), which can only be held by a 'citizen of the United States' as defined in DOT regulations (See 14 CFR Section 119.33).

As participants in these innovation programmes move to prove their concepts, they must use FAA's existing Part 135 (Air Carrier and Operator Certification) certification process, which consists of five phases,[95] some of which the FAA has adapted for drone operations by granting specific exemptions for rules that do not apply to drones, such as the requirement to carry the flight manual on board the aircraft. The FAA issues air carrier certificates to US applicants based on the type of services they plan to provide and where they want to conduct their specific operations. Before they can start these operations, operators must obtain airspace authorizations and air carrier operating certificates. Part 135 certification is currently (2020) the only path for small drones to carry the property of another for compensation BVLOS, according to the FAA.

Certificates are available for four types of Part 135 (Package Delivery by Drone) operations:

– Part 135 Single Pilot. A single pilot operator is a certificate holder that is limited to using only one pilot for all Part 135 operations.
– A Single Pilot in Command certificate is a limited Part 135 certificate. It includes one pilot in command certificate holder and three second pilots in command. There are also limitations on the size of the aircraft and the scope of the operations.
– A Basic operator certificate is limited in the size and scope of their operations. A maximum of five pilots, including second in command. A maximum of five aircraft can be used in their operation.
– A Standard operator holds a certificate with no limits on the size or scope of operations. However, the operator must be granted authorization for each type of operation they want to conduct.[96]

---

95 Phase – 1 Pre-application, Phase – 2 Formal Application, Phase – 3 Design Assessment, Phase – 4 Performance Assessment, Phase – 5 Administrative Functions.

Operators of commercial drones are entering the market. The biggest obstacles to the commercial use of drones in the United States have been a lack of clear and appropriate regulations as well as the slow process of development. At first, the FAA banned all commercial use of drones in the United States. Its main concerns with industrial use were flight altitude, whether to allow drone flights at night-time and whether to allow drone flights beyond the operator's field of sight. Concerning getting Part 135 certification, it does not automatically clear the way for drone deliveries across the United States.

Concerning compliance with aviation rules, the FAA has been facing local ordinances attempting to regulate the operation of UAS. At the same time 14 CFR Part 107 was released, an analysis by the National Conference of State Legislature (NCSL) has found that more than 40 states have created their own laws and regulations to govern local UAS operations.

The proliferation of drone operations has caused policymakers to question the extent to which the traditional 'exclusive sovereignty' of the FAA over manned aircraft that take off and land from aerodromes and fly over 500 ft applies to unmanned aircraft that take off and land from virtually anywhere and fly under 400 ft.

On 21 September 2017, a federal court, for the first time, struck down local ordinance attempting to regulate UAS operations within its jurisdiction. State and local governments have passed laws of their own, but subnational regulation presents a distinct problem: a drone cannot fly freely across city and state lines if inconsistent laws interfere with its path. But because federal law is supreme, cities and states do not have the final word.

It was the U.S. District Court for the District of Massachusetts in Boston that invalidated parts of an ordinance passed by the City of Newton, Massachusetts, which were challenged by a local UAS operator. For state and local governments wishing to regulate some aspects of UAS operation within their jurisdictions, this decision may be useful as an indicator of where federal courts are likely to draw the line when faced with pre-emption challenges in this area. Although the court's ruling is not binding in other jurisdictions, *Singer* has the potential to guide the outcomes of future pre-emption challenges to local drone laws.

The judge in the *Singer v. Newton* case found that the City of Newton's drone ordinance was pre-empted on all counts included in the challenge, while the unchallenged portions of the Newton ordinance remain in effect. Specifically, the judge found that the following provisions of the City's drone ordinance were pre-empted:
- Local registration requirements applicable to owners of all pilotless aircraft;
- a ban on the use of pilotless aircraft below an altitude of 400 ft over private property without the express permission of the owner of the private property;

---

96 Package Delivery by Drone (Part 135), FAA 1 October 2019. The FAA issued the first Part 135 Single pilot air carrier certificate for drone operations to Wing Aviation, LCC in April 2019.

- a ban on the use of a pilotless aircraft BVLOS of the operator; and
- a ban on the use of a pilotless aircraft over the City of Newton's property without prior permission.[97]

In March 2015, FAA proposed regulations would allow most commercial drone flights, although under strict conditions based on drone laws. In fact, the FAA was at that time and still is a long way from drafting rules for automated commercial drone activities such as package delivery.

In order to fly safely with drones, many rules, *in casu* drone laws, and systems will be needed that, however, do not yet exist. Drone laws in the United States can be broken up into drone law statutes, created through a legislative process, and drone regulations, created through a rule-making process. The US government has through the legislative process created multiple federal legislative laws that apply to traditional manned aircraft as well as unmanned aircraft, and also some of them that specifically address drones.

Through a similar state process, the states have also created legislative state drone laws, which, however, set different requirements. Federal agencies, such as the National Transportation Safety Board (NTSB) and the FAA under the U.S. DOT, and state agencies create regulations through the rule-making process, which makes it, with respect to drones, rather complex. Moreover, there is no sequential order of all drone regulations.

Fortunately, all federal regulations regarding aviation are located in 14 CFR Aeronautics and Space and 49 CFR Transportation. Multiple parts of the Federal

---

97 See Roberson, J.E., 'Local Drone Law Struck Down by Federal Preemption', *Holland & Knight Aviation Law Blog*, 27 September 2017. *Singer v. City of Newton*, Case No. 17-100071-WGY (D. Mass., 21 September 2017). *See also Singer v. City of Newton* Massachusetts District Court Find Portion of Local Drone Ordinance Preempted by FAA Regulation, *131 Harv. L. Rev. 2057*, 10 May 2018.
  On 19 December 2016, Newton passed an ordinance regulating UAS operations within the city. The ordinance was designed to allow beneficial uses of drones while protecting the privacy of residents throughout the city, and was intended to be read and interpreted in harmony with all relevant rules and regulations of the FAA.
  On 21 September 2017, in what is believed to be the first federal court ruling on the issue of local drone regulation, the U.S. District Court for the District of Massachusetts in *Singer v. City of Newton* overturned a 2016 ordinance passed by the Newton, MA, City Council regulating pilotless aircraft within Newton city limits. Dr. Michael S. Singer, a Newton resident and FAA-certified small unmanned aircraft pilot who owned and operated multiple drones but did not operate or register them as a hobbyist, challenged four subsections of Newton's prohibition on the uses of drones: 1. Below an altitude of 400 ft over any private property without the express permission of the property owner, 2. Over the City of Newton property without prior permission, 3. Beyond the drone operator's visual line of sight, and 4. Without first registering the drone.
  With the continued proliferation of state and local laws, the *Singer v. City of Newton* case drew considerable attention, with some even contending that the ruling establishes a rock solid affirmation that the federal government holds jurisdiction over the drone industry.
  While the ruling does bode well for proponents of federal pre-emption in the NAS and can be interpreted as a solid first step, its impact is rather limited. Where state and federal law conflict, federal law prevails and state law is pre-empted (Art. VI, Section 2 of the Constitution).

Aviation Regulations (FARs) could apply to commercial drone flights, but the number of common areas of regulations are Part 47 – Aircraft Registration, Part 48 – Registration and Marking Requirements for Small Unmanned Aircraft (Certificates of Aircraft Registration for Small Unmanned Aircraft), Part 91 – General Operating and Flight Rules (Set of Operating Regulations for Manned and Unmanned Aircraft), Part 93 – Special Air Traffic Rules (Special Air Traffic Rules for Certain Locations), Part 107 – Small Unmanned Aircraft Regulations (Operating requirements, Registration, Pilot certification, Drone certification, Other requirements, Airspace authorizations and FAA DroneZone), Part 135 – Air Carrier and Operator Certification (Package Delivery by Drone), and Part 137 – Agricultural Aircraft Operations (Certification Process for Agricultural Aircraft Operations).[98]

In 49 CFR Transportation, FARs regarding civil and public drone operations can be found in Subtitle VII – Aviation Programs, Part A – Air Commerce and Safety, Subpart iii – Safety, Chapter 448 – Unmanned Aircraft Systems, Sections 44801-44810.

In addition, there are other regulations from different federal agencies involving the preservation and protection of national wildlife that could restrict (commercial) drone operations above specific areas. For example, U.S. Fish and Wildlife Service Regulations: 50 CFR Section 27.34 – Aircraft, 50 CFR Section 27.71 – Commercial Filming and Still Photography and Audio Recording, 50 CFR 224.101 – National Marine Fisheries Service, Enumeration of Endangered Marine and Anadromous Species and, 15 CFR Part 922 – National Marine Sanctuary Program Regulations.

Commercial drone operations are focused to provide services linked to a certain range and within urban areas, BVLOS of the operator. The buzzword for flying without VLOS is BVLOS. A crucial factor for the emerging success of BVLOS is the creation of an airspace adapted to the particular characteristics of drones. A pure see and avoid principle with the well-known evasive action rules for the visual drone flight in the airspace Class G does not work in the case of BVLOS, and, indeed, this means a potential hazard to manned aircraft. In other words, an unacceptable unsafe condition. A requirement for BVLOS operated drones is a sense and avoid system, next to other additional state-of-the-art safety requirements, such as e-identification. The idea is to create a special airspace category for drones from ground level up to 500 ft AGL, in principle away from sanctuaries, obstacles and airports.

One step further is the integration of drones into non-segregated airspace. The vision of the FAA concerning full integration of drones into the NAS entails drone operating harmoniously, alongside traditional manned aircraft, occupying the same, non-segregated airspace and using many of the same air traffic management systems and procedures.

---

98 See also FAA Advisory Circular (AC) 137-1B, 21 August 2017.

This vision goes well beyond the accommodation practices currently in use, which, however, are largely relying on operational segregation to maintain systematic aviation safety. This effective vision, which will result in a complex elaboration, requires intensive collaboration across industry, government and academia. Both the FAA vision and elaboration on the FAA DroneZone system show similarity with the current and proposed developments on UAS services applications in U-space within the European Union.[99]

In the two regions, different providers in the field of UTM, communications and data link as well as commercial drone services pursue the same objectives. Ultimately, parallel operation of drones and manned aviation is considered feasible at low and even high altitudes, supported by applicable rules, procedures and systems.

The FAA Drone Advisory Committee (DAC) is a broad-based long-term federal advisory committee that provides the FAA with advice on key UAS integration issues by helping to identify challenges and prioritize improvements.

The Committee assists in creating broad support for an overall integration strategy and vision. Membership comprises CEO/COO-level executives from a cross section of stakeholders representing a wide variety of UAS interests, including industry, research and academia, retail and technology.[100]

The FAA UAS Data Exchange is an innovative, collaborative approach between government and private industry facilitating the sharing of airspace data between the two parties. Under the FAA UAS Data Exchange umbrella, the FAA will support multiple partnerships, the first of which is LAANC.

Through the UAS Data Exchange, the capability facilitates the sharing of airspace data between the FAA and companies approved by the FAA to provide LAANC services. The companies are known as UAS Service Suppliers, and the desktop applications and mobile apps to utilize the LAANC capability are provided by these suppliers.

The FAA has developed a safety statement describing some of the rules, regulations and safety tips consumers need to know when operating UAS or drones for recreational or commercial use. A federal law requires manufacturers to provide a safety statement with sUAS at the time of delivery. The safety statement is intended to serve as an example that manufacturers may use to satisfy that requirement.

Section 2203 (Safety statements) of the FAA Extension, Safety, and Security Act of 2016 (P.L. 114-190) requires manufacturers of small unmanned aircraft to make available to the owner a safety statement that satisfies requirements detailed in that Section. Although compliance with this provision of the Act is not yet required, it is, in the interest of flight safety, important that all small unmanned aircraft manufacturers begin to make safety statement information available.

---

99 https://faadronezone.faa.gov/#/.
100 www.faa.gov/uas/programs_partnerships/drone_advisory_committee/.

To ensure the widest education and safest integration of UAS into the NAS, the FAA encourages manufacturers to instantly provide safety statements to their consumers. The IPP is assisting the U.S. DOT and the FAA in drafting new rules that support more complex low-altitude operations by:
- Identifying ways to balance local and national interests related to drone integration.
- Improving communications with local, state and tribal jurisdictions.
- Addressing security and privacy risks.
- Accelerating the approval of operation that currently require special authorizations.

The IPP has created a meaningful dialogue on the balance between local and national interests related to drone integration and provides actionable information to the U.S. DOT on expanded and universal integration of drones into the NAS, well regarded in line with the objectives of the European SESAR Joint Undertaking with respect to drone integration into the Single European Sky.[101]

The IPP lead participants are cities, state departments of transportation, industry, innovation and entrepreneurship investment authority, universities and airport authorities. Industry partners, such as Amazon, will help bridge the gap between industry and the test sites to tackle some of the most difficult technological and operational challenges by, among others, assisting the UAS test sites to demonstrate or validate technologies essential to the safe integration into the NAS.

In other words, UAS test sites support UAS integration by providing an avenue for the UAS industry and stakeholder community to conduct more advanced UAS research and operational concept validation.

The selected companies must have the technical capability to work on these essential integration technologies:
- Develop and enforce geographic and altitude limitations (geofencing);
- Provide for alerts by the manufacturer of a UAS regarding any hazards or limitations on flight, including prohibition on flight as necessary;
- Sense (or detect) and avoid capabilities;
- BVLOS or for specific operations, such as agricultural monitoring, extended visual line of sight (EVLOS);
- Night-time operations;
- Operations over people;
- Operations of multiple sUAS;
- UAS traffic management;

---

101 SESAR JU – Single European Sky ATM Research Joint Undertaking, founded by the European Commission and EUROCONTROL on 27 February 2007. Since then 15 organizations have signed membership agreements. SESAR JU is the technological pillar of the SES. It aims to improve ATM performance by modernizing and harmonizing ATM systems through the definition, development, validation and deployment of innovative technological and operational ATM solutions.

- Other critical resource priorities; and
- Improve privacy protections through the use of advances in UAS technology.

The FAA Extension, Safety and Security Act of 2016 established the UTM Pilot Program (UPP) to define an initial set of industry and FAA capabilities required to support UTM operations in response to the need of new applications for sUAS, including goods or package delivery, infrastructural inspection, search and rescue and agricultural monitoring. Previously, there was limited infrastructure available to manage the widespread expansion of those operations within the NAS, which was the main cause of the need to set appropriate rules.

The primary goal for the UPP, an important component for defining and expanding the next set of industry and FAA capabilities required to support UTM, is to enable the development, testing and demonstration of a set of UTM capabilities and to provide an infrastructure to allow for future testing of new UTM capabilities. These capabilities support the sharing of information that promotes situational awareness and deconfliction such as cooperative separation. Some of the UTM capabilities successfully demonstrated in the UPP include:

- Sharing of operational intent between operators.
- The ability for a USS to generate a UAS Volume Reservation (UVR).
- Providing access to FAA Enterprise Services to support shared information.

The focus of the demonstration and evaluation activities is on the following capabilities of the UTM framework:

- Operation planning for participating UAS operators.
- Capability demonstrations including VLOS (14 CFR Part 101(e) & Part 107) and BVLOS operations in uncontrolled airspace under 400 ft (AGL) in remotely-populated areas away from airports, with minimal UAS/manned traffic and low risk to people and property on the surface. VLOS Part 101(e)/107 operators are not required to share their intent but may voluntarily do so in promotion of shared situational awareness.
- Shared situational awareness between participating UAS operators.
- This includes sharing intent and state information among UAS operators and between UAS operators and Remote Pilots in Command (RPICs). Both capability demonstrations, as mentioned above, include the same environmental conditions.
- Automated airspace authorization for 14 CFR Part 107 Operations.
- Capability demonstrations include 14 CFR Part 107 operations occurring within controlled airspace at low altitude (under 400 ft AGL).
- UVRs and their effect on UAS Operations.

– Capability demonstrations include VLOS (14 CFR Part 101(e) & Part 107) and BVLOS operations in controlled airspace, with other environmental conditions similar to those above.

The purpose of UPP is to evaluate results (Phases 1 and 2) and determine the appropriate next steps, moving towards the development and deployment of prototype enterprise services into the FAA framework to support initial UTM operations. These enterprise services will be used to share intent and situational awareness information with the FAA and UTM operators. Stakeholders will be informed about the results, enabling deployment of enterprise capabilities. The lessons learned from UPP will support ongoing policy and technology advancement efforts towards enabling BVLOS operations.

UPP is a congressional directive to the FAA and NASA to establish a Research Transition Team (RTT) and partner with industry to help advance the safe integration of unmanned aircraft into the NAS. IPP is a presidential directive to the Secretary of Transportation and FAA to create a partnership framework for private sector and local/state/tribal governments to help direct broader national policy.[102]

In 2015, the FAA announced the UAS Focus Area Pathfinder Program, which was an industry partnership programme to develop and validate operational concepts for certification, operations and safety beyond established or proposed policies and procedures. CNN, PrecisionHawk, which is a commercial drone data company, and BNSF Railways (formerly called Burlington Northern and Santa Fe Railway), one of the largest freight railroad networks, forming the industry partners, focused their work on operational expansion of VLOS operations over people, EVLOS and BVLOS operations in rural areas and BVLOS operations over right-of-ways.

The objective was to develop operational concepts in manageable segments while providing the safety and validation of risk mitigation actions. In 2017, the focus areas had all met the planned specific objectives, namely to define the parameters to allow safe operation of drones in the NAS; obtain operational approval for the Pathfinder industry stakeholder to perform routine, limited operations; and to define the conditions as well as constraints under which similar operations may be approved for future applicants.

The FAA Modernization and Reform Act of 2012 required the FAA to develop a plan, the Arctic Implementation Plan, to designate permanent areas in the Arctic where small unmanned aircraft could perform research and commercial operations.[103] In November 2012, the FAA published its plan, signed by the Secretary of Transportation, to inform interested parties, operators, federal agencies and international communities of its plans

---

102 www.faa.gov/uas/research_development/traffic_management/utm_pilot_program/.

CHAPTER 2   LEGAL BASIS FOR DRONE OPERATIONS

to establish permanent operational areas and corridor routes in the Arctic for the operation of sUAS.

The Arctic sUAS Implementation Plan, mandated by the 2012 FAA Modernization and Reform Act, required the FAA to:

> Initiate a process to work with relevant federal agencies and national and international communities to designate permanent areas in the Arctic where small unmanned aircraft may operate 24 hours per day for research and commercial purposes and SAR operations. The plan for operations in these permanent areas shall include the development of processes to facilitate the safe operation of unmanned aircraft beyond line of sight (BLOS), in compliance with Section 335 Safety studies under Subtitle B Unmanned Aircraft Systems of the 2012 FAA Modernization and Reform Act. Such areas shall enable over-water flights from the surface to at least 2000 ft in altitude, with ingress and egress routes from selected coastal launch sites.[104]

From 2013 to 2015, a number of operations took place in the Arctic carrying out surveys, environmental assessments and pipeline and infrastructure inspections. These operations, ranging from the NASA-funded Marginal Ice Zone Observations and Ocean Experiment (MIZOPEX) in the summer of 2013, supported by the ScanEagle UAS and the Data Hawk UAS for marine mammal and ice surveys, oil spill and SAR exercises to communication procedures for commercial sUAS BVLOS operations, were made possible through authorizations from the FAA and cooperation among other US government agencies and the academic and private sectors.[105]

Mid-2019, the FAA, NASA and their US industry partners successfully completed the UPP demonstrations, which consisted of a series of preparation flights and final flight demonstrations, consisting of live UAS flights combined with simulated UTM operations at each UAS test site.[106] The results of the UPP demonstrations will be used to mature UTM to support the continued development of UTM policy, standards, capabilities and requirements development. The progress achieved with the UPP is critical to the public

---

104 *See* Unmanned Aircraft Systems (UAS) Lessons Learned in the Arctic, Summer 2013, FAA UAS Integration Office. *See also* FAA Modernization and Reform Act of 2012, Conference Report to Accompany H.R. 658, 1 February 2012, Washington: U.S. Government Printing Office, 2012, p. 3.
105 FAA Integration of Civil Unmanned Aircraft Systems (UAS) in the National Airspace System (NAS) Roadmap: A Five-year roadmap for the introduction of civil UAS into the NAS, 3rd Edition 2020, pp. 7-8.

and private sector entities to provide data on the future activities necessary to support the successful implementation of the UTM infrastructure and supporting systems.

Communication is paramount in the UPP. The flight activities were executed while participating vehicles, both real and simulated, were connected to the Flight Information Management System (FIMS) via communication with a USS, and with that USS connected to the UPP Demonstration Platform. FIMS provides an interface for data exchange between FAA systems and UTM users, enabling the exchange of airspace constraint data between the FAA and the USS Network. The interface is also used by the FAA as an access point for information on active UTM operations. FIMS, which is managed by the FAA and being part of the UTM ecosystem, also plays a role regarding post hoc/archived data on UTM operations to FAA stakeholders for the purposes of compliance audits and/or incident or accident investigation.

Through the conduct of the UPP, the FAA and industry partners collected significant quantities of data and performance metrics for post-operations analysis. These will be used to refine system and performance requirements for UTM in the next process phase, as these requirements will form the foundation for following UPP activities.

The overall success of the UPP demonstrations, in the preparation and execution phases, can be attributed to many factors such as the following: the early development and coordination of the UPP partners with both NASA and the FAA through the Research Transition Team led to the teams having UAS platforms that were proven and ready for the demonstrations; by participating in early NASA Technology Capability Level (TCL) activities, the UPP partners had demonstrated necessary maturity levels leading up to the UPP; and collaboration among the team members throughout the process helped to facilitate communication and the sharing of ideas that led to overall UPP success.[107]

As required by the FAA Reauthorization Act of 2018, UPP is required to meet additional objectives prior to completion (Phase 2). These objectives include testing of Remote Identification (RID) technologies and operations with increasing volume and density. The testing will be conducted in cooperation with NASA, FAA UAS test sites, industry stakeholders and IPP participants. UPP Phase 2 moves towards the development and deployment of RID technologies in increasingly complex environments to enable a UTM ecosystem.

The FAA collaborates internally and maintains extensive partnerships across governments, industry and academia to develop integrated research plans that support

---

107 Source: FAA NASA Unmanned Aircraft Systems (UAS) Traffic Management (UTM). UTM Pilot Program (UPP) UPP Summary Report, October 2019.
107 Source: FAA NASA Unmanned Aircraft Systems (UAS) Traffic Management (UTM). UTM Pilot Program (UPP) UPP Summary Report, October 2019.

the development of regulations, policies, procedures, guidance and standards for UAS operations. Research activities such as flight tests, modelling and simulation, technology evaluations, risk assessments and data gathering and analysis provide the FAA with critical information in areas such as detect and avoid, UAS communications, human factors, resource management, system safety and certification, all of which enable the FAA to make informed decisions on safe UAS integration.

The Alliance for System Safety of UAS through Research Excellence (ASSURE) is a multi-university centre designated by the FAA as its Center of Excellence (COE) for Unmanned Aircraft Systems, bringing together, like university think tank partnerships, the best minds in the nation to conduct research to educate, train and work with the FAA towards solutions for aviation-related challenges.

This CEO for UAS collaborates with the US academic community and its affiliates by fostering cooperative research and developing intellectual capabilities of primary interest to the FAA and UAS community. Congress mandated the FAA to establish the COE under the Consolidated Appropriations Act of 2014.[108]

ASSURE comprises 23 of the world's leading research institutions and a hundred leading industry and government partners, directed by the FAA-selected Mississippi State University, along with a number of core and affiliate universities. The focus is on research, education and training in areas critical to safe and successful integration of UAS into the NAS.

ASSURE possesses the expertise, infrastructure and outstanding track record of success that the FAA COE demands. In this configuration, the COE for UAS is an academic body dedicated to supporting current and future UAS integration initiatives for a period of 10 years from 2015.[109]

The FAA COE for UAS contract is intended to focus on research in areas critical to the safe, secure as well as successful integration of UAS into the NAS. The contract vehicles will produce specific deliverables critical to the development of government policy, guidance and regulations. In the same way, this world-class, public-private partnership will assist the FAA to focus on challenges and opportunities associated with UAS and educate a cadre of unmanned aircraft professionals well into the future.

The research focus areas are ATC interoperability, airport ground operations, control and communication, detect and avoid, human factors, low-altitude operations safety,

---

108 Consolidated Appropriation Act 2014, H.R. 3547 (113th Congress 2013-2014), nicknamed the Cromnibus, is an omnibus spending bill that packages several appropriation bills together in one larger bill (source: Wikipedia).
109 Core member universities are Mississippi State University, Drexel University, Embry Riddle Aeronautical University-Prescott, University of Kansas, Kansas State University, Montana State University, New Mexico State University, The Ohio State University, University of Alabama-Huntsville, University of Alaska-Fairbanks, University of California-Davis, University of North Dakota, Wichita State University and Oregon State University. Affiliate member universities are Auburn University, Sinclair Community College, Louisiana Tech University, Concordia University, University of Southampton, Technion – Israel Institute of Technology, Tuskegee University and Indiana State University.

noise reduction, spectrum management, unmanned aircraft crew training and certification (including pilots), UTM, which is a collaborative research concept between NASA, the FAA and industry to address high-volume small-drone operations in low-altitude airspace, and UAS wake separation standards for UAS integration into the NAS.

UAS RID (Remote ID), currently (2020) in the process of proposed rule-making, is the ability of a UAS in flight to provide identification information that can be received by other parties. UAS are fundamentally changing aviation, and the FAA is committed to working on full UAS integration into the NAS. Safety and security are top priorities for the FAA, whereas RID of UAS is crucial in controlled and uncontrolled non-segregated airspace. RID would assist the FAA, law enforcement and federal security agencies when a UAS appears to be flying in an unsafe manner or in an area where the UAS is not allowed to fly. The development of RID builds on the framework established by the small UAS registration rule and the LAANC capability to lay the foundation for a UTM that is scalable to the national airspace.

The FAA has made significant progress in integrating UAS into the NAS so far. However, much more must still be accomplished to achieve the FAA's vision for full integration. Tremendous growth has occurred in the UAS sector in the past several years, and the growing interest in using UAS for business applications will continue with the implementation of the small UAS rule.

It must be fully considered that each novel aspect of an operation must be folded into routine operations. Lessons learned from each new stage must be continuously applied to make informed decisions for subsequent steps. UAS integration must consider risk and mitigation and, above all, must ensure that the safety of the current airspace system and its users is maintained as progress is made.[110]

On 28 December 2020, the FAA released its ruling on RID for drones along with a final rule on flights over people and at night (Press Release – U.S. Department of Transportation Issues Two Much-Anticipated Drone Rules to Advance Safety and Innovation in the United States). The new rules make way for the further integration into non-segregated airspace by addressing safety and security concerns. Remote pilots have three ways of complying with RID, which, in its simplest form, is the concept that a drone should have a digital licence plate:
- Operate a standard ID drone that broadcasts identification and location information of the drone and RPS;
- operate a drone with a RID broadcast module, which broadcasts identification, location and take-off information; or

---

110 *See* National Academies of Sciences, Engineering, and Medicine, 'Assessing the Risks of Integrating Unmanned Aircraft Systems into the National Airspace System', Washington: The National Academies Press, 2018, pp. 33-35.

- operate a drone without RID but at specific FAA-recognized identification areas (FRIAs).[111]

The Operation of Unmanned Aircraft Systems Over People Final Rule is the next incremental step towards further integration of UAS in the NAS. It regulates the ability to fly at night and over people, contingent on the risk factor of each drone flight. The final rule allows routine operations over people and routine operations at night under certain circumstances. The rule applies strictly to those with Part 107 certification. It eliminates the need for pilots to acquire individual Part 107 waivers from the FAA for these particular operations.[112]

The final rule establishes new categories (Categories 1 to 4 eligible) of small unmanned aircraft for routine operations over people. It also allows for routine operations over moving vehicles.

The near-term challenges of UAS integration are significant. As a result, the FAA's strategic goals and activities are increasingly focused on bridging the knowledge and technological gaps. Establishing performance and design standards to inform rule-making and policy development, as well as ensuring the addressing of network, cyber and other security issues, will be areas of intense focus over the coming years. Solving these challenges requires flexibility and a willingness to consider new and novel approaches to share challenges. The pace of UAS integration into non-segregated airspace will require the FAA to be agile and responsive to non-traditional (out of the box) thinking, while its commitment to safety remains firm.

2.5   FUTURE CONSIDERATIONS

Commercial drone usage seems to be inevitable and, with regard to the future, indispensable. However, current restrictions make practical application of a number of commercial drone operations rather arduous, despite the overwhelming prospects of the NextGen drone industry. The process of rule-making, the initiation, including a clear definition and scope, regulatory impact assessment, drafting of rules, consultation, review of comments and, finally, the adoption and implementation of a comprehensive set of international regulations to govern various drone operations worldwide, is essential for a safe environment.

---

111 Murphy, K., 'FAA Releases Final Rule on Remote ID and Operations Over People/Night Flights', *DPReview*, 29 December 2020. *See also* FAA Executive Summary – Final Rule on Remote Identification of Unmanned Aircraft (Part 89), 28 December 2020, and Final Rule on Operation of Small Unmanned Aircraft Systems Over People, 28 December 2020.
112 DOT – FAA 14 CFR Parts 11, 21, 43, and 107 [Docket No.: FAA-2018-1087; Amdt. Nos. 11-64, 21-105, 43-51, 107-8], RIN 2120-AK85, Operation of sUAS Over People.

The further development of drones and their integration in non-segregated airspace will pose new challenges in the coming years. While today flying a single drone in non-segregated airspace with cooperative aircraft can be done with appropriate coordination and special procedures, operation of multiple drones simultaneously, possibly in conjunction with non-cooperative aircraft, will be much more complicated and will require additional measures with a view to maintaining a high level of flight safety. The Certified category, mainly for a number of professional operators, should ultimately lead to a situation where almost anything becomes possible when it comes to unmanned aviation and urban air mobility in particular. Certification is a key prerequisite to properly manage drone operations with a high-risk potential.

A reason why the introduction of the Certified category is delayed is the dependence on U-space. In Europe, U-space must be developed into an umbrella system within which UTM providers offer services to drone operators. However, the political and technical complexity is still gigantic. If, in the foreseeable future, unmanned cargo aircraft and air taxis operate exactly in the same manner as traditional passenger and cargo aircraft, an accelerated implementation of U-space is possible, at least at the local level.

In the course of 2021, EASA is expected to come up with an initial concept with respect to the further operational development of the Certified category towards its 31 Member States. If the regulatory foundation has been laid for U-space, and legislation to operate in the Certified category is adapted, unmanned cargo aircraft and urban air mobility development, including the realization of smart infrastructure works, will then go at a fast pace.

The concept of composite operations will need to be further developed to address the issues related to operations of fleets of drones (drone swarms), operating on multiple different frequencies, in non-segregated airspace. These fleets of drone operations, *in casu* the magnitude, will pose new challenges hitherto unexplored with manned aircraft operations. This complex integration will need to be done in full coordination with the expected development of the ICAO ASBU being implemented by the SESAR programme in Europe.[113]

The key research areas for the integration in non-segregated airspace are as follows:
- Detect and avoid
- Airspace and airport access
- Command and Control (C2) communications

---

113 ICAO's Global Air Navigation Plan (GANP) presents a framework for harmonizing avionics capabilities and the required ATM ground infrastructure as well as automation. This framework, the ASBUs, is a package of capabilities (modules), including a set of operational improvements for harmonization. The ASBUs are programmatic and flexible, allowing ANSPs to advance their air navigation system based on their individual operational requirements. Source: Introduction to the ASBU Modules: Strategic Planning for ASBU Modules Implementation, CANSO (Civil Air Navigation Services Organization).

- Human factors
- Contingency
- Security
- Autonomy

This will need a significant amount of further research to be performed by, in particular, SESAR and the European Defence Agency (EDA). Coordination will be necessary to augment synergies and avoid duplication.

The following could be some of the factors to be taken into account:
- Transfer of drones from one control station to another: some drones do have a significant range, such as medium to very large unmanned cargo-only aircraft, and the transfer between subsequent control stations (ground, airborne or even space) must be envisaged. The present SESAR experimentations in this area have already shown that such transfers should not coincide with the transfer from one ATC sector to another.
- Operational control of several drones from one control station: this is a real possibility and would lead to formation flights, with coordinated flights of the various drones, for example, to efficiently fight a fire or for crop spraying.
- ATC and operational control done by the same person: this would be an extension of the previous case but will entail new risks and pose new liability issues.
- Communications with ATC with an acceptable time of latency.
- Full autonomy and cooperative operations, such as operation in swarms or network-centric operations.
- Extreme endurance, even months, at very high altitude (20,000 m): how to maintain the necessary vigilance to face emergencies.

Integration in non-segregated airspace will require for the ANS and the operators:
- Minimum navigation, communication and surveillance performance standards.
- Adaption of the infrastructure.
- New procedures.
- Adapted training.

ICAO predicts that by 2030 a large number of UAS, in particular RPAS, in any capacity, will share the airspace with manned aviation, even flying under IFR. While some RPAS operations will be conducted in accordance with IFR, either for a portion of their flight or the entire flight (instrument meteorological conditions (IMC) or visual meteorological conditions (VMC) conditions), others will only operate under VFR (VMC conditions). Similarly, RPAS will operate within national airspace and or transit through international airspace (cross-border flight) as well as controlled and uncontrolled airspace.

These RPAS may depart from less congested aerodromes and arrive at corresponding destination aerodromes, while others may use congested aerodromes. All RPAS will be expected to comply with the applicable procedures and national airspace requirements defined by the state, including emergency and contingency procedures and plans to be adhered to, which should be established and coordinated with the respective ANSPs. As airspace is a scarce and sought after resource, states must follow a balanced approach that harmonizes and meets the needs of all airspace users.

The 40th Session of the ICAO Assembly, held in 2019, from 24 September to 4 October, directed ICAO to continue processing the regulatory framework for the safe integration of UAS, including RPAS, and to engage with all players, including those that are not traditionally involved with ICAO, so as to promptly deliver their benefits to civil societies. In 2019, industry studies pointed to the European UAS market being worth over 10 billion euros annually in 2035, and over 50 billion euros in 2050. Similar positive and significant impacts are predicted for the US market. However, despite these unprecedented forecasts, the ICAO Secretary General, Dr. Fang Liu, warned about the challenges the integration of these UAS poses to national regulators.[114]

ICAO has already started updating its standards to answer this call, and it has already hosted a series of so-called Drone Enable events, bringing together innovators from the private sector and regulators from the public sector to assist in realizing effective global solutions to these challenges. The Secretary General noted that the scaling up of UAS air services, such as humanitarian aid and urban mobility, faces a variety of challenges, including the varying legislative requirements in states, and uncertainty surrounding applicable roles and responsibilities. In this area, the private sector has an important role to play, noting that coordination and consolidation around UAS would facilitate consensus-building among ICAO Member States.

The rapid growth of the UAS industry has resulted in significant and multiple challenges for states to deliver their mandate and meet the needs and expectations of the industry. Such challenges include the following:
− Managing the expectations of the UAS industry.
− Completing regulatory projects within established timelines.
− Supporting test site development to enable R&D with new technologies.
− Providing training materials at UAS events in order to educate operators.

---

114 ICAO Secretary General contributes to World Economic Forum (WEF) discussions on 21st century mobility, unmanned aircraft applications and cleaner skies, Davos 28 January 2020. The Secretary General contributed to a range of WEF sessions on topics related to drones and urban mobility, medical applications for unmanned aircraft, including emergency supply deliveries and epidemic control, and current and future aviation emissions reduction efforts.

- Advancing harmonization with international counterparts.
- Developing training and guidance material on UAS operations.
- Enhancing relationships with different governmental agencies for an understanding of the respective roles.
- Engaging legal authorities to strengthen enforcement capacity with law enforcement agencies.
- Managing large volumes of new operators or new types of operations.

In May 2019 the FAA released its forecast of the aviation scenario between 2019 and 2039. Particularly noteworthy is that the market for commercial drones is growing faster than anticipated and could triple until 2039, while the market for non-commercial drones appears to be slowing down. The FAA NextGen office released an initial overarching CONOPS for UTM that presented a vision and described the associated operational and technical requirements for developing a supporting architecture and operating within a UTM ecosystem.

UTM is defined as the manner in which the FAA will support operations for UAS operating in low-altitude airspace. Like the FAA's UTM CONOPS, EASA's support for conflict detection through the flight authorization service recognizes the ability of USSPs and the UTM ecosystem to enable safe operations today and in the future.

According to EASA, unmanned aircraft or drones represent a rapidly developing sector of aviation with a considerable potential to create new jobs and economic growth in the European Union. This is why the European Union adopted Regulation (EU) 2018/1139 to safely integrate remotely piloted drones into the European airspace in the near future. EASA recently published a draft opinion on the future of U-space that embodies a fundamental principle of the aviation industry, stating that the sky is a shared resource that, when overseen safely and fairly, promises profound benefits for all. The EASA framework offers a trajectory for Europe's aviation infrastructure to leverage new technologies and make air transport in any form smarter, safer and globally accessible.

The volume and diversity of drone operations to come would put tremendous strain on the current ATM. There will be more aircraft, flying in more places, on demand, with more unique form factors and types of missions than in the past. To support this scale, EASA acknowledges the value of an open and competitive marketplace. An ecosystem of multiple and diverse USSPs will develop innovative services that meet the needs of diverse UAS operators and enable future applications for unmanned aviation.

As UAS are regarded as aircraft within the implication of the Chicago Convention and are considered to engage in international civil aviation any time in the future, international rules pertaining to the safety and operation of aircraft and other instruments of international air law such as the 1971 Montreal Convention, the 1952

Rome Convention and the 2001 Cape Town Convention may apply. Aspects such as unmanned aircraft and third-party damage and liability, unlawful acts regarding pilotless aircraft passenger transport, such as urban air mobility, and unmanned aircraft equipment are to be considered as corresponding.

This implies that elements of the proposed regulatory framework for UAS certainly already exist as much as unmanned aircraft are considered as aircraft. In other words, the major portions of the regulatory framework established for manned aviation will be directly applicable.[115]

Relevant articles of the Chicago Convention refer to UAS, such as the notion of pilotless aircraft, and the special authorization needed for UAS to overfly the territory of a contracting state in accordance with the terms of such authorization, as mentioned in Article 8. Article 20 requires aircraft to bear registration and nationality marks, and Articles 31 and 33, respectively, are dealing with airworthiness, while Article 29 requires aircraft to carry documents on board such as a certificate of registration, certificate of airworthiness, journey logbook, crew member licences, aircraft radio station licence, passengers and cargo manifest and detailed declarations of the cargo.

All these issues are equally applicable to UAS, although the term onboard documents may be seen as electronic versions of these documents, either on board or at the corresponding remote control station(s).

Every aircraft engaged in international navigation shall be provided with a certificate of airworthiness issued or rendered valid by the state in which it is registered (Chicago Convention, Art. 31). Airworthiness certification for a UAS, being an unmanned aircraft, is equivalent to that for a manned aircraft, except for the command and control data link between the aircraft and the remote pilot at the control station or a chain of control systems, generic control stations, spread out like a network, able to control more UAS or different types of UAS as well as to have the potential to control consecutive unmanned flights, throughout the world's shared airspace, by means of handover, taking into account aspects such as operational responsibility, reliability and liability.

Typical issues such as handover, legal matters related to certification, licensing and recognition of documents have to be addressed in this scenario. Remote pilot control stations and data link communication facilities will require aviation safety and security oversight by the appropriate state authorities.

The essential organization and maintenance issues of UAS, including licensing of personnel involved, would not dramatically differ from manned aircraft organizations (traditional air operators). Concerning UAS safety, even in high-density operations, the

---

115 1971 Montreal Convention. Convention for the Suppression of Unlawful Acts against the Safety of Civil Aviation. 1952 Rome Convention. Convention on Damage by Foreign Aircraft to Third Parties on the Surface. 2001 Cape Town Convention and Cape Town Protocol on Aircraft Equipment. Convention on International Interests in Mobile Equipment/Protocol to the Convention on International Interests in Mobile Equipment on Matters Specific to Aircraft Equipment.

overall qualitative safety objective for this system must be the reduction of the risk of UAS catastrophic events to a level comparable to the risk existing with manned aircraft of equivalent categories in similar safe environments.

The objective of the regulatory framework is the protection of third parties, both on the surface and in the air. In other words, risks to third parties should be limited to an acceptable level by risk mitigation measures. In this respect, collision avoidance and ATM should be considered to be critical issues relating to operational safety, undoubtedly subject to full compliance with the stringent requirements of acceptable (continuing) airworthiness and certification.

The certification task involved in converting existing heavy civil aircraft into UAS is greatly eased by relevant basic aircraft designs and tests having previously complied with a comprehensive code of airworthiness requirements, which were traditionally linked to a hitherto crystallized conventional kind of operation. When an aircraft is modified in service to meet a new UAS role, it must be demonstrated that the modified aircraft continues to comply with the certification requirements, confining the new justification of airworthiness to the aircraft modification and its effects on the 'machine'.

Continuously evolving technologies will make flight automation play an increasingly important role. Well considered, it is multidisciplinary technology (mechatronics) that enables automation. Automation systems in both manned and unmanned aircraft are capable of controlling the aircraft throughout its full flight regime, including take-off, optimum climb, cruise, descent profiles, balancing fuel, transmitting and receiving data, identifying conflicting traffic and providing resolution advisories by means of a detect and avoid system, more sophisticated than ACAS II version 7.1, either self-governed or monitored by (remote) pilots.[116]

Critical decision areas with regard to autonomous flights are the automatically performed take-off roll, especially go/no-go decision-making in this quite dynamic situation (the operational significance of V_1) and during low-visibility landings, the applicable CAT-III(c) autoland procedure augmented by synthetic vision systems (SVSs), the combined use of synthetic and visual cues (by cameras). For optimal and safety-proof operations, it must be demonstrated that each individual UAS is in conformity with the certified design throughout its operational life span.

Article 5 (Airworthiness) of EU Regulation (EC) No. 1592/2002 is primarily intended for manned aircraft. That is to say, the basis for airworthiness certification should follow the principles applied to manned aircraft, but in consequence, and by deducing, existing certification procedures should also be applied to UAS wherever appropriate. It is stated that aircraft products shall have a Type Certificate (TC) issued by the State of Design. A product will be issued with a TC when the applicant has shown that the product complies with the TC basis. In principle, the State of Design is responsible for the overall systems

---

116 *See* Commission Regulation (EU) No. 1332/2011 of 16 December 2011, laying down common airspace usage requirements and operating procedures for airborne collision avoidance, *OJ* L 336/20, 20 December 2011.

design of the UAS, while the State of Registry will be responsible for the operation and continuing airworthiness of the UAS.

The safe integration of UAS operations in non-segregated airspace may take quite some time as essential technologies are not yet fully mature and screened for implementation. Therefore, there must be a progressive update of the EU SERA in this regard:

- In the first phase, SERA will be reviewed to identify potential issues that could hamper the development of UAS and could propose limited rule changes or guidelines to resolve these issues. However, comprehensive rule changes are envisaged only in a second phase;
- in the second phase, more detailed rules of the air will be developed, including (whenever available) requirements for the safe integration of UAS into non-segregated airspace.[117]

Today, a drone is well known as data capture apparatus, but in the near future improved drone technology will perform the full life cycle: capturing and analysing data and taking action on the basis of processed information. However, innovative developments do have their challenges. This applies to drones like no other, especially the question of how to make the operation of high-tech drones as safe as possible in global airspace. After all, safety in aviation is highly valued. Therefore, when it comes to robotic unmanned aircraft operations, human intervention, such as applied rule-making and regulation, remains indisputably necessary at all times.

---

117 *See* EASA Terms of Reference for rule-making task RMT.0230, Regulatory framework to accommodate unmanned aircraft systems in the European aviation system, Issue 2, 4 June 2018, p. 4.

Chapter 3 Commercial, Private and Sports Use

3.1 Commercial Drone Utilization

Over the past years, drones have become central to the functions of a variety of commercial activities and industries as well as (non-)governmental organizations. A commercial drone could be defined as any drone used commercially in connection with a business. Nowadays, drones are used for a wide range of commercial purposes. This is reflected in the fact that major companies but also small businesses come up with new ingenious ideas to use drones for their varied services. Drones are proving to be extremely beneficial at locations that are beyond human reach or where tasks cannot be performed in a timely and efficient way.

The potential of drones underlies the fact that they possess the capability to reach the most remote and impassable areas with extremely low or no manpower needed and require the least effort, valuable time and energy. Moreover, they have the potential in commercial applications to dramatically alter a number of industries. With their ability to transport loads, deliver goods and collect data, they also change the way we think, perform our tasks and reconsider our physical environment.

Globally, customized drones offer industries increased work efficiency and balanced productivity, decreased workload and production costs, improving accuracy, proportioning customer relations and services and resolving security issues on a large scale, to name just a few benefits. Today, multiple industries are working with these kinds of drones as part of their day-to-day regular business functions. While drone technology is constantly evolving, new applications will become a reality in the near future.

In the field of commercial drones, apart from the users, there are various stakeholders all with their own involvement, influence, interests and regulatory tasks. Governmental regulatory entities, judicial bodies, drone manufacturers, R&D institutes, service providers, technology designers and developers, lease and insurance companies, non-profit organizations acting in the public interest, privacy protectors and activists for and against drones, public establishment drone users and other drone-related professionals together form a complex and diversely challenging global aviation activity.

Regulation of drone operations, especially commercial drone operations, is highly necessary given the hazards involved. The primary concern when commercial drones, with any assignment, are flying over public space is that the associated risk is not imaginary, and crashes could happen. Crashes of drones, even the smallest ones, pose a real threat to health and property of the public. Generally speaking, drones could put lives in danger by crashing into public infrastructure or committing an airspace infringement, especially in regard to congested airspace, such as a control zone (CTR) controlled by the air traffic controller (ATCO), in most cases prohibited for drones.

In regard to the usage of drones, privacy and safety are two key elements that concern people. Safety concerns are much more serious since drones could jeopardize people's lives and property in the event of collision accidents. Drones, deployed for security purposes, are conducting possible unwarranted surveillance flights in public places surrounded by private property without fear of repercussion, but at the expense of assumed privacy. People are worried about the protection of their personal data. This has created uncertainty about violating privacy laws by an in-depth monitoring option, but has not yet been legally legitimized.

To regulate the use of commercial drones appropriately, in order to ensure the protection of individual property rights and public safety, a number of stakeholders such as the national CAAs and regional aviation organizations, industry and consumers are involved, all with their own motivations and responsibilities. Undeniably characteristic in this process, as in other materializing technology-based products, businesses want to manufacture and sell their products unimpeded while meeting the needs of customers, who in turn want choice and access to the market.

While the number of drones shows an unprecedented increase, commercial applications have expanded accordingly. However, any benefit has its disadvantage. Surveillance technology has become increasingly sophisticated and far more portable and thus suitable for any drone use, particularly commercial drone operations. The downside of this is their increasingly adverse impact on privacy. In other words, the issue is whether this proposed use of drone surveillance has a lawful basis and is justified, necessary and proportionate.

Applications of drones depend largely on the quality of images that are taken by cameras installed on them, as well as the quantity and sophistication of data collected by installed sensors. By operating commercial or government drones, specially designed and applied for security duties and equipped with state-of-the-art personal data gathering sensors and real-time aerial surveillance cameras, certain universal rights may come under threat. However, not all data captured by drones consists of personal data, and even where the data being recorded is technically personal, the risk to privacy depends mostly on the reason why the drone is used and what is done with the data collected.

No one shall be subjected to arbitrary interference with respect to his privacy, family, home or correspondence or to attacks on his honour and reputation. According to Article 12 of the Universal Declaration on Human Rights (UDHR), everyone has the right to the protection of the law against such interference or attacks, while in Article 3 is enshrined everyone's right to life, liberty and the security of person.[1]

Currently, the use of drones, both commercially and privately, in segregated and non-segregated airspace has triggered concerns about the challenges to these basic human rights. Privacy is an evolving concept that depends on society's conceptions and technological factors. A large volume of information is recorded about people, often without their being aware of it, especially pertaining to the exact location where we currently are, whom we are talking to, what we are buying, how healthy we are and what our political and sexual preferences are.

There is a broad consensus on the consideration of privacy as a fundamental right, a condition of being free, intricately connected with dignity, which means to respect the need to have one's own space or comfort zone and one's own secrets. Privacy has evolved in a more complex right that enables the free development of one's personality and the building of personal identity.[2]

Security versus privacy. In general, drones can be highly privacy intrusive. Drones should not normally be used to identify individuals without their consent or to capture close-up images of private areas such as houses, gardens or offices without the consent of the owner, unless these areas can be seen from a public vantage point or there is a public interest in showing them. Society is highly concerned about the privacy invasion issues that might be caused by commercial drone use. A breach of privacy could have tremendous consequences, while, on the other hand, security surveillance by drones, domestically used, may enhance neighbourhood safety, protect the borders and minimize security threats, albeit inevitably in certain cases contrary to privacy issues.

In the transportation sector, the logistics and distribution infrastructure is, in fact, still dependent on roadways, railways, waterways, airways and pipelines. However, with the advance of drones and associated technology, it is possible to enable a new form of transportation, including delivery, and this can completely change conventional rules within the sector. Especially with a view to overcoming issues such as the absence of paved roads or railroads and places where roads are long blocked for various reasons, many companies have started to plan using drones as the new mode of delivery. However, it places a burden on the regulators to achieve the highest level of safety regarding random drone delivery, mostly performed in very low-level airspace. On the other hand, there has already been societal acceptance for certain drone applications such as delivery medicines and food during catastrophes.

Currently, drone technology is far ahead of drone regulation, and hence the commercial use of drones is still severely restricted, even for research and development

---

1   See also European Convention on Human Rights (ECHR), Art. 5 – Privacy and Art. 8 – Liberty and Security.
2   Pauner, C., Viguri, J., 'A Legal Approach to Civilian Use of Drones in Europe: Privacy and Personal Data Protection Concerns', Roma: Democracy Security Review Anno V, No. 3, 27 October 2015, pp. 92-93.

purposes. Companies that deliver all kinds of goods, including fast-food services, to consumers just cannot launch their drones without the approval of the CAA, mostly because of an inadequate regulatory framework and expertise. The idea that tens of thousands of commercial delivery drones intersect across urban areas, flying below 400 ft and BVLOS fully automated, is quite frightening.

The chance of a collision with obstacles such as buildings and power lines, with other drones, with small or large traditional civil aircraft in the vicinity of airports or with people on the surface is a realistic threat. In other cases, potential loss of control over drones is conceivable because the data transmission or data control link between the controlling device, e.g. an RPS, and the drone could be interrupted or intentionally jammed.

EASA is working at an unprecedented pace to issue rules and guidelines on drone activities to meet the demands from industry for the basic rules for drone operations, both commercial and recreational. The new drone regulatory framework, to be established by EASA and adopted by the European Commission in December 2020, addresses societal concerns. In that sense, it is quite special for aviation safety legislation because it even goes beyond the safety principle. The regulatory framework tries to provide answers to the questions concerning how to deal with issues in relation to security, privacy and data protection as well as noise and emissions.[3]

In recent years, EASA has been working on legislation that will focus on urban airspace, known as U-space, the label used by the European Union to refer to unmanned traffic management. U-space will provide support to BVLOS operations and will be the fundamental basis for dense operations in urban areas below 120 m (400 ft). The regulation will lay down the principles that will allow multiple types of drone traffic, including commercial drones delivering e-commerce products, to interact safely within an urban airspace, taking account of other airborne and ground traffic, as well as people, in the same environment.

Drone technology is constantly evolving as new innovations and substantial investments aid its technological improvements. Based on the current technology, a potential new generation of drone technology is within reach and will contain innovative elements such as complete commercial suitability, fully compliant safety and regulatory standards-based design. Other elements are platform and payload interchangeability, automated safety modes, enhanced intelligent piloting models and full flight autonomy, full airspace awareness, including triple detect and avoid capability and comprehensive auto action during take-off, landing and mission execution.

In its forecast for the next two decades till 2039, the FAA anticipates what is to come for the civil aviation community, which includes the domestic US and international

---

3 Speech by Joachim Luecking, Head of Unit Aviation Safety in the Directorate-General for Mobility and Transport of the EU, during the EASA High Level Conference on Drones, at Amsterdam, on 5 and 6 December 2019.

airline markets, air cargo and space traffic and drones. Remarkably, the market for commercial drones is growing faster than anticipated and could triple by 2023, while the market for non-commercial, private drones appears to be slowing down. The accelerated growth of the commercial drone market is confirmed by new business models initiated by leading companies such as Amazon, Google, Walmart and the medical world, all experimenting with deliveries by drones.[4]

From 31 December 2020, national rules on unmanned aircraft in the EU Member States were replaced by a common EU Regulation. This basically means that once drone pilots have received valid authorization from their State of Registry, they will be allowed to circulate freely within the European Union. As a result of the Covid-19 pandemic, the European Commission decided to postpone the implementation of the rules and procedures of the operating UAS, allowing the national drone operating rules to apply for a further six months in 2020, is replaced by new EU drone rules starting on 31 December 2020. How society will see the drone community in the future will depend largely on how drone pilots, responsible for safe operations, especially but not exclusively in the commercial sector, will respond to the new rules and regulations and how they will respect them.[5]

The civil drone strategy, developed by the European Commission, aims to support the progressive development of the unmanned aircraft market in Europe. It will also address common concerns about safety, security, privacy, liability and general public acceptance.

The new EU Regulations remove the difference between commercial and non-commercial drone operations, adding three main categories that include other subcategories. In many EU Member States, the use of drones as part of a commercial activity is allowed only as long as responsible operators respect some very strict conditions. Failure to comply with EU drone rules may result in significant financial and legal consequences. Flying a drone for a commercial activity, such as delivery of products or food delivery, and urban air mobility in the foreseeable future, is allowed in many European states. Commercial drone operators holding an RPAS Operator Certificate will generally operate in the Specific category. They need an authorization or

---

4   Liptak, A., 'The FAA Says the Commercial Drone Market Could Triple in Size by 2023', *The Verge*, 4 May 2019. *See also* Khan, S., 'The Drone Market Could Triple in Size by 2023, Says the FAA', *The Science Times*, 24 May 2019. Corrigan, J., 'FAA Predicts the Commercial Drone Market Will Triple by 2023', *Nextgov*, 3 May 2019.
5   Commission Implementing Regulation (EU) 2020/746 of 4 June 2020, Art. 1: Implementing Regulation (EU) 2019/947 is amended as follows: (1) in Art. 20, '1 July 2022' is replaced by '1 January 2023'; (2) Art. 21 is amended as follows: (a) in Para. 1, '1 July 2021' is replaced by '1 January 2022'; (b) in Para. 2, '1 July 2021' is replaced by '1 January 2022'; (c) in Para. 3, '1 July 2022' is replaced by '1 January 2023'; (3) in Art. 22, 'two years' is replaced by '30 months'; (4) Art. 23 is amended as follows: (a) in Para. 1, the second subparagraph is replaced by the following: 'It shall apply from 31 December 2020'; (b) Para. 3, Para. 3 of Art. 15 shall apply from '1 January 2022'.

licence from the corresponding national CAA before they can start planning any drone operation.

In addition, data and privacy protection may play a paramount role since they must comply with the related EU rules. In order to avoid any sort of trouble, an operator must be aware of the rules that apply to the applicable category and how to register the drone flying activities related to his or her business.

The following are some general rules with respect to commercial drone operations:
- Fly respectfully and consider privacy.
- Fly safely and follow the flight safety rules.
- Fly responsibly and be insured.
- A commercial drone operator is obliged by the national law to respect the corresponding safety and operational rules in order not to interfere with aviation safety, endanger individuals or cause damage to property.
- In Europe, every citizen enjoys a fundamental right to privacy and to the protection of their personal data. A commercial drone operator must always respect these rights and strictly comply with the applicable privacy and data protection regulations.
- In the event of an accident, the commercial drone operator is responsible for the drone and has to compensate for the damage caused by it. Thus, European aviation law requires commercial drone operators to be adequately insured. A commercial drone operator should be aware of the applicable insurance and liability requirements.

Just to give an impression of a specific national regulation for the operation of drones, including commercial RPAS operations, the following regulation was in force within the Kingdom of the Netherlands, being a European Member State. From 31 December 2020, national regulations were replaced by the common regulatory framework on drones in the European Union, which is established on a risk-based categorical classification approach.

The Dutch national regulation on drones provides as follows:
- Flying a drone is allowed only in airspace class G, under applicable air traffic rules. This restricts flights in many areas of the Netherlands. A map including no-fly zones for drone operators is available.
- Drones may not fly more than 120 m (400 ft) above the ground or water.
- Drone pilots must give priority to all other aircraft, such as aeroplanes, helicopters, gliders, etc. This means that the pilot must land the drone immediately on seeing an aircraft approaching.
- Drones must fly at a safe distance from people and buildings.
- Drone pilots must maintain a visual line of sight (VLOS) with their drones during operations.
- Drones may not be flown at night.

CHAPTER 3 COMMERCIAL, PRIVATE AND SPORTS USE

The following are the rules for commercial drone operations:
- Commercial drone operations require the drone pilot to hold a pilot's licence (RPA-L) and the company/organization overseeing the operation to hold an RPAS Operator Certificate permit to fly.
- If you operate a drone weighing no more than 4 kg, you may apply for a light permit (ROC-Light), which means adapted rules: maximum flight altitude 50 m AGL; maximum distance between the pilot and RPA 100 m; VLOS, daylight only and a minimum visibility of 1,500 m; uncontrolled airspace only; minimum distance to roads, contiguous buildings, people and obstacles; not within 3 km distance from a controlled airport, unless permission is granted; and not under the influence of drugs, alcohol or medicines.
- Drone insurance is required for commercial drone operations in the Netherlands.

Additional rules within the Amsterdam flight information region (FIR):
- A flight with a remotely piloted aircraft (RPA) with a mass between 0 and 150 kg and not being a model aircraft (so its flight is for purposes other than air display, recreational or sports activities) is not allowed to operate unless the Remotely Piloted Aircraft Systems (RPAS) operator and RPAS pilot and the RPA have a valid specific permission/exemption of the inspectorate department of the CAA of the Netherlands (CAA-NL/ILT).
- Exemptions. RPAS operators based outside the Netherlands can apply for exemptions by filing the special form based on Article 8 of the Chicago Convention and described in ICAO Annex 2, appendix 4 Remotely Piloted Aircraft Systems, and in ICAO Circular 328 AN/190 and ICAO Manual on Remotely Piloted Aircraft Systems (RPAS) Doc 10019 AN/507.

Please note that the specified documents such as RPAS Operator Certificate and an operational plan are essential. Please note that permissions will be possible only for the following operations:
- flights in visual flight rules (VFR) daylight, VLOS, extended visual line of sight (EVLOS), in uncontrolled airspace;

- outside prohibited and restricted areas; drone map for permanent prohibited and restricted areas is available;
- with a safe distance (<150 m for RPAS with MTOM >4 kg and >50 m for RPAS with MTOM <4 kg during flights up to 50 m AGL) to populated areas (the congested areas of cities, towns or settlements or over an open-air assembly of persons), moving cars, trains and vessels; and
- below 120 m above ground or water (AGL).

RPAS operators have to convince CAA-NL that they are qualified to operate their RPAS safely.[6]

Additional rules within the Curaçao FIR and San Juan FIR:
- Please note that the airspace above the BES islands (Dutch Caribbean: airspace above the islands Bonaire, St. Eustatius and Saba) is prohibited airspace or controlled airspace (control zone – CTR or aerodrome traffic zone – ATZ). It is not allowed to fly there with aircraft, including RPA, without the permission of ATC or Aerodrome Flight Information Service (AFIS).

The following are FAA requirements for commercial and other (incidental business and public) drone operations:

Pilots requirements:
- Must have Remote Pilot Airman Certification.
- Must be sixteen years or older.
- Must pass Transportation Security Administration (TSA) vetting.

Aircraft requirements:
- Must be less than 55 lbs.
- Must be registered if over 0.55 lbs.
- Must undergo pre-flight checklist.
- Location requirements:
- Class G airspace without ATC permission.
- Classes B, C, D and E airspace require ATC permission.

---

[6] The national rules are subject to change when the new European Regulation on drones comes into effect. However, there are transitional provisions about authorizations and transitional applicabilities mentioned in Arts. 14 and 15 of the new Regulation: As of two years after entry into force of this Regulation, economic operators and UAS placed on the market shall comply with this Regulation. As of three years after entry into force of this Regulation, all unmanned aircraft shall be operated in accordance with this Regulation. Within three years of entry into force of this Regulation, all operators shall convert their existing authorizations into authorizations or declarations as required by this Regulation. *See also* Commission Implementing Regulation (EU) 2020/746 of 4 June 2020.
National authorizations, certificates and declarations are fully converted to the new EU system as of 1 January 2022. All operations in the Open category are conducted according to this amending Regulation as of 1 January 2023.

CHAPTER 3   COMMERCIAL, PRIVATE AND SPORTS USE

- Operating rules:
- Must keep aircraft in VLOS.
- Must fly under 400 ft.
- Must fly only during daylight hours.
- Must fly at or below 100 mph.
- Must yield right of way to manned aircraft.
- Must not fly over people.
- Must not fly from a moving vehicle.
- (The requirements under Operating rules are subject to waiver.)

3.2   PRIVATE DRONE USE

One of the biggest hurdles to mass adoption of drones is the numerous regulations that restrict their operation. One of the most prevalent restrictions is the so-called line of sight rule, which mandates that drone operators keep the drone within eyeshot at all times. This clearly removes any potential application for drones in the delivery space, not only because delivery by drones is normally a commercial activity, but also because the need to keep a drone in line of sight at all times defeats the purpose of sending a drone to drop a product at a consumer's location. In any case, the regulations for commercial and private/recreational drone use differ, but the VLOS remains pivotal, at least as long as there are no reliable tests and adequate rules prove otherwise.

Drones are quite enticing with their versatile deployment possibilities, their simple handling and their relatively low price, at least in the private sector. Owing to the exponential increase in privately used drones, adequate regulations were initially needed to curb excessive and dangerous usage. In various states, practically all over the world, national legislatures issued drone-related rules, primarily to ensure safety. However, the problem is that users are often unaware of any rules for the use of drones. Thus, information, harmonization and modification of regulations at the national level, and especially at the international level, are extremely necessary to regulate and contain the risk to aviation safety and security, especially near airports and in congested airspace.

In the past, at the national level, the public was informed about the content of new regulations for the use of civil drones, both private, public and commercial. An example of such new regulations was those issued in 2015 by the German Federal Ministry of Transport and Digital Infrastructure (Bundesministerium für Verkehr und digitale Infrastruktur, BMVI) and quoted in a position paper on civil drones regarding private and commercial use:

To avoid dangers in airspace or to prevent injuries to persons on the surface, the private use of drones needs to be re-regulated. Private drone flights shall be prohibited at an altitude of more than 100 m, beyond the visibility of the controller, over industrial installations, above prisons and military installations, prohibited around large crowds, disasters or disaster areas and places of deployment of police or other security authorities or organizations, and near facilities in the energy production and distribution sector as well as federal roadways and railway lines. Regarding commercial and private use, drones with a weight of 0.5 kg and up shall be subject to label in the future in order to be able to identify the user in case of misuse or accidents.

For commercial use: to enhance opportunities for use in agriculture or traffic monitoring, the scope of application should be extended. In the future, Länder (State) aviation authorities will be able to permit flights outside the visibility of the user; however, only if it can be proven to be operated in a safe manner. Until now, the operation is generally prohibited outside the visual range. There will be a user's license for commercial use of drones. Knowledge of aviation and aviation regulations must be demonstrated in a test. The license is issued by the Federal Aviation Office (Luftfahrt Bundesamt, LBA).[7]

At the European level, the European Commission presented in 2015 its strategy for air transport, intended to ensure the safe operation of drones, based on the so-called risk-based approach. The issued safety requirements determined the size of a drone, the airspace in which it operates and how it is deployed.

To achieve harmonization, the national regulations on drones of Germany and all other EU Member States are to be quickly overtaken, and or added to, in some parts by the introduction of a common regulatory framework for drone operations within Europe. The European Commission assigned EASA to draw up appropriate proposals to integrate drones regardless of their size, with the intent to establish an EU-wide standardized drone regulation. What applies to commercial drone operations will also apply to privately operated drones: as of 31 December 2020, national rules of EU Member States were replaced by common European rules.

The purpose of this reform is to create a truly harmonized drone market in Europe with the highest level of safety. In practice, it means that once a drone pilot has received an authorization from his or her State of Registry, he or she (or a legal person) will be allowed to circulate freely within the European Union. Operations in the Open category, especially intended for private drones, do not require prior authorizations or a pilot licence. However, they are limited to the following operations: flights in VLOS, below

---

[7] Position Paper: Civil Drones, October 2016, Bundesverband der Deutschen Luftverkehrswirtschaft e.V. (BDL), pp. 2-3.

120 m altitude and performed with a privately built drone or a drone compliant with the technical requirements defined in the regulation.[8]

To demonstrate this compliance, drones that can be operated in the Open category will bear a class identification label. Additional operational restrictions apply to each class of drones, in particular with regard to the distance that must be maintained between the drone and non-involved persons, based on the low-risk approach.

At the international level, ICAO issued in 2011 Circular 328 AN/190 that called on contracting states to provide comments regarding the subject on civil drones in an effort to proceed with the development of a fundamental regulatory framework through SARPs, with supporting PANS and guidance material to underpin routine operations of drones globally in a safe, harmonized and seamless manner comparable to that of traditional manned aviation operations. In summary, it can be said that the discussions about the provisions of Article 8 of the Chicago Convention led to this circular.

ICAO is the natural agency to bring together the best and brightest from government and industry to define how drones can be safely integrated into modern airspace and in a way that optimizes their benefits globally for the wide range of public and private sector operators. ICAO continues to process the regulatory framework for the safe integration of drones, including RPAS.

The FAA Reauthorization Act of 2018 describes how, when and where one can fly drones for recreational purposes. A recreational user is considered a person that flies a drone for fun. It is important to know when and where a recreational user can fly and how to register the drone.[9]

Flying drones safely for private, including recreational, use is defined as follows:
– Register the drone, mark it on the outside with the registration number and carry personal proof of registration.
– Fly only for recreational purposes. The pilot will not be paid or receive any compensation for the flight. The flight cannot be performed as a service, paid or unpaid, for any person or organization.
– Fly the drone at or below 400 ft AGL when in uncontrolled (Class G) airspace.
– Obtain authorization before flying in controlled airspace (Classes B, C, D and E). The pilot can obtain authorization in three ways:

---

8 See Commission Implementing Regulation (EU) 2019/947 of 24 May 2019 and Commission Implementing Regulation (EU) 2020/639 of 12 May 2020, both under Annex UAS Operations in the Open and Specific Categories, Part A UAS Operations in the Open Category.
9 FAA Reauthorization Act of 2018 (One Hundred Fifteenth Congress of the United States of America at the Second Session, 3 January 2018), Section I, Title II FAA Certification Reform, Title III Safety, Subtitle B – Unmanned Aircraft Systems (One Hundred Fifteenth Congress of the United States of America at the Second Session, 3 January 2018).

    a. LAANC
    b. DroneZone
    c. A written agreement with the FAA for fixed flying sites.

Note: Flying drones in certain airspace is not allowed. Classes of airspace and flying restrictions can be found on the FAA B4UFLY app.
- Keep the drone within VLOS or within the visual line of sight of a visual observer who is co-located (physically next to) and in direct communication with the pilot.
- Do not fly at night unless the drone has lighting that allows the pilot to know its location and orientation at all times.
- Give way to and do not interfere with manned aircraft.
- Never fly over any person or moving vehicle.
- Never interfere with emergency response activities such as disaster relief, any type of accident response, law enforcement activities, firefighting or hurricane recovery efforts.
- Never fly under the influence of drugs or alcohol. Many over-the-counter medications have side effects that could impact the pilot's ability to safely operate the drone.
- Do not operate the drone carelessly or recklessly.

The law also requires:
- Drone operators to pass an online aeronautical knowledge and safety test and to carry proof of having passed it.
- The FAA to issue guidance for how it will recognize community-based organizations.[10]

Recreational pilots should know that if they intentionally violate any of these safety requirements, and/or operate in a careless or reckless manner, they could be liable for criminal and/or civil penalties.

    For all recreational flights the following basic items apply:
- Keep UAS within sight.
- No flying over people.
- No flying over stadiums and sport events.
- No flying near other aircraft.
- No flying over moving vehicles.
- No flying near emergency response efforts.
- Check for airspace conditions.
- Check local regulations.

---

10 The FAA is incrementally rolling out these features and requirements (www.faa.gov/uas/).

– Fly only in reasonable weather conditions.[11]

Until the end of 2020, recreational and professional drone pilots in Europe had to adhere to the rules set at the national level by all EU Member States. Before the implementation of the EASA regulatory framework, there were a multiplicity of rules, which not only caused a lot of confusion among the affected people (and companies), who simply wanted to take their drones abroad, but also inhibited the fast-developing international drone industry. Licences and permits were hardly interchangeable. Moreover, several key safeguards were not addressed in a coherent way.

All this will change with the introduction of a European regulatory framework on drones and its subsequent implementation. Implementation means not only that there will be comprehensive work for the policymakers and enforcers of the government ministries concerned, but also that drone operators must make their licensing form suitable for the newly created situation. However, there will be a two-year transition period. This new European legislation will bring an overarching structure and uniformity to the current fractured legislative landscape. Following the full implementation in all EU Member States, it is clear what the European requirements for drone operations will look like. The European legislation, especially the implementing rule, prevails over the local rules. The EU Member States cannot make the rules stricter, but still have the freedom and flexibility to define drone zones, although at this point more uniformity is desirable.

Common European rules have a major impact on the recreational drone pilots' community. From 31 December 2020, they must adhere to theoretical and practical requirements set in the Open category and subcategories, albeit with a transition period. For example, there will be a registration requirement for pilots flying drones heavier than 250 g or equipped with a camera. For a weight category between 900 g and 4 kg, theory training must be followed, which is concluded by a test consisting of 40 questions.

In the Open category, no distinction is made between recreational and commercial drone pilots. Commercial enterprises that want to operate flights with a higher risk will fall into the Specific or Certified categories.

The EASA regulatory framework timeline for recreational and other drone users is showing the introductory phases of new rules that have been developed. These newly developed common European rules must ensure the free circulation of drones and a level playing field within the European Union. The approach taken is to apply the highest safety standards already achieved in traditional manned aviation to drones as well. These rules are based on an assessment of the risk of operation and strike a balance between the obligations of drone manufacturers and those of operators in

---

11 www.faa.gov/uas/recreational_fliers.

regard to safety, respect for privacy, the environment, protection against noise and need for security.

The new rules ensure that both recreational and professional drone operators will have a clear understanding of what is allowed and what is not. The rules will cover each operation type, from those not requiring prior permission to those involving certified aircraft and operators, as well as minimum remote pilot training requirements. The regulatory framework timeline started in February 2019 when the EASA Committee voted for the European Commission's proposal for an Implementing Act regulating the operation of UAS in the Open and Specific categories and subsequent adoption by the European Commission of the Implementing Act and Delegated Act in March, defining the technical requirements for drones, published in mid-June to enter into force 20 days later. These acts are the tools for the transition of the Regulation on UAS operations in the specified categories.

The EU rules build on national rules that were in place and now provide a harmonized framework across the European Union. On 12 March 2019, the Commissioner for Mobility and Transport Violeta Bulc said:

> Today's decision is vital for the further development of the European drone sector. We wholeheartedly support the development of these new technologies and services, which are essential for the digitalization and decarbonization of the European economy. However, above all, we have to ensure that they are safe for other airspace users and people on the ground. The rules adopted today are a first building block for a comprehensive set of rules, which will ensure safe, secure and green drone operations throughout the European Union.

This EU regulatory regime on unmanned aircraft operations will be applied gradually during the transition after publication. By 2022 the transitional period will be completed, which means that as of January 2023 all operations in the Open category and all drone operators must comply fully with Regulation (EU) 2019/945 and Regulation (EU) 2019/947. By the end of 2019, EASA published the AMC and GM for the Regulation, and the Opinion called Standard scenarios for UAS operations in the Specific category. The following timeline requirements will be applicable to recreational and other drone operators as from 2020:

- Registration of UAS operators and certified drones becomes mandatory. Starting from 31 December 2020, all drone operators shall register themselves for using a drone:
  o in the Open category with a weight of more than 250 g or less than 250 g when it is not a toy and it is equipped with a sensor able to capture personal data; and

CHAPTER 3   COMMERCIAL, PRIVATE AND SPORTS USE

  o in the Specific category.

All certified drones, operated in high-risk operations, shall be registered as well. The registration number needs to be displayed on the drone.
- A drone user without class identification label can continue to operate in the limited Open category under Article 22 of Commission Implementing Regulation (EU) No. 2019/947 between 31 December 2020 and 31 December 2022:
  o drones with a weight of less than 500 g may be operated in an area where it is reasonably expected that no uninvolved person is overflown;
  o drones with a weight up to 2 kg may be operated up to 50 m horizontal distance from people (also in low-speed mode);
  o drones with a weight of up to 25 kg may be operated at 150 m horizontal distance of residential, recreational and industrial areas, in a range where it is reasonably expected that no uninvolved person is overflown during the entire time of the operation.[12]
- As of 31 December 2020, operations in the Specific category may be conducted after authorization has been given by the national CAA.
- From 31 December 2021, national authorizations, certificates, declarations are fully converted to the new EU regulatory system. This means that EU Member States need to complete the definition of geographical zones where drones are prohibited or where special authorization is needed. In other words, EU Member States must have available information on geographical zones for geo-awareness in a digital format harmonized between these states.
- From 31 December 2022, all operations in the Open category will be conducted according to the EU Regulations. All model (also considered to be drones) clubs and associations should receive an authorization by the respective national CAA. EU Member States may provide model clubs and associations allowing their members to deviate from all requirements of the applicable EU Regulation.

On 4 March 2020, EASA published the Easy Access Rules for Unmanned Aircraft Systems (EU regime, Regulation (EU) 2019/947 and Regulation (EU) 2019/945),

---

12 *See* http://vdwouw.net/drones/eu_drone_rules.jpg based on www.dronewatch.nl for a more detailed overview of requirements in the subcategories of the Open category, from 31 December 2020. An uninvolved person is one who is not part of the drone operation.

consisting of UAS eRules (IR+AMC&GM+DR), which means that this comprehensive document, applicable to all types of drone operations, covers Regulation (EU) 2019/947, the related AMC and GM as well as Regulation (EU) 2019/945 on unmanned aircraft systems and on third-country operators of unmanned aircraft systems.[13] As a matter of fact, it is a regularly updated document, containing the rules and procedures for the operation of unmanned aircraft displayed in a consolidated, easy-to-read format with advanced navigation features.

EASA eRules, aviation rules for the 21st century, developed and implemented in close cooperation with EU Member States and aviation industry, will offer easy (online) access to all rules and regulations as well as new and innovative applications such as rule-making process automation, stakeholder consultation, cross-referencing and comparison with ICAO and third countries' standards.

3.3 DRONES IN SPORTS

There is no more striking example of the unbridled increase in drone applications than the boom in drone air sports, especially drone racing, which is one of the fastest growing sports in the world. One of the many new drone sport disciplines, it began in Australia in late 2013 and early 2014 with a number of amateur pilots getting together for semi-organized drone races in Brisbane and Melbourne, equipped with an onboard camera, which feeds back to the remote pilots' first-person view (FPV) goggles.

Drone racing is the newest air sport within the FAI (Fédération Aéronautique Internationale), and, driven by the development of easily available technology, drones have brought tens of thousands of new people into the world of air sports very quickly. In states all over the world, whether it is flying a drone for photography, using drones for business, but especially drone racing, t a whole new world of aerial activity is clearly opening up.

In a drone race, pilots race against each other around a dedicated drone track. There can be two or more pilots on each heat. Typically, a race will see pilots launch their drones from the ground and then navigating a race track, dodging slalom poles and ducking under gates at staggering speeds. The aim is to get around in the fastest time like a Formula One car. Marked by high and low gates and other obstacles, tracks go up and down as well as from side to side, and the pilot must learn quickly to fly the best line.

---

13   Revision from November 2020, published in December 2020, incorporates the changes introduced with the following regulations: Regulation (EU) 2020/639 and Regulation (EU) 2020/1058 introducing the standard scenarios and two new UAS classes, and Regulation (EU) 2020/746 postponing applicability of Regulation (RU) 2019/947. *See also* EASA Explanatory Note to Decision 2019/021/R, Introduction of a regulatory framework for the operation of unmanned aircraft systems in the Open and Specific categories. The draft text of this Decision has been developed by EASA, assisted by a UAS expert group, and based on the input provided by Joint Authorities for Rulemaking on Unmanned Systems (JARUS).

Skills required include good hand-to-eye coordination, quick reactions and a mechanically sympathetic mind to work with the drones.

Races will be performed outdoors as well as indoors, and some drone races have been held in spectacular city centre locations, where thousands gather to watch. Because the action on the racing field happens so quickly, expert judges watch the live video feed from each competitor to make sure the run is clean. If gates are missed, the judge will apply a penalty or let the pilot immediately know to go back around. Cameras could be attached to the drones, allowing fans to see what their favourite pilots are seeing live in HD quality.

From 2016, drone racing has really exploded over the last three years and has been the basis for numerous highly successful FAI competitions, including a real Drone Racing World Cup. This World Cup is a unique event offering fun and excitement for competitors and spectators alike. It brings together drone racers from all over the world and gives them a platform from which to show off their considerable skills, while pitting their drones against other top-flight pilots.

The drone sport, which is evolving to include new formats and larger drones, has many features that appeal to the younger generation: it is fast paced, it comes across well online and it has an element of gaming-style virtual reality thanks to the special goggles worn by the pilots. Drone racing is inextricably linked to electronics and technology. Unsurprisingly, therefore, there is a great deal of cutting-edge technology at work behind the scenes at drone racing events.

Flying small radio-controlled multicopters via video goggles for an FPV is becoming increasingly popular. FPV races are based on a completely different concept. A racer should always be a multicopter with at least three motors and should weigh no more than 1 kg, including batteries. An optimized weight-power ratio makes for agile and dynamic racers' movements in the air. Power and manoeuvrability are the key factors, which entail a major consideration when a multicopter is being designed for racing; in addition, it should also be crushproof and able to take a fair amount of punishment.

The size of these racers is defined by the distance between motor axes. Common sizes are between 200 and a maximum of 330 mm. Propellers with two, three or even four blades may be used. The video transmission system consists of a small camera, a 5.8 GHz transmitter and a circular antenna and is used to transmit the video signals from the copter to the video goggles. The goggles include a receiver that is also equipped with a circular antenna. So-called diversity receivers using a circular antenna and a patch antenna to receive the video signal from the copter are also available and provide improved reception.

The copter is controlled using a conventional 2.4 GHz radio controller. The racing circuit is 250 m long and has to fit into an approximately 180 × 100 m rectangle marked on the ground. Obstacles must be clearly visible. The entire race course has to be set up to avoid accidents and to ensure that there is no danger to any persons. The racing circuit must include three, four or five air gates. The crossing dimensions of the air gates must be adapted to the configuration of the circuit, depending especially on the natural obstacles.

In early 2016, a new F3U class (Radio Control Multi-rotor FPV Racing) for drone racing was created by the FAI. The rules specify a number of details so that national and international events can be governed by common rules. Events in this exciting racing class can be held outdoors as well as indoors and will be attractive to spectators and the media. Multicopter drone racing consists of successive races with several radio-controlled model aircraft (generally 4) flying together on a racing circuit. Each model aircraft is operated by an FPV pilot assisted by a helper. The FPV pilot steers the model from the video picture of the onboard camera transmitted in real time to the goggles.

An FPV racing contest, to be flown in one or two days, is usually organized in three stages:
- Qualification stage to define the placing for the first round of the elimination stage.
- Elimination stage with successive rounds up to semi-finals.
- Final with the best-placed FPV pilots of the semi-finals.

Drone racing contest sites could be an outdoor field or indoor place, such as sports hall or aviation hangar, equipped, if possible, with grandstands for the public. For the racing circuit, a minimum developed length of 250 m within a 180 × 100 m rectangle is recommended on an outdoor field. A minimum developed size or length of 80 m is recommended for an indoor circuit. The circuit must contain air gates to cross. In addition, natural or artificial obstacles can be part of the circuit.

Following a decision taken at the 2018 CIAM Plenary Meeting to establish a new category dedicated to drones, all drone-related matters have, since 1 January 2019, been brought under the F9-Drone Sport.

The class F9U is based on an electric-powered multimotor (model aircraft equipped with three power-driven propeller devices at least) with a maximum total flight weight of 1 kg. The running of an F9U contest, like the FAI World Drone Racing Championship Grand Final (WDRC), requires officials such as the contest director, circle marshal, judges, timekeepers, local officials and a nominated FAI jury in order to guarantee safety and to verify that the competition is conducted in compliance with the rules. The FAI jury is also in charge to manage protests when required.[14]

The flourishing popularity of the drone sport is an exciting development throughout the world. However, the trend of airspace restrictions, which could potentially be placed on

---

14 The rules for the FAI World Drone Racing Championship Grand Final are based on the F9U (RC Multi-Rotor Drone Racing) class rules. The FAI provisional class F9U rules are part of the FAI Sporting Code – Section 4 Aeromodelling – Volume F9 Drone Sport, recognized for the Drone Racing World Cup (source: FAI Sporting Code Volume F9 Drone Sport 2020 Edition, Chapter A Drone Racing World Cup Rules and Chapter C F9U Provisional Class). *See also* www.fai.org/world-cups/drone-racing-documents.

CHAPTER 3   COMMERCIAL, PRIVATE AND SPORTS USE

all air sports, particularly drones of all variants, has, unfortunately, become increasingly commonplace in our skies. Airspace allocation for recreational and competitive air sports has already been adversely affected in recent years. This rather bad scenario is a well-founded reason why the FAI, also known as the World Air Sports Federation, a non-governmental, non-profit-making international organization founded in 1905, quite recently published an airspace manifesto calling on ICAO and its Member States to ensure continued and fair airspace access for all air sports. Considering its history of promoting innovation, and its decades of diverse competitive air sports and regulatory experience, the FAI is especially perfectly placed to lead the way in the development of the emerging drone air sports.[15]

The 2018 FAI International Drones Conference and Expo, which concluded on 2 September, and was held at the Ecole Polytechnique Fédérale de Lausanne (EPFL) in Switzerland, offered a unique platform for sports organizations, businesses, governmental authorities and end users to discuss how drones are, and could be, used by everyone from hobbyists to huge enterprises and top-flight drone racers.

The debates hinged on three main subjects: safety, innovation and sports. Within these areas, the discussion ranged from airspace regulation, which is of crucial importance to the FAI and its members, to the phenomenal growth of eSports, and how drone racing looks set to change over the next ten years.

Among the many potential directions explored at the conference were both the 'Freespace Drone Racing' plan to develop races involving much larger drones capable of speeds of up to 220 km per hour and the Drone Combat's ambition to produce televised 'cage fighting with drones'.

The conference concluded with the statement that drones are undoubtedly going to have a big impact on both competitive air sports and recreational flying over the next few years. The FAI wants to remain at the forefront of the drone community, a position from which it is able to protect the rights of all its members to continue using the airspace for their chosen activities.[16]

Earlier, in 2016, the FAI Executive Board fully supported an initiative of the FAI Aeromodelling Commission (CIAM) to establish and implement a common FAI strategy for drones. The initiative included the following points, which are still valid:
– To promote FAI as the reliable partner to global and regional rule-making authorities and to also empower National Aero Clubs (NACs) to be reliable partners to their respective CAAs.

---

15 Schnitker, R.M., van het Kaar, D., *Preserving Airspace Access for Air Sports: The International Regulation of Air Sports*, Amsterdam: Berghauser Pont Publishing, 2018, Foreword by Alvaro de Orléans-Borbón, FAI Executive Director, Chapters Airspace and Manifest Justification, pp. 59-85.
16 Shaping the Future at the FAI International Drone Conference 2018. Alongside the Conference innovative drone design, technology and applications were on show at the FAI Drones Expo, the EPFL Robotics Showcase and the Drone Innovators Session – all part of the EPFL Drone Days. EPFL is a leading technology university in Switzerland.

- To partner with drone manufacturers with the objective of connecting them to the air sports community.
- To differentiate between the recreational and sporting activities that are governed by FAI-CIAM and its NACs, from the commercial activities that require a specific approval procedure from authorities in the respective countries.
- To develop a pool of best practices that others can benefit from (e.g. sharing of existing educational awareness materials, etc.). It is also intended to develop educational awareness material for global use, if suitable from the authorities' point of view and subject to availability of funding. Such material is currently available at a national level, and the content is different on many occasions, based on the respective regulations.
- To coordinate submissions on drone regulations with Europe Air Sports (EAS) and any other appropriate air sport-interested body.
- To empower the aeromodelling community to:
  1. Deal with the authorities in order to protect the existing aeromodelling structures because drones can be considered to be model aircraft if they are operated in the Open category.
  2. To effectively protect existing aeromodelling privileges because drone regulations may create regulatory overlaps requiring common guidelines to be framed.[17]
  3. Sensibly integrate drones into airspace use.
  4. Attract new members that are novices to FPV/Drone sports flying.

Europe Air Sports is an overarching organization representing all air sports organizations, including drones, in Europe. EAS is the voice and long-term promotional entity of sports and recreational aviation at the European level.[18] EAS has

---

17 See also EASA Drones – regulatory framework background: A general concept for an operation-centric, proportionate, risk-based and performance-based regulatory framework for all unmanned aircraft was proposed with the publication of A-NPA 2015-10, in July 2015, and a Technical Opinion, in December 2015. This Opinion includes 27 concrete proposals for a regulatory framework and for low-risk operations of all unmanned aircraft irrespective of their maximum certified take-off mass (MTOM). It also provides special alleviations for people flying model aircraft (also considered to be drones) to recognize the good safety records in aeromodelling by identifying three options:
  1. EU Member States may issue a special authorization to model clubs and associations defining deviations from the UAS regulation;
  2. Operations can be conducted in specific zones designated by EU Member States; or
  3. Operations can be conducted in the Open category according to operational limitations defined for subcategory (A3).
18 European Air Sports has been established in 1988 as a non-profit organization and, since 1994, has been affiliated to the FAI. Its current membership includes the National Aero Clubs of 20 states, including most of the EU Member States, plus the European Gliding Union (EGU), the European Hang Gliding and Paragliding Union (EHPU), the European Microlight Federation (EMF), the PPL/IR Group Europe, the European Federation of Light Experimental and Vintage Aircraft (EFLEVA), the European Power Flying Union (EPFU) and the European Model Flying Union (EMFU). Together, EAS represents the interests of some 650,000 active sport and recreational airspace users.

been involved in the regulatory process on the regulation of U-space from the beginning. In the first part of 2020, EAS had the chance to discuss remaining issues with the European Commission's Directorate General in charge of transport and mobility.

Following the publication of EASA Opinion 01/2020, the European Commission is going ahead with its policy for the safe integration of drones into airspace. Based on the EASA Opinion, it has developed a draft Implementing Regulation on a regulatory framework for the U-space, which will first be discussed with EU Member State experts at the end of June 2020, and then brought into additional meetings with EU Member States to vote on the regulation for adoption, presumably in early 2021, depending mainly on the outcome of the Covid-19 pandemic.

Exchanging opinions with the European Commission was positive and provided an opportunity to reiterate the four key principles that should be applied in order to ensure a fair and collaborative coexistence of air sports and other forms of recreational aviation together with commercial drones in U-space airspace. These principles demand that access must be:

- Safe, according to the principle of Regulation (EU) 2018/1139 that 'a high and uniform level of civil aviation safety should be ensured at all times'.
- Free, as the only beneficiary of the provided services are commercial drones. EAS is unaware of any traditional manned aircraft operations that have any need for U-space.
- Simple, by ensuring that the administrative and operational requirements for access do not add a layer of complexity to the planning and conducting of a flight.
- Technologically feasible, considering the very limited resources of light aircraft, in particular non-motorized ones, such as gliders and hang-/paragliders or even aeromodels.

During the meeting, EAS underlined the importance of safe access to airspace and the large number of approximately 650,000 airspace users who could be affected by the designation of U-space airspace. The European Commission provided an assurance that it was well aware of these needs and was willing to accommodate them, as long as the objective of developing a drone market could also be met. Safety, it was generally agreed, must be the number one priority. The European Commission, furthermore, stressed that the latest draft of the regulation ensures free access to U-space airspace by traditional manned aviation, such that flying activities could continue as always.

However, it stressed the need for electronic conspicuity, i.e. the requirement for all airspace users to communicate their position electronically and with a technology still to be defined in acceptable means of compliance and guidance material.

On this basis, U-space airspace should be understood not as a restricted area but rather as being similar to a transponder mandatory zone (TMZ). According to the European Commission, only drone flights shall require authorization, and it will ultimately be the responsibility of drone operators and the USSPs to ensure they avoid manned air traffic.

In summary, EAS was of the opinion that it would appear that tangible improvements have been made between the first drafts of the U-space concept and the latest versions of the draft regulation. EAS is generally positive that their needs are being taken on board, although EU Member State experts have yet to make their findings and further recommendations.[19]

---

19 Schubert, T., 'Drones: Work on the U-space Regulation Advances', *Newsletter EAS*, July 2020, pp. 2-3.

Chapter 4 Integration into Airspace

4.1 Access to Airspace

Airspace should not be designed as either purely civil or purely military airspace, but should rather be considered as one continuum, three-dimensional, in which all users' requirements have to be accommodated to the maximum extent possible.

It is a fundamental and universally recognized principle of international law that every state has complete and exclusive sovereignty over the airspace above its territory.

Article 1 of the Chicago Convention, 1944:

> Sovereignty.
> The contracting States recognize that every State has complete and exclusive sovereignty over the airspace above its territory.

The concept of sovereignty is the keystone on which virtually all air law is built, since every flight in international air navigation requires the prior consent of the state overflown, which is generally granted by treaty.

Article 2 of the Chicago Convention, 1944:

> Territory.
> For the purposes of this Convention the territory of a State shall be deemed to be the land areas and territorial waters adjacent thereto under the sovereignty, suzerainty, protection or mandate of such State (authentic text).

The corollary of this principle, the international status of the airspace above the high seas, is equally well established. The airspace of the high seas, like the subjacent waters, is not subject to the territorial sovereignty of any state. The airspace of the high seas is the airspace above all parts of the sea that are not included in the exclusive economic zone (EEZ), in the territorial sea or in the internal waters of a state.

Since the high seas are open to all states, the legal regime is characterized by the principle of freedom or innocent passage. One element of the freedom of the high seas is the freedom of overflight. However, the freedom of overflight is not absolute. Freedom must be regulated in the interests of all who are entitled to enjoy it.[1]

Article 12 of the Chicago Convention, 1944:

> Rules of the air.
> Over the high seas, the rules in force shall be those established under this Convention. Each contracting State undertakes to insure the prosecution of all persons violating the regulations applicable (partial text).

At the domestic level, a landowner in any particular state has private law ownership rights in the usable air column above his or her land, as stipulated in virtually all jurisdictions in the world, either by legislation or by some other source of law, such as case law.[2] However, as states have, since the beginning of aviation, claimed sovereignty over the airspace above national territory, the right to overfly a given territory or property is a function of this public sovereignty. Sovereign states have asserted legislative competence to legislate with respect to the private rights of the landowners in airspace. In other words, with respect to airspace, public predominance prevails over private rights,

---

1   *See* Grief, N., 'The Legal Principles Governing the Control of National Airspace and Flight Information Regions and their Application to the Eastern Mediterranean', Report, Larnaca: European Rim Policy and Investment Council, 23 October 2009, pp. 1-3. *See* Wallace, R.M.M., *International Law*, Third Edition, London: Sweet & Maxwell, 1997, pp. 148-163. *See also* United Nations Convention on the Law of the Sea, Art. 89 *Invalidity of claims of sovereignty over the high seas*: No State may validly purport to subject any part of the high seas to its sovereignty. Art. 87 *Freedom of the high seas*: The high seas are open to all States, whether coastal or land-locked. Freedom of the high seas is exercised under the conditions laid down by this Convention and by other rules of international law. It comprises, *inter alia*, both for coastal and land-locked States: (b) freedom of overflight; [...].
These freedoms shall be exercised by all States with due regard for the interests of other States in their exercise of the freedom of the high seas, and also with due regard for the rights under this Convention with respect to activities in the Area. Art. 2(4) of the Geneva Convention on the High Seas, 29 April 1958 states: Freedom to fly over the high seas.

2   *See also* On 21 March, a federal judge in the Western District of Kentucky dismissed, on jurisdictional grounds, a federal lawsuit seeking a declaratory judgment to define airspace rights of aircraft operators and property owners. Case No. 3:16-cv-6-DJH, *Boggs v. Merideth*, also known as the 'Drone Slayer' case, arose from a landowner shooting down a drone that was flying 200 ft above his property. The landowner claimed the drone was trespassing and invading his privacy, while the pilot asserted he was in navigable airspace under the jurisdiction of the federal government. The dismissal of this case further delays answering one of the most important questions for the (commercial) drone industry: who owns low-altitude airspace? (source: Greenberg, J., 'Who Controls Low-Altitude Airspace?', *Los Angeles & San Francisco Daily Journal*, 4 May 2017).

although it is bound by rules.³ Minimum heights for safety reasons, obstacle clearance and nuisance, for instance, are prerequisites.⁴

In 1906, at a meeting of the *Institut de Droit International*, the legal status of the airspace was an opportunity for new discussions. The reason was that aviation and the use of airspace had become issues of topical interest and concern, owing in particular to the successful flights accomplished by the Wright brothers from 1903 onwards. The fact that powered flying was emerging exited the public imagination. Legendary aviators offered sightseeing flights to citizens for remuneration. To impress, or possibly scare the public, it was fairly common practice to fly at very low altitudes with sputtering engines over built-up areas and spectators.

However, the majority of municipal authorities were not amused. Not only was there a need for rules regarding aviation activities at the local level, but also national authorities decided to adopt rules for expert oversight regarding flight demonstrations, thereby protecting the population from possible accidents. Authorities, still rather unfamiliar with the phenomenon of aviation, have been guided in drafting the first national aviation laws. Since the increasingly popular aviation sector started to cross national borders, conflicting situations concerning the status of airspace had to be resolved internationally.

In the early years of the 20th century, with respect to the issue about the status of airspace in public international law, there were two different standpoints. On the one hand, there was freedom of the air, by analogy with the freedom of the high seas, so that overflight ought to be free for all, and, on the other hand, there was the concept of sovereignty over the airspace, which means assimilating airspace to the territory underlying the airspace, concluding that flight over national territory is subject to the authorization and conditions set by the sovereign underlying state.

In 1910, the French government convened an international conference, the Paris International Air Navigation Conference, on the subject matter, chiefly to discuss the operation of flights into airspace over foreign territory in order to establish regulatory procedures to avoid international confrontations.

Until the year 1910, no acceptable coherent policy existed for international flight regulation. The successive putative airspace infringements above French territory by German balloons, in particular, indicated that regulation of the airspace borders should therefore be the subject of studies and consultation. No customary international law governed any mode of transport in the atmosphere above the surface of the Earth. One broad opinion maintained that the atmosphere surrounded planet Earth and that maritime territories bordered the sea. Therefore, the same rules applied to the air as

---

3 Haanappel, P.P.C., *The Law and Policy of Air Space and Outer Space*, The Hague: Kluwer Law International, 2003, pp. 1-3.
4 *See* Ann. 2 to the Chicago Convention, Rules of the Air: Chapter 3 General Rules, 3.1.2 Minimum Heights, Chapter 4 Visual Flight Rules, and Chapter 5 Instrument Flight Rules.

commonly to the sea. Since the freedom of the high seas had been established in international law, freedom of the atmosphere was a logical consequence. However, the theory of freedom of the air was during the prelude to, and certainly at, the outbreak of World War I not in favour any more, according to the convincing general tendency at that time.[5]

Another opinion maintained that states exercised absolute sovereignty over and beneath the surface of their respective territories and were entitled to exercise similar jurisdiction regarding the atmosphere above their territories. Under this doctrine, the theory of air sovereignty, the owner of the territory, *in casu* the state, was the owner of the whole airspace above it without any limits whatsoever.

Consequently, protection of the airspace is considered to be an integral part of the protection of the national territory. In this light, national airspace will be protected to safeguard safety and security of flight, observance of aviation regulations and of the life and property on the surface. Each contracting state, party to the 1910 Paris Conference, would admit the flight of aircraft of other contracting states within and above its territory, subject to certain restrictions. This conception, although formulated differently by supporting states on essential issues, was a starting point in the discussion, which, however, raised delicate questions. The draft convention of the 1910 Paris Conference made no clear pronouncement on the choice between the two opposite principles, sovereignty over national airspace or freedom of the air. As a matter of fact, in view of developing international political tensions and the real prospect of armed conflict in Europe, national interests and national security gained momentum.[6]

Nevertheless, the various positions of the delegates who attended the Paris Conference have been of paramount importance with regard to the further development of international air law. A plausible outcome of the Paris Conference was, apart from several issues essential for the future regulation of international air navigation, that states were able to test their respective opinions on this unprecedented split issue about airspace. In this respect, the 1910 drafted convention actually formed the basis for subsequent air law conventions. The Paris Convention of 1919, formally called the Convention Relating to the Regulation of Aerial Navigation, in fact contains provisions compiled during the 1910 Paris Conference. Moreover, the 1944 Chicago Convention, in turn, is influenced by the draft convention of the 1910 Paris Conference and the

---

5   Verzijl, J.H.W., *International Law in Historical Perspective*, Volume III, Leyden: Sijthoff, 1970, Part III State Territory, Chapter II, Section 4 The Air Column, pp. 75-77.
6   Giemulla, E.M., Weber, L. (Eds.), *International and EU Aviation Law*, Selected Issues, Alphen aan den Rijn: Kluwer Law International, 2011, pp. 7-8.

provisions of the 1919 Paris Convention as well as the USA-instigated 1928 Havana Convention, dealing with traffic rights, which would amount to multilateral granting of the five freedoms of the air, practically a concept that gained momentum only years later.[7]

When the 1919 Paris Convention accepted that states have sovereign rights over the airspace above their respective territories, direct government intervention in cross-border air navigation became inevitable. In other words, while sovereignty over the airspace above their territories was asserted as a right of all states under customary law, freedom of passage for foreign aircraft was set forth merely as a contractual right under the 1919 Paris Convention.

After World War II, international civil aviation has expanded significantly year after year and is predicted to increase even more rapidly in the near future, even though there will be years when the expansion is checked by economic crises, political upsets or other conditions unfavourable to travel.

The downside of growth is that the airspace becomes overcrowded. More and more areas in the world have to deal with increasing air traffic in a finite amount of airspace. Commercial as well as military aviation are demanding a considerable portion of the available airspace. Unfortunately, the lower priority airspace users will have much less airspace available, today and certainly tomorrow. Regulations built around safety buffers, a rigid airway system, complicated arrival and departure routes, holding patterns, restricted, prohibited and danger areas, military low-level flying routes, air defence training missions and real-time exercises, nature preservation, will all raise constraints for unmanned aircraft, unless a comprehensive framework of regulations will be implemented to integrate these airspace users in a way that will avoid impairing the safety of flight and ensuring risk is kept to a bare minimum.

Available airspace is a critical resource, which it is worthwhile to make every effort to conserve. Unfortunately, there are numerous examples of airspace restrictions having been implemented that have later been proven to be rather unnecessary or over-regulated. Unnecessary restrictions of airspace benefiting traditional commercial and military aviation result in loss of valuable airspace for other activities such as unmanned aviation. The result of the current design, management and use of airspace is that critical and complex air traffic flows, at a sustainable safety level, can hardly accommodate any additional air traffic. Therefore, a redesign of the airspace infrastructure is absolutely required, next to stringent integration regulations for unmanned aircraft and the airspace management concept of flexible and dynamic use of airspace.

---

7 Pan-American (or Inter-American) Convention on Commercial Aviation (Havana Convention) of 20 February 1928, entered into force on 13 June 1929. *See* Chicago Convention, Art. 80 Paris and Habana Conventions. *See also* Milde, M., *International Air Law and ICAO*, Essential Air and Space Law Volume 4, Series Editor Benkö, M.E., Utrecht: Eleven International Publishing, 2008, p. 13.

This specific airspace management concept, Flexible Use of Airspace (FUA), is described by ICAO, and developed by EUROCONTROL.[8] The current airspace structure and management still lacks a policy framework and procedures for FUA, thereby hampering airspace design and management by not allowing the application of an optimum airspace infrastructure and the use of optimum flight paths.

The limitations that have been identified include the existence of permanently restricted and reserved airspace, primarily for military aviation purposes, which, although justified from a national security point of view, impose undesirable constraints on airspace planning, preventing direct flights between (inter)national airports. The endeavour, made using FUA principles, should permit civil flights through such reserved areas, when not being utilized by the military. All users can have access, and, on the basis of actual needs, their requests should be managed to achieve the most efficient use of airspace. Wherever possible, permanent airspace segregation should be avoided.[9]

FUA, replaced by the Advanced Flexible Use of Airspace (AFUA) concept, by adaptable airspace strategy and utilization, could offer a wealth of possibilities, particularly when using the currently available technical systems. Coordination and cooperation between civil and military authorities shall be organized at strategic, pre-tactical and tactical management levels, which are separate, though closely interdependent management functions, and therefore need to be performed coherently to ensure efficient use of airspace. These airspace management levels are aimed at increasing airspace safety and capacity as well as improving the efficiency and flexibility of air operations.[10]

The AFUA concept aims to improve network performance and provide safe, efficient and accurate information/data flows. The improved concept is an airspace management concept, based on civil-military partnership to enhance the efficient use of airspace. It is expected to provide more flexibility on the basis of dynamic airspace management in all flight phases, from initial planning to execution. The implementation of AFUA has already benefited aviation in the form of increased flight economy offered through a reduction in distance, time and fuel consumption, which implies less CO2 emissions into the atmosphere, the establishment of an enhanced air traffic service (ATS) route network, a reduction in delays and a more efficient real-time civil-military coordination at the local and network levels. Further benefits include the definition and use of temporary airspace reservation, which are more closely in line with military operational

---

8 Commission Regulation (EC) No. 2150/2005 of 23 December 2005 laying down rules for flexible use of airspace, OJ L 342/20, 24 December 2005. The EUROCONTROL concept of FUA is that airspace is no longer designated as purely 'civil' or 'military' airspace but considered as one continuum and allocated to user requirements. Any necessary airspace segregation is temporary, based on real-time usage within a specific period. Contiguous volumes of airspace are not constrained by national boundaries.
9 ICAO Circular 330 AN/189 Civil/Military Cooperation in Air Traffic Management, 2011, pp. 7-11.
10 Resolution A 37-15 Appendix O Coordination and Cooperation of Civil/Military Air Traffic.

requirements, and a reduction in airspace segregation needs, which should significantly improve access for UAS into non-segregated airspace.

States around the world are recommended to include the following principles in compliance with ICAO's Guidelines on Airspace Management (ASM):
- All available airspace should be managed in a flexible way, whenever feasible;
- airspace management processes should incorporate dynamic flight paths and provide optimal operational solutions;
- when conditions require segregation, based on different types of operations and/or aircraft, the size, shape and time zones of said airspace should be determined to minimize impact on operations;
- the use of airspace should be coordinated and monitored in order to accommodate the conflicting requirements of all users and minimize any constraints on operations;
- airspace reservation should be planned in advance with changes made dynamically whenever possible. The system also needs to accommodate short-notice unplanned requirements; and
- the complexity of operations may limit the degree of flexibility.[11]

All users of the airspace can have access, and, on the basis of actual needs, their requests should be managed to achieve the most efficient use of airspace.

'The sky is the limit' is a general expression meaning that there are no limits and that anything is actually possible. Unfortunately, for air traffic there really is a limit to the sky. As more aircraft fill the already busy airspace, air traffic control concepts, redesign, procedures, equipment and rules will continue to evolve. Apart from the (A)FUA concept, there are more developments that might allow for more efficient use of the overcrowded airspace.

NextGen required aircraft navigation, communication and surveillance equipment initiatives, such as Automatic Dependent Surveillance-Broadcast (ADS-B) and Mode S, which includes equipping aircraft with secondary surveillance radar transponders having the capabilities set out in Part A of Annex II of Commission Implementing Regulation (EU) No. 1207/2011, Performance-Based Navigation (PBN), Area Navigation (RNAV) and Required Navigation Performance (RNP), have expanded area navigation techniques, largely developed for civil air transport, originally centred on lateral navigation accuracy only to a more extensive statement of required performance. This

---

11 Source: ICAO Cir 330 AN/189, Civil/Military Cooperation in Air Traffic Management. *See also* www.icao.int/NACC/Documents?Meetings/2016/SAR/SARMTG-P07.pdf.

is related to accuracy, integrity and continuity, along with the way in which such performances are to be achieved in terms of civil aircraft functionalities and flight crew requirements.[12]

RNP extends the capabilities of modern aircraft navigation systems by providing real-time estimates of navigation uncertainty, assurance of performance through its containment concepts, and features that ensure the repeatability and predictability of aircraft navigation. This precise characterization of aircraft performance is key to designing more efficient airspace routes and procedures. Furthermore, ensured navigation performance and standardized functionality of RNP allow new procedures to be designed for airports where infrastructure or terrain makes it difficult or impossible to use some runways. RNP also allows for effecting improvements to procedures that are burdensome for flight crews.

ICAO defines PBN as area navigation based on performance requirements for aircraft operating along an ATS route, on an instrument approach procedure or a designated airspace. The ICAO PBN concept aims:
- to ensure global interoperability through the standardization of RNAV and RNP system performance through internationally agreed RNAV and RNP specifications; and
- to limit proliferation of navigation specifications in use worldwide.

PBN can potentially enable operational benefits in the area of safety, flight efficiency and airspace capacity. PBN also has the potential to effectuate a reduction in the volume of commercially occupied airspace because of the system accuracy. In that respect, PBN can be a decisive factor in enabling UAS to get access to airspace portions, previously being segregated and thus off limits. However, within the lower regions of airspace, representing the generally suitable flight area for most of UAS, the beneficial effect of PBN is considered to be much less significant. High-altitude long-range remotely piloted aircraft system (RPAS) operations, integrated into non-segregated airspace, could benefit from PBN, substantially similar to traditional manned aircraft operations.

The Continuous Descent Approach (CDA) procedure, also known as Optimized Profile Descent (OPD) procedure, is another operational tool, originated because of the technological advancements in the aviation industry. It enables aircraft operators and air navigation service providers to increase airspace capacity and flight safety while reducing the environmental footprint.

---

12 Commission Implementing Regulation (EU) No. 1207/2011 of 22 November 2011 laying down requirements for the performance and the interoperability of surveillance for the single European sky, OJ L 305/35, 23 November 2011. *See also* Commission Implementing Regulation (EU) No. 1028/2014 of 26 September 2014 amending Commission Implementing Regulation (EU) No. 1207/2011, OJ L 284/7, 30 September 2014, and Commission Implementing Regulation (EU) 2017/386 of 6 March 2017 amending Implementing Regulation (EU) No. 1207/2011, OJ L 59/34, 7 March 2017.

Continuous Descent Operation (CDO) in the arrival phase is enabled by airspace design, special procedures and facilitation by ATC. Arriving aircraft will fly from top of descent to the final approach, a continuous descent profile with reduced engine propulsion, in low drag configuration, along a predictable optimum flight path, without intermediate level-off to the final approach fix, resulting in reduced fuel burn, lower gaseous emissions, noise and fuel costs, without any adverse effect on safety. This largely also applies to the Continuous Climb Operation (CCO) procedure, which allows aircraft to climb continuously to the greatest extent possible. Aspects of the airspace and route system to be used, capacities, flight characteristics and limitations of aircraft performing the CDO or CCO are to be known by all stakeholders.

A positive side effect of these procedures is that the needed airspace volume will shift from the outer section to the more inner section of the airport TMA/CTR (terminal control area/control zone), leaving airspace away from, and low airspace more close to, the airport available for other traffic. Airspace design for CDO and CCO is of utmost importance, not only for the benefits that these procedures entail for traditional manned aviation as well as noise abatement, but especially for low-level controlled unmanned aircraft activities in the vicinity of the airport.[13]

Additional potentials to generate more airspace are as follows:
- downgrading and harmonization of airspace classifications in special airspace segments. In this way, the unnecessary strict classification should be adjusted, which together with simplified and proportionate rules will enable easier access to appropriate airspace segments without sacrificing flight safety;
- the Transition Altitude (TA), if applicable, could be raised and also harmonized in certain regions, such as the European Union, with divergent TAs, to create more airspace and mitigate complications and error-prone situations; and
- flexible boundaries of TMAs, CBAs (Cross-Border Areas) and CTAs (Control Areas).[14]

4.2 Safe Integration of Drones into the Single European Sky

Civil aviation contributes to an increased integrated logistical transport chain that aims to better serve citizens and society. It adds value by offering fast, reliable and resilient

---

13 EUROCONTROL CCO and CDO, towards a flexible, optimum flight path that delivers major environmental and economic benefits. Status of Task Force work flows following the TF#6 meeting (September 2019). *See also* ICAO Doc 9992 Manual on the Use of Performance Based Navigation (PBN) in Airspace Design-Overview, ICAO Doc 9931 AN/476 Continuous Descent Operations (CDO) Manual First Edition 2010 and ICAO Doc 9993 AN/495 Continuous Climb Operations (CCO) Manual First Edition 2013.
14 In the United States and Canada, the TA is 18,000 ft (5,500 m). ICAO's definition of TA (ICAO Doc 8168 PANS-OPS): the altitude at or below which the vertical position of an aircraft is controlled by reference to altitudes.

connections in a global network. However, the expectation is that by the year 2050, many different aircraft categories, diverse in size, performance and type, will be operating, some still having a pilot on board but most remotely piloted, controlled or fully automated. Thus, opening of the European market to RPAS, or the civil (commercial) use of drones, is an important step towards the aviation market of the future.

In 2050, European aviation will have achieved unprecedented levels of safety and will continue to improve. Manned, unmanned, legacy and NextGen autonomous aircraft and all types of rotorcraft operate simultaneously in the same airspace and in almost all weather conditions. A holistic, total system approach to aviation safety is integrated across all components and stakeholders. This is supported by new safety management, safety assurance, certification techniques and advanced technologies that account for all system developments.

A major challenge remaining for manufacturers, regulators and authorities alike is the need to build the trust of citizens and consumers. The fact that unmanned aircraft or drones have been in the public eye more often for their misuse than for their accomplishments makes transparency and effective communication imperative to prepare citizens for the approaching (autonomous) drone age.

The occurrence and impact of human error will be reduced significantly through new designs and training processes and through applicable new technologies that support decision-making. The just culture concept has been adopted uniformly across Europe and beyond as an essential element of the ongoing safety process. Comprehensive and consolidated test, demonstration and validation infrastructures are harmonized, interoperable and available across Europe to support the transition to automated, autonomous and integrated systems and beyond, in particular for the purpose of eliminating the likelihood of mid-air collisions or any other potential hazard regarding manned aviation.[15]

The number of drones that will use airspace is expected to increase exponentially over the coming years. Unfortunately, drones are hard to detect and often fly literally below the radar. Without the current restrictive regulation, chances of conflicts between drones and traditional air traffic or other objects and between drones themselves would be considerably high. Yet commercial pilots more and more often spot drones during the critical phases of flight: take-off and landing. The growing risk of a mid-air collision with a drone also applies to emergency rescue helicopters, which often fly at low altitudes.[16]

---

15 *See* Flightpath 2050, Europe's Vision for Aviation – Maintaining global leadership and serving society's needs – Report of the High-Level Group on Aviation Research, 2012. *See also* Polloczek, D., 'An Accident Waiting to Happen', ECA (European Cockpit Association) Editorial of 21 September 2015.
16 *See* Small Remotely Piloted Aircraft Systems (drones) Mid-Air Collision Study, Military Aviation Authority (MAA), British Airline Pilots' Association (BALPA) and the Department for Transport, 2016.

CHAPTER 4   INTEGRATION INTO AIRSPACE

On the other hand, stakeholders greatly desire to ease this regulation, although this can only be accomplished if a sufficient level of safety can be guaranteed. An extremely important condition is that the location of all drones in the airspace can be known and displayed. To mitigate the chances of conflicts between drones and manned air traffic, Single European Sky ATM Research (SESAR) called for a project to merge existing technologies to build the core functions of an Unmanned Traffic Management System (UTMS).[17]

The Clear Air Situation for UAS (CLASS) is the answer to increase the maturity level of the main technologies required for surveillance of UAS traffic. CLASS, a project funded as part of SESAR 2020, focused on functionalities that include real-time tracking and display of both cooperative and non-cooperative drones, aggregation of relevant aeronautical data, providing adjusted services to each stakeholder and advanced functions such as geofencing, geocaging, conflict detection and resolution. Whether a drone is cooperative or not has no bearing on whether that drone is flying rogue at its current location. Drones that transmit their location themselves are called cooperative, whereas for non-cooperative drones the locations are observed and tracked by the external system. Based on these functionalities, a real-time centralized UTMS will be developed.[18]

The CLASS project, complying with U-space services called U1, U2 and U3, as defined in the U-space initiative, enables deconfliction, assistance for separation management, dynamic geofencing and protection of restricted areas.[19]

U-space is a set of services and procedures relying on a high level of digitalization and automation of functions to support safe, efficient and secure access to airspace for a large

---

17 The Unmanned Aircraft System Traffic Management (UTM) operational concept aims to describe the operational ATM environment in which manned and unmanned aircraft must coexist safely, including the airspace below 500 ft.
18 The CLASS project is spearheaded by Airbus Defense and Space. International partners Aveillant, École Nationale de l'Aviation Civile (ENAC), Norwegian University of Science and Technology-Norges teknisk-naturvitenskaplige universitet (NTNU) and Unifly, a leading provider of UTM software in Europe, join forces to research and evaluate the ground-based technologies' potential to monitor and separate drone traffic in a real-time UTMS.
19 U1 foundation services provide e-registration, e-identification and geofencing. U2 initial services support the management of drone operations and may include flight planning, flight approval, tracking, airspace dynamic information and procedural interfaces with ATC. U3 advanced services support more complex operations in dense areas and may include capacity management and assistance for conflict detection. U4 U-space full services.

number of drones. It provides an enabling framework to support routine drone operations and addresses all types of missions, including operations in and around airports. Ultimately, U-space will enable complex drone operations with a high degree of automation to take place in all types of operational environments.[20]

Typical Norwegian University of Science and Technology (NTNU) CLASS scenarios are GNSS failure leading to intrusion at an airport, conflict in an emergency situation (2 drones), aerial work near high-voltage lines, drone Instrument Landing System (ILS) calibration (2 drones), gliding rogue drone and urban pollution sampling.[21]

In both cases, relevant aeronautical data is aggregated, and the data from multiple trackers, both on the drones and on the ground-based systems, is merged through data fusion so that the location of all drones in the airspace can be known and displayed. In other words, the UTMS will provide an overall view of both the planned and the current real-time UAS traffic situation. This information will be centralized in real time in an UTMS to create an overall solution with advanced functions such as geofencing, where the drone pilot is automatically warned if he or she trespasses into an unauthorized zone; geocaging, where the drone pilot is warned that he or she is leaving a pre-defined zone; conflict detection; and resolution. The performance of these cooperative and non-cooperative drone detection and tracking technologies will be assessed through live experiments. It will provide the basis on which to develop services tailored to end users such as drone operators, ANSPs and authorities.[22]

Although drones have the potential to transform business models and tackle societal challenges practically all over the world, governments are struggling to find ways to regulate and manage drones in controlled airspace while maintaining public safety and

---

20 U-space Supporting Safe and Secure Drone Operations in Europe: A preliminary summary of SESAR U-space research and innovation results (2017-2019), p. 6. *See also* The Drone Amsterdam Declaration of 28 November 2018 urged that priority is given to the implementation of the European drone regulations and called for timely delivery of the U-space regulatory framework and invited the relevant EU organizations to join the effort to develop an institutional, regulatory and architectural framework for a competitive U-space services market (https://ec.europa.eu/transport/sites/transport/files/2018-drones-amsterdam-declaration.pdf).
21 *See* Project insight: Clear Air Situation for UAS (CLASS), 15 November 2018, Workshop on Autonomous Aerial Vehicles, Trondheim, Krzysztof Cisek, research fellow NTNU. GNSS stands for Global Navigation Satellite System, referring to a constellation of satellites providing signals from space that transmit positioning and timing data to GNSS receivers. The receivers then use this data to determine location. *See also* SESAR JU European ATM Master Plan: Digitalizing Europe's Aviation Infrastructure, Executive View, 2020 Edition, December 2019, pp. 65-85 about U-space services and GNSS. SESAR 2020 is a programme for air traffic management modernization, within the framework of Horizon 2020 (2014-2020), Europe's biggest research and innovation programme aimed at securing its global competitiveness. SESAR, the technological pillar of the Single European Sky initiative, aims to modernize and harmonize air traffic management in Europe.
22 Unifly. Clear Air Situation for UAS. Objectives and deliverables of the CLASS project.

confidence. More than today, drones will be a significant part of our future. Rapid changes in drone technology hold enormous promise for the future use of airspace and aviation at large as the digital transformation expands skyward. This will require a change in airspace traffic management. Enabling several thousand traditional aircraft and potentially hundreds of thousands of highly connected and automated aerial vehicles in any capacity to fly concurrently in the airspace every day will require novel designs of airspace management and physical infrastructure.

Yet the primary objective in integrating UAS or drones into the airspace is at least to maintain today's ultra-high level of safety. Unlike traditional aircraft, drones use a different flight model by not operating point to point between fixed airports but enabling a more dynamic use of airspace, requiring limited physical infrastructure. Technological developments relating to unmanned aviation are currently moving much faster than those for traditional manned aircraft.

This rapid growth in the use of drones has increased the demand for access to non-segregated airspace. In particular, there is strong pressure on VLL operations, contrary to the current rules of the air. With respect to this groundbreaking concept of operations, the market is driven by new business opportunities, such as delivery and data services and urban air mobility. Many procedural and technological areas require further development, and this lies behind the U-space concept.

The future U-space airspace and traffic management needs to be flexible enough to be applied in all airspace segments, and not only the discussed very low-level (VLL) airspace below 500 ft, as, for instance, for urban air mobility. Drones operating between 500 ft and 60,000 ft, or even higher, will have to be integrated into conventional air traffic management using current instrument flight rules (IFR). Highly automated drones, such as urban air mobility vehicles, will require new forms of traffic management and air-ground system integration. At the same time, interest is growing in the potential for specifically operating vehicles, such as communication and cargo RPAS at very high altitudes, which need access to and from the stratosphere via managed airspace.[23]

SARPs are under development for such operations by ICAO with the adoption foreseen in 2020, hopefully leading to operations from 2023. Equally important when attempting to develop a long-term approach is the applicability of any new airspace management throughout all airspace where manned and unmanned aircraft will be operating together.[24]

With regard to the access of drones into non-segregated European airspace, there are two mainstreams: the Roadmap for the safe integration of drones into all classes of airspace,

---

23 UAS ATM Integration: Operational Concept, Edition: 1.0, 27 November 2018, EUROCONTROL/EASA, pp. 10-15.
24 SESAR JU European ATM Master Plan: Roadmap for the safe integration of drones in all classes of airspace, 2018, pp. 4-5.

in particular to fit into the European ATM Master Plan, and the Roadmap for the integration of civil RPAS into the European aviation system, both with their associated innovative, operational, technological, procedural and societal aspects.

From an EU policy point of view, the access of drones may also appoint two interlinked principles:

- The urgent need to develop and use drones in Europe for a wide, and, as yet, unlimited range of purposes; and
- Regulatory and technical impediments to the introduction and routine use of drones in EU airspace must be overcome. In this respect, drones refer to UAS, including, as a subset, RPAS.[25]

The European ATM Master Plan is the agreed road map that connects ATM R&D activities with deployment scenarios in order to achieve the European Sky performance objectives, such as modernizing ATM. This modernization needs to reflect a greater focus on increased efficiency and effectiveness while sustaining or even improving the levels of safety and security and at the same time recognizing the need to provide solutions to address critical capacity bottlenecks.[26]

The European ATM Roadmap will support the allocation of resources for the development and the deployment of drone operations in all types of operational environments. It outlines which drone-related R&D activities should be prioritized in order to support the expansion of the drone market and achieve the smooth, safe and fair integration of these relatively new civil aircraft systems into European airspace. It also provides an ambitious roll-out for these technological developments.

The Roadmap for the integration of civil RPAS into the European aviation system covers RPA of all types except model aircraft. RPAS belong to the wider family of UAS, which also comprises semi-autonomous RPAS, which means no human action is necessary after the take-off phase. The Roadmap has been prepared by the European RPAS Steering Group (ERSG), set up by the European Commission in 2012, and was launched on 20 June 2013 at the Paris Air Show.[27] The Roadmap identifies all the

---

25 Roadmap for the integration of civil Remotely-Piloted-Aircraft Systems into the European Aviation System. Final report from the European RPAS Steering Group (ERSG), June 2013. *See also* Eurodrones Inc. A report by Ben Hayes, Chris Jones and Eric Töpfer, Transnational Institute – Statewatch, 1. Introduction.

26 On 22 September 2020, the European Commission proposed an upgrade of the Single European Sky regulatory framework as a result of the European Green Deal. The objective is to modernize the management of the European airspace and to establish more sustainable and efficient flight paths. This can reduce up to 10% of air transport emissions. Key enablers to secure, safe and cost-effective traffic management services are strengthening the European network to avoid congestion and suboptimal flight routes to achieve optimal use of airspace, the need for data services for a better ATM, streamlining economic regulation of ATS to stimulate greater sustainability and resilience, and better coordination for the definition, development and deployment of innovative solutions (source: EC Mobility and Transport, Air: Single European Sky: for a more sustainable and resilient air traffic management).

27 The ERSG is a group of stakeholders gathering the main organizations and experts interested in the integration of RPAS into the European aviation system.

issues to be addressed and establishes a step-by-step approach to address them. The complete document includes three annexes entitled:
- Regulatory Approach
- Strategic Research Plan
- Study on the Societal Impact

By presenting a clear way forward towards the integration of RPAS, the Roadmap is expected to facilitate the decisions to be taken by the different organizations involved, to provide transparency and efficiency in the planning of different initiatives and support the coordination of the related activities in Europe.

Together with the SESAR JU drafted U-space blueprint, both documents cover all essential requirements considered for the integration of all drone operations. This U-space blueprint aims at enabling complex drone operations with a high degree of automation to happen in all types of operational environments, particularly in an urban context. When fully deployed, a wide range of drone missions that are currently being restricted will be possible owing to a sustainable and robust European ecosystem that is globally interoperable.[28]

The European Commission introduced the U-space initiative to establish an efficient framework for all individuals and businesses to operate drones. It refers to the low-level airspace and covers the ecosystem of services and specific procedures necessary for reliable and safe drone operations.

Within the framework of the Single European Sky, a pan-European initiative, launched in 2004 to deliver a solid ATM system for the continent, the European ATM Master Plan is the main planning tool for defining ATM modernization priorities and ensuring that the SESAR ATM Target Concept becomes a reality.[29]

The smooth and safe handling of flights in Europe's airspace is guaranteed by ATM. This specific work is accomplished by ground-based controllers who direct aircraft on the ground and in the air. Their primary tasks are to prevent collisions and to organize and expedite the flow of air traffic uninterruptedly round the clock. This system has worked very well in the last few decades. However, ageing technology, together with significant increases in the volume of air traffic, higher environmental awareness and the need for

---

28 SESAR JU U-space Blueprint, Luxembourg: Publication Office of the European Union, 2017.
29 SESAR European ATM Master Plan: The Roadmap for Delivering High Performing Aviation for Europe, Executive View, Edition 2015. Single European Sky (SES): the EU's main objective is to reform ATM in Europe in order to cope with sustained air traffic growth and operations under the safest, most cost- and flight-efficient and environmentally friendly conditions. This implies de-fragmenting the European airspace, reducing delays, increasing safety standards and flight efficiency to reduce the aviation environmental footprint, and reducing costs related to service provision. The SES legislative framework consists of four Basic Regulations (No. 549/2004, 550/2004, 551/2004 and 552/2004) covering the provision of air navigation services, the organization and use of airspace and the interoperability of the European Air Traffic Management Network (European Commission > Transport > Transport modes >Air > Single European Sky).

cost efficiency are calling for a fundamental change to the way in which traditional aircraft and drones, including RPAS, are directed in the future. ATM technology is in dire need of major improvements to cope with these challenges.

SESAR is the technological pillar of the SES initiative. The European ATM Master Plan is an evolving road map and the result of strong collaboration between all ATM stakeholders. The modernization, the key of which shall be the digitalization of the ATM system, is and will be the cornerstone of the implementation of the SES initiative and any future SES-related projects. The Master Plan sets the framework for the development activities performed by the SESAR JU and EASA, such as specific regulation and services needed for a safe, secure and efficient integration of drones into European airspace.

While the SESAR JU faces enormous challenges to effectuate the comprehensive Single European Sky objective, the safe, efficient and seamless integration of drones, including RPAS, into all classes of the European airspace will be an almost bigger and rather laborious task to materialize.

The European vision of the safe and seamless integration of drones is not carried out in isolation but in a global context. European efforts and initiatives to collaborate and coordinate at a worldwide level promote convergence of approaches, sharing of experiences and, ultimately, target global interoperability for the integration of drones.

Cooperation between Europe and the United States is achieved through the memorandum of cooperation (MoC) on civil aviation R&D, which includes a specific cooperation plan on UAS. In this framework, the SESAR JU, the FAA and NASA aim to deliver a joint vision for the safe integration of drones in all classes of airspace, including U-space and UTM. This cooperative framework also allows an exchange of views concerning common operational and deployment challenges, including the standardization and regulatory road maps.

4.3 RPAS Integration Alongside Manned Aviation

In the first decade of the 21st century, people with a visionary perspective identified the emergence and proliferation of civil UAS, including RPAS, in bringing civil aviation in the realm of the Third Industrial Revolution. This strongly incentive tipping point could create highly qualified jobs in the manufacturing sector, in R&D, in operations and exploitation of data information acquired through RPAS.

It was recognized that the emerging technology of RPAS applied to the development of non-military aviation applications could help boost industrial competitiveness, promote entrepreneurship and create new businesses to generate growth and jobs, especially, but not only, with respect to the European aviation market.[30]

However, at that time the potential of RPAS was, unfortunately, limited by the fact that RPAS flight authorizations were still issued on a case-by-case basis through burdensome procedures, based on national regulations, unfortunately not necessarily aligned with one another. In addition, RPAS were limited to segregated airspace only, which caused a suboptimal situation in Europe. The need arose to remove the fragmentation by developing a seamless regulatory framework covering all RPAS, enhancing the coordination of various R&D initiatives and achieving a broad, safe and swift integration of RPAS of all sizes into non-segregated airspace.

One basic principle underpinning not just the European but, in fact, the global integration of RPAS applicable at the time and even now, perfectly aligned with the ICAO principles, is that RPAS have to be treated just as manned aircraft while duly considering the specificity of RPAS. RPAS operations have to be compliant with existing aviation regulations, and their integration into the ATM system should not impact current airspace user operations and levels of safety.

RPAS behaviour should therefore be equivalent to manned aviation and should comply with the communications, navigation and surveillance (CNS) requirements applicable to the airspace class within which they are intended to operate. RPAS should also comply with evolutions in the ATM operational concepts, such as trajectory management, being researched within SESAR, as they are deployed. The full potency of RPAS can be realized only if these types of UAS become an integral part of the civil aviation system, regardless of the conditions set. For instance, IFR RPAS must be transparent (alike) to ATC and other airspace users.[31]

However, RPAS rules must be as light as necessary, in order to avoid unnecessarily burdening the emerging industry. Not only are RPAS tailored rules important, but also RPAS integration requires adequately addressing the societal impact of RPAS applications by covering meaningful and responsible elements such as liability, insurance, privacy, etc.

Integration in non-segregated airspace requires mature and standardized related key technologies for RPAS. Experts around the world agree that the integration of RPAS will be gradually and evolutionary, for example, initially restricted access under specified

---

30 SESAR European Drones Outlook Study: Unlocking the Value for Europe, November 2016, pp. 3-4. *See also* COM(2014) 207 final (2015/C 012/14), Brussels 8 April 2014 Communication from the Commission to the European Parliament and the Council, A new era for aviation. Opening the aviation market to the civil use of RPAS in a safe and sustainable manner, Para. 2.
31 PJ. 13 W2 IFR RPAS ID: SESAR-IR-VLD-WAVE2-11-2019, 10 January 2019.

conditions to cope with flight safety and subsequent alleviation of the restrictions as soon as R&D, technology, regulation and societal acceptance are in a progressive mode.

Today, there are a wide array of types of RPAS. Many copy the designs and flight characteristics of traditional civil aircraft. This is particularly true where RPAS may be integrated in traditional manned aviation operations, such as large commercial cargo transport. The opportunities in design, owing to the pilot no longer being situated within the aircraft, mean that novel architectures are possible, although well-adapted traditional aircraft, converted to unmanned aircraft, can also suffice in the RPAS category.

However, unique applications of airframes, power plants, (bio)fuels or any other energy sources and materials can result in flight characteristics that are quite different from traditional manned aircraft, most notably extreme flight endurances, very high altitudes and low-speed flight.

RPAS are themselves multisystems and involve a very wide variety of associated equipment and payloads. Beyond the RPAS manufacturers and system integrators, the RPAS industry also contains a broad supply chain that provides an extensive range of enabling technologies such as flight control, communication, propulsion, energy, sensors, telemetry, etc. In addition, RPAS will generate the emergence of a new, sophisticated service sector. Finally, the development of RPAS technologies is likely to create civil spin-offs with significant impact in many sectors.

The potential for civil RPAS in regard to mobility and transportation purposes in the years to come has considerable implications for airspace management. With increasing demand for this category of RPAS, SESAR affiliates are investigating in Europe the best way to integrate these vehicles into non-segregated airspace alongside traditional manned aviation and even military traffic. The safe integration of RPAS will also need to encompass ground operations, particularly at airports where automated taxiing capabilities are required. The ERSG Roadmap for the integration of civil RPAS into the European Aviation System so far will not focus on fully autonomous aircraft because they lack the capability of a remote pilot in command and his/her associated responsibilities.[32]

---

32 Roadmap for the integration of civil Remotely-Piloted-Aircraft-Systems into the European Aviation System, Final report from the European RPAS Steering Group, June 2013, including the Roadmap and three Annexes. *See also* Drones done right: UK testing integration of drones with manned GA traffic. The first flight tests to combine unmanned aerial drones flying from an airport with regular manned air traffic will be conducted in UK airspace early 2021 by the newly launched Aircraft Innovation Center in Goodwood, Sussex. The UK government has awarded funding for the project. The live trial shows BVLOS UAS operations in non-segregated airspace. Drone operations management company ANRA Technologies, ATM company Trax International and avionics supplier uAvionix are participating in the project (source: Drones IAOPA Newsletter).

CHAPTER 4 INTEGRATION INTO AIRSPACE

The RPAS Steering Group, set up as an outcome of the consultation on the future of RPAS in Europe, conducted by the European Commission between 2009 and 2012, received a mandate to draft the Roadmap for the safe integration of civil RPAS, actually with more substantive means to accommodate RPAS integration into non-segregated ATM environments, such as airspace and aerodromes, on a European scale.[33]

The Roadmap, whose design was completed in 2013, identified all the issues to be addressed and established a step-by-step approach to address them. So far, its aim has been to establish an initial RPAS integration by 2016 and to cover not only the regulatory and R&D perspectives, but also the societal and liability perspectives. By presenting a clear way towards the integration of RPAS, the Roadmap is expected to facilitate the decisions taken by the different organizations, which were involved in the preparation of the Roadmap, to provide transparency and efficiency in the planning phases of various initiatives while supporting the coordination of the related activities within Europe.

It is envisaged that RPAS will ultimately operate in the airspace and ATM environments, mixed with a variety of manned aircraft, from gliders to large airliners, under IFR or visual flight rules (VFR) adhering to the requirements of the specified airspace in which they are operating.

While commercial air transport (CAT) normally flies to move passengers, cargo or mail from one airport to the other, following a profile that includes a take-off and step climb segment, en route to relatively high altitudes composed of essentially straight cruise segments, descent and approach segments, followed by a landing, RPAS comprise a much wider range of possible operations, and in many ways similar to the operations of the general aviation (GA), aerial work, rotorcraft and military or other governmental missions. However for RPAS, able to fly even a few metres above the ground, the Roadmap uses the following taxonomy:

1) VLL operations (alias non-standard VFR or IFR operations) below the typical IFR and VFR minimum flight altitudes for manned aviation: i.e. not to exceed 400 ft AGL; they comprise:

A. VLOS in a range not greater than 500 m from the remote pilot, in which the remote pilot maintains direct unaided visual contact with the remotely piloted aircraft;

B. EVLOS where, beyond 500 m, the pilot is supported by one or more observers, in which the crew maintains direct unaided visual contact with the remotely piloted aircraft (in both VLOS and EVLOS the remote crew shall also be able to see incoming threats);

---

33 The Roadmap is the result of the ERSG, co-chaired by DG Enterprise & DG Mobility & Transport. In addition to the SESAR JU, the Steering Group consists of EASA, EUROCONTROL, JARUS, ECAC, EDA, European Space Agency (ESA), Aerospace and Defence Industries Association of Europe (ASD), UVSI, an international lobby group for the drone industry, European Research Establishments in Aeronautics (EREA), EUROCAE and ECA.

C. BVLOS where the operations are also below 400 ft but where beyond visual line of sight operations require additional technological support.
2) RPAS operations in VFR and IFR, above 400 ft and above minimum flight altitudes; they comprise:
A. IFR (or VFR) operations in radio line of sight (RLOS) of the remote pilot station (in non-segregated airspace where manned aviation is present). The key capability of detect and avoid is required in relation to cooperative and non-cooperative nearby air traffic (otherwise, specific procedures and restrictions would apply);
B. IFR (or VFR) operations beyond radio line of sight (BRLOS) operations, when the RPA can no longer be in direct radio contact with the remote pilot station, and therefore wider range communication (COM) services, including via satellite, are necessary. In this case COM would typically be offered by a COM service provider.[34]

The Roadmap, in helping to address the challenges of RPAS integration in Europe, identifies the actions that should be taken in the areas of regulation, research and the societal impact, taking into account the necessary coordination and interdependencies between these three main streams of activities. Each of these areas is developed in a specific annex to the Roadmap:
– Annex 1 provides a Regulatory Work Plan identifying the improvements to the existing regulatory framework considered necessary to allow RPAS operating outside segregated airspace.
– Annex 2 presents a Strategic R&D Plan identifying the technology enablers and the research activities necessary to achieve a safe integration of RPAS.
– Annex 3 analyses aspects of the societal impact of RPAS.

Annex 1, entitled 'A Regulatory Approach for the integration of civil RPAS into the European Aviation System', has been structured to initially provide an introduction and the high-level objectives, followed by a work programme required to achieve full RPAS integration. The work programme is organized in four time frames, linked to the ICAO Global Air Navigation Plan (GANP) and the Aviation System Block Upgrades (ASBUs), with initial priority for harmonization of rules to safely open the internal market for light RPA (MTOM below 150 kg) and parallel extension of scope of EASA, paving the way for common rules to be published soon after 2018.

---

34 UVS International Remotely Piloted Systems: promoting International Cooperation & Coordination. Outline of the ERSG Roadmap, Ann. 1 A Regulatory Approach for the integration of civil RPAS into the European Aviation System, p. 7 (The altitudes that are identified for the aforementioned operations are of a generic nature, ignoring national differences notified to ICAO or exemptions).

The first two time frames include a description of the activities in three layers:
- Layer 1: Regulatory Improvements (RI);
- Layer 2: detailed actions to achieve each RI and expected deliverables;
- Layer 3: intentions of the contributing organizations.

The latter two time frames in the first edition of the REG Roadmap are described only in terms of RI.

Annex 2, entitled 'A Strategic R&D Plan for the integration of civil RPAS into the European Aviation System', has been structured to initially provide an introduction of the objectives and the high-level principles governing the R&D Roadmap, followed by the identification of the integration requirements, as well as the identified operational and technological system gaps of enablers that are required to achieve full RPAS integration. R&D activities have, on the basis of these findings, been grouped in specific operational and technical gaps around specific types of foreseen operations not only considering the specific time frames according to the European ATM Master Plan, which is already linked to the ICAO GANP and the ASBUs, but also bearing in mind possible early opportunities or quick wins. The R&D Roadmap includes a first analysis of the risks related to the successful implementation of the complete set of identified R&D Roadmap activities required to achieve full RPAS integration.

Annex 3, entitled 'A study on the societal impact of the integration of civil RPAS into the European Aviation System', provides a first analysis of the impact the development of RPAS applications could have on society. The main topics addressed include:
- In case of accident: liability, including issues like enforcement and impact of automation, and insurance;
- the protection against abusive use: data protection, privacy and security; and
- public acceptance of RPAS applications: benefits, acceptable risk/safety, end-user forum, demonstrations, etc.

Its aim is to provide the European Commission with preliminary views on some of the actions that might be required to address the RPAS impact, allowing society to benefit from innovative technology, while minimizing potential threats. Information is given concerning the overall legal framework defining responsibility/liability at the national and international levels.

RPAS are covered in Europe by Directive 95/46/EC (Data Protection Directive) on the protection of fundamental rights and freedoms of natural persons, and, in particular, their right of privacy with respect to the processing of personal data wholly or partly by automatic means, and to the processing other than by automatic means of personal data, which form part of a filing system or are intended to form part of a filing system.

Subsequently, added coverage has been instigated by two Commission Proposals in the same area, COM(2012) 10 final and COM(2012) 11 final.³⁵

Benefits for citizens highlight the possible use of RPAS for civil protection and environmental monitoring. The industry insists on the need to develop specific rules allowing these applications to develop. The study also proposes ideas to increase public awareness on the benefits of RPAS.

The Roadmap envisages that EASA will produce, as soon as practically possible, RPAS rules within the remit of its current competencies. In parallel, national CAAs in the European Union are expected to further develop and/or harmonize their national regulations on the basis of the recommendations and guidance materials developed by the Joint Authorities for Rulemaking on Unmanned Systems (JARUS) and published by EASA. Because of their specific experience and resources, national CAAs in the EU are also invited to contribute actively to the work of JARUS.

The Roadmap for the safe integration of civil RPAS identifies 27 regulatory improvements to be achieved, according to subsequent time frames: 2013, 2014-2018, 2019-2023 and 2024-2028. Possible disruptive delays, occurring in a specific activity, do not mean that the sequence of activities will have to change but that only the suggested dates will have to be adjusted. For each regulatory improvement a detailed planning system will identify the necessary deliverables, the responsible organization, dependencies and deadlines.³⁶

As the required technologies were not yet available during the presentation of the Roadmap, it identified technological gaps in six activity areas:

---

35 Directive 95/46/EC of the European Parliament and of the Council of 24 October 1995 on the protection of individuals with regard to the processing of personal data and on the free movement of such data, OJ L 281/31, 23 November 1995. COM(2012) 10 final, 2012/0010 (COD), Brussels, 25 January 2012 Proposal for a Directive of the European Parliament and of the Council on the protection of individuals with regard to the processing of personal data by competent authorities for the purposes of prevention, investigation, detection or prosecution of criminal offences or the execution of criminal penalties, and the free movement of such data. COM(2012) 11 final, 2012/0011 (COD), Brussels, 25 January 2012. Proposal for a Regulation of the European Parliament and of the Council on the protection of individuals with regard to the processing of personal data and on the free movement of such data (General Data Protection Regulation).

36 ERSG Roadmap, Chapter 4, Para. 4.2 Resulting Airspace Access. Planning issues in specific timeframes. Timeframe 2013 light RPA (<150 kg) operations in VLOS and EVLOS in a number of EU Member States. Timeframe 2014-2018. VLOS and EVLOS operations of light RPA will have become a daily occurrence, thanks to the progressive harmonization of national rules. Timeframe 2019-2023. In this timeframe, licensed remote pilots, under the responsibility of certified RPAS operators, would be able to operate approved RPAS, comprising an airworthy RPA, under IFR in almost all airspace classes. Common and proportionate rules developed by EASA, progressively apply to civil RPAS, comprising RPA of any MTOM. Timeframe 2024-2028. In this timeframe, among other things, besides the evolution of technical and operational rules, which will lead to alleviation of residual restrictions, RPAS are expected to operate in most non-segregated airspace, mixed with manned aviation, following the same ATM procedures and ensuring the same level of safety and security.

- Integration into ATM and airspace environments.
- Verification and validation.
- Data communication links including spectrum issues.
- Detect and avoid systems and operational procedures.
- Security issues.
- Operational contingency procedures and systems.
- Surface operations, including take-off and landing.

The Roadmap reiterates that achieving the full integration of all types of RPAS requires the development of appropriate regulations in the three essential domains of airworthiness, flight crew licensing (remote pilots) and air operations. These are essential prerequisite safety requirements for integration into non-segregated airspace. Since this task is considered extremely complex, the Roadmap proposes to address this issue through a stepwise approach lasting over 15 years, well synchronized with the ICAO ASBU concept and ensuring a close coordination with R&D plans and the development of the necessary technologies.[37]

The ERSG has suggested that all R&D initiatives supporting the safe integration of civil RPAS into the aviation system need to be addressed under the umbrella of the SESAR programme. This will enable an efficient coordination of all R&D efforts at the European level and will assist the coordination with other initiatives of relevance to this aviation sector, in particular the military ones, as many of the enabling technologies for RPAS integration are dual-use.

Last but not the least, the ERSG is of the opinion that the R&D activities that have been identified for the purpose of the integration of RPAS into the general airspace, in particular non-segregated airspace and ATM environments, could as well serve the evolution of operational procedures and technical systems for manned aviation to further enhance flight safety and efficiency and improve environmental friendliness.

Between 2009 and 2012, the European Commission identified many other issues to be addressed in the near future simultaneously with the safe integration of RPAS, in order to ensure the societal acceptance of this new advancing technology. Securing societal acceptance is entirely dependent on a tailored legal framework concerning third-party liability and insurance, security and privacy and protection of personal data.

The objective of the Roadmap still is to support the development of RPAS applications, while ensuring the safety, security and privacy of citizens as well as the safety of other airspace users. Nevertheless, accidents might happen, occasionally causing damage to third parties, including people or property on the surface, and to other airspace users. If

---

37 ICAO Aviation System Block Upgrades (ASBUs) provide a consensus-driven modernization framework for integrated planning based on performance. ASBUs will increase the capacity and improve the efficiency of the global civil aviation system.

an accident is caused by an RPAS operation, there is a need to adequately compensate for any injury, casualty or damage to property, similar to manned aviation.

Regarding RPAS and the issue of security, it is quite obvious that RPAS run the risk of being hijacked and de facto used as a lethal weapon against other airspace users or specific targets on the surface. Terrorists are also able to crash their own RPAS into preordained, vital targets or jam or spoof GPS signals to other RPAS or traditional aircraft, causing serious hazards to aviation safety. These malicious acts could be achieved by any means, such as physical attacks on the RPS or the remote pilot(s), and electronic attacks such as jamming or spoofing of data links or different satellite navigation systems.

On the other hand, signal-jamming systems could deter unwanted flight operations. Developed by Airbus Defense & Space, a so-called Counter-UAV System is able to detect illicit intrusions of UAS into critical airspace segments, such as aerodrome CTRs and TMAs at long range, and offers electronic countermeasures minimizing the risk of collateral damage.

This quick response protection system can disable signals between an RPA and its operator or, in some cases, jam its navigation system to legally intervene, allowing a takeover of the operation to prevent prohibited airspace infringements. It can also be used against cyberattacks on specific information networks or the hacking of vital RPAS C2 systems, the consequences of which could represent a major challenge for future large-scale RPAS operations such as air cargo transportation.[38]

The increased use of low-cost RPAS, which is the result of their progressive, unobtrusive and playful integration into the airspace together with their attractive purchase price, flexibility and even more sophisticated sensors, is making RPAS unique tools in the area of privacy. However, they may raise serious and unparalleled privacy and data protection concerns in society, thereby undermining the overall benefits of this innovative technology, although privacy and data protection are enshrined in a comprehensive legal framework consisting of national laws, the EU treaty and directives and international fundamental rights charters. RPAS operators do have to comply with the rules and regulations of this versatile decisive legal framework, although ensuring compliance with these legal rules is primarily a responsibility of the EU Member States.

Eventually, large cargo air vehicles (CAVs), expected to be RPA (the platform) with an authorized operator and licensed remote pilots, will fly under IFR. With regard to air traffic avoidance, these large drones are required to have a detection system such as the airborne collision avoidance system (ACAS). If this system diagnoses a risk of impending

---

38   *See* Counter-UAV System from Airbus Defence & Space protects large installations and events from illicit intrusion, 16 September 2015.

collision, it issues a resolution advisory (RA) to the remote pilot, which directs the remote pilot how best to regulate or adjust the vertical rate so as to avoid a collision. Naturally, these drones must, among others, adhere to the international airspace infrastructure (semi circular cruising system), and ATC alerting instructions pertaining to intruder aircraft.

Under VFR, which means weather conditions equal to or better than the minimum requirement for a flight under these visual flight rules, visibility must be such that the remote pilot of an RPA must be capable to detect and avoid another aircraft. This detection and avoid technology is assumed to be similar to the human capability of see and avoid.

Another evolving technology must provide RPA with capabilities to perceive adverse weather conditions to be able to take subsequent corrective actions in the interest of flight safety. This technology must be a substitute for the human eye, judgment and experience. In terms of aviation rules, all RPAS will be expected to comply with the applicable procedures and airspace requirements such as rules of the air defined by the state and/or ICAO, including contingency and emergency procedures, which should be established with the respective ANSPs.

The behaviour under abnormal, contingency conditions could be very different from regular flight profiles and performance characteristics, but some degree of predictability and conformance to existing defined procedures will be needed to minimize conflict with other traffic. In other words, where RPAS are able to comply in a manner similar to manned aviation, they should follow the conventional system with the responsibility to fly safely. No doubt, RPAS have to comply with the aviation rules, especially but not limited to the rules of the air, which means that RPAS integration should not impact on the traditional airspace users. As a matter of fact, this requirement excludes degradation of the achieved safety level in the air, disruption of current operations, modification of ATC procedures and any additional mandatory equipment caused by RPAS.

Under any circumstances, RPAS should be able to operate safely alongside manned aviation, respecting ICAO's key principles expressed in Circular 328-AN/190, as stated in its RPAS Concept of Operations (CONOPS) 2017.[39] RPAS must comply with the communication, navigation and surveillance requirements applicable to the class of airspace within which they intend to operate as well as the trajectory management concept envisaged in the SESAR system and associated ATC rules and procedures as expressed in the following restrictive points:
- In order to integrate seamlessly into the airspace, RPAS must, as far as possible, comply with the operational procedures that exist for manned aircraft. Flight

---

39 ICAO Remotely Piloted Aircraft System (RPAS) Concept of Operations (CONOPS) for International IFR Operations, March 2017, pp. 1-5.

operations must not present an undue hazard or burden to persons, property or other aircraft.
- RPAS operations must not degrade the current level of aviation safety or impair manned aviation safety or efficiency. This applies to all operators and all drones.
- RPAS should conform to manned aircraft standards to the greatest extent possible. When the ICAO key principles are not achievable, owing to unique RPAS designs or flight characteristics, and no alternative means of compliance are identified, the operation of such RPAS may be subject to safety risk mitigations, such as restricting operations to remain within segregated airspace.

When these principles are not achievable because of the unique design or flight characteristics, and no alternative means of compliance are identified, the operation of such RPAS may be subject to safety risk mitigations, such as restricting operations to segregated airspace. The key assumptions, which can be considered to apply to all RPAS operations, are described as follows:
- Access to the airspace remains available to all, providing each RPA is capable of meeting pertinent conditions, regulations, processes and equipage defined for that airspace;
- new types of operations may need additional or alternative considerations, conditions, regulations, processes and operating procedures; the objective should be to add only the minimum necessary to achieve safe operation;
- the RPA has the functional capability to meet the established normal and contingency operating procedures for the class of airspace, aerodrome, etc, when such procedures are available;
- the flight operation does not impede or impair other airspace users, service providers, such as air traffic management, aerodromes, etc, or the safety of third parties on the surface and their property, etc;
- the RPA must operate in accordance with the rules of the air;
- the RPAS must meet the applicable certification, registration and approval requirements;
- the operator must meet the applicable certification and approval requirements; and
- the remote pilot must be competent, licensed and capable of discharging the responsibility for safe flight.

Continuously evolving technologies will give flight automation an ever-increasing role. After all, it is multidisciplinary technology (mechatronics and robotics) that enables automation. Automation systems in both manned and unmanned aircraft are capable of controlling the aircraft throughout its full flight regime, including take-off, optimum climb, cruise and descent profiles, approach and landing trajectory, balancing fuel, failure management, transmitting and receiving data, identifying conflicting traffic and providing traffic and resolution advisories by means of a detect and avoid system, more sophisticated than ACAS II, either self-governed or monitored by (remote) pilots.[40]

Critical decision areas regarding autonomous or remotely piloted flights are the take-off roll, especially go/no-go decision-making in this very dynamic transition (the operational significance of V1), and the applicable CAT IIIc autoland procedure augmented by synthetic vision systems (SVSs), the combined use of synthetic and visual (internal and ambient cameras) cues to meet the intent of see and avoid, comparable to a pilot on board. Considering RPAS, the remote pilot will get all the inputs to be able to conduct a successful trajectory all the way.

That does not alter the fact that nowadays technology is so advanced that, with the actuation of a single push button in the (remote) cockpit, a fully automatic approach and landing without any further human aid or input will be accomplished. The application is primarily intended in the event of an emergency situation. The avionics system automatically tunes its transponder to the 7700 code, alerting the ground stations, and will select a route to a safe and suitable destination by using its onboard obstacle and terrain databases and satellite-delivered destination weather and forecast, and the GPS approach feature. During descent and approach, the system communicates automatically by means of a digitalized voice with ATC and uses detect and avoid. Nearing the selected airport, the system reduces airspeed, sets the altimeter to the landing field elevation and the aircraft in the landing configuration with flaps and landing gear down, spoilers and autobrakes armed, and then executes an autoland and roll-out to a full stop followed by engine shutdown.[41]

The see and avoid requirement, which is both implicit and stated in the Annexes to the Chicago Convention, presents a unique challenge to those wishing to operate RPAS in international non-segregated airspace. As an RPA has no pilot on board to provide the see and avoid capability that is self-evident for manned aviation, in other words, the ability to visually perceive other traffic, processing the information as only a human is able to do, followed by taking the necessary action to avoid a collision, no airborne see and avoid system has been certified yet as being capable of replacing the ability of a

---

40 Airbus has successfully performed the first fully automatic vision-based take-off using an Airbus Family test aircraft (A350-1000) at Toulouse-Blagnac airport on 16 January 2020. Airbus' Autonomous Taxi, Take-off & Landing (ATTOL) project.
41 Ostrower, J., 'Emergency Autoland puts Garmin on the Bleeding Edge of Autonomous Flying', *The Air Current*, 3 November 2019.

human pilot on board the aircraft to provide the see and avoid capability that is required for flights in international airspace.[42]

For optimum and safe operating conditions, it must be demonstrated that each individual RPAS is in conformity with the certified design throughout its operational life span.

In order to achieve integration with manned aviation, a phased approach is envisaged:
- Phase 1: IFR RPAS in classes A-C: RPAS will be able to operate in airspace classes A-C under IFR, with a detect and avoid system that provides collision avoidance and situational awareness in relation to cooperative traffic. RPAS will be able to communicate with ATC. Navigation and surveillance equipment will be proportional to the airspace in which the drone is operating. Special provisions will be needed for ground operations at most airports. Procedures and technology for dealing with contingency situations will be in place.
- Phase 2: IFR RPAS in classes A-G: RPAS flying under IFR will have detect and avoid capability, enabling them to integrate with other IFR and VFR traffic, both cooperative and non-cooperative, in airspace classes A-G. Communication with ATC will use an appropriate architecture, addressing integrity and security requirements.
- Phase 3: RPAS in classes A-G (IFR and VFR): RPAS will be able to operate in controlled and uncontrolled airspace, both under IFR or VFR, and safely integrate with cooperative and non-cooperative traffic. Increased use of data link for ATC communications is likely. Work on broadening the range of drone types and missions continues, and the ATM environment starts to evolve as routine operations diversify.

Phase 1 and phase 2 correspond to the so-called ICAO accommodation period, while phase 3 equates to the so-called ICAO integration period. Accommodation refers to the condition when RPAS can operate along with some level of adaption or support that compensates for its inability to comply within existing operational constructs. This may be necessary during normal operations, abnormal or problem scenarios, and when emergency situations arise. Integration refers to a future when RPAS may be expected to enter the airspace routinely without requiring special provisions.

Suitably equipped RPAS can therefore integrate as soon as the aircraft and the supporting ATM environment allow such integration. The integration phase foresees a

---

42 FAA. Detect and Avoid Unmanned Aircraft Systems Operational Assessment: Visual Compliance. Purpose: The research associated with Detect and Avoid (DAA) UAS Operational Assessment Visual Compliance will: Identify how a UAS will meet the need to visually comply with regulations and ATC clearances. Background: It is difficult for DAA systems to obtain operational and airworthiness approval because these systems are new and their intended function needs to be defined in the context of DAA systems and associated UAS. UAS will need to visually comply with ATC clearances and regulations, and the impact of such operations (source: www.faa.gov/uas/research_development/information_papers/).

time when all European ATM environments can support routine RPAS operations; however, this does not prevent early adopters from operating.[43]

As in manned aviation, the Roadmap considers that an RPAS operator will obtain permission to operate only when essential prerequisites are to be in place to safeguard the entire aviation safety system. The three following basic prerequisites are expected to apply to RPAS:
1. RPAS must be approved by a competent authority. According to ICAO, they are systems comprising an RPA or platform, one or more associated remote pilot stations (RPS), the required C2 links, including those supported by satellite communications, and any other components as specified in the type design of the RPAS.
2. The RPAS operator must hold a valid RPAS Operator Certificate.
3. The remote pilot must hold a valid licence.

The highest possible and uniform level of safety, the achievement and maintaining of which is one of the principal objectives of the aviation regulatory framework, shall be set through essential requirements adopted by the legislature, following substantial consensus by all involved parties during the rule-making process. The risk must be considered in relation to the type of RPAS operation involved and the different sizes of RPAS that are designed, manufactured, operated and maintained in such a manner that the risk to people and property on the surface and other airspace users is considered to be at an acceptable level.

Enabling successful safe operations of RPAS BVLOS in either controlled or uncontrolled airspace will require the availability of a variety of technologies that are suggested to require not only European but worldwide support to an effective integration.
Operational technology requirements:
- Detect and avoid capabilities are seen as a key enabler for drone operations in all classes of airspace and are expected to have a positive impact on safety and social acceptance. Depending on the flight rules: in IFR, the detect and avoid system performs the collision avoidance function against cooperative and non-cooperative traffic.

---

43 SESAR JU European ATM Master Plan: Roadmap for the Safe Integration of Drones in All Classes of Airspace, 19 March 2018, pp. 9-10.

- Datacom and spectrum issues are critical to enabling BVLOS or even BRLOS and long-endurance RPAS cargo flights to be conducted in safe conditions.[44] Appropriate data links are necessary for C2 as well as, in a potential sense, for communication with ATC. Major challenges when it comes to data links are the identification, allocation and protection of the necessary spectrum.
- Security and cyber resilience is a priority area of development to mitigate the risk that RPAS could be subjected to malicious or accidental takeovers of data links leading to accidents, theft or deliberate use of the aircraft to damage infrastructure or hurt civilians.
- Those significant issues could have a severe negative impact on public acceptance. Clear concepts of operations, requirements and standards are needed to drive research into a more advanced and coordinated phase.
- Human factors and training will need additional R&D efforts to ensure that the situational awareness of remote pilots matches that of pilots in the cockpit. Additionally, there will be a requirement to manage the transition from RPAS to more automated drones that are only monitored. In order to achieve those purposes, effective solutions with respect to contingency, failure management, etc. will need to be put in place. Harmonization of the operator's environment is likely to lead to more appropriate training and a higher level of safety.
- Training and qualification is an underlying topic that requires immediate action from the European Union to provide new, well-trained remote pilots. Achieving EU-wide accepted remote pilot licences would accelerate the creation of RPAS commercially operated airlines.
- Validation and demonstration will be important to increase public acceptance of RPAS operations and will support the regulatory work. Although some validation exercises are performed at the national level, broader authorized and safe testing environments to perform integrated demonstrations, involving manned and unmanned aircraft, especially RPAS, operating simultaneously, will be needed.
- ATM requires further R&D. All previously mentioned research and development topics depend on how ATM will integrate RPAS in all classes of airspace. The basic principles of drone traffic management, especially RPAS, as defined by the CONOPS, will lead to precise requirements on which industry standards will be developed, thereby assuring a strong basis for future investments and partnerships across private industry players and public EU Member States and stakeholders.

---

44 BRLOS refers to any configuration in which transmitters and receivers are not in RLOS (radio line of sight). BRLOS thus includes all satellite systems and possibly any station where an RPS (remote pilot station) communicates with one or more ground stations via a terrestrial network that cannot complete transmissions in a time frame comparable to that of an RLOS system (source: ICAO Remotely Piloted Aircraft System (RPAS) Concept of Operations (CONOPS) for International IFR Operations, March 2017, pp. 7-10).

4.4 U-Space

Practically all over the world, the use of drones is a steadily growing business, technically capable of providing services in all environments, including urban areas. It is poised to generate significant economic growth and societal benefits. The challenge will be to create a legal framework that will facilitate the growing market while also handling the increased drone traffic alongside traditional civil aviation in a safe and efficient manner. This is where U-space comes, according to a notion which was first mooted by Violeta Bulc, European Commissioner for Mobility and Transport at the 2016 Warsaw High Level Conference, also attended by Executive Directors of EASA, SESAR, the Polish CAA and a number of DGCAs from EU Member States, as well as representatives of ICAO, international associations, European aviation bodies, agencies together with leaders of the industry, resulting in the Warsaw Declaration.[45]

The Warsaw High Level Conference called for the development of the concept of U-space on access to low-level airspace, especially in urban areas and all related aspects such as a regulatory framework, including the timely delivery of industry standards, the efficacy and funding of drone integration projects and the development of the U-space framework.

U-space is a set of new services and specific procedures designed to support safe, efficient and secure access to airspace for a large number of drones. These services rely on a high level of digitalization and automation of functions, whether they are on board the drone itself or are part of the ground-based environment. As such, U-space is enabling a framework designed to facilitate any kind of routine mission, in all classes of airspace and all types of environment – even the most congested – while addressing an appropriate interface to manned aviation, ATM/ANS service providers and authorities.

The establishment of the U-space airspace and the provisions for U-space services are considered essential to respond to the anticipated proliferation of unmanned aircraft operations, especially today in low-level airspace, which is expected to outpace the volume of traffic currently seen with manned aircraft. Because in 2021 and beyond, apart from undue delay, the ATM system is already reaching its limits, and as the expected UAS traffic and flying characteristics of the unmanned aircraft – the pilot is not on board and the level of automation is higher – are different from those of manned aircraft, ATM cannot be seen as the only appropriate means to safely and efficiently manage the upcoming UAS traffic.

---

45 Warsaw High Level Conference on 23-24 November 2016. The conference called for a number of well-coordinated actions to develop the EU drone ecosystem and to deliver it by 2019, building on the guiding principles set forth in the Riga Declaration on Remotely Piloted Aircraft (Drones), 'Framing the Future of Aviation', Riga, 6 March 2015. The conference concluded on 24 November 2016 with the Warsaw Declaration 'Drones as a leverage for jobs and new business opportunities'. (https://ec.europa.eu/transport/sites/transport/files/drones-warsaw-declaration.pdf).

Consequently, in the coming years there is a need to complement existing European regulations for UAS operations in the Open and Specific categories with a European regulatory framework that enables harmonized implementation of U-space and is adapted to the task of ensuring safe and sound management of UAS traffic.

Indeed, U-space is the enabler to manage more complex and longer-distance operations and to ensure that operations such as BVLOS operations or urban air mobility are supported with services that enhance safety, security, privacy and efficiency of these operations. Given the tremendous increase in UAS traffic and its complexity aspect, the need for U-space airspace and U-space services is expected to increase and may cover the entire airspace in which BVLOS and operations of UAS with a higher level of autonomy are conducted.

The U-space airspace and U-space services are also needed to ensure fair access of UAS operators to the airspace in a cost-effective manner through a competitive U-space service market. The European approach will facilitate this competitive model by providing the basis for common data exchange protocols, establishing a cooperative environment where all the necessary information is available and transmitted to those who need it, in order to ensure seamless exchange of aircraft operators' positions and UAS operators' intent, operational constraints and other data critical for safety and security purposes.[46]

The U-space framework comprises an extensive and scalable range of services relying on agreed EU standards and delivered by service providers. These services do not replicate the function of ATC, as known in ATM, but deliver key services to organize the safe and efficient operation of drones and ensure a proper interface with manned aviation, ATC and relevant authorities. They may include the provision of data, supporting services for drone operators such as flight planning assistance and more structured services such as tracking or capacity management.

U-space is therefore not to be considered as a defined volume of airspace, which is segregated and designed for the sole use of drones. U-space covers altitudes of up to 150 m (500 ft AGL) and will pave the way for the development of a strong and dynamic EU drone services market. The design makes it capable of ensuring the smooth operation of drones in all operating environments and all types of airspace (in particular, but not limited to, VLL airspace). It addresses the needs to support all types of missions and may concern all drone users and categories of drones. Furthermore, the U-space system will provide information for highly automated drones to fly safely and avoid obstacles or collisions in all types of operational environments, particularly in an urban context.

The ultimate objective of U-space in its final stage is to prevent collisions between manned and unmanned aircraft and mitigate the air and ground risks. The final stage of U-space is when all the necessary U-space services are completely defined, developed,

---

46   EASA Opinion No. 01/2020 High-level regulatory framework for the U-space, RMT.0230, 13 March 2020, p. 5, with the Annex to EASA Opinion No. 01/2020: draft Commission Implementing Regulation (EU).

demonstrated, validated, available and deployed. Another key objective is to create a competitive U-space services market that leads to safe and sustainable operations in the U-space airspace. Only a clear EU regulatory framework can establish a competitive European U-space services market to attract business investments in both the UAS and U-space services markets. An effective and enforceable regulatory framework should support and enable operational, technical and business developments, and provide fair access to all airspace users, so that the market can drive the delivery of the U-space services to cater to the needs of UAS operators.

The U-space regulation should support a level of environmental protection, security and privacy that is acceptable to the general public. In particular, privacy is considered as a major threat to the development of the UAS market as UAS operations can be and are conducted closer to the ground and therefore closer to people. At the same time, it should provide enough flexibility for the drone industry to evolve, innovate and mature as many of the technical solutions and U-space services are still under development and demonstration phases.

Therefore, the U-space regulation should be not only performance based but also risk based. It should ensure interoperability and consistency with the existing Regulation (EU) 2019/947 and Regulation (EU) 2019/945 and provide the necessary flexibility to allow for local implementation at the level of the EU Member State or even at regional/local level that is suitable for and adapted to the local UAS traffic environment and expected traffic complexity. Still, the implementation should be sufficiently harmonized across the European Union.

The main objectives of the U-space services are to:
- Prevent collision between UAS and between UAS and manned aviation;
- expedite and maintain an orderly flow of UAS traffic;
- provide information and instructions relevant to the safe and efficient conduct of UAS operations;
- notify appropriate organizations regarding emergency or abnormal situations with the UAS that may endanger people and property on the surface or manned aviation; and
- ensure that the environmental, security and privacy requirements, applicable in the Member States, are met.

The delivery of U-space relies on the following key principles:
- To ensure the safety of all airspace users operating in the U-space framework, as well as people on the surface.
- To provide a scalable, flexible and adaptable system that can respond to changes in demand, volume, technology, business models and applications, while managing the interface with manned aviation.

- To enable high-density operations with multiple automated drones under the supervision of fleet operators.
- To guarantee equitable and fair access to airspace for all users.
- To enable competitive and cost-effective service provision at all times, supporting the business models of drone operators.
- To minimize deployment and operating costs by leveraging, as much as possible, existing aeronautical services and infrastructure, including the GNSS, as well as those from other sectors, such as mobile communication services.
- To accelerate deployment by adopting technologies and standards from other sectors where they meet the needs of U-space.
- To follow a risk-based and performance-driven approach when setting up appropriate requirements for safety, security (including data-, information- and cybersecurity) and resilience (including failure mode management), while minimizing environmental impact and respecting the privacy of citizens, including data protection.[47]

Cybersecurity architecture should be established at an early stage of U-space development. It is obvious that the future ATM system and U-space will rely on an increase in interconnected systems based on novel technologies, quite different from the current ATM system, consisting of many bespoke systems and networks, operating mainly according to national and proprietary standards. Building on current cybersecurity best practices in the information technology domain, a number of guiding principles should be defined for the operational and technical measures that are needed to strengthen cyber resilience. Interoperability is a key factor in delivering operational improvements through a shared view of all aeronautical information.

Two key concerns that threaten these benefits have been identified:
- Increased interconnectivity and integration will create new vulnerabilities to cyberattacks, for example through third-party access to ATM systems and networks.
- Interoperability implies an increased use of commercial off-the-shelf components and, without careful planning, a corresponding loss of diversity. This increases the likelihood of introducing common vulnerabilities into the system even if, by using open standards, there is also a larger group of users who are actively finding and fixing vulnerabilities.

---

47 *See also* EASA Notice of Proposed Amendment (NPA) 2019-07 Management of information security risks RMT.0720, – In order to ensure appropriate proportionality of the risks involved, the proposed requirements shall not apply to the following organizations: operators of unmanned aircraft systems (UAS) that belong to the Open and Specific categories (as per Opinion No. 01/2018), NPA 2019-07, pp. 13-14.

UAS traffic management is a concept that brings an automated ATM-like system to VLL airspace, which will be occupied primarily by unmanned aircraft or drones. Development is under way in a number of states, mainly in Europe and in the United States, at universities, international aviation organizations and by large aviation corporations and new start-up tech companies. In the United States, UTM is a so-called traffic management ecosystem that is separate from, but complementary to, the FAA's ATM system. The UAS business sector is growing rapidly, but in Europe today this sector is held back by the absence of a harmonized approach for the integration of UAS into VLL airspace. The CORUS (Concept of Operation for European UTM Systems) project gathers experts from manned and unmanned aviation, research and academia to develop a reference to CONOPS for UTM in VLL airspace within Europe.

Building on the state of the art, today and tomorrow, CORUS will develop an operational concept enabling safe interaction between all airspace users in VLL considering contingencies and societal issues. Specifically, CORUS will:

1. Establish a CONOPS for nominal situations, developing use cases for major scenarios.
2. Address drone operations in the vicinity of airfields and controlled airspace and for transfer between controlled and non-controlled airspace segments.
3. Describe how losses of safety in non-nominal drone situations can be minimized.
4. Examine non-aviation aspects, identifying key issues for society and offering solutions to ease societal acceptance.
5. Identify necessary technical developments, quantifying the level of safety and performance required.

The broad acceptance of the CORUS CONOPS is paramount. To this end, CORUS will establish a 'UTM community network', drawing on a wide range of stakeholders, to guide and review the development through a series of workshops. A subset of this network will form an advisory board to review draft documents and answer questions. Through these bodies coordination with other ongoing research and rule-making initiatives from the European Commission, EUROCAE, EASA, JARUS and NASA's UTM research project will be ensured, as well as the regular interaction with the Work Area 2 projects of the same 'Call for proposal'.[48]

Comprehensive communication and dissemination activities will be implemented to ensure the widest possible outreach of the project outcomes throughout the project's life. Duration of the project: September 2017-November 2019, Status: Complete (Parent programmes: H2020-EU.3.4. – Horizon 2020: Smart, Green and Integrated Transport).

---

48 Partners of CORUS: EUROCONTROL (the project's main contributor and coordinator), Unifly, Hemav Technology SL, Direction des Services de la Navigation Aérienne (DSNA), ENAV S.p.A. (Italian ANSP), Deutsches Zentrum für Luft- und Raumfahrt e.V. (DLR), NATS (En Route) PLC, Universitat Politècnica de Catalunya, and DFS Deutsche Flugsicherung GmbH. Call for proposal: H2020-SESAR-2016-1.

A variety of national and international organizations such as ICAO and EASA, bodies such as JARUS and EUROCAE, and initiatives such as NASA UTM, NASA Urban Air Mobility and the Global UTM Association (GUTMA) have been formed in recent years. The objectives range from the provision of legal framework conditions for a future UTM and possible CONOPS for the use of UAS to technical and operational requirements for the architecture of a future UTM system.

In early 2017 in the European Union, SESAR continued to develop a blueprint regarding U-space in preparation for the SESAR JU project. This project is making progress on the development of U-space, the European framework for safe and secure drone operations in VLL airspace. The SESAR Information Management Portal to Enable the Integration of Unmanned Systems (IMPETUS) project, one of the SESAR Very Large Scale Demonstration (VLD) projects, being part of the vast applicable demonstrator network, is investigating and testing information management solutions for U-space. The purpose of the U-space demonstrator network is to reduce red tape, de-risk implementations, accelerate lead time to the market, share lessons learned and best practices and provide a platform for public authorities and industry.[49]

Initially, the project identified the information needs of drone operators by reviewing the entire drone operational life cycle, starting with mission and individual flight planning, continuing via traffic planning, mission and flight execution and ending with the end customer who receives the service. The project also proposes technologically and commercially feasible solutions to address those information management needs. Drone information services will be significantly more detailed, diverse and dynamic.

Safety-critical information, for instance, will be needed at a much higher fidelity than in today's solutions, such as geospatial information services to ensure surface clearance, local weather information to calculate drone trajectory uncertainties and non-conventional navigation sources, such as signals of opportunity and vision-based navigation, to allow for more precise navigation on a local scale.

In June 2017, SESAR JU, whose role it is to develop the new-generation European ATM system following a request by the European Commission, unveiled its U-space blueprint setting out the vision on how to make U-space operationally possible. The vision aims to enable complex drone operations with a high degree of automation to happen in all types of operational environments, in particular in an urban context. In addition, the blueprint will ensure that drone use in low-level airspace will be safe, secure and environmentally friendly.

---

49 On 19 October 2019, the European Commission launched the European Network of U-space Demonstrators to support U-space projects and solutions. It is a forum to share knowledge on how to keep drone operations safe, secure and green. It focuses on U-space, which is a system that connects all drones flying in the air and that makes all drones visible for authorities and citizens. For red tape reduction attempts regarding drones in a number of states, see: Hodgekinson, D., Johnston, R., *Aviation Law and Drones: Unmanned Aircraft and the Future of Aviation*, Milton Park, Abingdon, Oxon: Routledge, 2018, p. 35.

Delivering services in urban areas, collection of data for a wide range of industries, infrastructure inspections, precision agriculture, transportation and logistics are just some of the possible applications of drone technology. When fully deployed in the foreseeable future, a wide range of drone missions, which are currently being restricted in most areas, will be made possible with the help of a sustainable and vigorous European ecosystem that is globally interoperable.[50]

The progressive deployment of U-space is linked to the increasing availability of blocks of services and enabling technologies. It is foreseen in an incremental manner: each new phase will propose a new set of services and appropriate capabilities while including an upgraded version of the services already existing from the previous phase. The roll-out of each new phase should be seen as a high-level sequence for EU-wide harmonization; however, implementations can be fast-tracked in parallel at the local level and for certain types of operations of lower risk and complexity.

As the range of mission types expands, and U-space services are deployed and enhanced, drones of all types and the supporting ground-based infrastructure will need to have capabilities that evolve accordingly. Over time, U-space services will evolve and scale up as the level of automation of the drone increases and advanced forms of interaction with the environment are enabled (including manned and unmanned aircraft) mainly through digital information and data exchange.

Three U-space services (4 sets of U-space services are discussed in further detail) have already been identified as foundational or basic services that incorporate capabilities to enable U1 U-space services:

- Electronic identification (e-identification). Ability to identify the drone and its operator in the U-space system.
- Electronic registration (e-registration). Ability to register the drone and its operator in the U-space system.
- Geofencing. Ability to comply with geographical, altitude and time restrictions defined by the geofencing service. This capability covers the technology, processing and any required communication links, as well as management and use of geofencing information used in the provision of this service.[51]

---

50 SESAR JU U-Space Blueprint, 9 June 2017 (www.sesarju.eu/u-space-blueprint).
51 A Geo-Fence contains a Hard Fence and a Soft Fence. Hard Fence: the border of the three-dimensional area that shall not be crossed. Soft Fence: the border of the area on which action must be taken to prevent crossing the Hard Fence. The area within the Soft Fence is the Nominal three-dimensional Area of Operation. The Hard Fence and the Soft Fence can be dynamic. The area between the Hard Fence and the Soft Fence is defined as the buffer. The buffer must take into account all elements that can have an influence on the size of the buffer such as latency, accuracy, wind, altitude, UA performance, etc.
Geo-Fence can be interpreted as an expanded Performance Based Navigation (PBN) confined to a defined area. It may be part of future Procedures for Air Navigation Services (PANS) rules (source: JARUS CS-UAS Recommendations for Certification Specification for Unmanned Aircraft Systems (2019), 1.6.1 Definition of the Geo-Fencing Function, pp. 15-16.

- Security. Ability to protect vehicle and data (interaction with other vehicles and infrastructure) against attacks on information technology and communication systems.
- Telemetry. Ability to transmit measurement data from the drone-to-drone operator and/or service provider to meet the demands of relevant services.
- Communication, navigation and surveillance. Ability for drones to meet the communication, navigation and surveillance performance requirements for the specific environment in which they will operate. This capability involves the combination of onboard sensors and equipment, such as data link, voice radio relay, transponder, laser, GNSS, and cellular, as a means of achieving the required performance.
- C2. Ability of drones to communicate with the ground control station to manage the conduct of the flight, normally via a specific data link.
- Operations management. Ability to plan and manage drone missions. This includes access to and use of all aeronautical, meteorological and other relevant information to plan, notify and operate a mission.

Capabilities incorporated to enable U1/U2 U-space services are:
- Tracking. Ability of the drone to provide flight parameters including at least its position and height.
- Emergency recovery. Ability of drones to take account of failure modes, such as C2 link failures, and take measures to ensure the safety of the vehicle, other vehicles and people and property on the surface. This includes identification of possible problems (autodiagnostic) and all equipment required to manage solutions.

Capabilities incorporated to enable U3 U-space services are as follows:
- Vehicle to Vehicle communication (V2V). Ability for drones to communicate information to each other. The nature of the information exchanged, and its performance requirements, will depend on the application.
- Vehicle to Infrastructure communication (V2I). Ability for drones to share information with infrastructure components.
- Detect and avoid. Ability for drones to detect cooperative and non-cooperative conflicting traffic, or other hazards, and take the appropriate action to comply with the applicable rules of flight. This includes collision avoidance, situational awareness and remain well clear functionalities during airborne and ground operations (aircraft, vehicles, structures or people on the ground), and other hazards like (high) terrain and obstacles, hazardous meteorological conditions, such as thunderstorms, icing,

turbulence and windshear as well as other airborne hazards like aircraft wake-induced turbulence, birds or volcanic ash.[52]

Current initiatives envisage that electronic registration is mandatory for drone operators (except operators of drones weighing below 250 g) as well as some classes of drones used in the Open category, and all classes of drones used in the Specific category. Electronic identification will allow authorities to identify a drone flying and link it to information stored in the registry.

The e-identification supports safety and security requirements, as well as law enforcement procedures. The principle of e-identification is that a cooperative drone regularly broadcasts a unique identifier and the current position through a radio frequency digital message. This enables authorized parties to detect, identify, locate and track drones anywhere at any time, even in the absence of network connectivity or other infrastructure. Reliable identification is also a basic element of airspace and traffic management, be it UTMS, Low Altitude Authorization and Notification Capability (LAANC), e-identification mandatory zones (IMZ), or a safe integration into current airspace used by and shared with manned aviation. Electronic identification is a key pillar in U-space foundation services of SESAR.

The U-space blueprint proposes the implementation of four sets of services to support the EU aviation strategy and regulatory framework on drones:
- U1: U-space foundation services covering services called e-registration, e-identification and geofencing (planning 2019).[53]

The main objectives of these services are to identify drones and operators and to inform operators about known restricted areas. With the development of the U1 foundation services, more drone operations are enabled, especially in areas where the density of manned aviation traffic is very low. The administrative procedures for permission to fly and the authorizations for some specific missions will be facilitated. The range of VLOS routine operations will be extended and will support extended VLOS flights, including VLOS operations in an urban environment. BVLOS operations will still be constrained

---

52   *See* ICAO Manual on Remotely Piloted Aircraft Systems (RPAS), Doc 10019 AN/507 First Edition 2015, Chapter 10.2.3.
53   EUROCONTROL defines geofencing as "[a] technology that supports dynamic security alerts and the means to prevent surface and aerial intrusion into or out of a defined area. Geofence describes geographical and temporal airspace barriers that unmanned aircraft should/may not cross, to reduce nuisance and ensure operational safeguards. Geolimitation is the act of restricting the movement of an unmanned aircraft by the use of geofence, notably through exclusion or caging. Geo-exclusion prevents unauthorized unmanned aircraft from flying inside a predetermined sensitive area whilst authorized unmanned aircraft can freely operate in accordance with their agreed mission. Geocaging prevents an unmanned aircraft from flying outside of a predetermined volume".

but will become more and more possible.
- U2: U-space initial services refer to an initial set of services that support the safe management of drone operations and a first level of interface and connections with ATM/ATC and manned aviation. The services include flight planning, flight approval, tracking, airspace dynamic information and procedural interface with air traffic control (planning 2021).

Where appropriate, U2 will make use of existing infrastructure from ATM, but new opportunities for drone operations will be enabled by the exploitation of technologies from other sectors such as long-term evolution (LTE) standards for data communication. The range of operations at low levels will be increased, including some operations in controlled airspace. Drone flights will no longer be necessarily considered on a case-by-case basis, and some examples of BVLOS operations will become routine, albeit with some constraints.
- U3: U-space advanced services will build on the experience gained in U2 and will unlock new and enhanced applications and mission types in high-density and high-complexity areas. U-space advanced services include capacity management and assistance for conflict detection. Indeed, the availability of automated detect and avoid functionalities, in addition to more reliable means of communication, will, as can be expected, lead to a significant increase in operations in all environments (planning 2025).

New technologies, automated detect and avoid functionalities and more highly reliable means of communication will enable a significant increase in drone operations in all environments and will reinforce interfaces with ATM/ATC and manned aviation. This is where the most significant growth of drone operations is expected to occur, especially in urban areas, with the intention of new types of operations, such as air urban mobility.
- U4: U-space full services, in particular services offering integrated interfaces with ATM/ATC and manned aviation, supports the full operational capability of U-space and will rely on a very high level of automation, connectivity and digitalization for both the drone and the U-space system. It is expected that the need for new services will arise during the roll-out of U3. U4 means the full integration of drone flights into controlled airspace (planning 2030+).

In fact, the U-space blueprint initiative dates back to 2015, when the European Commission mandated SESAR JU to draft the document. Since then, SESAR JU has received a further mandate to carry out research and demonstration activities in translating the blueprint into reality.

Following the publication of the U-space blueprint, The SESAR programme has launched 19 projects covering demonstration activities related to U2 initial services, the exploration of U3/U4 and, importantly, the development of CORUS, a project led by EUROCONTROL. The development of the CONOPS is closely associated with the other SESAR projects related to U-space and is integrated into the European ATM Master Plan, delivered in 2019 according to the timeline.

In the planning phase, SESAR has to deliver some preoperational SESAR demonstrations of the initial U-space services (U2), as well as first results from SESAR R&D projects, which pave the way for the roll-out of U-space (U2-U4). Project demonstrations and trials and their results were finalized in late 2019, early 2020, to be followed by sequential roll-outs indicating the levels of increasing drone connectivity and automation. The roll-out of each phase should certainly be seen as a high-level sequence for EU harmonization.

To make the Single European Sky more efficient, deployment of SESAR innovative projects, such as unleashing the potential of the drone market by setting up EU-wide rules to ensure safe drone operations for all airspace users, to protect citizens' privacy and to offer legal certainty, means a paramount prerequisite.

The U-space blueprint, the European ATM Master Plan and the U-space CONOPS form the basis for establishing the principles for the U-space architecture. These principles will guide the U-space projects in their setting and in their final reporting, as well as supporting U-space implementers by establishing a common approach to defining and realizing U-space. Finally, the U-space services will evolve to enable the growth in the number and variety of drone operations, supported by an appropriate interface with ATM. As time goes on, the whole aviation environment is expected to evolve into a fully integrated environment supporting manned and unmanned operations in all classes of airspace. The services are designed to minimize the risk to third parties on the surface, other airspace users and passengers. The services are supported by appropriate safety management systems and processes.

The U-space architecture has to support the vision of the U-space blueprint and related principles: The U-space relies on a very high level of automation, connectivity and digitalization for both the drone and the U-space systems.

From the architecture perspective, a U-space service is the contractual provision of one non-physical object by one entity for use by one or more others. It is also a discrete unit of functionality that can be assessed remotely, acted upon and updated independently. A service has four properties:

1. It logically represents a self-contained business activity with a specified outcome.
2. It is self-contained, in that users do not need additional services to benefit from its output.
3. It is a black box for its consumers.
4. It may make use of other underlying services.

From the perspective of a service provider, each service has three aspects: the business aspect (why), the operational aspect (what) and the technical aspect (how).

The U-space services are grouped according to the main actor involved:
- Services to service providers
    o Any service that is provided by an authority to the U-space service providers (USSPs) or between two service providers (e.g. AIMP to USSP).
    o This includes provision of services to enable safe and secure interoperability between U-space and ATM (e.g. ANSP to USSP), between U-space providers and services that support cross-border operations.
    o This includes the provision of certified services for safety oversight.
- Supplemental data services
    o Any service that provides additional data to other services from different sources; e.g. terrain, weather, surveillance, obstacle, cellular coverage, etc.
- Services to drone operators
    o Any service that is provided by service providers to the operators prior to the execution, during or after the flight (e.g. flight plan preparation, optimization assistance, strategic deconfliction).
    o Some services are provided by service providers directly to the pilots (human or onboard system) during the execution of the flight; e.g. tracking, tactical deconfliction.[54]

The SESAR VLD projects for U-space within the European Union are the main factors for a rapidly expanding drone market to generate economic and societal benefits for Europe. The benefits to European society and economy will be as follows:

Drone users/operators:
- Offer fair, flexible and open access to the airspace.
- Open up drone services market.

Regulatory authorities:
- Maintain control over airspace.
- Ensure safety, privacy, security and environmental protection.
- Enforce registration and identification of drones.
- Protect safety and security-critical areas.

Citizens:
- Offer new and innovative drone services.

---

54 *See* SESAR JU Initial View on Principles for the U-space Architecture, Edition 01.04, 29 July 2019, pp. 5-9. Aeronautical Information Management Provider (AIMP). U-space Service Provider (USSP).

- Ensure safe and secure drone operations.
- Safeguard privacy and ensure environmental protection (noise and visual pollution).

Businesses:
- Enabling the development of new business models.
- Spurring jobs and market growth.
- Support move towards automation and digitalization.

To illustrate that Europe is on course with its implementation of U-space, an initiative that must ensure safe and secure drone traffic management, a series of drone demonstrations were conducted during the second half of 2019 at urban and rural locations in various EU Member States, supported by the SESAR JU within the framework of the EU's Connecting Europe Facility (CEF) programme.[55] Stakeholders under the auspices of SESAR, such as start-ups, research institutes, universities, drone operators, service providers, airports, authorities at local and city level, law enforcement agencies and civil aviation authorities participated in order to show the readiness of initial U-space services to manage a broad range of drone operations and related services and their interaction with manned aviation.

These operations range from transportation and logistics, such as parcel deliveries between two dense urban locations, urban air mobility, medical emergencies, police interventions to maritime search and rescue and forestry inspections. Attention has also been paid to recreational drone users with projects demonstrating how these private operators too can benefit from U-space services. The operations are also aimed at demonstrating different levels of automation that are possible, as well as seamless information exchange between multiple drone operators and service providers.

U-space is an enabling framework designed to facilitate any kind of routine mission, in all classes of airspace and all types of environment, including the most congested, while addressing an appropriate interface with manned aviation and air traffic control units. When fully deployed, a wide range of drone missions that are currently being restricted will be possible because of a sustainable and sturdy European ecosystem that is globally interoperable. An essential prerequisite for this structure is the timing for U-space, given the speed at which the drone market is growing.

The different drone services projects, including demonstrations, are the first batch of drone-centric activities selected and funded by the SESAR JU to foster the development of the U-space system, which aims to enable complex drone operations with a high

---

55 Connecting Europe Facility (CEF) is a key EU funding instrument to promote growth, jobs and competitiveness through targeted pan-European infrastructure investment in transport, energy and digital projects that aim at a greater connectivity between EU Member States (ec.europa.eu/inea/en/connecting-europe-facility).

degree of automation in all types of operational environments. The foundation services (U1) like e-identification, registration and pre-tactical geofencing must be running by the end of 2019. However, further U-space services and their corresponding standards need to be developed in the near future. The basic services activities were supposed to have a planned duration of two years before implementation. A number of services, whose gradual implementation is planned in phases U1 (2019+) to U3 (2025), will be analysed and evaluated before the final implementation phase U4 (2030+).[56]

All projects have their own particular demonstration and exploration disciplines and research methods, approaches, results and perspectives concerning future drone operations in U-space, but, above all, they share knowledge, skills, resources, best practices and the safe, secure and flexible integration of U-space services to make the economical and societal promises of U-space a reality.

The various SESAR JU U-space exploratory research projects within the European Union that have been completed so far are as follows:
- CORUS, which stands for Concept of Operation for European UTM Systems, is a project established within the context of SESAR. This project developed and has written a CONOPS for U-space, the European system for the management of drones, taking into account that a harmonized approach to integrating drones into VLL airspace is vital if the rapidly growing drone industry is to fulfil its economic and societal potential. Gathering experts from civil aviation, research and academia, under the guidance of a 21-member stakeholder advisory board, the CORUS consortium developed the CONOPS for U-space by considering the use-cases of U-space, starting with the most frequent. The CONOPS is a living document, and thus the expectation is that updates will be required in order to take into account the evolution towards urban air mobility operations.

CORUS sees U-space as an environment that enables business activity related to drone use while maintaining an acceptable level of safety and public acceptance. The concept describes how VLL airspace will need to be organized and what rules and regulations will need to be put in place so that drones may bring about the full potential they offer to many aspects of life in the 21st century in safety and security, with respect to the environment and the privacy of people. The CONOPS details drone operations in uncontrolled VLL airspace and in and around controlled and/or protected airspace such as airfields. It also describes an initial architecture that identifies the airspace classes, services and technical development necessary for the implementation of the CONOPS, quantifying the levels of safety and performance required. CORUS also communicated and cooperated with more than 70 organizations involved in other

---

56 A total of 16 services will be implemented in phases U1, U2 and U3. U4 services are not yet defined.

related projects looking at specific drone and U-space technologies. Finally, it proposes solutions for easing social acceptance of drones by examining safety, privacy, noise and other societal issues.[57]

- SECOPS: an integrated SECurity concept for drone OPerationS. Its headline is 'Security is key to safe operations in VLL airspace'. Given the highly automated nature of drone operations, cybersecurity is particularly important, and thus security risks in U-space need to be assessed and mitigated to an acceptable level. Secure drone operations need to be supported by a combination of different security functions at different levels in the drone end-to-end system, managed by a dedicated set of procedures and supported by clear regulations.

By establishing an integrated security concept, drones can operate in accordance with appropriate procedures and regulations, while any drones that divert from their flight plan can be detected and acted upon.

To this end, SECOPS defined an integrated security concept for drone operations, including addressing resistance of drones against unlawful interference, protection of third parties and the integration of geofencing technology. The research reviewed technological options for both airborne and ground elements and considered legal as well as regulatory and social aspects.

A preliminary cybersecurity risk assessment was performed to determine the risks concerning confidentiality, integrity and availability (CIA) of the U-space information flows. By assessing and prioritizing potential security risks, the SECOPS Integrated Security Concept defines requirements and proposes potential security controls. An experimental proof of concept integrating common off-the-shelf technologies of the consortium partners was executed in order to prove the feasibility of parts of the integrated security concept and co-operability of the more mature technical solutions, including detection of rogue drones and typical air defence solutions.

Among critical issues, SECOPS found the trustworthiness of drone track and position information to be important. A key priority is knowing where data comes from and assuring data integrity of global positioning and geofence information, for example, as are the timeliness of reactions to events to ensure law enforcement is informed.

SECOPS concluded that drone countermeasures are likely to be a combination of different technologies and suggests further research to identify appropriate solutions for various applications. It also recommends a legal framework setting out the responsibilities and roles of enforcement agencies.[58]

---

57 CORUS participants: ENAV, EUROCONTROL (Coordinator), DFS, DLR, HEMAV, NATS, DSNA, Universitat Politècnica de Catalunya (Polytechnic University of Catalonia UPC) and Unifly.
58 SECOPS participants: Delft Dynamics BV, NLR Royal Netherlands Aerospace Centre (Coordinator), Sensofusion OY and Unifly.

- IMPETUS: Information Management Portal to Enable the inTegration of Unmanned Systems. This project, aiming at new technologies to support U-space information needs, analysed the information management needs of drone operations in VLL airspace. Its approach is based on the analysis and identification of the needs of future drone operators and service providers to define a conceptual model of drone information microservices and a cloud-based architecture that will answer the identified needs. Safety-critical information, for instance, will be needed at a much higher fidelity than in today's solutions and will include geospatial information services to ensure surface clearance, local weather information to calculate drone trajectory uncertainties and non-conventional navigation sources, such as signals of opportunity and vision-based navigation, to allow for more precise navigation on a local scale. Services of this level of fidelity will require the movement of massive amounts of data to a wide array of users spread over a large geographical area.

The information management architecture based on microservices contrasts with legacy monolithic applications that are centralized, uniformly packaged and single-language-based programs that quickly reach overwhelming complexity as they grow to meet consumer demand. Microservice-based applications avoid issues as the entire application is split into small, independent but highly interconnected services.

The project also proposed technologically and commercially feasible solutions to address those needs. IMPETUS will advance the state of the art in two main areas:
1. Drone information life cycle that best supports the flight life cycle.
2. Proposal for a technological solution to deliver the U-space services.

The solution developed in the IMPETUS project builds on existing traffic management information systems addressing key issues such as data quality assurance, data integration needs with the ATM systems and scalability of the drone information services to multiple users with diverse business models.

IMPETUS has taken into consideration drone market needs and previous emerging technologies to propose a cloud-based serverless environment based on the use of the smart concept and the application of microservices and Function as a Service (FaaS) paradigms to deliver a solution that will be cost-effective, scalable and capable of enabling both market-based mechanisms for information provision and public governance and oversight required for safety and regulatory compliance.

The framework of the IMPETUS solution is based on a federated architecture with a layered distribution of responsibilities. It is made up of a central actor that provides a single point of truth of the airspace situation, an intermediate interface composed of multiple USSPs and an external layer for the end users (drone operators). The IMPETUS platform supports testing of various U-space services. IMPETUS replicated aspects of this architecture and concluded that it can meet relevant U-space challenges.

For example, one experiment explored how a drone deconfliction service can interact with other services in the system to maximize the airspace capacity for drones on the basis of dynamic volumes. IMPETUS looked at whether this is not only technically possible, but also a viable option when realized in coordination and conjunction between services. This approach fully supports U-space objectives of flexibility, availability and scalability and is an enabler of high-density operations requiring agile responses and adaptability to change.[59]

– DREAMS: DRone European Aeronautical information Management Study. Much like manned aviation, unmanned flights rely on accurate aeronautical information to stay informed about weather, airspace restrictions and regulations during a flight. The variety and complexity of drone operations require a different approach to managing this aeronautical information.

The DREAMS project set out to identify gaps between existing information used by manned aviation and new needs coming from U-space. Unmanned aviation will require a comparable level of information with the same level of integrity and reliability as manned aviation. In this respect, DREAMS assessed the present and future needs of aeronautical information to support the growth of unmanned aviation and ensure the safety of operations. The gap analysis carried out by the DREAMS partners analysed operational and technical aspects, environmental scenarios, technologies, safety and security impact in order to identify U-space data, including airspace structure, drone data, flight plan, obstacles and weather, and related service providers and facilities required by drones. The work was validated through simulations and examined how information might be sourced, managed and disseminated.

It also looked at technologies needed to support remotely piloted flights, such as geofencing and flight planning management functionalities. It recognized the importance of information quality for drone operators and the need to provide sufficient information on active drones for other airspace users.

The project concluded that aeronautical information available today is insufficient to support U-space operational needs without some extension or tailoring and additional research. It confirmed, for instance, that U-space will need new aeronautical features such as geofencing and geocaging (to instruct a drone where it can fly), geovectoring (how to fly) and speed vectors. Several data formats were identified, for example the aeronautical

---

59 IMPETUS participants: Altitude Angel Limited, Boeing Research &Technology Europe S.L.U., C-ASTRAL (Proizvdna zračnih in vesoljskih plovil d.o.o.), Centro de Referencia de Investigación, Desarrollo e Innovación ATM A.I.E. (CRIDA) (Coordinator), Ingenieria y Economia Del Transporte S.A. (INECO) and Jeppesen GmbH. FaaS is a category of cloud computing services that provide a platform allowing customers to develop, run and manage application functionalities without the complexity of building and maintaining the infrastructure typically associated with developing and launching an app. FaaS is about running back-end code without managing your own server systems or your own long-lived server applications (source: Roberts, M., Serverless Architectures, 2016, martinFowler.com).

information exchange model (AIXM) and GeoISON, which will be needed to ensure data quality and performance. Similarly, several protocols will be necessary to enable data exchange with different client capabilities.

DREAMS also concluded that the aeronautical data exchange service should provide data querying capability in terms of feature type and attribute and that data suppliers should include data sources in keeping with the open-data environment. In terms of preferred development, the research partners concluded that a microservice approach would be the best option and fully compliant with SESAR JU and CORUS CONOPS architecture principles.[60]

– CLASS: CLear Air Situation for uaS. In the context of exploratory research projects, this description and the findings of CLASS are more extensive than previously discussed.

Reducing the risk of conflict between airspace users becomes more important as more drones enter the airspace. The CLASS project examined the potential of ground-based technologies to detect and monitor cooperative and non-cooperative drone traffic in real time. The consortium fused surveillance data obtained using a drone identifier and tracker as well as a holographic radar to feed a real-time UTM display.

CLASS tested tracking and display of cooperative and non-cooperative drones in six operational scenarios, ranging from an out-of-control recreational drone, conflicts with emergency operations and incursions by rogue drones. Various scenarios were carried out by project partners to benchmark the surveillance and data fusion technology and achieve the lowest rate of false alarms.

The functionalities provide the basis for a real-time centralized UTM system, which can be used by all stakeholders, from drone operators to ANSPs, authorities and airports. The functionalities were also designed to support advanced services, such as geofencing, geocaging, conflict detection and resolution.

As a result of the demonstrations, CLASS was able to define and detail the functional and technical requirements for tracking, monitoring and tactical deconfliction. For example, tracking requirements will vary from statically managed to dynamically managed airspace, where real-time decisions are necessary because of conflict or new dynamic geofenced volumes. CLASS also found variations in the performance of tracking technology and recommended the development of standards for different U-space services. For example, there is a difference between tactical deconfliction services and onboard detection and avoid systems, which means these must operate effectively to manage the wide range of drone types and sizes.

---

60 DREAMS participants: IDS Ingegneria Dei Sistemi S.p.A. (Coordinator), EuroUSC España S.L., Topview SRL and TU Delft-Delft University of Technology.

Further research is recommended to scale up the operational scenarios to simulate surveillance in more dense environments, initially involving dozens of drones.[61]
- TERRA. The Technological European Research for RPAS in ATM project explains that the CNS infrastructure is designed to support the needs for manned aviation and that the requirements of the emerging drone sector are different and will rely on new and existing technologies to perform effectively. The TERRA project set out to identify relevant ground technologies and to propose a technical ground architecture to support drone operations. TERRA started by defining the performance and functional requirements of ground-based systems for drones, analysing, in particular, the strengths and weaknesses of CNS technology to support safe, effective and efficient VLL operations.

Three business cases were selected (agriculture, infrastructure inspection and urban delivery), and small-scale trials were conducted using new and existing technologies. A qualitative evaluation was performed for all the presented technologies using a set of performance characteristics, together with an assessment of their pros and cons for drone operations. Additional work was carried out to assess whether machine learning can help to monitor VLL operations, including early detection of off-nominal conditions such as trajectory deviations.

The research considered different sizes and types of drones operating VLOS and BVLOS, in urban and rural environments, in terms of the applicability of technologies. It also examined continuity of service, coverage, data security, bandwidth, latency, update rate, integrity and availability. Further, it applied artificial neural network (ANN) modelling to demonstrate successful conflict prediction in urban environments and used rule-based reinforcement learning to mitigate against frequent follow-on conflicts with other traffic.

The analysis showed that machine-learned application of traffic rules performed relatively well under higher traffic densities. TERRA concluded that in environments with a low density of drones and a low level of complexity the current CNS technologies are sufficient to support U-space services. However, existing technologies present some drawbacks, which limit their application to complex scenarios like urban environments and high drone densities.

To allow full U-space deployment, improved technologies are required. These kinds of technologies include making use of 5G wireless communications, technologies enabled by Galileo and the European geostationary navigation overlay service (EGNOS) like augmented satellite positioning data to cover gaps. Additionally, ANNs modelling has shown the potential benefits of machine learning for use in predicting and classifying

---

61 CLASS participants: Airbus Defence &Space SAS (Coordinator), Aveillant Limited, Ecole Nationale de l'Aviation Civile (ENAC), Norwegian University of Science and Technology, and Unifly.

drone trajectories in the urban scenarios.[62]
- PercEvite : Percevoir et Eviter – Detect and Avoid. The headline of the project findings is: Developing an autonomous sense and avoid package for small drones.

Given the number of drones forecasted to take to the skies in the coming years, a key priority will be to ensure they stay clear of other airspace users, people and property on the surface. A smart solution is needed that allows drones to detect and avoid other obstacles autonomously, and it would be beneficial if this solution were also suitable for large groups of small drones.

To address this challenge, the PercEvite project focused on the development of a sensor, communication and processing suite for small drones. The main requirement was that the chosen solution could detect and avoid ground-based obstacles and flying air vehicles without necessitating human intervention.

The work centred around developing a low-cost, lightweight, energy-efficient sensor and processing package to maximize payload capacity. The package features a mixture of mature concepts such as collaborative separation and less mature but high-potential technology like hear and avoid. The work started with designing the hardware and software to support these functionalities before combining the technology into a single unit capable of operating on small drones.

Activity then transitioned to live demonstrations using innovative concepts to test the different functionalities. For example, cameras were used to identify objects such as automobiles, people and obstacles, while embedded microphones were used to differentiate between objects in the airspace and identifying a fixed-wing aircraft as opposed to a helicopter. The tests looked at different methods of communication, ranging from software-defined radio to LTE 4G wireless broadband. The aim was always to find low-cost, lightweight solutions suitable for use by small drones.

The PercEvite partners developed two systems, one designed for extremely small drones weighing as little as 20 g, and another more comprehensive solution, weighing 200 g, suited to drones commonly used in commercial activities such as inspection services, photography, surveillance and package delivery. Development work continued in 2020 as the research partners endeavoured to produce integrated solutions for these applications.[63]
- DroC2om. Drone Critical Communications indicates that reliable communications are central to safe drone operations. Drones rely on a high level of digitalization to operate autonomously and depend on data link communications to achieve this. C2 information needs to be reliably transferred in support of functions and specific

---

62 TERRA participants: C-ASTRAL, CHPR BV-Center for Human Performance Research, CRIDA, INECO (Coordinator), Leonardo S.p.A., NLR Royal Netherlands Aerospace Centre.
63 PercEvite participants: Katholieke Universiteit Leuven-KU Leuven, Parrot Drones and Delft University of Technology (Coordinator).

procedures, enabling drones and manned vehicles to operate safely in the same airspace.

The DroC2om project reviewed the capability of the existing cellular and satellite infrastructure that supports C2 data link communications, using live flight trials and simulations to test availability and performance. The research led to the definition of an integrated communications concept incorporating cellular and satellite data links, which is contributing to EUROCAE and 4G/5G standardization work. Project partners assessed the reliability of the combined cellular-satellite radio network architecture and radio mechanisms. One of the noted challenges is the operating conditions for drone radio channels, which are reasonably known for satellite communication channel commonly used by large drones.

The DroC2om project included experimental investigations to bring further clarification on this project in order to design radio technology that will make the C2 link operate with specified reliability with specific reference to service-level compliance and latency.

Based on DroC2om initial investigations, the project partners found that interference management presents a challenge to the reliable operation of the C2 data link and proposed solutions for further simulation and research.

Proposals to address connectivity issues include the following: increasing the number of antennas on the drone, with simple selection mechanism, and adding different network connections and operators. The solutions are moderately complex and designed for situations of drone density increases. The project provided solid empirical evidence on the drone to cellular networks channel in urban areas and validated dual LTE C2 performance using live trials. It also tested multi-link connectivity and beam switching to ensure drone C2 link quality is maintained in highly loaded cellular networks. It concluded a hybrid cellular-satellite architecture, combining low latency and coverage of cellular with reliability of satellite communications, contributes to robust C2 performance.[64]

- AIRPASS. The Advanced Integrated RPAS Avionics Safety Suite project indicates that identifying onboard technology is necessary for drones to share the airspace. Drones of all shapes and sizes will provide services in the short and medium future, ranging from an automated external defibrillator (AED), small medical deliveries, inspection services and package deliveries to larger urban taxis and remotely operated systems. To interact safely with all other airspace users and services, AIRPASS partners defined a high-level architecture for the onboard equipment they need to carry.

---

[64] DroC2om participants: Aalborg Universitet-Aalborg University (Coordinator), ATESIO GmbH, Nokia Solutions and Networks Danmark A/S (Bell Labs) and Thales Alenia Space France SAS.

This architecture considers communications, CNS systems, as well as technology specific to drone operations such as autopilot and detect and avoid systems.

AIRPASS performed an analysis of available onboard technologies and identified gaps between these systems and technologies necessary to operate drones. The project matched every U-space service to the main avionics components of a drone, specifically automated flight control and databases, navigation and communications. This was used to compile over 60 basic requirements for an onboard system concept for drones in a U-space environment.

The research enabled the partners to develop different subsystems relating to specific activities and define a general functional architecture, which can be applied to different missions. Among the key technologies, the project addressed pre-tactical, tactical and dynamic geofencing; tactical deconfliction, e-identification in communications systems; emergency management; and tracking and monitoring. Owing to the variety of drone types and airspaces, AIRPASS defined a general functional architecture that can be applied to multiple applications and that has no implications for hardware.

These findings are now being used by standardization groups to develop a standardized onboard architecture available for use by every drone using U-space services.

In summary, the AIRPASS functional architecture supports the development of U2 services in simple environments and paves the way for the integration of every drone into U-space. The project identified some gaps in currently available onboard technologies, especially when it comes to scalability and operations in high drone densities, underlining the importance of the quality of U-space services and CNS capabilities.

Certification will be a critical part of implementing U2 services, especially for the all-important BVLOS, which is expected to become the standard way of flying in U-space.[65]

The various demonstrations by the SESAR VLD projects within the European Union that have been conducted are:
- DIODE: D-flight Internet of Drones Environment. This project aims to demonstrate how the implementation of the full set of the U-space services up to U3 ensures a safe flow of drones that pursue specific business or recreational intents, fully integrated with manned aviation, and in all types of environment. The demonstrations have taken place in a specific area in the vicinity of Rome, known as *umbilicus italiae*, with several different geographical situations, including rural, mountainous and remote territories and industrial, urban and semi-urban regions. The demonstrations covered a wide range of applicable drone operations, such as parcel delivery, road traffic patrol, professional photography, railway and power lines

---

65 AIRPASS participants: Avular BV, DLR (Coordinator), Israel Aerospace Industries Ltd., NLR Royal Netherlands Aerospace Centre, Università degli Studi di Napoli 'Parthenope', SAAB AB, Technische Universität Braunschweig and The Central Aerohydrodynamic Institute (TsAGI).

surveillance, search and rescue, airport operations, interaction with GA and firefighting.

The flights were carried out in combination with manned flights and took account of third parties on the surface. The demonstrations adopted a risk-based approach to the provision of initial and advanced U-space services aligned with the expectation of drone operators.

The drones were monitored using D-Flight, a dedicated platform that provides e-registration, e-identification and static geofencing in compliance with European regulations to be introduced at the end of 2020. The risk assessment followed the SORA methodology used for complex drone operations and looked at new competences and technology to support the growth of drone services. DIODE demonstrated emerging and mature capabilities on board drones, which support the deployment of a risk-based and an operation-centric concept of U-space. The project considered a huge range of drones and highlighted opportunities where the drone market can also contribute to the development of more advanced U-space services.[66]

- DOMUS: Demonstration Of Multiple U-space Suppliers. This project aims to illustrate the full set of core U2 services, as well as the demonstration of specific U3 services, such as tactical deconfliction and collaboration with ATM. The demonstrations involved three specific USSPs interacting with an ecosystem manager and many drone operators equipped with drones from different manufacturers. The planned operations have taken place in Andalucía, Spain. In this approach, the ecosystem manager is the principal USSP and provided data integrity to the system as a single point of truth: ensuring safety, security, privacy and secrecy and easing the entry of new service providers into the system. It also provided the single interface with ATM. The service providers operate in parallel to deliver U-space and value-added services to the various drone operators, who need to exchange data to carry out their operations.

Such data includes optimum operation profiles, fleet management, log records and additional flight information. During the flights conducted by DOMUS partners, three service providers were connected to the ecosystem manager and simultaneously provided services to five different drone operators in close proximity, and at a certain distance, in two different locations: Lugo and Jaen, Spain. In one example, integration with manned aviation was also demonstrated.

Thanks to the ecosystem manager, DOMUS demonstrated some of the initial services detailed in U1 and U2 definitions of U-space, including e-registration, e-identification,

---

66 DIODE participants: ENAV, Leonardo, Telespazio, IDS Ingegneria Dei Sistemi S.p.A., e-GEOS, Nextant Applications & Innovative Solution (NAIS), Aiview Group, Poste Italiane, EuroUSC Italia S.r.l. and TechnoSky.

geofencing, flight planning, tracking, dynamic flight management and interfaces with ATC. Some U3 services, such as tactical deconfliction between two drones, and dynamic geofencing, for example around manned aircraft, in collaboration with ATM, were also tested. Activities included mapping, normal and urgent deliveries, building inspections and integration of recreational drone flights. The project also demonstrated the feasibility of connecting U-space operations to the smart city platform.

The live trials showed how a federated architecture can support multiple service providers under the management of an ecosystem manager for efficient deployment of U-space services. This is possible using current technology and interoperable U-space services provided by different service providers and different drone operators.[67]

– EuroDRONE: a European UTM test bed for U-space. Demonstrations were aimed at connecting various stakeholders, such as operators, regulators, law enforcement agencies and product developers, and different systems in a unified environment in order to test U-space functionalities up to U3. Test location was Missolonghi, Greece. The EuroDRONE drone architecture is made up of cloud navigational software (DroNav) and hardware elements, including a transponder, to be installed on drones. It consists of a sophisticated self-learning system operating in a distributed computing environment, offering multiple levels of redundancy, fail-safe algorithms for conflict prevention/resolution (traffic alert, collision avoidance and resolution advisory) as well as assets management.

EuroDRONE conducted highly automated unmanned flights using a cloud-based UTM system connected to a miniature, intelligent transponder processing board on drones fully capable of flight mission planning. The tests used an innovative vehicle to infrastructure link (communications), integrated to a self-learning UTM platform, with the capability to share flight information in real time.

The flights demonstrated end-to-end UTM applications focusing on both VLOS and BVLOS logistics and emergency services. Among the main activities, the project identified key user needs and regulatory challenges and compared the results with the CONOPS. The findings were used to define a practical, automated cloud-based UTM system architecture using simulation and live demonstrations.

In conclusion, the project demonstrated robust end-to-end UTM cloud operations, including BVLOS medical deliveries over a 10-km range in coordination with ATC and commercial operation. It also demonstrated innovative vehicle to infrastructure and state-of-the-art vehicle to vehicle communications, equipped with operational detect

---

67 DOMUS participants: ENAIRE, Air Map Deutschland GmbH, Sociedad Estatal de Correos y Telégrafos S.A., CRIDA, Earth Networks, Everis Aeroespacial y Defensa S.L.U., Fundación Andaluza para el Desarrollo Aeroespacial (FADA-CATEC), FuVeX Civil SL, GMV Aerospace & Defence S.A.U., Indra Sistemas, INECO, Ingeniera de Sistemas para la Defensa de España S.A. S.M.E. M.P. (ISDEFE), Pildo Consulting, SOTICOL Robotics Systems SL and Vodafone España.

and avoid algorithms. The flights were able to demonstrate high levels of autonomy using cloud-based infrastructure envisaged for an advanced UTM environment. The demonstrations ranged from sea areas to the scenery of rural areas and urban environments and tested LTE communications links.[68]
- GOF-USPACE: Safe drone integration in the Gulf of Finland (Finnish-Estonian Gulf of Finland very large U-space demonstration GOF U-space). The initial flight trials were aimed at establishing a preoperational FIMS with an interoperability architecture capable of integrating existing commercial off-the-shelf UTM components.

In different live cases, representing the most typical VLOS and BVLOS missions, FIMS capabilities have been tested to demonstrate that safe and integrated (large-scale) drone operations are possible, building on established and existing systems in open and interoperable environments. Flight trials have been undertaken on the following:
- International parcel delivery between two major cities (Helsinki and Tallinn, Estonia).
- Dense urban drone fleet operations in Helsinki with police intervention.
- Dense urban drone fleet operations in Tallinn in controlled airspace.
- 100 km+ BVLOS multisensory inspection flights in forestry and utility inspection.
- Cooperation with GA and recreational users at an uncontrolled airport.
- Maritime traffic surveillance combined with search and rescue over the Gulf of Finland.
- Drone taxi flight from Helsinki-Vantaa airport to the city of Helsinki.

As air traffic continues to rise in numbers and kinds, especially with the arrival of unmanned aircraft and air taxis, the technology and rules for using especially very low-level airspace needs updating.[69]

The GOF U-space architecture integrated USSP microservices that enabled a collective and cooperative management of all drone traffic in the same geographical region. A microservice-oriented data exchange layer provided standard protocols to connect various U-space services from different service providers, and the capabilities of service provision were demonstrated during the trials; furthermore, integration between FIMS and USSPs, FIMS (Estonia) and FIMS (Finland) and USSPs to ground control services was established with a link to receive data from the ATM systems, demonstrating interoperability between systems.

The demonstrations showed commercial off-the-shelf UTM components to be suitable for purpose to demonstrate all phases of drone operations with a focus on pre-

---

68 EuroDrone participants: Aslogic, Cranfield University, Dronsystems Limited, Hellenic Civil Aviation Authority (HCAA), Hellenic Post S.A. (ELTA), University of Patras (UPAT) and Romanian Post (CNPR).
69 Maria Tamm, GOF project coordinator of Estonian Air Navigation Services.

flight and flight execution. The exercise proved that service providers and operators were able to connect to the open platform to access FIMS and ATM data, while noting the need for additional work to develop tracking solutions and improve resilience to poor mobile network coverage. The project demonstrated the need for single truth, where all airspace users can access one source of reliable airspace and aeronautical information, and common standards for communication between systems.[70]

- SAFIR, Safe and Flexible Integration of Initial U-space Services in a Real Environment. The SAFIR consortium has been selected by SESAR JU to demonstrate integrated drone traffic management for a wide range of drone activities in Belgium. The goal of SAFIR is to contribute to the EU legislative process in regard to drones and to the implementation of interoperable, harmonized and standardized drone services in Europe.

So far SAFIR has carried out multiple studies and demonstrations for drone operations that are viable, robust and ready to implement throughout Europe, such as inspection flights at the Port of Antwerp (including container terminal inspections and oil spill inspections), drone delivery, medical transports between hospitals, power line mapping and pylon inspection, all flights conducted at the ultra-modern Drone Test Center of DronePort in the city of Sint-Truiden and in the larger Antwerp area, including the Port of Antwerp.

The project consists of a broad range of operations and services up to U3 linking smart mobility, including flights in both controlled and uncontrolled VLL airspace, flights in VLOS and BVLOS and an evaluation of the use of telecom technology for data communication between manned and unmanned aircraft. A specialized radar developed by the CLASS project was deployed to detect rogue drones in critical areas and provide a live feed for the USSPs. SAFIR's federated model enabled information sharing between multiple interoperable services, categorized according to their function.

SAFIR proved the ability of drones to safeguard critical areas, such as an international port or an urban environment. It was demonstrated how the Port of Antwerp could request a drone to inspect a certain area should there be reason for concern as well as create no-drone zones to manage safety in the port. The project also showed how multiple USSPs can operate in the same geographical area at the same time thanks to UTM systems that have the potential to be interoperable.

---

70 GOF U-space participants: Lennuliiklusteeninduse Aktsiaselts (EANS), Altitude Angel Limited, Air Map Deutschland GmbH, Air Navigation Services Finland (ANS Finland), Avartek R. Lindberg Ky Kb, BVdrone Oy, CAFA Tech OÜ, Estonian Police and Border Guard Board (PPA), Finnish Transport and Communications Authority (TRAFICOM), The Finnish Air Rescue Society (SLPS), Fleetonomy.ai Oy, Frequentis, Helsinki Police Department (Helsinki PD), Hepta Group Airborne OÜ (HGA), Robots Expert Finland Oy (REX), Threod Systems, Unifly, VideoDrone Finland Oy and Volocopter.

SAFIR demonstrated full availability of the following services: e-identification, pre-tactical, tactical and dynamic geofencing, strategic and tactical deconfliction, tracking and monitoring. The project successfully tested initial advanced and full U-space services and made recommendations for further research. For example, it concluded that tracking data sourced from different places needs to be fused, full integration is needed between UTM and drone operators on the ground and interaction with ATC is important, preferably in an automated way.

Flight authorization is complex, and SAFIR expects European regulation to help clarify drone categories. It also found satellite mobile connectivity performed quite well, but 4G unfortunately degrades at higher altitudes and would benefit from a dedicated 4G drone overlay network, particularly relevant to BVLOS operations.

SAFIR findings will contribute to the EU regulatory process and deployment of interoperable, harmonized and standardized drone services across Europe.[71]

- VUTURA. Validation of U-space by Tests in Urban and Rural Areas is a SESAR CEF[72] project supporting U-space, the European vision for the safe, secure and efficient handling of drone traffic and a key enabler for the growing drone market to generate economic and societal benefits. VUTURA is one of SESAR's VLD projects and is part of the vision of the European Commission to increase the speed of implementing unmanned traffic services to drive economic benefits stemming from the use of drones. U-space services for flight planning and geofencing will be the first to be implemented.

VUTURA is focusing on four major goals:
o Validating the use of shared airspace between existing airspace users (manned aviation) and drones.
o Validating more than only one USSP providing U-space services in a specific airspace, and the procedures needed to support drone flights, including the involvement of ATC.
o Ensuring alignment of regulation and standardization between SESAR developments and USSPs.
o Increasing the pace by which European cities and companies exploit emerging technologies related to drones. This will improve quality of life in cities, create concrete socio-economic outcomes and help European companies to take a leading position in the new smart city market.

---

71 SAFIR participants: Unifly (Coordinator), Amazon Prime Air, Skeyes, DronePort, Proximus 4G, Port of Antwerp, Helicus BVBA, SABCA, Elia System Operator, Explicit APS, C-Astral, Tekever II Autonomous Systems and Aveillant.
72 See Regulation (EU) No. 1316/2013 of the European Parliament and of the Council of 11 December 2013 establishing the Connecting Europe Facility, amending Regulation (EU) No. 913/2010 and repealing Regulations (EC) No. 680/2007 and (EC) No. 67/2010, OJ L 348/129, 20 December 2013.

Directed by NLR, the VUTURA consortium conducted BVLOS demonstration flights involving multiple USSPs in rural, urban and smart city environments.[73] Each scenario featured two service providers coordinating their services where interoperability was a major focus. Manned aviation, different levels of automation, commercial and leisure or recreational drones, off-the-shelf drones as well as custom-made ones all featured in the scenarios.

Information was shared allowing all stakeholders to access the data via a Web interface. In the tests, drones gave way to high-priority drones autonomously, for example medical deliveries, and the USSPs facilitated the drone traffic deconfliction using interoperable systems.

The work done by VUTURA demonstrated that commercial drone traffic can safely coexist with traditional air traffic in different types of environments and that the technology to safely manage drone traffic is feasible, scalable and interoperable. It also flagged up areas in need of further research. This includes closer alignment of flight planning activity by USSPs and a set of procedures for cross-border flight planning, a common interface for exchanging information and acceptable transmission delay and reliable detect and avoid capability.

Among key findings, VUTURA concluded that airspace users need to be registered in order to share airspace, be identifiable and meet geofencing requirements before the industry can move closer to supporting urban air mobility.[74]

- GEOSAFE. GEOfencing for Safe and Autonomous Flight in Europe. The project focused on avoiding no-fly zones in busy low-level airspace. To allow safe, efficient and secure access to airspace, U-space uses the geofencing system. Both geofencing and geocaging are critical to keeping complex low-altitude airspace safe. By securing the flight pattern of drones to avoid determined zones, geofencing solutions are key safety enablers. They are notably mandatory to ensure that drones adhere to rules put in place by EU Member States and do not fly in perimeters around critical infrastructure, such as power plants, airports and city centres. Geofencing solutions form part of the foundational services for the deployment of drone operations.

In October 2019, in France, GEOSAFE partners conducted a series of demonstrations on making use of geofence technologies in a simulated search and rescue operation to locate a missing hiker. The participants successfully demonstrated three tiers of geofencing aligned with U-space capability levels. The project was based on a one-year-long flight-test campaign, which assessed a number of commercially available geofencing solutions in order to propose improved geofencing systems for the near future and technological

---

73 First Dutch U-space Test Shows Positive Results, Amsterdam Drone Week, 26 September 2019.
74 NLR Royal Netherlands Aerospace Centre (Coordinator), Delft University of Technology, the City of Enschede, UAV International BV, AirHub BV, LVNL, Unifly, AirMap, Unisphere and Robor Electronics BV.

improvements for drones. The research included 280 flight tests in France, Germany and Latvia, which tested representative situations that a drone would face in urban and rural areas. They covered a range of missions including agriculture operations, inspections, emergency events and deliveries.

Geofencing consists of managing the avoidance of restricted areas both in drone mission planning and during the drone's flight. Geofencing is essential to ensuring that drones comply with airspace restrictions. Geofencing prevents drones from entering no-fly zones and keeps them away from protected areas. Geocaging, on the other hand, does not allow drones to fly beyond a set boundary.

The flights tested foundational and advanced geofencing services with reference to pre-tactical flight (a core competency required for entry into U-space, U1 foundation services), tactical operations (required for slightly more advanced U-space, U2) and dynamic situations (necessary for U3). Project partners considered issues such as technology performance, pilot warnings, communication failure, weak satellite positioning signals, restricted area updates during flights, tracking and drone navigation system performance. The results were used to identify ways in which the technology can be used to support safe interaction with all airspace users.

The project concluded that most drones meet the requirements for pre-tactical geofencing and demonstrated that existing technology is ready for initial U-space services even though no single solution is aligned with regulations in different states.

Solutions are also available to support tactical geofencing necessary to deliver advanced U-space services despite the lack of standardization so far. However, technology capable of supporting dynamic geofencing is not sufficiently mature to meet full U-space service levels, although this is expected to develop rapidly in the near term, not least because dynamic geofencing is a key function for unmanned vehicles operating BVLOS.

The results are helping to inform the European Commission, EASA and EUROCAE of best practices for integrating drones into European airspace; in particular, the development of performance requirements will be used for the ongoing standardization process.[75]

– PODIUM. Proving Operations of Drones with Initial UTM is a SESAR Horizon 2020 project, supporting U-space, the European vision for the safe, secure and efficient handling of drone traffic and a key enabler for the growing drone market to generate economic and societal benefits, just like the VUTURA project.

Drones have many possible uses. They have the potential to bring enormous added value to our daily lives in various areas, such as agriculture, the media, maintenance, deliveries,

---

75 GEOSAFE participants: Thales Alinea Space France SAS (Coordinator), Aeromapper, AirMap, Air Marine, ATechsys and SPH Engineering.

surveillance and inspection. However, they are relatively small and hard to detect. Left unmanaged, the increasing drone traffic can easily pose a threat to bystanders and manned aviation.

The PODIUM project highlights the important role of unmanned traffic management in providing a mutual traffic situational awareness for the involved local actors, including ATM, as a means to facilitate their daily drone management. Mutual traffic situational awareness means drones are aware of the other air traffic around them and vice versa: local air traffic as well as air traffic controllers know where the drones are.

A key aspect of the project is the use of software to manage the drone traffic. As part of the project, validation data was collected and analysed from 41 post-demonstration questionnaires completed by participants, five facilitated debriefing sessions and observations from validation experts and partners. The partners considered the maturity of services and technology and analysed the impact on flight efficiency, safety, security and human performance metrics.

Today, drone operators must perform many manual processes before they can fly, all of which takes extra time and effort, potentially impacting the commercial viability of drone operations. PODIUM looked to reduce the risk inherent to the operational and industrial deployment of U-space by demonstrating a Web-based UTM system, including an open cloud-based solution and a secure gateway solution, using tracking systems based on ADS-B 1090 MHz, UNB L-Band and GSM networks.

Drones operate in low-level airspace, requiring compliance with local restrictions and regulations and consideration of changing circumstances such as the weather. The PODIUM Web-based platform enables drone operators and authorities to follow drone operations in real time and connect the pilot where necessary. After performing extensive demonstrations of U-space services and technologies across five sites in Denmark, France and the Netherlands, the project's main deliverables were published.

PODIUM concluded that there is a very strong demand from all stakeholders for U-space solutions that can ease the burden of obtaining flight authorizations for drone flights and, furthermore, that increased situational awareness enables safety and efficiency benefits during flight execution. It found U-space services for the pre-flight phase almost ready for deployment but concluded that significant action is needed to ensure that U-space services can really take off in the flight execution phase. In particular, PODIUM made recommendations relating to tracking, the human-machine interface for drone pilots and the access to trustworthy data, with implications for standardization, rules and regulation, and further R&D.[76]

- SAFEDRONE. Unmanned and Manned Integration in VLL Airspace. The objective of SAFEDRONE was to demonstrate how to integrate GA, state aviation, optionally piloted aircraft and drones into non-segregated airspace in a multi-aircraft and

---

76 The main PODIUM partners are EUROCONTROL, Airbus, Delair, Drone Paris Region, DSNA, NLR Royal Netherlands Aerospace Centre, Orange and Unify.

manned flight environment. The project was to accumulate evidence and experience about the required services and procedures necessary to operate drones in a safe, efficient and secure way within U-space. SAFEDRONE sought to define and detail pre-flight services, including e-registration, e-identification, planning and flight approval as well as in-flight services such as geolimitation or geofencing, flight tracking, dynamic airspace information and automatic technologies to detect and avoid obstacles in order to demonstrate how to integrate manned aviation and drones into non-segregated airspace.

SAFEDRONE partners carried out demonstrations involving eight different aircraft types ranging from drones to fixed-wing and rotary-wing light aircraft, flying simultaneously in the same airspace. The flights were carried out in rural and semi-urban areas in southern Spain, recreating situations such as delivery of medical supplies, aerial mapping and surveying and operating BVLOS.

The project performed flight operations with initial and advanced U-space services, in addition to technologies required for full U-space services, including autonomous detect and avoid capabilities and multi-drone operations by a single operator at the ATLAS test flight centre located in Villacarrillo (in the neighbourhood of Jaén, Spain). The project also considered higher levels of autonomy necessary to operate in non-segregated airspace to carry out dynamic in-flight activities such as onboard replanning trajectories within the U-space approved flight plan, and autonomous generation of coordinated trajectories within an approved U-space area of operation. It assessed the viability of using 4G networks for communication during BVLOS flights and GNSS technologies enabled by Galileo to estimate the drone's height. The demonstrations focused on U1 and U2 services and a limited version of U3 advanced services, including automated detect and avoid technologies.

Finally, the research included a pre-risk assessment scenario of the CONOPS based on the technical, safety and operational requirements as detailed in the specific operational risk assessment drone GM. Lessons learned and results from the technologies tested have been passed to EASA and standardization bodies EUROCAE and the GUTMA, a non-profit consortium of worldwide UTM stakeholders based in Lausanne, Switzerland, to help develop the standards that will enable the safe integration of different drone categories under U-space.[77]

- USIS. U-space Initial Services ensures easy access to the airspace and the safety and security of U-space services. In the near future, mankind will experience the transformation of lives by drone services. The implementation of U-space services requires the progressive integration of UAS into the European ATM environment.

---

77 SAFEDRONE participants: CATEC, CRIDA, Enaire, IAI, Indra Sistemas, Unifly and the University of Seville.

USIS especially targets regulations and coordination with ATC units. USIS research sought to validate the services that will be provided by U-space service providers to drone operators and third parties, including the authorities in charge of the airspace, to demonstrate their readiness at a European level.

The USIS project considered initial U-space services of e-registration and e-identification, as well as more advanced flight planning, authorization and tracking service necessary for BVLOS and operations above people. It also looked at scheduling, including flight permissions, and dynamic airspace management such as no-fly zones and restricted areas most likely enforced by dynamic geofencing.[78]

USIS partners carried out live demonstrations using a secure and resilient cloud-based platform at locations both in France and Hungary. A dedicated application allows drone operators to submit flight requests that are then analysed and approved or dedicated by the appropriate authority. An embedded hardware connected to the mobile phone network was used to securely identify and track the equipped drones.

In France, the trial focused on current use cases. For example, drone operators in the Lille region participated while conducting regular operations such as aerial videos in rural and subrural environments. A few dedicated flights were also organized around Lille airport. In Hungary, the trial focused on future use cases. Dedicated flights were carried out in a rural environment, exploring search and rescue, parcel delivery, agriculture surveying and surveillance scenarios.

The research validated the use by a platform of a national registry (using the example of the French Alpha Tango service) and confirmed the technical feasibility of secured identification and tracking of drones through embedded hardware connected to mobile phone networks. This was used to monitor the compliance between the position of the drones and the approved operations.

The project showed that initial U-space services can support multiple numbers of drone operations without creating additional workload for an operator or impacting the safety of the airspace. It highlighted the need for flexibility when carrying out flight planning and approval management processes to cope with different national and local regulations.

Further examples by active drone operators will contribute to future R&D. The actual and expected proliferation of drones, including the related services, requires the

---

78 e-Identification enables information about the drone and other relevant information to be verified without physical access to the unmanned aircraft. e-Registration means the interaction with the registrar to enable the registrations of the drone, its owner, its operator and its pilot. Different classes of users may query data, or maintain or cancel their own data, according to defined permissions. Geofence provision, including dynamic geofencing, means an enhancement of geo-awareness that allows geofence changes to be sent to drones immediately. The drone must have the ability to request, receive and use geofencing data (source: CORUS Intermediate Concept of Operations for U-space, Enhanced Overview. GEOSAFE, U-space project successfully demonstrated geofencing technologies, SESAR.

continuous development, validation and implementation of U-space services to provide safe, equal and efficient access to airspaces all across Europe.[79]

U-space will open up new business opportunities within the European Union and, potentially, raise the quality of life of European citizens. The SESAR research and innovation programme has brought together many key players across Europe and has provided a sound basis that allows regulators, ANSPs, standardization bodies, industry and researchers to continue to build this new environment, and the results show real progress from almost nothing to initial deployment of certain features in only two years of study, research, tests and demonstrations.

The (preliminary) findings from 19 projects take Europe several steps closer to implementing a safe, initial drone operating environment and provide the necessary building blocks for more advanced U-space services to full integration together with manned aviation. Stakeholders in some of the projects, such as DIODE, DOMUS, GOF U-space and SAFIR, are already working with the authorities in their respective states to exploit solutions to deploy U-space.

In addition, initial deployments that reflect the findings from U-space projects are either being planned or in execution in a number of states across Europe.

However, there is much that still needs to be done. The findings make it clear that while much has been achieved in the past two years, more work is needed on developing and validating drone capabilities and U-space services to ensure safe and secure drone operations. For the U3 concept to be realized, complex issues that these SESAR JU projects have started to address need to be resolved, including detect and avoid, C2 link, geo-awareness, contingency procedures, dynamic interface with ATM, etc.

These issues must continue to be addressed in cooperation with international partners, including ICAO, and the traditional manned aviation community, whose operations are impacted by the rapid appearance of drones.

Additionally, the scope of the U-space projects needs to be widened to include, inter alia, the following areas:
- Urban air mobility operations;
- extension of U-space services beyond the VLL limit;
- altitude references;
- U-space interoperability with ATM, including the development of a collaborative decision-making process between the urban operations, ATM and city authorities;
- higher levels of automation, including machine learning and AI; and
- fundamental aviation tenets, such as airspace classification and the rules of the air.

---

79 USIS participants: Altametris, DFS, DSNA, ENAC, HungaroControl, Thales Alinea Space France SAS (Coordinator) and Unifly.

The SESAR JU has hitherto been the focal point of U-space research. Exciting and important work is being done by many stakeholders, and it is essential that this continues. The European Network of U-space Demonstrators, co-chaired by the European Commission, EUROCONTROL, EASA and SESAR JU, has created a powerful and well-attended forum to support the cross-pollination of ideas between all stakeholders involved in the development of U-space.[80]

However, full value from past work and the Network discussions can be realized only against the background of a R&D plan coordinated at the European level and integrated into the global developments taking place elsewhere.

It is not without reason that 14 European cities and regions, members of the UAM Initiative Cities Community (UIC²), presented their 'Manifesto on the Multilevel Governance of the Urban Sky' at the Amsterdam Drone Week Hybrid 2020, acknowledging the role of cities and regions in the multilevel governance of U-space and giving them a deciding role as competent authority, along with other pertinent stakeholders, in the governance of U-space, or UAM, operations in their territories.[81]

At this virtual conference, Patrick Ky, executive director of EASA, had a clear statement:

> The first drone delivery in Europe will take place in 2023 or 2024. In the same year, we will see drone taxis in European cities. But they will still have a pilot on board. I don't expect unmanned air taxis before 2025.[82]

Rob Welten, Chairman of Euregio Netherlands/Germany, stated:

> U-space will open up a new chapter for cities and regions. The activities in low level airspace are going to interact with the city on the ground, and this brings new opportunities and responsibilities for our cities. With the manifesto, we want to kickstart our collaboration with other aviation and non-aviation authorities and stakeholders to make sure U-space is going to be a success.

---

80 On 19 October 2019, the European Commission launched the European Network of U-space Demonstrators to support U-space projects and solutions. The Network is a forum to share knowledge on how to keep drone operations safe, secure and green. It focuses specifically on projects with a clear business case that build on mature technologies but need some further operational and regulatory demonstrations before starting commercial operations (source: EUROCONTROL).

81 The Urban Air Mobility Initiative is part of the European Innovation Partnership in Smart Cities and Communities (EIP-SCC). Effective 1 December 2020, the fourteen cities and regions are Aachen, Amsterdam, Nouvelle Aquitaine, Ingolstadt, Hamburg, Ljubljana, Liège, Malaga, Tampere, Northern Hesse, Oulu, Enschede, Trikala and Metropolis GZM.

82 The World gathers virtual during ADW Hybrid 2020, Wednesday, 9 December 2020. *See* Cities and Regions of the EU's UAM Initiative present the 'Manifesto on the Multilevel Governance of the Urban Sky', sUAS News, the business of drones, 2 December 2020. *See also* www.amsterdamdroneweek.com/manifesto.

And Dr. Christian Scharpf, Lord Mayor in the City of Ingolstadt, Germany, stated:

> In Ingolstadt we welcome UAM as an innovative mobility solution. Whether it is about air taxis or the transportation of medical supplies with drones, it is important that we anticipate and design UAM services that are safe, reliable and fit in with local needs and circumstances. Which is why we support this manifesto.

U-space has been born and is developing fast. The SESAR JU will continue to participate in and support further developments as part of a focused and motivated pan-European team that will create a safe and productive operating environment for manned and unmanned aircraft alike. In the near term, research needs to be done towards more complex U3 and U4 operations, keeping operations safe, secure and green, and integrating the urban dimension, through learning in this Network from the management expertise of the SESAR JU and the air traffic management expertise of EUROCONTROL as well as, under the competence of EASA, the adoption of a comprehensive U-space Regulation to further materialize U-space.[83]

4.5 Preserving Airspace Access

A frequently asked question is, who controls low-altitude airspace? Another more intriguing and controversial question is, who owns low-altitude airspace?

The latter question represents one of the most important issues for the commercial drone industry. Although international aviation organizations created regulatory frameworks for drone operations, a great deal of confusion still prevails over the question of what constitutes a legal flight under state law and international rules. Organizations such as the FAA and EASA take the position that each independent state controls its airspace from the ground up. In other words, states believe they have regulatory sovereignty over 'every cubic inch of outdoor air'.

However, what remains quite unclear is where navigable airspace begins, an issue that has major implications for airspace users. Airspace may normally be used at or above 500 ft, which is the minimum safe altitude for flight in non-congested airspace. The airspace below 500 ft is not empty, even in areas far from aerodromes. Many other users share the airspace, and this use must be taken into account. In many cases these other users may be anywhere in the airspace. This is the case for GA, including gliders. On the other hand,

---

[83] Sources: SESAR JU U-space: Supporting Safe and Secure Drone Operations in Europe. A Preliminary Summary of SESAR U-space Research and Innovation Results (2017-2019) SESAR JU 2020. What is the EU doing to deliver the U-space? Joachim Lucking, Head of Unit Aviation Safety DG Move, Madrid 13 March 2019. SESAR JU U-space Demonstrations (https://sesarju.eu/node/3346).

there are areas where such use is likely to be more prevalent: around uncontrolled airports and corresponding departure/arrival paths; near hospitals equipped for air ambulances; near rural areas used as starting points for paragliders or balloonists, etc; military low-level routes and low-flying areas; and simulated forced landing areas, permitted by regulations, procedures or specific (ad hoc) exemption. Needless to say, aircraft committed to executing an actual emergency landing are committed to using this particular airspace segment without any alternative.

Other airspace users need to be aware of drone flights in their vicinity and vice versa. When preparing an airspace assessment, questions such as what interface is needed between drone operators and GA or how a glider pilot would be made aware of a planned drone operation along the cliff where he or she is intending ridge soaring need to be answered. In most cases, all users will need to inform a central system where they will be flying. The means of disseminating this information, nowadays most likely through one or more cloud-based mobile apps, should be included in an airspace assessment.

Technically, drones, helicopters and different air sports can take off and land on any property, but owing to the significant proliferation of drones, boundaries are required to define where private property rights end and navigable airspace starts. In this light, courts in many states try to address the question of determining the exact boundary between one's property and public airspace, let alone defining navigable airspace in the context of drones. To benefit from the full potential of the commercial drone industry, the boundaries and jurisdiction of low-altitude airspace must be defined. However, more drones operating at or below 1500 ft in uncontrolled airspace, if so permitted by regulation, might interfere with other traffic, mainly GA, usually flying in that airspace segment. This extremely important safety issue will unfortunately increase owing to the reduction of available airspace.[84]

Increasing questionable closures of airspace parts and environmental constraints raise a discussion about who, in fact, is the owner of the airspace. In this discussion, the crucial element is still the sovereignty of the state over its own territorial airspace. The principle of sovereignty stems from the state's responsibility for safety, in this particular case state security in the absence of physical airspace borders, which may entail conceivable airspace infringements or unlawful incursions, especially in times of war, and aircraft safety risks that, already in the initial phase of aviation, necessitated, among others, airworthiness requirements and rules of the air.

The Chicago Convention is playing an extremely important and harmonizing role in regard to international air traffic. However, the Chicago Convention is intended primarily for commercial aviation. It is therefore not surprising that the use of national airspace is granted to commercial aviation and, as part of a national defence task, military

---

84 See Greenberg, J., 'Who Controls Low-Altitude Airspace?', *Los Angeles & San Francisco Daily Journal*, 4 May 2017.

aviation. Remarkably enough, the articles of and annexes to the Chicago Convention are silent on the rights of the GA sector, including recreational flying, air sports and drones. Likewise, in EU legislation, there are no specific rules or recommendations about the use of airspace by national air sports and drones. However, airspace is obviously within the public domain entrusted to the state to be managed in the interest of all citizens. Not surprisingly, recreational aviators, air sporters and drone operators want to have just as many rights to use the airspace as commercial and military aviation.

Naturally, they are well aware of the prioritization of air traffic, as well as nature protection and conservation, although that does not imply that they can just be put aside without any form of participation or consultation, let alone compensation. In other words, they should not become a victim of the impetuous growth of CAT and arbitrary, stringent environmental policies of non-transparent state authorities.

The imposition of high fees by larger airports, owing to increasing air traffic intensity, is an attempt to prevent these particular airspace users from using the full infrastructure. There is a strong tendency by authorities/regulators to impose airspace restrictions, often without proper consultation, thereby regularly dramatically limiting these airspace users. Although not all regions in the world are facing airspace congestion, airspace restrictions will be a global issue any time in the future owing to a significant increase in world air transport, even despite short-term economic setbacks.

Available airspace is a critical resource that deserves every effort to be conserved. Unfortunately, there are numerous cases where restrictions have been implemented and have later been proved to be completely unnecessary or over-regulated. Therefore, any future airspace restriction must be tailored to impose the least burden on airspace users.

A common occurrence is the unnecessary allocation of airspace segments solely for commercial or military aviation activities, thereby practically blocking the GA, including air sports, recreational flying and drone activities in those specific airspace segments, often for no valid or substantiated reason. The result of the current design, management and use of airspace is that the critical and complex air traffic flows, at a constant safety level, can hardly accommodate any additional traffic. Therefore, a redesign of the airspace infrastructure, linked to advanced technologies, is absolutely required.

Restructuring airport CTRs, TMAs and CTAs is a prerequisite. The overall result will be piled-up CTAs, compact at the surface level and more extensive at higher levels. The shape will give the impression of an 'upside-down wedding cake', making more lower airspace available to specific airspace users such as drone operators.

To secure the rights, albeit undervalued, of this individual aviation sector, its interests must be addressed to international organizations such as ICAO, EASA and the European Commission, and other influential entities in the world, so that the activities of this sector can be conducted under proportional and simplified regulations, the greatest possible freedom and in balanced interaction with other, more privileged air transport operations. In this context, the responsible regulators and authorities with respect to airspace management should observe the need for flexibility and predictability in the availability of airspace, ensuring improved, and therefore easier, airspace access for this sector. This is especially applicable to primarily segregated airspace, unnecessarily blocked for the purpose of air transport operations and military missions.

It is common practice that CAAs simply enforce ICAO Standards for this sector in the absence of customized regulations. The ICAO SARPs are considered to be the legal framework for the entire aviation industry. That may be true for certain rules, such as rules of the air, search and rescue, aerodromes, and aircraft accident investigation, but other elements of aviation regulations require simplification and proportionality to meet the needs of this sector for special treatment and specific rules in order to reduce cost and facilitate future growth.

International aviation organizations recognize that more rules and regulations will not necessarily mean more aviation safety. EASA, for example, rejects heavy regulation and red tape. Instead, the Agency proposes to introduce flexibility and simplification regarding airworthiness certification and a dedicated oversight system for small and low-risk aircraft, to delegate licensing, certification and oversight responsibilities towards approved third parties such as National Aero Clubs or equivalent organizations, and to introduce provisions that will allow possible deviations from existing requirements, where appropriate.

While in many states increasing pressure exists on the availability of airspace because of the multitude of air traffic, at the same time, nature conservation organizations are claiming airspace above designated nature protection areas to restrict overflight up to a certain altitude, much higher than the code of conduct almost universally adopted by the GA sector. Everyone is convinced that nature conservation is of utmost importance to flora and fauna as well as to society. However, this often unjustified measure results in increasing air traffic density, or more diverse, mixed air traffic in less airspace. This might easily lead to a situation where nature prevails over flight safety. In many states, courts of justice are the appropriate legal institutions to have to decide on appeals about this controversial issue.

In a world where the decaying environment, the greenhouse effect and global climate change, in other words, the broad impact of human activities on resources and nature and the evidence of man-made contribution to climate change, are really hot topics, GA aircraft, including drones, are, in fact, minuscule contributors of pollution to the environment. The almost negligible contribution of the GA sector to total emissions of air pollutants is even decreasing at a rate surpassing that of most other aviation disciplines, mainly owing to rather low emission, innovative electric flying by solar and battery power associated with a strong reduction in noise pollution. This new way of flying creates the possibility to use more airspace allowed above nature reserves.[85]

In the ideal flexible future, CTRs, TMAs and CTAs will be divided into blocks that could be activated and deactivated with flexible boundaries according to and depending on the demand and use. The (de)activation should happen in real time using data link communication that graphically shows the activated and deactivated airspace blocks. The determination of the period and size of deactivated airspace will be done by analysing the actual demand using the FAA NextGen SWIM (System Wide Information Management) concept of 4D trajectory. In other words, three spatial dimensions plus the time factor as a fourth dimension, meteorological information and aerodrome operational status.[86]

When the runway operation changes, for reasons of weather, noise abatement or preference, the airspace demand by commercial traffic will change, which in turn will result in the opening and/or closure of a designated airspace sector for non-IFR traffic. This action could very well be done automatically. If all aircraft, including drones, are equipped with a data link system, these aircraft will know exactly to what time a certain airspace sector is open, which makes their operation more flexible. For the time being, the ANSP is the body that determines the best solution for flexible use of airspace that fits within the airspace structure.

The regulating bodies and authorities, responsible for airspace management, should observe the following:
- Continued access to currently available airspace should be a clearly stated high-priority objective;
- all actions to restrict access to airspace for the GA sector, including drones, should be subject to a formal procedure involving all relevant stakeholders ensuring that only absolutely necessary validated restrictions are implemented;
- structured programmes should be established with the objective of improving and regaining access to airspace unnecessarily blocked in favour of CAT and military activities; and
- greater flexibility and predictability in the availability of airspace should be a stated, high-priority objective ensuring improved airspace access for the GA sector, including drones.

---

85 Verstraete, D. (University of Sydney), 'Climate Explained: Why Don't We Have Electric Aircraft?', *The Conversation*, 20 September 2019.
86 ICAO Doc 10039 AN/511 Manual on System Wide Information Management (SWIM) Concept, 2015: The System Wide Information Management Concept consists of standards, infrastructure and governance enabling the management of ATM-related information and its exchange between qualified parties via interoperable services. SWIM enables seamless information access and interchange for all providers and users of ATM information and services. It takes information management business practices from the ICT sector such as Service-Oriented Architecture (SOA) and the use of open standards and Web technologies and applies them to ATM (www.eurocontrol.int/concept/system-wide-information-management).

States shall through their CAAs:
- Formulate the national policy for airspace management taking into account the requirements of national and international airspace users and ANSPs;
- reassess the national airspace structure and ATS route network with the aim of planning, as far as possible, for flexible airspace structures and procedures;
- periodically review the national airspace requirements and, where applicable, cross-border airspace utilization;
- establish negotiation procedures and priority rules for airspace allocation at FUA level 2;
- review the procedures and efficiency of FUA level 2 and FUA level 3 operations; and
- provide operational transparency across national boundaries through collaborative airspace planning and harmonized airspace management with neighbouring states.

FUA level 1: the strategic level is the high-level definition and review of the national airspace policy, taking into account national and international airspace users and air traffic service provider requirements. Related tasks include the establishment of the airspace organization, the planning and the creation of permanent and temporary airspace structures, and the agreement of airspace use priorities and negotiation procedures.

FUA level 2: the pre-tactical level is the conduct of operational airspace management within the framework of the structures and procedures defined at level 1. Pre-tactical tasks include the day-to-day allocation of airspace and the communication of airspace allocation data to all the parties concerned.

FUA level 3: the tactical level at which state authorities establish enhanced supporting coordination equipment and real-time civil-military coordination procedures in order to activate, deactivate or reallocate in real time the airspace allocated at level 2, resolve specific airspace issues and traffic situations between civil and military ATS units and controllers, provide access to all necessary flight data, including controller's intentions, and fully exploit the FUA concept at levels 1 and 2.

By using variable time frames for (initial) planning/execution as a reference, the levels of FUA can be explained more in detail as follows:

Level 1 is the long-term management of flexible airspace. This level of flexibility is planned from one year to a week prior to operation. The main activity at this level is the planning of airspace and route usage. For flexible solutions, the authority in charge, as a rule the National High-Level Airspace Policy Body, the permanent body for strategic airspace management, has to look at individual situations and determine the best solution that fits within the airspace structure using currently available technology.

An example is the ICAO HX (no specific working hours) classification. By using this type of classification, the airspace in question will fall back to the (less strict) airspace classification of the surrounding airspace, or other if specified. The HX classification principle could easily be applied to CTRs of airports that are closed on weekends (military CTRs) or at airports with scarce traffic. The HX classification could also be operated at level 2 or level 3 flexibility.

The main activity in level 2 flexibility is the allocation of the airspace and route structure. This happens in the period between a week to one day prior to operation. The responsible organization is the Central Flow Management Unit (CFMU) or the national Airspace Management Cell (AMC). Related tasks include the day-to-day allocation of airspace and the communication of airspace allocation data to all parties concerned.

Level 2 flexibility does not offer any more chances for the GA sector, including drones, except for the operation of the HX classification; however, that would benefit this sector more if it were used on an hourly basis, which, in fact, is level 3 flexibility. Since aircraft, including drones, being part of the GA sector, are not flying according to a fixed schedule, and mostly not via a specific route, it is impracticable, if not impossible, to plan flexibility too far in advance. This, however, makes it possible for this sector to be able to adjust their route or activity in real time, if airspace is, or shortly will be, (de)activated. Two systems that help to (de)activate distinct airspace are the automated regional flight information service (REFIS) and the military aerodromes status information system (MASIS).

These systems, applied in different states, send automated information via fixed frequencies to radio-equipped airspace users. The automated REFIS provides information about the regional barometric pressure (QNH), significant meteorological information (SIGMET), if applicable, the latest regional airspace information and other information likely to affect safety, clearly unable to be covered at short notice by a Notice to Airmen (NOTAM).

The MASIS is a trigger-activated loop of information that broadcasts on the military tower frequency outside opening hours, providing airport information and crossing clearance of the CTR. The information provided is quite similar to that of automated terminal information service (ATIS), normally used 24/7 at civil airports.

Level 3 flexibility is the short-term flexibility and is planned a day to three hours prior to the operation. The main activity at this level is the activation of airspace and route structure. Responsible entities are the supervisors of civil and military ATC centres. In the ideal situation, level 3 flexibility offers a wealth of opportunities, although full flexibility entails complex technical challenges. Level 3 flexibility, which currently exists, occurs according to previously made agreements and covenants between ATC, the government, in particular the CAA, and the airspace users. Communication is done by VHF radio or by telephone.[87]

---

[87] See The EUROCONTROL Concept of the Flexible Use of Airspace, October 2002 (www.eurocontrol.int/eatmp/fua/index.html).

Airspace block availability is examined on a daily basis. Some airspace blocks are to be used flexibly only under certain conditions. When conditions regarding usage of multiple flexible airspace blocks differ, the situation could become rather complex. Publication on a specific website could make it easier for airspace users. In the future, sharing of information concerning (de)activation of airspace blocks could well be improved by using newly developed technological systems that could bring the FUA concept to serve a wider airspace use, especially at level 3 flexibility.

The REFIS system could, in combination with the HX classification, create CTRs and TMAs, as well as other airspace segments or volumes that can be used by the GA sector without the need for additional, expensive (technical, digital) electronic equipment. In the future, however, the REFIS systems will eventually be replaced, in the context of aeronautical system modification, by the use of data link communication. Comprehensive aeronautical flight information can also be obtained from the digital aeronautical flight information file (DAFIF).

With respect to the FUA concept, ATS units and users make the best possible use of available airspace to meet commercial flight efficiency and military mission effectiveness, although security of national airspace shall be paramount and will not be compromised at any stage.

Airspace reservation for exclusive or specific use of certain categories of aircraft, including drones, shall be temporarily applied during limited periods, depending on actual use, and shall be disregarded as the activity that motivated the exclusive airspace use ceases to exist. Eventually, it shall follow the procedures set forth in applicable ICAO Annexes and documents.

The FUA concept has evolved to become the AFUA concept, which, as mentioned before, stands for advanced flexible use of airspace. This improved concept is an airspace management concept based on civil-military partnership to enhance the efficient use of airspace. It is expected to provide more flexibility on the basis of dynamic airspace management in all flight phases, from initial planning to execution. Furthermore, it is aimed at providing a responsive approach in a more complex environment within which air traffic growth needs to be accommodated.

AFUA is based on extended civil-military cooperation, more proactive and performance oriented to achieve the optimum mission effectiveness and commercial flight efficiency, as is the case with FUA. The AFUA concept will introduce free route airspace, which will actually be part of the European SES programme, real-time information sharing and common situational awareness. The concept will be of utmost importance for unmanned aircraft, especially IFR equipped, to integrate and operate safely within the existing air traffic environment in a harmonized manner alongside traditional manned aviation.

A two-step approach is defined for IFR-capable drones in controlled airspace, with accommodation possible mostly through FUA/AFUA techniques during ASBU Block 1, most probably until 2025, and then full integration with the necessary developed SARPs from ASBU Block 2, from 2025. In Europe, the accommodation phase can easily be maintained owing to the relatively small number of drone operations yet. VFR operations pose additional challenges compared with IFR operations. The traditional see and avoid principle used for separation and collision avoidance in uncontrolled airspace must be replaced by a technical detect and avoid system of the same level of confidence as, and compatible with, the current see and avoid principle. Despite promising results towards finalizing such a system and operationally validating it, it is unlikely that full integration into VFR airspace can occur before around 2030 (ASBU Block 3). Owing to the limited use of airspace above FL 600 so far, by both manned aviation and prospective UAS, UAS operations in this particular airspace may be accommodated in the foreseeable future.[88]

In the context of UAS integration, regulations, procedures and safety levels, ICAO has specified four main requirements for UAS-ATM integration:
- The integration of UAS shall not imply a significant impact on current users of the airspace;
- UAS shall comply with the existing and future regulations and procedures laid out for manned aviation;
- UAS integration shall not compromise existing aviation safety levels or increase risk more than an equivalent increase in manned aviation would;
- UAS operations shall be conducted in the same way as those of manned aircraft and shall be seen as equivalent by ATC and other airspace users.

Two new sets of flight rule-based operations are to be recognized: low-level flight rules (LFR), below the normal minimum VFR height of 500 ft in what is termed VLL, and high-level flight rules (HFR), above FL 600, taken as a soft boundary between the top segment of the upper information region (UIR) and the Kármán Line, depending on state-specific regulations. The fact is that between the middle latitudes and the equator, FL 600 (18,3 km) is the approximate top of the troposphere, and most aerospace activities occur in this lower part of the atmosphere.

Both manned and unmanned air operations above FL 600 are, apart from inefficient aerodynamic characteristics, limited by technological, physiological, physical and administrative constraints. The HFR will cover all operations on manned and unmanned aircraft operating within this ultra-high-level airspace as commercial point-to-point suborbital flights and high-altitude, long-endurance (HALE) flights and must be compatible with IFR but may warrant additional requirements such as satellite-based navigation systems. Furthermore, altitudes above FL 600 pose a much higher safety risk to both manned and unmanned aircraft operations, especially in the event of

---

88 *See* IATA Vision 2050 Report, Singapore, 12 February 2011.

malfunctions. Therefore, there is a strong need to develop new legal and regulatory regimes, while their impact on existing international agreements will require global consideration regarding the development and implementation of an effective functioning Space Traffic Management (STM) system that encompasses unmanned operations above, below and across the Kármán Line.[89]

It is assumed that all drones operating as IFR/VFR traffic within airspace classes A-G will comply with the relevant airspace requirements in the same manner as manned aircraft. Operations in the airspace where commercial air transport aircraft normally operate could demand additional operational performance requirements covering speed, reaction time, turn performance and climb/descent performance. The general principle for the integration of drones into airspace where IFR/VFR traffic is operating is that capabilities should be available that prevent collisions between drones themselves or between drones and manned aircraft. In cases where such capabilities are not available or are degraded, the airspace should be so organized and allocated as to guarantee that there is no risk of collision. ASM/FUA-AFUA concepts and airspace structures defined by ICAO would be the primary means of achieving such an airspace organization.[90]

---

89 Hunter, S.K., Lt. Col. (Air Force Space Command), 'Safe Operations Above FL 600', *Space Traffic Management Conference*, Embry-Riddle Aeronautical University, 2015.
90 UAS ATM Integration Operational Concept, European Organization for the Safety of Air Navigation (EUROCONTROL), Directorate of European Civil-Military Aviation (DECMA) and Aviation Cooperation and Strategies Division (ACS), Edition: 1.0, 27 November 2018, pp. 7-14.

Chapter 5 Safety Requirements in UAS Operations

5.1 Introduction

Drones, or unmanned aircraft systems (UAS), equipped with a wide range of technological products, systems and services, are one of the most advanced societal tools in the area of robotics, aeronautics and electronics. Drones will definitely be part of our future. Some expert predictions even mention a predominant social role. Obviously, drones will perform an extensive range of useful but also necessary societal applications, creating significant benefits in many sectors. However, inappropriate use of drones poses a constant concern for public authorities and regulators. Drones are considered aircraft and should be able to operate in airspace, along with a variety of traditional manned aircraft under instrument flight rules (IFR) or visual flight rules (VFR), adhering to the requirements of the specific airspace class in which they are operating.[1]

Drones have to comply with aviation rules. As for manned aircraft, a uniform implementation of and compliance with rules and procedures should apply to operators, including remote pilots, of unmanned aircraft (systems), as well as for the flight operation of such aircraft and systems. The rules and procedures applicable to drone operations should be proportionate to the nature and risk of the operation or activity and adapted to the operational characteristics of drones concerned.

Considering the specific characteristics of drones and the nature of the area of operations, such as the population density, the presence of buildings and other obstacles as well as surface conditions, they should be as safe as those in manned aviation. A wide range of possible drone operations are accomplished by advanced technologies. Requirements related to the degree of airworthiness, the organizations, operations and the personnel involved should be drawn up in order to ensure safety for third parties on the surface and in the air.

Integration into non-segregated airspace should not impact on the current airspace users. In other words, there should be no disruption of current air operations, no modification of ATC procedures, no additional mandatory equipment because of

---

1   UAS, or drones, are legally defined as aircraft by ICAO Ann. 2. See De Florio, F., *Airworthiness: An Introduction to Aircraft Certification,* Second Edition, The Boulevard, Langford Lane, Oxford: Butterworth-Heinemann, 2011, pp. 82-85. See also De Florio, F, *Airworthiness: An Introduction to Aircraft Certification and Operations,* Third Edition, The Boulevard, Langford Lane, Kidlington, Oxford: Butterworth-Heinemann, 2016, pp. 471-476.

increasing drone operations and no degradation of safety in the air. Achieving the full integration of all types of drones requires the development of appropriate regulations in the three essential domains of airworthiness, flight crew licensing and air operation. These are crucial prerequisite safety requirements., Commercial drone pilots, in particular, fall under strict regulation. Situational awareness for pilots of drones must match that of traditional pilots in cockpits. Additionally, there will be a requirement to manage the transition from remotely piloted drones to more automated drones that will only be monitored.

Current national drone certificates of airworthiness, personnel licensing and operations within the EU should be adapted to certificates, licences and authorizations complying with the requirements set by EASA. The FAA has been creating adjusted rules and procedures concerning operational limitations, certificate of airworthiness standards, aeronautical knowledge and safety tests, licences and authorizations and community-based organizations in order to reform and authorize rules and to set harmonized standards throughout the United States.[2]

In any region of the world, apart from the United States and the European Union, national drone regulations differ dramatically,, although the elements of regulation are largely similar from state to state. These elements are licensing, aircraft registration, restricted zones for drones, risks and insurance. The level of restrictiveness of each element varies widely, depending on the favourable introduction of new technologies or a stricter approach to safety first. In a number of states, operating a drone is still considered illegal. However, depending on government approval of applicable regulations, developed in line with ICAO, states will soon lift the ban on drones.

The goal of ICAO in addressing unmanned aviation is to provide the fundamental international regulatory framework through SARPs, with supporting PANS and guidance material, to underpin the routine operation of UAS throughout the world in a safe, harmonized and seamless manner comparable to that of manned aviation, including the main elements such as rules of the air, certification, licensing, operations, communications and environmental considerations.

5.2 Remote Pilot Requirements

The FAA has created its first and only airman certificate specifically for the use and operation of small UAS, known as the remote pilot certificate with a small UAS rating. A small UAS includes a small unmanned aircraft, with an MTOM of less than 55 lbs,

---

[2] *See also* 49 U.S.C. 44809 Exceptions for limited recreational operations of unmanned aircraft (text contains those laws in effect on 7 September 2020), from Title 49 – Transportation, subtitle VII Aviation Programs, Part A Air Commerce and Safety, subpart iii safety, Chapter 448-UAS (New FAA Recreational Drone Laws, May 2019).

CHAPTER 5   SAFETY REQUIREMENTS IN UAS OPERATIONS

including inboard payload or anything attached to the aircraft.[3] Eligibility for a remote pilot certificate requires that the individual meet the minimum age condition of 16 years and be able to read, understand, speak and write the English language. In addition, eligibility depends on whether he or she knows or has reason to know of a physical or mental condition that would interfere with the safe operation of the small UAS.

There are different methods for obtaining a remote pilot certificate from the FAA, depending on whether the applicant is a pilot or non-pilot. An applicant is a pilot if he or she holds a pilot certificate, which means any grade, except student pilot, for any aircraft category, issued by the FAA under Part 61 of the Federal Aviation Regulations, and has accomplished a flight review within the past 24 calendar months. If these two requirements are not met, the applicant is considered a non-pilot.

EASA Opinion 01/2018, which was published on 6 February 2018, is proposing a new European regulation for UAS operations in the Open and Specific categories. This proposed regulation defines, among other issues, the technical and operational requirements for unmanned aircraft, for example the remote pilots' qualifications.

In accordance with Paragraph 8 of Article 56 (Compliance of unmanned aircraft) of Regulation (EU) 2018/1139 "This Section (Section VII Unmanned aircraft) shall be without prejudice to the possibility for EU Member States to lay down national rules to make subject to certain conditions to the operations of unmanned aircraft for reasons falling outside the scope of Regulation (EU) 2018/1139, including public security or protection of privacy and personal data in accordance with the law of the European Union (Union law)".[4]

UAS operators and remote pilots should ensure that they are adequately informed about applicable EU rules and national rules relating to the intended operations, in particular with regard to safety, security, privacy and data protection, liability, insurance and environmental protection.

The responsibilities of the operator and of the remote pilot have been clearly separated. For example, the obligation to register is one of the operator's responsibilities, which are of a structural nature. The remote pilot's responsibilities are of a tactical nature; for example, the remote pilot should fly the unmanned aircraft within the limits of its user manual. One important task, in addition to others, is to ensure safe separation from manned aircraft. Although this is different from what is defined in the

---

3   Payload means instrument, mechanism, equipment, part, apparatus, appurtenance or accessory, including communications equipment that is installed in or attached to the aircraft and is not used or intended to be used in operating or controlling an aircraft in flight, and is not part of an airframe, engine, or propeller. Maximum take-off mass (MTOM) means the maximum UA take-off mass, including payload and fuel, as defined by the manufacturer or the builder, at which the UA can be operated. *See* Art. 2 Definitions, Commission Implementing Regulation (EU) 2019/947 of 24 May 2019 on the rules and procedures for the operation of unmanned aircraft, *OJ* L 152/45, 11 June 2019.

4   Regulation (EU) 2018/1139 Section VII includes Art. 55, Essential requirements for unmanned aircraft; Art. 56, Compliance with unmanned aircraft; Art. 57, Implementing acts as regards unmanned aircraft; and Art. 58, Delegated powers.

Standardized European Rules of the Air, it can be explained by the fact that the unmanned aircraft remote pilot is better placed to detect a traditional manned aircraft than the reverse and also because of the typical smaller size of unmanned aircraft operating in the Open category. It should be noted that the FAA has adopted the same approach in its Part 107.[5]

According to ICAO, remote pilots and other members of the remote crew shall be trained and licensed in accordance with Annex 1 (Personnel licensing) to the Chicago Convention. Annex 1 establishes the minimum training, operation and licensing standards to be met by aviation personnel involved in international air navigation, both manned and unmanned aviation.

Therefore, licensing and training requirements will be developed similar to those for manned aviation and will include both the aeronautical knowledge and operational components. Specific adjustments may be needed considering the particular and unique nature and characteristics of the remote pilot environment and the specific unmanned aircraft applications.

The introduction of unmanned aircraft operations brings new dimensions to licences for remote pilots and other members of the remote crew in that they are outside the scope of Article 32 of the Chicago Convention.

Article 32 of the Chicago Convention, 1944:

> Licenses of personnel.
> - The pilot of every aircraft and the other members of the operating crew of every aircraft engaged in international navigation shall be provided with certificates of competency and licenses issued or rendered valid by the State in which the aircraft is registered.
> - Each contracting State reserves the right to refuse to recognize, for the purpose of flight above its own territory, certificates of competency and licenses granted to any of its nationals by another contracting State.

All RPAS personnel responsible for flight safety must be knowledgeable, adequately trained, experienced and otherwise qualified in their duties. Any person involved in the operation of an unmanned aircraft, including the remote pilot, shall possess the required knowledge and skills that are necessary to ensure the safety of the operation and that are proportionate to the risk associated with the type of operation. The person shall also

---

5   Commission Implementing Regulation (EU) 2016/1185 of 20 July 2016 amending Implementing Regulation (EU) No. 923/2012 as regards the update and completion of the common rules of the air and operational provisions regarding services and procedures in air navigation (SERA Part C) and repealing Regulation (EC) No. 730/2006, OJ L196/3, 21 July 2016.

demonstrate medical fitness, if this is necessary to mitigate the risk involved in the operation concerned.[6]

The qualifying requirements are manifest in personnel licences issued by the competent authority. Remote pilots are required to receive medical certification, complete training and demonstrate competency before being licensed to remotely fly an unmanned aircraft. The training requirements and degree of competency required depend on the complexity of the RPA being flown and the purpose of the flight.

Requirements for smaller, less complex RPA flown privately should be less stringent than the requirements for remote pilots flying large, complex RPA in high-density airspace. According to the ICAO, all remote pilots should possess knowledge of general aviation rules, rules of the air, regulations and procedures, although remote pilot certification qualifications may differ depending on the RPA type, size or operational environment. Different categories of RPA or remote pilot stations may require a certain class or type rating on the remote pilot licence, as considered necessary by the competent authority.

Class ratings pertain to systems that entail comparable handling and performance characteristics, while type ratings refer to systems requiring additional training beyond the initial licence, for example where the operation requires more than one remote pilot. A strict rule is that all remote pilots conducting international IFR operations must possess a remote pilot licence. The competent authority (licensing authority) of the state where the RPA is located will issue, renew or validate remote pilot licences for qualified applicants.[7]

The question arises as to whether the remote pilot is primarily affiliated with the unmanned aircraft or with the remote pilot station. If it is determined that the primary relationship is between the remote pilot and the remote pilot station, the conclusion can be drawn that the state of the remote pilot station rather than the State of Registry of the unmanned aircraft, if different, would grant or issue the licence. A clear assessment has to be made before a decision can be reached. In either case, the unmanned aircraft and the remote pilot station would be considered as a unit by the designated licensing authority, who, in addition, will have to consider the location and the configuration of the remote pilot station when issuing remote pilot licences. For example, a remote pilot station can be located in a building or can be vehicle based, ship based, airborne or handheld.

A number of significant differences with manned aircraft are observed when an unmanned aircraft is operating internationally. The remote pilot licence will be issued to an individual, located in the remote pilot station, who apparently will not be with the unmanned aircraft as it arrives in a foreign state. Authorities in the destination state will not have direct personal contact with the remote pilot or members of the remote crew.

---

6   Regulation (EU) 2018/1139 Ann. IX Essential requirements for unmanned aircraft.
7   ICAO Remotely Piloted Aircraft Systems (RPAS) Concept of Operations (CONOPS) for International IFR Operations, p. 20.

On the basis of the foregoing, current and previous national designations for personnel piloting unmanned aircraft need to be replaced by applicable terms as contained in ICAO Annex 1, appropriately modified to indicate their actual position being external of the unmanned aircraft, such as remote pilot, remote navigator or remote sensor engineer, each of which is a member of the remote crew. A new crew position unique to some VLOS operations is the RPA observer, an individual who, by visual observation of the RPA, assists the remote pilot in the safe conduct of the flight.[8]

In general, the remote pilot must be competent, properly licensed and capable of discharging the responsibility for safe flight.

Minimum age for remote pilots:

1. The minimum age for remote pilots operating a UAS, including RPAS, in the Open and Specific category shall be 16 years.
2. No minimum age for remote pilots shall be required:
   - when they operate in subcategory A1 as specified in Part A of the Annex to Regulation (EU) 2019/947, with a UAS Class C0 defined in Part 1 of the Annex to Regulation (EU) 2019/945 that is a toy within the meaning of Directive 2009/48/EC.
   - For privately-built UAS with an MTOM of less than 250 g;
   - When they operate under the direct supervision of a remote pilot complying with Paragraph 1 and Article 8.
3. EU Member States may lower the minimum age following a risk based approach taking into account specific risks associated with the operation in their respective territory;
   - for remote pilots operating in the Open category by up to 4 years;
   - for remote pilots operating in the Specific category by up to 2 years.
4. Where a EU Member State lowers the minimum age for remote pilots, those remote pilots shall only be allowed to operate a UAS on the territory of that EU Member State.
5. EU Member States may define a different minimum age for remote pilots operating in the framework of model aircraft clubs or associations and the authorization issued in accordance with Article 16 (UAS operations in the framework of model aircraft clubs and associations).[9]

Requirements for remote pilots applicable to all UAS operations in the Open category are defined as follows:

The remote pilot shall:
- have the ability to take control of the UA, except in case of a lost link;

---

8 ICAO Circular 328 AN/190 Unmanned Aircraft Systems (UAS), 2011.
9 Art. 9 of the Commission Implementing Regulation (EU) 2019/947 of 24 May 2019. *See also* Art. 8, Rules and procedures for the competency of remote pilots.

- have the appropriate competence for the subcategory of UAS operations (A1, A2 or A3); and
- comply with UAS.OPEN.10 and UAS.OPEN.20 if the remote pilot is also the UAS operator.

Except when operating a UAS Class C0, before starting a UAS operation, the remote pilot shall:
- obtain updated information, relevant to the intended operation, about any flight restrictions or conditions published by the EU Member State;
- familiarize themselves with the operating environment;
- ensure that the UAS is in a safe condition to complete the intended flight.

During flight, the remote pilot shall:
- comply with the requirements applicable to the subcategory of UAS operations;
- ensure the safe operation of the UA with respect to third-party activities on the ground or in the air;
- give way to manned aircraft;
- comply with the limitations on the area, zone or airspace defined by the EU Member State;
- operate the UAS within the performance limitations defined in the instructions provided by the manufacturer;
- keep the UA in VLOS or within a range such that the remote pilot, or an UA observer, situated within the line of sight of the remote pilot, maintains VLOS; clear and effective communication shall be established between the remote pilot and the UA observer;
- not use the UA to transport dangerous goods;[10]
- not fly close or inside areas where an emergency response effort is ongoing unless they have permission from the local authority; and
- respect other people's fundamental rights and operate the UAS in a considerate way to minimize nuisance to other people due to noise emissions.
- In order to ensure an adequate level of competency for remote pilots, the following approach was followed in Opinion 01-2018: since STS-01 (standard scenario) covers UAS operations with a low intrinsic risk, similar to the level for Open subcategory A2,

---

10 Dangerous goods are articles or substances capable of posing a hazard to health, safety, property or the environment in the case of an incident or accident, which the unmanned aircraft is carrying as its payload, including in particular, explosives, gases, flammable liquids, flammable solids, oxidizing agents and organic peroxides, toxic and infectious substances and corrosive substances.

a similar approach to the one used for that subcategory is followed for remote pilot competency.[11]

For the theoretical knowledge part, similarly to the requirements for Open subcategory A2, the student remote pilot will be granted a certificate issued by a competent authority or by an entity recognized by a competent authority of an EU Member State after:
- having passed the online theoretical knowledge examination as required for the Open subcategories A1 and A3; and
- having passed a classroom theoretical knowledge examination provided by the competent authority or by the entity recognized by the competent authority. Compared with the one defined for Open subcategory A2, more subjects and topics need to be covered, and two options are possible:
  1. if student remote pilots do not hold a certificate of remote pilot competency required for Open subcategory A2, the subjects to be covered by the examination are those listed in the proposed Attachment A to STS-01; or
  2. if student remote pilots hold a certificate of remote pilot competency for Open subcategory A2, they are only required to pass the examination on the reduced number of subjects indicated in point 1(b) of the proposed Attachment A to STS-01.

Requirements for remote pilots applicable to all UAS operations in the Specific category are defined as follows:

The remote pilot shall:
- not perform duties under the influence of psychoactive substances or alcohol or when he or she is unfit to perform his or her tasks owing to injury, fatigue, medication, sickness or other causes;
- have the appropriate remote pilot competency as defined in the Operation Authorization (OA), in the standard scenario defined in Appendix 1 or as defined by the Light UAS Operator Certificate and carry a proof of competency while operating the UAS.[12]

---

11 See Opinion 01-2018 p. 8: a standard scenario involves a pre-established risk assessment and includes mitigation measures. It may be followed by a declaration submitted by the UAS operator, if the implementation of the mitigation measures is considered to be simple, or by an authorization issued by the competent authority, if the implementation of the mitigation measures is considered to be complex.

12 The Light UAS Operator Certificate (LUC) has been introduced as an option. This allows more flexibility to operators performing operations covered by standard scenarios requiring an authorization by the competent authority or operations not covered by a scenario. In these cases, an operator may request a certificate from the competent authority, which is an LUC, with privileges to authorize these specific operations (Explanatory Note on Prototype Commission Regulation on Unmanned Aircraft Operations, 22 August 2016).

CHAPTER 5   SAFETY REQUIREMENTS IN UAS OPERATIONS

Before starting a UAS operation, the remote pilot shall comply with all of the following:
- obtain updated information relevant to the intended operation about any geographical zones defined in accordance with Article 15;
- ensure that the operating environment is compatible with the authorized or declared limitations and conditions;
- ensure that the UAS is in a safe condition to complete the intended flight safely, and, if applicable, check if the direct remote identification works properly;
- ensure that the information about the operation has been made available to the relevant air traffic service unit, other airspace users and relevant stakeholders, as required by the OA or by the conditions published by the EU Member State for the geographical zone of operation in accordance with Article 15.

During the flight, the remote pilot shall:
- comply with the authorized or declared limitations and conditions;
- avoid any risk of collision with any manned aircraft and discontinue a flight when continuing it may pose a risk to other aircraft, people, animals, environment or property;
- comply with the operational limitations in geographical zones defined in accordance with Article 15 of Regulation (EU) 2019/947;
- comply with the operator's procedures;
- not fly close to or inside areas where an emergency response effort is ongoing unless they have permission to do so from the responsible emergency response services.[13]

5.3   UAS OPERATOR REQUIREMENTS

Member States of the European Union shall establish and maintain accurate registration systems for UAS whose design is subject to certification and for UAS operators whose operation may present a risk to safety, security, privacy and protection of personal data or environment.

---

13   Commission Implementing Regulation (EU) 2019/947 Art. 15. Operational conditions for UAS geographical zones. 1. When defining UAS geographical zones for safety, security, privacy or environmental reasons, EU Member States may: (a) prohibit certain or all UAS operations, request particular conditions for certain or all UAS operations or request a prior operational authorization for certain or all UAS operations; (b) subject UAS operations to specified environmental standards; (c) allow access to certain UAS classes only; (d) allow access only to UAS equipped with certain technical features, in particular remote identification systems or geo-awareness systems. 2. On the basis of a risk assessment carried out by the competent authority, EU Member States may designate certain geographical zones in which UAS operations are exempt from one or more of the Open category requirements. 3. When pursuant to Paras. 1 or 2, EU Member States define UAS geographical zones, for geo-awareness purposes they shall ensure that the information on the UAS geographical zones, including their period of validity, is made publicly available in a common unique digital format.

The UAS operator shall comply with all of the following in the Open category:
1) develop operational procedures adapted to the type of operation and the risk involved;
2) ensure that all operations effectively use and support the efficient use of radio spectrum in order to avoid harmful interference;
3) designate a remote pilot for each UAS operation;
4) ensure that the remote pilots and all other personnel performing a task in support of the operations are familiar with the user's manual provided by the manufacturer of the UAS; and
a) have appropriate competency in the subcategory of the intended UAS operations in accordance with points UAS.OPEN.020, UAS.OPEN.030 or UAS.OPEN.040 to perform their tasks or, for personnel other than the remote pilot, have completed an on-the-job-training course developed by the operator;[14]
b) are fully familiar with the UAS operator's procedures;
c) are provided with the information relevant to the intended UAS operation concerning any geographical zones published by the EU Member State of operation in accordance with Article 15 of Regulation (EU) 2019/947.
5) update the information into the geo-awareness system when applicable according to the intended location of operation;
6) in the case of an operation with an unmanned aircraft of one of the classes defined in Parts 1 to 5 of Regulation (EU) 2019/945, ensure that the UAS is:
a) accompanied by the corresponding EU declaration of conformity, including the reference to the appropriate class; and
b) the related class identification label is affixed to the unmanned aircraft.
7) ensure that in the case of a UAS operation in subcategory A2 or A3 all involved persons present in the area of the operation have been informed of the risks and have explicitly agreed to participate.[15]

The UAS operator shall comply with all of the following in the Specific category:
a) establish procedures and limitations adapted to the type of the intended operation and the risk involved, including;
i. operational procedures to ensure the safety of the operations;
ii. procedures to ensure that security requirements applicable to the area of operations are complied with in the intended operation;

---

14 Commission Implementing Regulation (EU) 2019/947, Annex UAS operations in the Open and Specific categories, Part A UAS operations in the Open category, UAS.OPEN.020 UAS operations in subcategory A1, UAS.OPEN.030 UAS operations in subcategory A2 and UAS.OPEN.030 UAS operations in subcategory A3.
15 Commission Implementing Regulation (EU) 2019/947, Annex UAS operations in the Open and Specific categories, Part A UAS operations in the Open category under UAS.OPEN.050 Responsibilities of the UAS operator.

iii. measures to protect against unlawful interference and unauthorized access;
iv. procedures to ensure that all operations are in respect of Regulation (EU) 2016/679 on the protection of natural persons with regard to the processing of personal data and on the free movement of such data. In particular, it shall carry out a data protection impact assessment, when required by the National Authority for data protection in application of Article 35 of Regulation (EU) 2016/679;[16]
b) designate a remote pilot for each operation or, in the case of autonomous operations, ensure that during all phases of the operation, responsibilities and tasks, especially those defined in points (2) and (3) of point UAS.SPEC.060, are properly allocated in accordance with the procedures established pursuant to point (a) above;
c) ensure that all operations effectively use and support the efficient use of radio spectrum in order to avoid harmful interference;
d) ensure that before conducting operations, remote pilots comply with all of the following conditions:
i. have the competency to perform their tasks in line with the applicable training identified by the operational authorization or, if point UAS.SPEC.020 applies, by the conditions and limitations defined in the appropriate standard scenario listed in Appendix 1 or as defined by the Light UAS Operator Certificate;
ii. follow remote pilot training which shall be competency-based and include the competencies set out in Paragraph 2 of Article 8;[17]
iii. follow remote pilot training, as defined in the Operation Authorization for operations requiring such authorization, it shall be conducted in cooperation with an entity recognized by the competent authority;
iv. follow remote pilot training for operations under declaration that shall be conducted in accordance with the mitigation measures defined by the standard scenario;
v. have been informed about the UAS operator's operations manual, if required by the risk assessment and procedures established in accordance with point (a);
vi. obtain updated information relevant to the intended operation about any geographical zones defined in accordance with Article 15;
e) ensure that personnel in charge of duties essential to the UAS operation, other than the remote pilot itself, comply with all of the following conditions:
i. have completed the on-the-job training developed by the operator;

---

16 Regulation (EU) 2016/679 (General Data Protection Regulation), Art. 35 Data protection impact assessment.
17 Commission Implementing Regulation (EU) 2019/947 Art. 8, Para. 2: Remote pilots operating UAS in the Specific category shall comply with the competency requirements set out in the operational authorization by the competent authority or in the standard scenario defined in App. 1 to the Annex or as defined by the LUC and shall have at least the following competencies: (a) ability to apply operational procedures (normal, contingency and emergency procedures, flight planning, pre-flight and post-flight inspections), (b) ability to manage aeronautical information, (c) manage the unmanned aircraft flight path and automation, (d) leadership, teamwork and self-management, (e) problem solving and decision-making, (f) situational awareness, (g) workload management, and (f) coordination or handover, as applicable.

ii. have been informed about the UAS operator's operations manual, if required by the risk assessment, and about the procedures established in accordance with point (a);
iii. have obtained updated information relevant to the intended operation about any geographical zones defined in accordance with Article 15;
f) carry out each operation within the limitations, conditions and mitigation measures defined in the declaration or specified in the operational authorization;
g) keep a record of the information on UAS operations as required by the declaration or by the operational authorization;
h) use UAS which, as a minimum, are designed in such a manner that a possible failure will not lead the UAS to fly outside the operation volume or to cause a fatality. In addition, man-machine interfaces shall be such as to minimize the risk of pilot error and shall not cause unreasonable fatigue;
i) maintain the UAS in a suitable condition for safe operation by:
i. as a minimum, defining maintenance instructions and employing an adequately trained and qualified maintenance staff;
ii. complying with point UAS.SPEC.100, if required; and
iii. using an unmanned aircraft which is designed to minimize noise and other emissions, taking into account the type of the intended operation and geographical areas where the aircraft noise and other emissions are of concern.[18]

UAS.SPEC.100 Use of certified equipment and certified unmanned aircraft.
1. If the UAS operation is using an unmanned aircraft for which a Certificate of Airworthiness or a Restricted Certificate of Airworthiness (R-CofA) has been issued, or using certified equipment, the UAS operator shall record the operation or service time in accordance either with the instructions and procedures applicable to the certified equipment, or with the organizational approval or authorization.
2. The UAS operator shall follow the instructions referred to in the unmanned aircraft certificate or equipment certificate and also comply with any airworthiness or operational directive issued by the Agency.

The UAS operator shall provide the competent authority with an operational risk assessment for the intended operation in accordance with Article 11, or submit a declaration when point UAS.SPEC.020 is applicable, unless the operator holds a LUC with the appropriate privileges, in accordance with Part C of the Annex to Regulation (EU) 2019/947, entitled 'Light UAS Operator Certificate'. The operator shall regularly evaluate the adequacy of the mitigation measures taken and update them where necessary.

---

18 Commission Implementing Regulation (EU) 2019/947 of 24 May 2019, Annex UAS operations in the Open and Specific categories, Part B UAS operations in the Specific category, UAS.SPEC.050 Responsibilities of the operator, UAS.SPEC.060 Responsibilities of the remote pilot.

CHAPTER 5   SAFETY REQUIREMENTS IN UAS OPERATIONS

UAS.SPEC.020 Operational declaration

1) In accordance with Article 5 (Specific category of UAS operations), the UAS operator may submit an operational declaration of compliance with a standard scenario as defined in Appendix 1 to this Annex to the competent authority of the EU Member State of operation as an alternative to points UAS.SPEC.030 and UAS.SPEC.040 in relation to operations:
a) of unmanned aircraft with:
i. maximum characteristic dimension up to 3 m in VLOS over controlled ground area except over assemblies of people;
ii. maximum characteristic dimension up to 1 m in VLOS except over assemblies of people;
iii. maximum characteristic dimension up to 1 m in BVLOS over sparsely populated areas;
iv. maximum characteristic dimension up to 3 m in BVLOS over controlled ground area.
b) performed below 120 m from the surface of the Earth, and:
i. in uncontrolled airspace (class F or G), or
ii. in controlled airspace after coordination and individual flight authorization in accordance with published procedures for the area of operation.
2) A declaration of UAS operators shall contain:
a) administrative information about the UAS operator;
b) a statement that the operation satisfies the operational requirement set out in point (1) and a standard scenario as defined in Appendix 1 to the Annex;
c) the commitment of the UAS operator to comply with the relevant mitigation measures required for the safety of the operation, including the associated instructions for the operation, for the design of the unmanned aircraft and the competency of involved personnel;
d) confirmation by the UAS operator that an appropriate insurance cover will be in place for every flight made under the declaration, if required by Union law or national law.
1) Upon receipt of the declaration, the competent authority shall verify that the declaration contains all the elements listed in point (2) and shall provide the UAS operator with a confirmation of receipt and completeness without undue delay.
2) After receiving the confirmation of receipt and completeness, the UAS operator is entitled to start the operation.
3) UAS operators shall notify, without any delay, the competent authority of any change to the information contained in the operational declaration that they submitted.
4) UAS operators holding a LUC with appropriate privileges, in accordance with Part C of this Annex, are not required to submit the declaration.

Contingency and emergency procedures. The UAS operator is required to develop contingency and emergency procedures to be described in the Operations Manual, and the remote pilot is required to put them in place immediately in the following situations:
- contingency procedures: in abnormal situations, which include situations that can lead to the UA exceeding the limits of the flight geography; and
- emergency procedures: in emergency situations, which include situations that can lead to the UA exceeding the limits of the operational volume. Remote pilots are expected to react immediately, performing the relevant emergency procedures as soon as they have an indication of those situations. Furthermore, when the emergency situation is perceived as likely to lead to the UA being outside the operational volume, remote pilots are required to trigger the flight termination system (FTS) at least 10 m before the UA reaches the limits of the operational volume.
- An emergency response plan (ERP) is considered an important element to ensure that the UAS operator's personnel participating in an operation are aware of what to do in case of an emergency in order to avoid an escalation of the effects. Even for UAS operations with the lowest risk in the Specific category, this plan should be required. In Specific Operation Risk Assessment (SORA), there is a penalty when this plan is not available or does not achieve a sufficient level of integrity.

UAS.LUC.020 Responsibilities of the LUC holder
The LUC holder shall:
1) comply with the requirements of points UAS.SPEC.050 (Responsibilities of the UAS operator) and UAS.SPEC.060 (Responsibilities of the remote pilot);
2) comply with the scope and privileges defined in the terms of approval;
3) establish and maintain a system for exercising operational control over any operation conducted under the terms of its LUC;
4) carry out an operational risk assessment of the intended operation in accordance with Article 11 of Regulation (EU) 2019/947 (Rules for conducting an operational risk assessment) unless conducting an operation for which an operational declaration is sufficient according to point UAS.SPEC.020 (Operational declaration);
5) keep records of the following items in a manner that ensures protection from damage, alteration and theft for a period of at least three years for operations conducted using the privileges specified under point UAS.LUC.060 (Privileges of the LUC holder):
a) the operational risk assessment, when required according to point (4), and its supporting documentation;
b) mitigation measures taken; and
c) the qualifications and experience of personnel involved in the UAS operation, compliance monitoring and safety management;

6) keep personnel records referred to in point (5)(c) as long as the person works for the organization and shall be retained until three years after the person has left the organization.

Safety management requirements regarding a Light UAS Operator Certificate.
UAS.LUC.030 Safety management system:
1) A UAS operator who applies for a LUC shall establish, implement and maintain a safety management system corresponding to the size of the organization, to the nature and complexity of its activities, taking into account the hazards and associated risks inherent in these activities.
2) The UAS operator shall comply with all of the following:
a) nominate an accountable manager with authority for ensuring that within the organization all activities are performed in accordance with the applicable standards and that the organization is continuously in compliance with the requirements of the management system and the procedures identified in the LUC manual referred to in point UAS.LUC.040 (LUC manual);
b) define clear lines of responsibility and accountability throughout the organization;
c) establish and maintain a safety policy and related corresponding safety objectives;
d) appoint key safety personnel to execute the safety policy;
e) establish and maintain a safety risk management process including the identification of safety hazards associated with the activities of the UAS operator, as well as their evaluation and the management of associated risks, including taking action to mitigate those risks and verify the effectiveness of the action;
f) promote safety in the organization through:
i. training and education;
ii. communication;
g) document all safety management system key processes for making personnel aware of their responsibilities and of the procedure for amending this documentation; key processes include:
i. safety reporting and internal investigations;
ii. operational control;
iii. communication on safety;
iv. training and safety promotion;
v. compliance monitoring;
vi. safety risk management;
vii. management of change;
viii. interface between organizations;
ix. use of subcontractors and partners;
h) include an independent function to monitor the compliance and adequacy of the fulfilment of the relevant requirements of Regulation (EU) 2019/947, including a

system to provide feedback of findings to the accountable manager to ensure effective implementation of corrective measures if necessary;

i) include a function to ensure that safety risks inherent to a service or product delivered through subcontractors are assessed and mitigated under the operator's safety management system.

3) If the organization holds other organization certificates within the scope of Regulation (EU) 2018/1139, the safety management system of the UAS operator may be integrated with the safety management system that is required by any of those additional certificate(s).

Operators of RPAS generally will be responsible for ensuring:
- airworthiness of the RPA;
- C2 link services used during an operation meet appropriate performance requirements;
- flight crew members required for safety of flight are qualified and competent in their duties;
- arrangements with contractual entities, such as service providers, involved in the conduct of flight operations are appropriate;
- required records are established, managed and stored appropriately;
- compliance with all requirements established by the State of the Operator regarding its operation; and
- compliance with all international standards and air traffic management (ATM) instructions.

5.4 Technical Requirements

The overall target of ensuring safe operation of traditional manned aircraft is met by different means that are focused both on the aircraft and on the people on board. In other words, the flight crew will operate the aircraft safely within its approved envelope where airworthiness requirements are fulfilled. This safe operation prevents danger to third parties both in the air and on the surface. The airworthiness objective of an operation with a UAS is targeted primarily at the protection of human beings and property on the surface by not increasing the risk compared with traditional manned aircraft of equivalent category.

Airworthiness standards should be set to be no less demanding than those currently applied to comparable manned aircraft, nor should they penalize UAS by requiring compliance with higher standards simply because technology permits. Technologies for UAS allow a wide range of possible operations. Requirements related to the airworthiness, the organizations and the persons involved in the operation of UAS

CHAPTER 5   SAFETY REQUIREMENTS IN UAS OPERATIONS

should be set out in order to ensure safety for people on the surface and other airspace users.

All aircraft, whether manned or unmanned, share a high degree of commonality with regard to airworthiness. Airworthiness and certification considerations require many airborne systems to be provided in a redundant configuration for traditional manned aircraft. Achieving a similar level of redundancy for a UAS, especially an RPAS, involves the platform or RPA, RPS and the connecting C2 data links. For an RPAS, all systems and their constituent components may necessitate the same degree of redundancy or greater than those in manned aircraft. Likewise, many supporting systems will require a similar or greater level of redundancy, such as the flight recorders, which might be required for both the RPA and the RPS.[19]

A majority of UAS assessments will likely rely on what is already prescribed for manned aviation. Interestingly, the few areas unique to UAS that are addressed in current ICAO documents are more critical because of the potential magnitude of their impact. Review of these areas will likely result in dramatic changes to technology growth, international infrastructures, regulations and standards and operational procedures.

Many existing SARPs are applicable to UAS. Other standards may require interpretive or innovative solutions. Relief from regulations may be possible given the policy that should a condition not exist, then the requirement(s) do(es) not apply. As an example, the absence of the flight crew from the onboard environment will provide relief from seat belt requirements, life vests and life rafts, except when human passengers are on board (e.g. urban air mobility). Conversely, while the cockpit windscreens become irrelevant, the necessity of an undistorted field of vision may still have to be addressed in some (digital) way.

Article 31 of the Chicago Convention requires that every civil aircraft engaged in international aviation be issued with a certificate of airworthiness by the State of Registry. Article 33 of the Chicago Convention states that certificates of airworthiness must be based on compliance with at least the minimum international (airworthiness) standards established by Annex 8. Where there is a failure to comply with international airworthiness requirements, the certificate of airworthiness must be properly annotated on those areas of failure.

Article 33 of the Chicago Convention, 1944:

> Recognition of certificates and licenses.
> Certificates of airworthiness and certificates of competency and licenses issued or rendered valid by the contracting State in which the aircraft is registered, shall be recognized as valid by the other contracting States, provided that the requirements under which such certificates or licenses were issued or rendered

---

19   *See* ICAO Circular 328-AN/190, Unmanned Aircraft Systems, 2011, Remote Pilot Station(s) 6.21, p. 28.

valid are equal to or above the minimum standards which may be established from time to time pursuant to this Convention.

ICAO Annex 8 (Airworthiness of Aircraft, Twelfth Edition, July 2018) requires the following:
a. That the State of Design provide evidence of an approved Type Design by issuing a Type Certificate;
b. that an aircraft be produced in a controlled manner that ensures conformity to its approved Type Design;
c. that a Certificate of Airworthiness be issued by the State of Registry based on satisfactory evidence;
d. that the aircraft comply with the design aspects of the appropriate airworthiness requirements; and
e. that the State of Design, State of Registry and the UAS Type Certificate Holder collaborate in maintaining the continuing airworthiness of the aircraft.

Airworthiness is a determination of the suitability of an aircraft for safe flight. The direct use of the existing traditional manned aircraft airworthiness certification framework for the regulation of UAS, including RPAS, incorporates a number of specific limitations, such as collision and hazard avoidance, approval of RPAS as a complete system, technical protocols for automatic transfer of C2 data link authority, which in turn would require a log to record the unmanned aircraft and the connected RPS. Airworthiness with respect to an individual UAS takes into consideration all components of the system needed for operational safety, such as the unmanned aircraft (platform), the RPS and communication (C2 data link system). RPS/non-installed equipment is part of the UAS Type Design.

Airworthiness and certification are based on a well-established Airworthiness Design Standard (ADS) provided in Annex 8. However, performance standards currently in use for manned aviation may not apply or satisfactorily address UAS operations. The following UAS-related issues will have to be addressed:
a. SARPs are limited to aircraft over 750 kg intended for carriage of passengers or cargo or mail;
b. SARPs for RPS; and
c. provisions for C2 data links.[20]

The operation of a UAS may require external equipment that is not physically installed on the UA. However, for the time being, until fully standardized interface requirements for this non-installed equipment is available, it is required that the design and continued

---

20 ICAO Circular 328-AN/190, Unmanned Aircraft Systems, 2011, pp. 26-28.

airworthiness of this equipment remain under the control of the UAS Type Design Holder and therefore part of the UAS Type Design. This ensures the equipment is under the responsibility of the UAS Type Design Holder. Where the UA depends on an RPS for normal operation, several configuration options are possible:
1. 1 UA and 1 RPS.
2. 1 UA compatible with various RPS.
3. 1 RPS compatible with various types of UA.
4. 1 RPS for controlling multiple UA.
5. Multiple RPS for controlling multiple UA.

These multiple options can lead to issues that cannot be solved with the traditional methods used for manned aviation. For example, the UAS Type Certificate Holder is responsible for defining the acceptable configuration and handover process of the RPS when there is a chance of UAS control from one RPS to another. It is envisioned that the handover process would require a log to record the UA and connected RPS.

The new (proposed) ICAO Annex 8, in 2019, put forward by Working Group 1 (WG-1), which was established to develop airworthiness concepts, and part of the ICAO Remotely Piloted Aircraft Systems Panel (RPASP), states in Part II, Chapter 3, Section 3.2.1.2:

> 3.2.1.2 The Certificate of Airworthiness issued to a remotely piloted aircraft shall convey evidence of the airworthy status of the remotely piloted aircraft by reference to the appropriate remote pilot stations as well as a command and control link and any other components as specified in the Type Design, being part of the remotely piloted aircraft design complying with the appropriate airworthiness requirements.

This means that the RPS/non-installed equipment is part of the UAS Type Design and that although the certificate of airworthiness is issued by the CAA to an individual UA, this certificate will make reference to the type of RPS/non-installed equipment via the Type Design. To comply with Section 3.2.1.2 of the proposed Annex 8, the certificate of airworthiness should refer to the Type Design of the UAS that will include the RPS approved by the UAS Type Design Holder as part of the design. Therefore, this certificate contains by reference to the approved Type Design a list of possible RPS models.

As a result, the certificate of airworthiness is valid if the UAS is operated with a RPS model listed in the Type Design and the RPS, to which the UA is connected, is in a condition for safe operation, which should be granted by the continued validity of the Airworthiness Approval of the UAS. If during flight an RPS ceases or fails, meaning that it is not in a condition for safe operation, the UA is required to connect to an RPS that is in a condition for safe operation or initiate contingency procedures. This allows the UA to fly under the control of different RPS along the route, as long as they are part of the approved UAS Type Design and in a condition for safe operation all the way.[21]

Airworthiness certification takes into account system configuration, usage, environment and the hardware and software of the integral system. In order to adequately mitigate safety risks, design characteristics, flight tests and production processes, interoperability, reliability and in-service maintenance procedures are taken into account. To certify specific components of a system, agreed technical standards are recommended to be used.

Airworthiness certification is considered to address the intrinsic safety of the UAS. The detection and avoid feature falls outside this area, as its sole purpose is for anti-collision. The operating criteria, defined by the authorities responsible for the safety regulation of air navigation services, on which it relies to adequately perform its function, is dependent on the airspace being used and the aircraft flying into it. Once the operating criteria have been established, the design, production, installation and operation of the equipment, to ensure it functions correctly, would be subject to design approval, similarly to other installed avionic systems and equipment.

EASA is of the opinion that the definition of appropriate criteria for detect and avoid capability is a key issue to the introduction of unmanned aircraft in non-segregated airspace. Certification will be required for operations with an associated higher risk due to the kind of operation or might be requested on a voluntary basis by organizations providing services, such as remote piloting, or equipment, for instance, detect and avoid.

The organization responsible for the design, testing, production, maintenance and training shall demonstrate their capabilities by holding the respective approvals when required owing to the risk posed by the operation. The pilot shall be licensed, and the operator shall hold a Remote Operator Certificate (ROC). This certificate must ensure that all the equipment related to the operation, either in the air or on the surface, has been granted the appropriate design approval and complies with the limitations and conditions of the Type Certificate or Restricted Type Certificate (R-TC) and with the requirements for the airspace classification for which approval is requested.

Unmanned aircraft in the EASA-certified category are considered to be aircraft and, hence, in a way similar to traditional manned aircraft, need a Type Certificate. However, type certification does not address the detect and avoid feature. This Type Certificate should cover the airworthiness of the entire UAS/RPAS as specified in the Type Design. The UAS requirements shall be laid down in codes like the EASA Certification Specifications.

---

21 JARUS CS-UAS Recommendations for Certification Specification for Unmanned Aircraft Systems, Edition 1.0, 6 September 2019, pp. 13-14.

CHAPTER 5   SAFETY REQUIREMENTS IN UAS OPERATIONS

In the European Union, the technical requirements for the UAS classes are subject to revision as defined by the EASA Opinion 01-2018 amendments:
- For all classes, the manufacturer is required to include an information notice in the UAS package. This is an essential element in the promotion of safety, which provides UAS operators with basic information on what is in their ability to do or not to do, and a link to websites, instead of using leaflets, where they can register, receive the online training and obtain additional information. Manufacturers are required to include in each UAS package an information notice defined by EASA and available on its website.
- For UAS in class C0, a maximum speed of 19 m/s has been added for UAS that do not comply with Directive 2009/48/EC on the safety of toys. This will avoid fast UAS, which are typically used for (indoor) races, being classified as class CV0 and operated over people. These UA will be classified as class C3 and will be operated in accordance with subcategory A3 only. Another possibility is the use of a standard scenario as per EASA Opinion 05-2019.[22]
- For UAS in classes C1, C2 and C3:
- A new requirement has been added to mandate a smooth transition in the event of the activation of an automatic flight mode. This will apply to those manufacturers who voluntarily decide to implement functionality that automatically limits the access of the UA to certain airspace areas or volumes. It will ensure that the safety of the flight is maintained and that the remote pilot is provided with sufficient information when such automatic functionality is about to be engaged. This will prevent the UA from suddenly demonstrating unexpected behaviour during the transition to an automatic flight mode;
- Requirements related to the use of an electronic identification system have been introduced directly into each appendix, requiring the following information to be broadcast:
    o the UAS operator registration number;
    o the unique serial number of the UA or, if the e-identification is provided by a separate module to be added to the UA, the serial number of that module;
    o the geographical position of the UA and its height;
    o the geographical position of the point from which the UA has taken off; and
    o the timestamp of the data;
- It has been clarified that the information in the UA user's manual shall include at least the mass of the UA, its MTOM, the frequency of its electronic identification emissions, the general characteristics of allowed payloads in terms of their masses and dimensions, and a description of the behaviour of the UA in the event of a loss of the data link;

---

22   Directive 2009/48/EC of the European Parliament and of the Council of 18 June 2009 on the safety of toys, *OJ* L170/1, 30 June 2009.

- A new requirement has been introduced to mandate manufacturers to assign to each UA a unique serial number according to a standard to be developed. Together with the UAS operator registration number, this unique serial number will be fed to the identification systems for broadcasting.
- For UAS in class C1:
- Based on the large number of negative comments, the reference to the maximum resolution of a camera being 5 MP has been removed, and the requirement for e-identification and geo-awareness has been made mandatory for all UAS in this class;
- It has been clarified that the requirements for lights are linked to the controllability of the UA in daylight conditions during the night, if the UA is designed for night operations; if the manufacturer decides to install lights, their design shall be different from the design of the navigation lights of a traditional manned aircraft, so that these two types of aircraft cannot be confused.[23]
- For UAS in class C2, a new requirement has been introduced for a low-speed mode that is selectable by the operator and that limits the maximum cruising speed of the UA to a maximum of 3 m/s if the UA is intended to be operated in close proximity to people. This requirement will enhance the controllability of the UA and will allow UAS operators to fly their UA as close to uninvolved persons as 3 m.
- For UAS in class C4, a new requirement has been added to forbid automatic control modes. The rationale is to separate UA that are used mostly for leisure purposes or for pleasure flights (considered mostly model aircraft) from those that allow more automatic functions, where the payload, such as a camera, is at the centre of interest. It is recognized that imposing functions such as lost link management or height limitation on model aircraft would require the UA to be equipped with sophisticated flight control systems that most of the time would alter the nature of model aircraft. Therefore, forbidding automatic control modes will allow class C4 UAS to deal with model aircraft and limit the technical requirements imposed on them.

Appendix 5, which contains the technical requirements of UAS in class C4, only requires manufacturers to provide documentation. All other UAS will be classified as class C3, on which additional technical requirements are imposed.[24]

---

23 *See also* Annex to Commission Delegated Regulation (EU) 2019/945, Part 2, A C1 UAS shall comply with the following: (16) be equipped with lights for the purpose of: (a) the controllability of the UA, (b) the conspicuity of the UA at night, the design of the lights shall allow a person on the ground, to distinguish the UA from a manned aircraft.
24 For detailed UAS technical requirements: Annex to Commission Delegated Regulation (EU) 2019/945, Part 1 requirements for a class C0 UAS, Part 2 requirements of a class C1 UAS, Part 3 requirements for a class C2 UAS, Part 4 requirements for a class C3 UAS and Part 5 requirements for a class C4 UAS.

CHAPTER 5   SAFETY REQUIREMENTS IN UAS OPERATIONS

- In order to provide citizens with a high level of environmental protection, it is necessary to limit the noise emissions to the greatest extent. For UAS in class C1 and C2, the noise level requirement has been maintained at the same level. However, its expression has been corrected. The term sound power level has been changed to sound pressure level since it refers to the sound pressure measured at a certain distance from an object. Under certain standard conditions, a sound power level of 80 dB approximately equals a sound pressure level of 60 dB(A) measured at a distance of 3 m from the source.[25]

Moreover, A-weighting of the sound level has been introduced, as this is commonly used when describing the level of noise that is perceived by humans. While the technical basis for this limit, or any other, as well as the details of the underlying measurement procedure for small UAS remain rather undefined at present, it was decided to set a modest noise limit. Unmanned aircraft noise and emissions should be minimized, taking into account the operating conditions and various specific characteristics of individual EU Member States, such as the population density, where noise and emissions are of concern. In order to facilitate the societal acceptance of UAS operations, Regulation (EU) 2019/945 includes the maximum level of noise for unmanned aircraft operated close to people in the Open category. In the Specific category, there is a requirement for the operator to develop guidelines for its remote pilots so that all operations are flown in a manner that minimizes nuisances to people and animals.[26]

- For UA in classes C2 and C3:
- lights are made mandatory for the purpose of controllability or visibility; their design shall be different from the design of the navigation lights of a traditional manned aircraft so that these two types of aircraft cannot be confused;
- a new requirement has been introduced to mandate protection of the data link so as to prevent unauthorized access to the command and control functions of a UA;
- following the extension of the European Union competence to tethered aircraft with propulsion systems and with masses greater than 1 kg, as defined by Regulation (EU) 2018/1139, all the requirements have been reviewed to extend the applicability to those aircraft.

---

25   dB(A). A-weighting is the most common used of a family of curves defined in the International Standard IEC 61672:2003 and various national standards relating to the measurement of sound pressure level. A-weighting is applied to instrument-measured sound levels in an effort to account for the relative loudness perceived by the human ear, as the ear is less sensitive to low audio frequencies (source: Wikipedia).

26   *See also* Recital (22) of Commission Implementing Regulation (EU) 2019/947 of 24 May 2019.

A promising fact is that the Joint Authorities for Rulemaking on Unmanned Systems (JARUS), a group of experts from the civil aviation authority (CAAs) of the five continents, the European Organisation for the Safety of Air Navigation (EUROCONTROL) and EASA, recommends a single set of technical, safety and operational requirements for all aspects linked to the safe operation of UAS such as Certification Specifications for UAS (CS-UAS).[27] This requires review and consideration of existing regulations and other material applicable to traditional manned aircraft, the analysis of the specific risk linked to UAS and the drafting material to cover the unique features of UAS.

The recommendation by JARUS, which, however, is not developing legally binding or mandatory regulatory material, is based on public consultation of interested UAS stakeholders, including the industry. This independent consultation process is aimed at delivering better quality and harmonized proposals for regulation provisions, which could be utilized without any coercion by individual states or a regional organization.

Through the reorganization of the FAR/CS-23 Certification Specifications for normal, utility, acrobatic and commuters aeroplanes, a new concept of Objective Requirements was introduced to provide requirements proportionate to the UAS performance and complexity and the type of operation. With the new concept, supported by Airworthiness Design Standards, the existing recommendations of Certification Specification for Light Unmanned Rotorcraft Systems (CS-LURS) and Certification Specification for Light Unmanned Aeroplane Systems (CS-LUAS) can be used to comply with the requirements in CS-UAS.[28] The purpose of CS-UAS is to provide recommendations for design-independent Objective Requirements as CS for UAS. CS-UAS is intended to be used for the Certified category, but some or all may also be used for the Specific category depending on the outcome of the Total Hazard and Risk Assessment.[29]

The Certification Specification provides Objective Requirements, whose objectives are to provide directions for new developments, for the issuance of type certificates, and changes to those certificates, for UAS independent of their design under the following conditions:

- MTOM not to exceed 8,618 kg/19,000 lbs for UA without VTOL (Vertical Take-off and Landing) capability, or MTOM not to exceed 3,175 kg/7,000 lbs for UA with VTOL capability.

---

27 JARUS CS-UAS Recommendations for Certification Specification for Unmanned Aircraft Systems, Edition 1.0, 6 September 2019, pp. 19-42.
28 CS-LURS means Certification Specification for Light Unmanned Rotorcraft Systems. CS-LUAS means Certification Specification for Light Unmanned Aeroplane Systems.
29 *See* Farner, M., 'SORA: Risk Assessment for Unmanned Airborne Mobility', Manager Innovation and Advanced Technologies, *Federal Office of Civil Aviation FOCA* Winterthur, 2017, p. 51 Pillars of a New Risk Assessment: Risk Based Approach, New Culture. Holistic not Atomistic, and Total Hazard and Risk Assessment.

- Human transportation is excluded.
- The intended operation for which the UAS is designed is not in the Open category.
- Non-deterministic systems are excluded such as AI or Machine Learning.

CS-UAS covers the requirements for BVLOS operation with the exception that the performance requirements for any detect and avoid technology ensuring safe separation are not yet developed (as per 2019) and CS-UAS includes requirements for the RPS, launch and recovery equipment (LRE) and C2 link equipment.

Objective Requirements are design independent and applicable to the entire range of CS-UAS applicability. These Objective Requirements will be used as a basis for developing ADS where the design-specific details will be captured. ADS can be developed for a Type Certificate with or without operating limitations, but are nonetheless used to comply with the Objective Requirements.

According to the latest amendment to CS-23, the technical design-specific details are removed from the rules and moved to the AMC, which has been published in December 2017. The amendment alternatively provides what the objectives of the design should be. Thereby, new designs will not be hampered by detailed prescriptive rules, enabling innovative solutions to be developed that will enhance safety. In order to speed up the introduction of new AMC, the development of AMC introduces the possibility to use continuous cooperation between industry, users, EASA and other relevant authorities. This leads to more up-to-date industry standards, in addition to reducing red tape, valuable time and high certification costs for manufacturers. When consensus standards are developed in a transparent and accessible process, EASA can give credit and follow a short rule-making process to accept the use of those standards.

The first set of consensus standards are being developed in an international cooperation via ASTM International.[30] The change, based on the amendment, has almost simultaneously taken place in both the European Union and the United States (Part 23) in order to achieve the highest level of harmonization.

In the United States, the FAA established, through Order 8130.34D (09 August 2017), procedures for issuing special airworthiness certificates in the experimental category or special flight permits to UAS and manned aircraft integrated with UAS technology. This hybrid type of aircraft is referred to as Optionally Piloted Aircraft (OPA), which means that the method of controlling the aircraft is optional. Control of the aircraft can be accomplished by the pilot on board the aircraft as well as an RPS via control link. In

---

30 ASTM International, formerly known as American Society for Testing and Materials, is an international standards organization that develops and publishes voluntary consensus technical standards for a wide range of materials, products, systems and services. The organization offers global access to fully transparent standards development, resulting in the highest technical excellence in standardization (www.astm.org).

either case, the pilot in command always remains on board the aircraft, which excludes the definition of an unmanned aircraft, but in a way meets the characteristics of RPAS.

A special certificate of airworthiness may be issued for an aircraft that does not meet the airworthiness requirements for a standard certificate of airworthiness. FAA Form 8130-7 may be issued to UAS, OPA and OPA/UAS, which are aircraft intended to be flown either as OPA or as UAS, pursuant to Title 14 of the Code of Federal Regulations under specific conditions.[31]

A special certificate of airworthiness is defined as an experimental certificate when it is issued for the purpose of R&D, showing compliance with regulations, crew training, exhibition and/or market survey, as defined in 14 CFR 21.191 (Experimental certificates). A special flight permit may be issued for production flight testing new production aircraft as stated in 14 CFR 21.197 (Special flight permits), although a Type Certificate has not been issued for that particular aircraft.

5.5 Operational Use

New types of operations such as unmanned aircraft operations may need additional or alternative considerations, conditions, regulations, processes and operating procedures, taking into account the particular characteristics of those flight operations. Nevertheless, unmanned aircraft operations must not impede or impair other airspace users and air navigation service providers (ATM, CNS, SAR, airports, etc.) or the safety of third parties and properties on the surface.

Unmanned aircraft include very large aircraft, equivalent in size and complexity to traditional manned aircraft, but also very small consumer electronics aircraft for business or recreational use. Especially smaller unmanned aircraft are increasingly being operated in the European Union, but until recently under a fragmented regulatory framework.

More uniformity and an overarching structure are the main objectives of new EU legislation in a manner that unmanned aircraft operations performed by professionals and other users will deploy safely, solid and fast with less paperwork. In particular, the implementing rule prevails over the local rules, except for the EU Member State option to create specific drone zones that may deviate from the general rule. While new EU legislation, comprising the implementing rule and the delegated act, is valid in every EU Member State, local rules cannot be stricter.

The ability to locate RPS all over the world offers considerable opportunities for new business models but also raises legitimate questions. Issues like state-to-state oversight and cross-border relationships, especially jurisdiction on enforcement and liability, but

---

31 FAA Form 8130-7 is a special airworthiness certificate that is an FAA authorization to operate an aircraft in the US airspace in one or more of the following categories: primary, restricted, multiple, limited, light-sport, experimental, special flight permit and provisional.

also entry and clearance regulations in case of an intermediate stopover and recognition of certificates and licences, will have to be addressed.

RPA, operating internationally, must comply with the framework regulations and requirements defined under the Chicago Convention. At the highest level, this means the following:
- the operator must have obtained special authorization from all affected states;
- RPA must be so controlled as to obviate danger to traditional civil aircraft;
- operators must hold an RPAS (or Remote) Operator Certificate;
- RPA must hold a valid certificate of airworthiness, issued against the approved Type Design as recorded in the Type Certificate;
- RPA must meet the communications, navigation and surveillance requirements for the airspace in which it operates;
- the remote pilots must hold valid licences appropriate to the unmanned aircraft and the complete system;
- the flight plan must comply with the conditions set out in ICAO Annex 2 – Rules of the Air, Chapter 3.3 Flight plans; and
- RPAS must meet the detect and avoid capability requirements for the airspace in which the RPA will actually fly and the operations to be performed.

Additionally, RPAS operations will require approvals encompassing the processes, procedures, manuals and safety management systems applicable to the organization, its staff and method of operation. Although similar in arrangement to manned operators, distinction will exist in the information recorded in this approval document. The distinction will pertain primarily to the types and methods of flights permitted.

Obviously, every operation conducted by any aircraft type, whether manned or unmanned, carries a certain degree of risk to third parties. Regulation (EC) No. 1008/2008, amended by Regulation (EU) 2019/2, deals with common rules for the operation of air services in the Community. This Regulation does not apply to air carriers alone, but to aircraft operators too. Although the Regulation exempts, among others, model aircraft with an MTOM of less than 20 kg, and foot-launched flying machines, including powered paragliders and hang gliders, the current definition of an RPAS does not seem to be covered by these exemptions.[32]

Where RPAS are to be covered by the Regulation, the impact would be only with respect to insurance for third-party liability. The Regulation defines, through a table (Table 5.3, starting with category 1 for aircraft >500 kg), the minimum amount of

---

32 Regulation (EC) No. 1008/2008 of the European Parliament and of the Council of 24 September 2008 on common rules for the operation of air services in the Community (Recast), *OJ* L 293/3, 31 October 2008. Regulation (EU) 2019/2 of the European Parliament and of the Council of 11 December 2018 amending Regulation (EC) No. 1008/2008 on common rules for the operation of air services in the Community, *OJ* L 11/1, 14 January 2019.

insurance to be covered for the different categories of aircraft to be applied in accordance with their MTOMs. Although while the Regulation was being drafted it was not envisaged that significant numbers of aircraft would have very low MTOMs, it is now likely that a considerable portion of RPAS for civil use will be under 15 kg.[33]

With Regulation (EC) No. 1008/2008, insurance for these RPAS for third-party liability amounts to 0.75 million SDR. However, this Regulation should clarify the definition of model aircraft in order to establish that they are to be separated from RPAS. Another question regarding the applicability of Regulation (EC) No. 785/2004 to RPAS concerns the purpose and cover of Regulation (EC) No. 1008/2008, which provides the basis for the application of Regulation (EC) No. 785/2004. Regulation (EC) No. 1008/2008, which regulates the licensing and operation of air carriers, defines an air service as a flight or a series of flights carrying passengers, mail and/or cargo for remuneration and/or hire. RPAS, as it functions today, does not appear to match this description.

On the other hand, the definition of operating licence as an authorization granted by the competent licensing authority to an undertaking, permitting it to provide air services as stated in the operating licence, might give room for application to RPAS. This will be so if the RPAS undertaking, which provides the air services, acts as an operator. Moreover, as stated earlier, Regulation (EC) No. 785/2004 also applies to aircraft operators.[34]

Nevertheless, RPAS operations, like the operation of traditional manned aircraft, need to be accommodated within a clear legal framework providing for insurance requirements for third-party liability.

Operating requirements for UAS operations in the Open and Specific categories, in accordance with the proposals for the regulatory framework for drones and the regulation of drone categories, are presented in EASA documents.[35]

The Open category operation is low-risk and simple-drone operation, where the risk to third parties on the surface and to other airspace users is mitigated through operational limitations. The Open category operation is any operation with small drones under direct

---

33 *See* Final Report Mid-term Evaluation of Regulation (EC) No. 785/2004 on insurance requirements of air carriers and aircraft operators, London: Steer Davies Gleave, July 2012.
34 Regulation (EC) No. 785/2004, OJ L 138/1, 30 April 2004: Art. 1, Objective 1. The objective of this Regulation is to establish minimum insurance requirements for air carriers and aircraft operators in respect of passengers, baggage, cargo and third parties. Art. 2, Scope 1. This Regulation shall apply to all air carriers and to all aircraft operators flying within, into, out of or over the territory of a Member State to which the Treaty applies. Art. 3 Definitions, for the purpose of this Regulation: (a) air carrier means an air transport undertaking with a valid operating licence.
35 EASA Advance Notice of Proposed Amendment 2015-10. *See also* EASA Opinion No. 01-2018 Introduction of a regulatory for the operation of unmanned aircraft systems in the Open and Specific categories, Annex to the Prototype Commission Regulation UAS operations in the Open and Specific categories (PART-UAS).

VLOS with an MTOM of less than 25 kg operated within safe distance from persons on the surface and separated from other airspace users.

However, a zero-risk approach is not quite practical since a balance must be found between ensuring appropriate safety levels and practicing easy drone operations. The Open category drones should not require an authorization, normally by the CAA, for the flight, but rather should stay within defined limits for the operation. From a safety point of view, it is obligatory to maintain a safe distance from aerodromes, manned aircraft and persons on the surface.

Operators of unmanned aircraft are also required to be registered when they operate an unmanned aircraft that, in case of impact, can transfer, to a human, a kinetic energy of above 80 J, or that presents risks to privacy, protection of personal data, security or the environment.

Studies have demonstrated that unmanned aircraft with an MTOM of 250 g or more present risks to security, and therefore UAS operators of such unmanned aircraft should be required to register themselves when operating such aircraft in the Open category. Considering the risks to privacy and protection of personal data, operators of unmanned aircraft should be registered if they operate an unmanned aircraft that is equipped with a sensor that is able to capture personal data.

However, this should not be the case when the unmanned aircraft is considered to be a toy within the meaning of Directive 2009/48/EC of the European Parliament and of the Council of 18 June 2009 on the safety of toys.[36]

This Open category of operations would be subject only to a minimal aviation regulation system, focusing mainly on defining the limits of such a category of operations. No certification, approval, licence or other equivalent document is required in relation to the operation of drones, except in the case of more composite, complicated low-risk operations where adequate knowledge and skills need to be demonstrated.

To prevent unintended flights outside safety areas and to increase compliance with applicable regulations, it has been proposed to mandate geofencing and e-identification for certain drones and operation areas. Geofencing means the automatic limitation of airspace that a drone is normally able to enter. In principle, the geofencing feature, based on appropriate EASA standards, is already embedded in the most recent manufactured drone series, some of which require manual updating in a dynamic digital way to support operators and pilots in complying with temporary restrictions in the form of safe areas or airspace volumes created for environmental protection, response efforts and privacy or security tasks.

The competent authorities can define no-drone zones, where no operation is allowed without official approval, and limited-drone zones, where drones must provide a function

---

36 *See* Recital (16) of Commission Implementing Regulation (EU) 2019/947 of 24 May 2019.

to enable easy e-identification and automatic limitation of the airspace segment they can enter and should have a limited MTOM.

The current charts with drone no-fly zones are well known to drone pilots, especially hobbyists and professionals who are quite often flying their drones in the open air. As part of the newly introduced European drone regulations, these charts will be replaced by a new system of drone zones, not immediately but no later than one year after the transition to that new system.

The current drone no-fly zone charts, being derived from existing air navigation maps, are not very flexible. Some of the drone no-fly zones are very spacious, like aerodrome control zones (CTRs). Moreover, the charts make little or no distinction between people who, for a reason, fly their drones in the air for the first time and well-trained professionals who are very knowledgeable about civil aviation safety. There is also quite a difference between, on the one hand, the areas that drone manufacturers classify as no-fly zones through their geofencing system, and, on the other hand, the official aviation information system. That means that drones can take off from places where this action is not actually intended. Another restriction is that the drone no-fly zone charts are not interchangeable within the European Union (yet).

The new European system of drone zones should remedy this shortcoming. The idea is that drone zones are defined in a much more detailed manner than today's charts. Another difference is that a drone zone is not necessarily restrictive in nature. Through a drone zone, more options can be offered. It is also conceivable that a lower maximum flight altitude can be set via a drone zone, for example, in case of a nearby military low-flying area. In addition, the system of drone zones also offers the possibility for dynamic zones, for example, to set up a temporary no-fly zone around an event. And, finally, almost all drones flying in the Open category are intended to automatically recall the drone zones defined by the EU Member States.

Although the new European regulation on unmanned aircraft operations will be published on 31 December 2020, following the alleged postponement because of the Covid-19 pandemic, the European chart with new-style drone zones will probably not be ready by that date. Given the complexity of the topic, EU Member States have a year longer to complete all the drone zones for their own territory. The way in which these states accomplish this work differs considerably. In some states, the minister of transport determines the drone zones, whereas in others various stakeholders have been given the opportunity to present their views, although the ministers of transport and defence will have the powers to decide on the design and location of drone zones.

Temporary drone zones are likely to occur at major events, the expectation being that in those cases a distinction will be made between drones in the Open category and drones of operators in the Specific category. Within drone zones where small airfields are located for model aircraft, more is possible for drones, such as a flight altitude of 300 m. Hope is also set on drone test centres where drones are being allocated more options.

In the future, most drones will be required to be equipped with a technical device that automatically stores the new available drone zones. This technique already exists in the form of geofencing. However, until now it has actually been the manufacturers who have determined where altitude restrictions or flight limitations applied. In the new situation, EU Member States will be in control via a 'drone-zoning system'. Drones with the new CE label, mandatory in due course for the majority operating in the Open category, should, in principle, automatically know where and what is not allowed to fly. Existing drones and self-made drones will, two years after the introduction of the new EU regulations, be allowed to operate only in the A3 category, at a considerable distance from buildings and people.

In the longer term, some drone zones will be designated as U-space areas. To perform a flight in a zone designated as U-space, the drone operator will be obliged to be affiliated with a U-space service provider (USSP) so that the drone can be monitored remotely. It is expected that in the EU Member States all CTRs, and possibly also urban areas, industrial areas and seaport zones, will first be designated as U-space. This probably means that the operators in the Specific and Certified categories, unlike those in the Open category operators, will have to deal with U-space.[37]

In the near future, owing to advanced technologies, features such as interoperability with systems for manned aviation or autonomous cooperation and traffic management for low-level operations can be assumed and will most likely be required once traffic in urban environments increases significantly.

All drone operations in the Open category must be conducted within the defined limitations:
- the remote pilot keeps the unmanned aircraft in VLOS at all times except when flying in follow-me mode or when using an unmanned aircraft observer as specified in Part A of the Annex to Regulation (EU) 2019/947;
- only unmanned aircraft with an MTOM below 25 kg are allowed;
- no operation of unmanned aircraft in no-drone zones is permitted;
- unmanned aircraft operating in the limited-drone zones must comply with the applicable limitations;
- the pilot is responsible for the safe separation from any other airspace user(s) and shall give right of way to any other airspace user(s) according to standard rules of the air;

---

37 De Jager, W., 'EU Droneregels: systeem van "drone zones" gaat kaart vervangen' (EU Drone rules: system of drone zones will replace the chart), *Dronewatch*, 17 April 2020.

- during flight, the unmanned aircraft is maintained within 120 m (approximately 400 ft) from the closest point of the surface of the Earth, except when overflying an obstacle, as specified in Part A of the above mentioned Annex;
- during flight, the unmanned aircraft does not carry dangerous goods and does not drop any material;
- the pilot is responsible for ensuring safe operation and maintaining a safe distance from uninvolved persons and property (third parties) on the surface and from other airspace users and shall never fly the unmanned aircraft over assemblies of people, which means more than 12 persons. The pilot should not be negligent or reckless. Moreover, the pilot needs to be fit to fly, which also applies to the unmanned aircraft and the equipment.

In line with the present practice, there should be established subcategories for the Open category to allow for more flexible adaption to the risk. In fact, it is a further separation in risk classes, already observed in practice as a good average of the existing national regulations. The maximum drone mass or MTOM is chosen as a simple and enforceable criterion to separate (sub)categories of drones. Together with other uncomplicated thresholds for altitude and distance to persons, this enables the practical implementation of these risk classes.

From 31 December 2020, the distinction between recreational and professional drone pilots is no longer applicable. The question that really matters is no longer who is actually flying but the risk posed by the flight. The regulations indicate that determination is necessary concerning which drone can be classified in which subcategory of the Open category. Pilots who want to fly outside the limitations of these subcategories will automatically end up in the Specific category or even the Certified category. In the future, all ready-made drones will receive a new type of CE label with the designation C0 to C4 (C5 and C6 for the Specific category). This label determines the Open (sub) category and the exams to be taken.[38]

Open subcategory A1. Drone flights performed in this subcategory are allowed only with drones that pose very little risk to people on the surface; for instance, they are very light or are so constructed as to pose a negligible risk of injury in the event of a crash. Flying over assemblies of people is not allowed. In almost all cases, registration by the drone pilot or the operator is mandatory. The MTOM in this subcategory is 900 g, or 500 g if the drone does not have a Cx or CE label. A transitional arrangement of two years will apply to existing (earlier than 31 December 2020) drones. Operations with a drone weighing more than 250 g require pilots to take an online theory course and exams consisting of 40 multiple choice questions.

---

38 *See* Commission Delegated Regulation (EU) 2019/945 Annex Part 1 Requirements for a class C0 UAS, Part 2 Requirements for a class C1 UAS, Part 3 Requirements for a class C2 UAS, Part 4 Requirements for a class C3 UAS and Part 5 Requirements for a class C4 UAS, pp. 23-31.

Open subcategory A2. This subcategory is intended for drones with an MTOM of 4 kg (or if the drone has no Cx or CE label 2 kg) and must meet a number of technical standards. The minimum distance to people is 30 m (50 m for old version drones). New drones equipped with slow speed mode are allowed to approach people up to 5 m. In all cases, the operator has to register, and besides the online theory course and exams, an additional exam must be passed. A statement of having some practical experience must be provided.

For both Open subcategories A1 and A2, the condition is that for any operation over 50 m above the surface, the pilot needs to have basic aviation awareness, and any failures, malfunctions, defects or other occurrences that lead to severe injuries or fatalities of any person must be reported to the competent authority.

Open category A3. This subcategory is intended for more heavy (self-made) drones with an MTOM of up to 25 kg, model aeroplanes and FPV racers. Minimum distance to people and buildings is 150 m. From 1 January 2023, all drones that do not have a C0 up to and including C4 CE label will fall into this subcategory (except drones lighter than 250 g, which will remain in subcategory A1). Registration of the pilot or organization and the online knowledge exam are mandatory.

Additional requirements for subcategory A3 of small drones (<25 kg) are defined as follows: any drone sold as a consumer product that is heavier than 4 kg could comply with the applicable general product safety directive and shall have the means to automatically limit the airspace it can enter and the means to allow automatic identification. Operation in the limited-drone zones is not permitted in the Open category for drones with an MTOM above 4 kg.

In the Specific category, it is to be expected that operations of drones will be conducted BVLOS, sharing airspace with other users. The result is that the drone pilot is no longer able to guarantee separation with respect to other airspace users. From that moment on, this function relies on the safety equipment, such as detect and avoid, installed on the drone, or on specific operational procedures. Operations over high-density areas, such as city centres, could also fall into the Specific category.

Specific category operations may be conducted with an MTOM exceeding 25 kg, flying higher than 120 m above the surface with a higher risk of conflict with manned aviation, for instance nearby low-level flying routes or uncontrolled aerodromes. Concerning these more elaborate functions, it is foreseen that basic aviation awareness is required for the remote pilot. As soon as operations start posing more significant aviation-related risks to persons and properties overflown or involve sharing airspace with manned aviation, these operations are at all times placed in the Specific category. This is also the case when one or more safety constraints of the Open category are exceeded. In other words, for drone flights that do not fit within the limitations of the Open category, there is the Specific category.[39]

The Specific category is a tool to treat particular operations with safety requirements proportionate to the risk posed by drones that are capable of performing a certain drone operation with certain limitations. Each specific aviation risk needs to be analysed and mitigated through a safety risk assessment, and adequate mitigation measures need to be agreed by the CAA, which in turn issues an OA, materializing the approval to start the specific operation. Operational manuals, training and any standard scenarios and aircraft inspections are in many cases sufficient as mitigating measures, as required in the Specific category.

In the Specific category, there are three options when it comes to risk management:
- The first option is to work according to European standard scenarios (STS).
- The second option is to start from an already elaborated risk analysis, a Pre-Defined Risk Assessment (PDRA).
- The third option: anyone who wants to describe an operation from scratch, including all the relevant characteristics and events, will have to deal with SORA.

Finally, the EU Regulations also provide for a category for drone flights with a very high risk. These are mainly drones that transport parcels or even people. Such operations end up in the Certified category. The requirements imposed on companies that want to become active in this category are very strict, comparable to the requirements of manned aviation. While mandatory for the more burdensome Certified category, for the Specific category, a certificate delivered by the competent authorities for the operation of a drone, as well as for the personnel, including remote pilots and organizations involved in those activities, or for the drone pursuant to Regulation (EU) 2019/945, could also be required. Rule-making regarding the Specified category is ongoing.

Through Opinion 01-2018, EASA presented the concept of standard scenarios for drone operations in the Specific category that are characterized by a low risk. Those drone operations can be conducted on the basis of a declaration submitted by the drone operator to the CAA. The approach in the Opinion was to define in Regulation (EU) 2019/947 the process to allow such types of drone operations through the standard rule-making procedure and to include in the text of the Regulation the detailed description of the mitigating measures. In a survey declared and carried out by EASA, among all EU Member States, to identify drone operations that are allowed according to national regulations, experience and risk assessments, two types of drone operations were

---

39 All published provisions could be subject to amendment in the future owing to new developments, advancing technologies as well as practical feedback with respect to various drone operation experiences.

identified, resulting in the development of two standard scenarios: STS-01 and STS-02. Since it was decided to also impose for STSs the use of drones with particular CE class marks, an amendment to Regulation (EU) 2019/945 was also necessary, to define the requirements for the two new drone CE classes, which are C5 and C6, to be used with STS-01 and STS-02, respectively.

The two STSs are related to the following drone operations:
- STS-01: VLOS operations at a maximum height of 120 m, at a ground speed of less than 5 m/s in the case of untethered unmanned aircraft, over controlled ground areas that can be in populated, urban environments, using drones with MTOMs of up to 25 kg; and
- STS-02: BVLOS operations with the drone at not more than 2 km from the remote pilot, if visual observers are used, at a maximum height of 120 m, over controlled ground areas in sparsely populated environments, using drones with MTOMs up to 25 kg.

The requirements proposed in the STSs have been developed to ensure that the resulting level of risk of drone operations is consistent with the declarative regime defined in Article 5(5) and point UAS.SPEC.020 of the Regulation (EU) 2019/947.

The specific objective of Opinion 01-2018 is to:
- ensure that (emerging) safety issues are addressed;
- create a new regulatory framework that defines measures to mitigate the risk of operations in the Open category through a combination of limitations, operational rules, requirements for the competency of the remote pilot, as well as technical requirements for the drone, such that the operator may conduct the operation without prior authorization by the competent authority, or without submitting a declaration, and in the Specific category, through a system that includes a risk assessment being conducted by the drone operator before starting an operation, or an operator complying with a standard scenario or an operator holding a certificate with privileges;
- incorporate improvements that result from relevant developments in new technologies and from the application of both relevant Regulations;
- develop STSs for those drone operations in the Specific category that are considered mature enough, based on a declaration by the drone operator; and
- contribute to addressing citizens' concerns regarding security, privacy, data protection and environmental protection.

A safety risk assessment shall be performed by the operator taking into account all the elements that contribute to the risk of the particular operation. Key factors of the safety assessment are:
- Area of operation, which means population density or areas with special protection;

- with respect to airspace: class of airspace, segregation and ATC procedures;
- design of the drone: functions provided, redundancy and safety features;
- type of drone operation, which includes operational procedures;
- pilot competence; and
- organizational factors of the operator.

Regarding the safety assessment, the operator shall:
- provide to the competent authority (CAA) all the information required for a preliminary applicability check of the category of operation;
- provide to the competent authority a safety risk assessment covering both the drone and the operation, identifying all the risks related to the specific operation, and proposing adequate risk mitigation measures;
- compile an appropriate operations manual (OM), together with the safety assessment forming the basis for the Operation Authorization, containing all the required information, descriptions, conditions and limitations for the operation, including training and qualification for personnel, maintenance of the drone and its systems, as well as incident and accident occurrence reporting and oversight of suppliers. The Operation Authorization defines the limitations, a combination of airworthiness and operational limitations, under which the particular operation with particular equipment is safe in a given condition.

When the risks that are posed by an operation in the Specific category have to be mitigated by the technical characteristics of the drone involved, compliance of some functions or system in the drone may need to be demonstrated with the applicable CS or industry standards to ensure safe flight. In the Specific category only a clearly defined or identified type of operation is authorized, while in the Certified category the design of a drone is considered appropriate for a variety of operations.

The operation in the Specific category might be performed with drones or equipment that is certified or otherwise approved. The particular operation might exceed the operational limitations for the certified equipment when specifically authorized and when the operation ensures application of adequate risk mitigations as identified in the operational authorization.

It is expected that an operator may start operations under an OA with a drone in the Specific category with limited support from the drone manufacturer. When the number and variety of such OAs increase, the drone manufacturer could apply to EASA to obtain a TC for the drone design that the operator could use to support additional OAs, while the Certified category compliance of all functions and systems needs to be demonstrated with the applicable CS.

When the outcome of the operations safety assessment results in an unacceptable level of risk, mitigating measures need to be proposed by the applicant of an OA. Operators may voluntarily make use of suppliers or personnel holding certificates or voluntarily apply for an ROC detailing the means on how responsibilities are shared and having adequate privileges to authorize operations. An ROC is foreseen in the Certified category for high-risk operations of a wider scope that exceed the applicability of the safety risk assessment. Operators holding an ROC could be granted the privilege to authorize their own OAs and later changes in the Specific category when their capabilities are assessed and considered appropriate within a given scope.

Certification will be required for operations with an associated higher risk due to the nature of operation, or might be requested on a voluntary basis by organizations providing services or specific required equipment, such as detect and avoid. When unmanned aviation risks rise to a level similar to traditional manned aviation, a risk level considered to be fairly low in general terms, the operation is classified as a Certified category operation.

Operations in this Certified category should, as a principle, be subject to rules on certification of the operator and the licensing of remote pilots, in addition to certification of the aircraft pursuant to Regulation (EU) 2019/945.

As a consequence, these operations and the corresponding drones would have to be treated in the traditional, classic manned aviation way. As for manned aviation, multiple certificates would be issued plus some more certificates specific for drones. In other words, requirements in this category are comparable to manned aviation requirements.

The operations in the Certified category are envisaged for drone operations with a high risk together with a wider scope of operation than the Specific category. Applicability of the safety risk assessment process is the key factor with respect to the delimitation between the Specific and Certified category.

Article 6 of Regulation (EU) 2019/947:
1) Operations shall be classified as UAS operations in the Certified category only where the following requirements are met:
a) The UAS is certified pursuant to points (a), (b) and (c) of Paragraph 1 of Article 40 of Regulation (EU) 2019/945; and
b) the operation is conducted in any of the following conditions:
i. over assemblies of people;
ii. involves the transport of people;
iii. involves the carriage of dangerous goods, that may result in high risk for third parties in case of accident.
2) In addition, UAS operations shall be classified as UAS operations in the Certified category where the competent authority, based on the risk assessment provided for in Article 11 Rules for conducting an operational risk assessment (Regulation (EU) 2019/947), considers that the risk of the operation cannot be adequately mitigated

without the certification of the UAS and of the UAS operator and, where applicable, without the licensing of the remote pilot.

Article 40 (Requirements for UAS in the Certified and Specific category), Paragraph 1 of Regulation (EU) 2019/945:
1) The design, production and maintenance of UAS shall be certified if the UAS meets any of the following conditions:
a) It has a characteristic dimension of 3 m or more and is designed to be operated over assemblies of people;
b) It is designed for transporting people;
c) It is designed for the purpose of transporting dangerous goods and requiring a high level of robustness to mitigate the risk for third parties in case of accident.

UAS operations in the Specific and Certified category shall be subject to the applicable requirements laid down in Commission Implementing Regulation (EU) No. 923/2012, and, additionally, UAS operations in the Certified category shall be subject to the applicable requirements laid down in Commission Regulations (EU) No. 965/2012 and (EU) No. 1332/2011.[40]

International air cargo transport with large drones and transport of persons as well as any other operation where the risk assessment process of the Specific category does not sufficiently address the high risks involved in the operation are categorized as Certified operations. Oversight is performed by the CAAs in the field of issuing of licences, approval of maintenance, operations, training, air traffic management and air navigation services, as well as by EASA in the field of design and approval of foreign organizations.

In order to operate a drone in the Certified category, the airworthiness of the aircraft and its compliance with environmental standards shall be ensured in the same way as is presently done for manned aviation by issuing a TC or an R-TC for the type, and an R-CofA for the particular drone.

---

40 Commission Implementing Regulation (EU) No. 923/2012 of 26 September 2012 laying down the common rules of the air and operational provisions regarding services and procedures in air navigation and amending Implementing Regulation (EU) No. 1035/2011 and Regulations (EC) No. 1265/2007, (EC) No. 1794/2006, (EC) No. 730/2006, (EC) No. 1033/2006 and (EU) No. 255/2010, OJ L 281/1, 13 October 2012. Commission Regulation (EU) No. 965/2012 of 5 October 2012 laying down technical requirements and administrative procedures related to air operations pursuant to Regulation (EC) No. 216/2008 of the European Parliament and of the Council, OJ L 296/1, 25 October 2012. Commission Regulation (EU) No. 1332/2011 of 16 December 2011 laying down common airspace usage requirements and operating procedures for airborne collision avoidance, OJ L 336/20, 20 December 2011.

CHAPTER 5   SAFETY REQUIREMENTS IN UAS OPERATIONS

Until 2020, the certification basis of UAS has been either derived from manned aircraft Certification Specifications integrated with Special Conditions (SC) to address specific UAS aspects or defined with Special Conditions based on documentation developed and published by JARUS. In both cases the approach has been prescriptive. Objective-based Certification Specifications are deemed more appropriate for UAS.

Therefore, EASA decided to develop a dedicated Special Condition for light UAS, which will be applied in accordance with point 21.B.80 when the Agency has to determine the certification basis for light aircraft, considering that no existing Special Condition is applicable to those aircraft.[41]

On 20 July 2020, EASA published a proposal of airworthiness standards for the certification of the vast majority of light unmanned aircraft in Europe. These standards will contribute significantly to the safe operation of drones for a wide variety of services, such as parcel delivery in urban environments, railways and power lines inspection or delivery of essential supplies into crisis zones. The proposed standards are known as Special Condition Light UAS and will be applicable to unmanned aircraft under 600 kg operated in the Specific or Certified category in accordance with Regulation (EU) 2019/947.

The standards came into force on 31 December 2020. This Special Condition addresses airworthiness specifications for unmanned aircraft, not the authorization of operations in the Specific category. Nevertheless, as defined by Regulation (EU) 2019/947, some operations in the Specific category may be authorized by the national CAA only if the UAS operator demonstrates that he or she is operating an EASA-certified unmanned aircraft. Rule-making on the Certified category will follow. EASA has adopted AMC, which provide further guidance on when the Regulation requires the certification of the unmanned aircraft.

Until that particular date, most drones under certification in EASA will adopt this certification basis. The proposed airworthiness standards form part of EASA's wider initiative to ensure that drones can be operated safely and acceptably, particularly in areas that are densely occupied by people and moving or static objects.

The proposed Specification Certification is applicable to UAS:
– Not intended to transport humans.
– Operated with intervention of the remote pilot or autonomous.
– With MTOM up to 600 kg.
– Operated in the Specific category of operations, medium and high risk, or in the Certified category of operations.

---

41 Ann. I (Part-21) to Regulation (EU) No. 748/2012 of 3 August 2012: inserted point 21.B.80 Ann. I Type certification basis for a Type Certificate or Restricted Type Certificate.

With large parts of the economy looking at ways to use drones to streamline their operations, it is essential that there are strong rules in place to ensure there is no danger to people or property from drone usage. Setting certification standards for drones presents particular challenges. Design concepts vary hugely, technologies develop quite rapidly and there is strong economic pressure to bring new products to the market in an even faster way.

Publishing of the proposal for the future certification basis is expected to stimulate new design and certification initiatives for drones and to contribute to the safe integration into populated environments of BVLOS operations.[42]

For UA of higher MTOM, closer to traditional manned aircraft or capable of carrying persons, the certification basis may be established on the basis of existing manned aircraft Certification Specifications (CS-23 Normal, Utility, Aerobatic and Commuter Aeroplanes, CS-27 Small Rotorcraft, CS-25 Large Aeroplanes, CS-29 Large Rotorcraft), complemented with appropriate airworthiness standards from a CS-UAS, yet to be created, focused only on UAS-peculiar elements.

Owing to the Covid-19 crisis in 2020-2021, the following delay aspects are essential:
- As of 31 December 2020, registration of drone operators and certified drones becomes mandatory.
- As of 31 December 2020, operations in the Specific category may be conducted after authorization has been given by the national CAA.
- Between 31 December 2020 and 1 January 2023, drone users operating drones without class identification label can continue to operate in the limited category under Article 22 of Regulation (EU) 2019/947.
- As of January 2022, national authorizations, certificates and declarations must be fully converted to the new EU system.
- From 1 January 2022, EASA Member States must make available information on geographical zones for geo-awareness in a digital format harmonized between the EU states.
- As of January 2023, all operations in the Open category and all drone operators must fully comply with both Regulation (EU) 2019/945 and Regulation (EU) 2019/947 (amended regarding applicability by Regulation (EU) 2020/746.

---

42 EASA Special Condition Light Unmanned Aircraft Systems, Proposed Special Condition for Light UAS, 20 July 2020, p. iv.

Chapter 6 Privacy, Data Protection and Security

6.1 Privacy and Data Protection

Drone use by civilians, either recreational or professional, has increased tremendously worldwide. The applications of drone use in the service of society are versatile, ranging from subservient to, unfortunately, more obscure tasks. Drones are able to capture personal data. As soon as a drone is flown outdoors, any sensor attached to the drone will generally be directed outwards from the private setting. Increasingly sophisticated sensors are some of the characteristics that make drones unique tools for flexible, effective and discrete video surveillance and monitoring of all kinds of activities.

The intensified use of drones, resulting in their progressive integration into the airspace, may raise serious and unique privacy and data protection concerns in society and undermine the overall benefits of this innovative technology. The logical question is whether such a course of action will have a real adverse impact on the fundamental rights and freedoms of others, in particular their right to the protection of personal data.[1]

In our daily life, the use of drones, in any conceivable application, has the potential to dramatically change our attitudes, behaviours and feelings about safety and the physical environment. They will certainly create a big paradigm shift. Yet by means of authority-issued regulations and licences the integration of drones in our society has been legitimized. However, atypical features of drone technology have been identified that pose privacy concerns.

In this context, the following characteristics are mentioned: the invisibility of the technology, the particular privacy intrusive character compared with other data collection technologies, the ability to process data on very wide territories, the ability to process a massive volume of information, the ability to perform continuous surveillance, the ability to collect and store data indiscriminately and the evolving character of the technology. It is thus apparent that existing drone capabilities and applications raise a number of privacy, data protection and ethical issues.

On 4 November 2010, the EU Commission adopted a Communication entitled 'A comprehensive approach on personal data protection in the European Union'. The

---

1 *See* Recital (2) of Directive (EU) 2016/680 of the European Parliament and of the Council of 27 April 2016 on the protection of natural persons with regard to the processing of personal data by competent authorities for the purposes of the prevention, investigation, detection or prosecution of criminal offences or the execution of criminal penalties, and on the free movement of such data, and repealing Council Framework Decision 2008/977/JHA, *OJ* L 119/89, 4 May 2016.

Communication intends to lay down the Commission's approach to the review of the EU legal system for the protection of personal data in all areas of the EU activities, focusing on the challenges resulting from globalization and new technologies such as drones. The Communication represents an important step towards such a legislative change, which in turn would be the most important development in the area of EU data protection since the adoption of Directive 95/46/EC, which is generally considered as the cornerstone of data protection within the European Union.[2]

The Communication was sent to the European Data Protection Supervisor (EDPS) for consultation in accordance with Article 41 of Regulation (EC) No. 45/2001. Before the adoption of the Communication, the EDPS was given the possibility to give informal comments, followed by a comprehensive Opinion by the EDPS, in which the EDPS concluded that a review of the legal framework for data protection in the European Union was necessary by replacing Directive 95/46/EC, in order to ensure effective protection in a further developing information society. The review of data protection rules occurred at a crucial and historic moment. The Communication described the context extensively and convincingly. On the basis of this description, the EDPS has identified the four main drivers of the environment in which the review process should take place.[3]

The first driver is technological development. Technological phenomena like cloud computing, social networks, road toll collection, geolocation devices and sensor-equipped drones profoundly changed the way in which data is processed and pose enormous challenges for data protection.

The second driver is globalization. International data processing has become ubiquitous owing to advanced information and communication technologies (ICTs),

---

2   Directive 95/46/EC of the European Parliament and of the Council of 24 October 1995 on the protection of individuals with regard to the processing of personal data and on the free movement of such data (Data Protection Directive).
3   Regulation (EC) No. 45/2001 of the European Parliament and of the Council of 18 December 2000 on the protection of individuals with regard to the processing of personal data by the Community institutions and bodies and on the free movement of such data, OJ L 8/1, 12 January 2001, Art. 41 European Data Protection Supervisor, 1. An independent supervisory authority is hereby established, referred to as the European Data Protection Supervisor. 2. With respect to the processing of personal data, the European Data Protection Supervisor shall be responsible for ensuring that the fundamental rights and freedoms of natural persons, and in particular their right to privacy, are respected by the Community institutions and bodies. The European Data Protection Supervisor shall be responsible for monitoring and ensuring the application of the provisions of this Regulation and any other Community act relating to the protection of the fundamental rights and freedoms of natural persons with regard to the processing of personal data by a Community institution or body, and for advising Community institutions and bodies and data subjects on all matters concerning the processing of personal data.

such as delocalized processing of large quantities of data on a global scale for international police and judicial operations in combating terrorism, cross-border crime and other international organized crimes, supported by a tremendous exchange of information for law enforcement purposes.[4]

The third driver is the Lisbon Treaty (Treaty on the Functioning of the European Union, TFEU), specifically TFEU Article 16 (ex Art. 286 Treaty establishing the European Community, TEC), providing for a direct legal basis for a strong EU-wide data protection law.[5] It allows for a comprehensive legal framework for data protection applicable in the private sector, the public sector in the EU Member States and the EU institutions and bodies, targeted as the main subjects of regulation.

The fourth driver is represented by parallel developments taking place in the context of international organizations. Where personal data moves across borders it may pose an increased risk to the ability of natural persons to exercise data protection rights themselves from the unlawful use or disclosure of that data.[6] At the same time, supervisory authorities may find that they are unable to pursue complaints or conduct investigations relating to the operations outside their borders. Their efforts to work together in the cross-border context may also be hampered by insufficient preventive or remedial powers and inconsistent legal regimes. There is therefore a need to promote closer cooperation among data protection supervisory authorities to help them exchange information with their foreign counterparts. Adoption of international standards on the protection of personal data and privacy, preferably leading to a binding global instrument on data protection, must ensure effective and consistent protection in a modern technologically driven and globalized environment.

Owing to the remarkably rapid proliferation of the use of drones, more and more questions arise about the privacy aspects associated with drone activities in today's

---

4   Directive (EU) 2016/680, Art. 3 Definitions. For the purposes of this Directive: (2) 'processing' means any operation or a set of operations which is performed on personal data or on sets of personal data, whether or not by automated means, such as collection, recording, organization, structuring, storage, adaptation or alteration, retrieval, consultation, use, disclosure by transmission, dissemination or otherwise making available, alignment or combination, restriction, erasure or destruction.

5   TEC Art. 286: 1. From 1 January 1999, Community acts on the protection of individuals with regard to the processing of personal data and the free movement of such data shall apply to the institutions and bodies set up by, or on the basis of, this Treaty. 2. Before the date referred to in paragraph 1, the Council, acting in accordance with the procedure referred to in Art. 251, shall establish an independent supervisory body responsible for monitoring the application of such Community act to Community institutions and bodies and shall adopt any other relevant provisions as appropriate.

6   *See also* Regulation (EU) 2016/679 (General Data Protection Regulation), Art. 4 Definitions. For the purpose of this Regulation: (23) 'cross-border processing' means either: (a) processing of personal data which takes place in the context of the activities of establishments in more than one Member State of a controller or processor in the Union where the controller or processor is established in more than one Member State: or (b) processing of personal data which takes place in the context of the activities of a single establishment of a controller or processor in the Union but which substantially affects or is likely to substantially affect data subjects in more than one Member State.

society. After all, the use of drones can infringe on privacy and will therefore have some far-reaching consequences. First of all, it is quite important to distinguish between the protection of privacy and personal data. The right to respect for one's private and family life, home and correspondence is, among other things, enshrined in the European Convention on Human Rights (ECHR), formally the Convention for the Protection of Human Rights and Fundamental Freedoms. This right protects not only personal data, but also our spatial, relational and physical privacy. The right to protection of personal data is considered part of the right to privacy.[7]

The question that arises is, when does the use of drones violate the right to privacy? Provided that there is an infringement of the right to privacy, this does not mean that the infringement is not permitted. By its very nature, privacy legislation is quite abstract, as it is not possible to provide a specific rule for every situation where privacy is at stake. Therefore, it mainly contains criteria on the basis of which a specific consideration must be made in a concrete situation, in which, for example, the use of drones is involved.

To answer the question of when the use of drones does infringe the right to privacy, as laid down in Article 8 ECHR (Right to respect for private and family life), it is most important to consider whether the use of drones affects the private sphere. The private character of this sphere derives from its coverage of the intimate aspect of a human being's personality. The private sphere is delimited from the public sphere by physical boundaries, such as the walls of a property, personal relationships with family, close friends, colleagues or good acquaintances and by selected fields of information (personal, sensitive or embarrassing information). Using a drone to monitor someone within his or her own private sphere, in other words an intrusion from outside, undeniably implies an infringement of Article 8 ECHR.[8]

Whether the use of a drone in the public sphere is in violation of Article 8 ECHR depends on the circumstances. This should take into account the concept of a reasonable expectation of privacy of people in public places. Depending on the circumstances of a certain case, the violation of the right to privacy will then be assessed more or less drastically.

A public place is defined as:

> A place which can be in principle [be] accessed by anyone freely, indiscriminately, at any time and under any circumstances. Public areas are open to the public. In principle anyone at any time can have the benefit of

---

7   See also Charter of Fundamental Rights of the European Union (2012/C 326/02) (CFREU), OJ C 326/391, 26 October 2012, Art. 7 Respect for private and family life, and Art. 8 Protection of personal data.
8   Finn, R.L., Wright, D., Donovan, A., Jacques, L., De Hert, P., 'Study on Privacy, Data Protection and Ethical Risks in Civil Remotely Piloted Aircraft Systems Operations', Final Report, European Commission, Directorate-General Enterprise and Industries, Luxembourg: Publications Office of the European Union, November 2014, p. 58.

this area. A person benefits freely from public areas. Public areas are governed by public authorities whose power to enforce the law and intervene are wider than within private property.

In public areas (the public sphere), individual privacy is similar to the concept of non-privacy, because:

> When entering a public area or staying there implies that one is conscious that one will be at least seen, even recognized and that one's behaviour may be scrutinized by anyone in this public area, one may draw one's own conclusions with respect to these elements and decide to adapt one's behaviour accordingly. The European Court of Human Rights found that the mere monitoring in public areas does not interfere with Article 8(1) of the ECHR.[9]

This acknowledges that a lower degree of privacy may well be expected by any human being moving in public areas. Individuals can still hold privacy expectations, and thus they should not expect to be deprived of their rights and freedoms, including those related to their own private sphere and image. Therefore, Article 8(1) ECHR may also be applied in public areas if the individual concerned could reasonably expect a certain degree of privacy.[10]

The question of what a reasonable expectation of privacy is, for example when using a camera attached to a drone, can turn out differently when it concerns a fixed camera on the surface. After all, when images are shot with a fixed camera during an event, it will usually be easy to notice that camera and to focus on the person who is filming with it or on his assisting colleagues, if any, to learn the purposes and the context of the images, or at least to be able to ask what the images consist of, and possibly to object to being filmed.

On the other hand, the circumstances are completely different when a camera-equipped drone makes the images. People involved are not always aware or have not always been informed that they are being filmed by a drone or that their image can be reused on various media, such as the internet, television or written press, or for other purposes, such as journalism, reportage, promotion of events, etc. Even if they are aware

---

9   Case *Pierre Herbecq and the Association Ligue des droits de l' homme v. Belgium*. Decision of 14 January 1998 on the admissibility of the applications. Applications No. 32200/96 and No. 32201/96.
10 Study No. 404/2006 CDL-AD(2007)014 European Commission for Democracy through Law (Venice Commission), Opinion on Video Surveillance in Public Places by Public Authorities and the Protection of Human Rights Adopted by the Venice Commission at its 70th Plenary Session (Venice, 16-17 March 2007), on the basis of comments by: van Dijk, P., Dimitrijevic, V., Buttarelli, G., Strasbourg, 23 March 2007, pp. 3-7.

of the drone, it can be extremely difficult to find out and trace the drone operator to ask for clarification. The same considerations may also apply to surveillance with camera-equipped drones and will be discussed later.

On the basis of these considerations, it is plausible to provide a strict interpretation of the concept of reasonable expectations when using drones. As the use of drones in the airspace will be further liberalized, the possibility that an individual in the public space may be filmed by a drone may not automatically lead to the conclusion that the images are within the reasonable expectations of that individual. In other words, technological evolution should not lead to a citizen's expectations of privacy being diminished because the collection of their personal data has become easier, more discreet and less framed.

Against this background, it can be inferred from case law relating to Article 8 ECHR that the use of drones in the public sphere infringes the right to privacy if:

- A drone is used that records data about people in a systematic or sustainable matter, regardless of whether this is done covertly or overtly;
- an advanced camera is used, such as an infrared camera, a night camera, a thermal imager or a camera with built-in video analytics, even if this camera only monitors and does not capture images of people; or
- the information collected with the drone is made public.

Therefore, there will be no infringement of privacy in the public sphere if the use consists solely of monitoring activities, without images being captured, images being made public or advanced cameras being used. From the jurisprudence with regard to Article 8 ECHR, it can further be deduced that the use of drones that are able to determine locations using Global Positioning System (GPS) is considered less intrusive than the use of drones recording with cameras or those that intercept communication.

> GPS surveillance is by its very nature to be distinguished from other methods of visual or acoustical surveillance which are, as a rule, more susceptible of interfering with a person's right to respect for private life, because they disclose more information on a person's conduct, opinions or feelings.[11]

Article 8(2) ECHR states:

> There shall be no interference by a public authority with the exercise of this right except such as in accordance with the law and is necessary in a democratic society in the interests of national security, public safety or the economic well-being of the country, for the prevention of disorder or crime, for the protection of health or morals, or for the protection of the rights and freedoms of others.

---

11   Finn R.L. *et al*, p. 63.

If the government does infringe Article 8 ECHR with the use of a drone, this may be lawful if the conditions set out in the second paragraph of this article are met. These conditions are:
1. That one of the aims, as referred to in Paragraph 2, is pursued,
2. the infringement is provided by law, and
3. the measure is necessary in a democratic society.

The first condition can be met relatively easily, since the purpose of drone use is most likely to be one of the aims set out in Article 8(2) ECHR: the importance of national security, public security or the economic well-being of a State, the prevention of disorder and criminal offences, the protection of health or good morals or the protection of the rights and freedoms of others.

In the context of public safety or to prevent disorder and criminal offences, municipalities and the police may use drones as a form of camera surveillance. Emergency services can also use drones to protect health or the rights and freedoms of others. This could include the deployment of drones, for example in the event of an emergency or for the detection of missing persons.

The use of drones by the government that restricts privacy must also be provided by law. It will have to be taken into account that different sensors on drones have different infringements of the right to privacy. Depending on the intensity of the violation of the right to privacy, more detailed regulations with restrictions on the use of drones may be appropriate. It can be emphasized that it must be made clear to citizens under what circumstances the use of drones is possible and how that use can infringe on privacy.

The requirement of foreseeability is playing an emphatic role in technologies that are increasingly sophisticated and intrusive. The requirement that the use of privacy-restricting drones must be necessary means that there ought to be an urgent social need for such deployment. The measure must also be proportional, that is to say, the breach of the privacy of the data subject must not be disproportionate in relation to the purpose achieved by the breach (proportionality test). The government will therefore have to motivate what added value the use of drones will bring and how this use outweighs the interests of the right to privacy. It will also need to verify whether no less drastic resources are available (subsidiarity test). The ECHR will set limits to the restrictions on the right to privacy, imposed by governments.

The question now arises in regard to what differentiated limits criminal law is placing on the use of cameras on drones. When using a camera attached to a drone in the Netherlands, first of all, the provisions in the Dutch Criminal Code concerning the secret production of images are relevant. Covert filming in a home and in publicly inaccessible places has been made a criminal offence. It is also a criminal offence to make secret images of persons with an applied technical device in publicly accessible places. The element 'applied technical device' has been widely interpreted in legal history.[12]

By analogy, a camera attached to a drone can also be qualified as an applied technical device. With respect to drone use, one can think of a drone that hovers for some time in front of a window or above a garden (or backyard) to take images of a person in a confined place, whereby the garden is expressly referred to as a private area where someone basically feels unobserved. Legally established rules should serve to curb this literally transgressive behaviour at too low a height.

A frequently asked question in this context is, who controls low-altitude airspace? Another more intriguing and controversial question is, who owns low-altitude airspace? The latter question happens to be one of the most important issues of commercial and recreational drone operations.

Although international aviation organizations proposed and created regulatory frameworks for drone operations, there is still a great deal of confusion as to what constitutes a legal flight under state law and international rules. It is still unclear where navigable airspace begins, causing major implications for airspace users, in particular drone operators, including potentially duped people of low-flying drones equipped with technical devices such as cameras. The FAA rule that all airspace is publicly accessible navigable airspace and that drone operators may fly under FAA rules anywhere in navigable airspace means that there is no longer private airspace. Apart from minor

---

12 Criminal Code of the Kingdom of the Netherlands, Art. 139f: Any person who intentionally and unlawfully produces an image of a person who is present in a home or another place that is not open to the public by means of a technical device which is not clearly visible or notified, shall be liable to a term of imprisonment not exceeding twelve months or a fine of the fourth category. *See also* Art. 441b. Imprisonment for a maximum of two months or a fine of the third category will apply to anyone who, using an applied technical device, the presence of which has not been clearly indicated, unlawfully produces an image of a person present at a place accessible to the public.

substantive differences, these rules are similar to other national regulations and case law.[13]

Other punishable offences related to the broad interpretation of 'applied technical device' include telecommunication tapping and placement of eavesdropping instruments, which may also include the use of small drones for eavesdropping. Anyone who films in a private place with a drone is punishable only if he or she is deliberately and unjustly making an image of a person present.

The element 'unlawfully' unambiguously expresses the idea that investigative authorities or intelligence services are not punishable if they secretly use cameras attached to drones for the performance of their task within the applicable frameworks.

---

13 Case *Boggs v. Merideth*, Civil Action N0. 3:16-CV-00006-TBR Document 20 (W.D. Ky. 2017), 21 March 2017. A drone operator sued his neighbour for shooting down his drone. As a result, several issues pertaining to the boundaries of 'navigable airspace' and how that airspace interacts with the state property rights of landowners may be clarified. *See* Connot, M.J., Zummo, J.J., 'United States: Navigable Airspace: Where Private Property Rights End and Navigable Airspace Begins', *Fox Rothschild LLP*, 18 January 2016.
The federal government has exclusive sovereignty over U.S. airspace. Congress delegated to the FAA the ability to define 'navigable airspace' and the authority to regulate 'navigable airspace' of aircraft by regulation or order (49 U.S. C. Section 40103(b)(1)). According to Federal Aviation Regulations, 'navigable airspace' is defined as 'airspace at or above the minimum altitudes of flight prescribed by under this chapter, including airspace needed for safe take-off and landing' (14 C.F.R. Section 1.1 General definitions). While it is clear that 'navigable airspace' falls under the purview of the FAA, the boundaries of that airspace remain unclear.
Sovereignty and use of airspace: *see* Case *United States v. Causby*, 328 U.S. 256 (1946). The Supreme Court of the United States provided in 1946 guidance on where private property rights end and 'navigable airspace' begins. In Causby, a farmer lived adjacent to a military airport where aircraft flew as low as 83 ft over the farmer's property. As a result, the noise from the aircraft startled the farmer's chickens, causing them to fly into walls, causing their death. The Court found that the 'navigable airspace' that Congress had placed in the public domain was airspace above what was deemed the minimum safe altitude (MSA), and it put forth two key principles regarding airspace below the MSA.
First, landowners have exclusive control of the intermediate reaches of the enveloping atmosphere.
Second, landowners own at least as much of the space above the ground as they can occupy or use in connection with the land. The Court ruled in favour of the farmer but did not decide where the precise boundaries of public airspace above the farm meet the immediate reaches of the farmer's property and how high state government's rights extended. *See also* Case *Griggs v. Allegheny County*, 369 U.S. 84 (1963), Section 1 (24) of the Civil Aeronautics Act, 49 U.S.C.A., Section 4019240, defines 'navigable airspace' as follows: "Navigable airspace means airspace above the minimum altitudes of flight prescribed by regulations issued under this Act." Pursuant to authority granted by the Civil Aeronautics Act of 1938, the Civil Aeronautics Board (predecessor of the FAA) issued Civil Air Regulations (14 C.F.R. Parts 1-190). Among these Regulations, Section 60.17, Part 60 (Air Traffic Rules), which establishes minimum safe altitudes of flight at 1,000 ft over congested areas and 500 ft over other than congested areas, is prefaced with the following: "Except when necessary for take-off or landing, no person shall operate an aircraft below the following altitudes." The Supreme Court has held that "[t]he navigable airspace which Congress placed in the public domain does not include the path of glide for an airplane's take-off or landing. The path of glide governs the method of operating – of landing or take-off. The altitude required for that operation is not the minimum safe altitude of flight which is the downward reach of the navigable airspace. Hence the flights in question were not within the navigable airspace […]. If any airspace needed for landing or taking off were included, flights which were so close to the land as to render it uninhabitable would be immune."

Under certain conditions, the same can be said of journalists who covertly shoot images with drones. This activity is particularly related to freedom of information.

Circumstances that play a role are the importance of the topic to be revealed by means of a hidden camera, whether the journalist *in casu* at that particular time had other options available to gather the necessary information, and the nature and extent to which the hidden camera has infringed the privacy of the persons depicted. It is assumed that there is an image only if the person, which is photographed or filmed, is recognizable.

However, the question is whether people being photographed or filmed from above, for example, by a drone, will be recognizable. Filming or photographing is a covert activity if the presence of a camera is not clearly disclosed. The intent must be to produce an image, in particular an image of a person. Producing includes forms of digital streaming without image storage or preservation. A person may not be punishable if a great social interest is served in the secret making of recordings by means of a drone.

Last but not least, someone systematically tracing and tracking (monitoring) with a drone, or stalking, as it is better known today, has been criminalized. Stalking is the act or crime of wilfully and repeatedly following or harassing another person in circumstances that would cause a reasonable person to fear injury or death, especially because of express or implied threats.

This behaviour is interrelated with harassment and intimidation and may include following the victim either in person or by monitoring with a device such as a drone. In other words, the use of drones by private individuals is likely to disturb their privacy as drone operators engage in voyeuristic behaviours and/or harassment. The widespread availability of drones means that they empower pilots and/or operators (paparazzi and voyeurs) of onboard facilities, such as sensors and cameras, to be able to engage in voyeurism, intimidation, harassment, stalking, surreptitious observation for longer periods and even acts of gratuitous violence.[14]

Police and prosecution services make use of drones for investigation and prosecution purposes. Regulation (EU) 2016/679 (GDPR) does not apply to the police and judicial authorities when they perform their duties such as prevention, investigation, detection or prosecution of criminal offences or the execution of criminal penalties. Instead, Directive (EU) 2016/680 applies to the aforementioned activities.

---

14 Finn R.L. *et al*, p. 35.

This includes the tasks of protecting public safety. In regard to other tasks of the police and judicial authorities, for instance, the processing of personal data, Regulation (EU) 2016/679 does apply.[15] The question arises why different rules apply to the police and judicial authorities. Investigative services such as the police and the public prosecutor are subject to special rules because they are responsible for safeguarding public safety and security and detecting and prosecuting criminal offences. They therefore have special powers to perform these public tasks.[16] At the same time, investigative services process very sensitive personal data of people in the public interest of crime fighting, often without their permission and knowledge. It is therefore all the more important that investigative services safeguard citizens' fundamental rights, such as the right to privacy. These services should very well secure all processed data.

While Regulation (EU) 2016/679 applies, inter alia, to the activities of the courts and other judicial authorities, Union law or EU Member State law could specify the processing operations and procedures in relation to the processing of personal data by their courts and other judicial authorities. The competence of the supervisory authorities, which are independent authorities established by the EU Member States pursuant to Article 51 of this Regulation, should not cover the processing of personal data when courts are acting in their judicial capacity, in order to safeguard the independence of the judiciary in the performance of its judicial tasks, including decision-making.

It should be possible to entrust the supervision of such data-processing operations to specific bodies within the judicial system of the EU Member State, which, in particular, should ensure compliance with the rules of this Regulation, enhance awareness among members of the judiciary of their obligations under this Regulation, and likewise handle complaints in relation to such data-processing operations.

Personal data is any data about an identified or identifiable natural person. The principles of data protection should apply to any information concerning an identified or identifiable natural person. A natural person is identifiable if the identity of this person can be reasonably established without disproportionate effort. An identifiable person is one who can be identified, directly or indirectly, by reference to an identifier such as a name, an identification number, location data, an online identifier or to one or more

---

15 *See also* Recital (8) Where this Regulation provides for specifications or restrictions of its rules by Member State law, Member States may, as far as necessary for coherence and for making the national provisions comprehensible to the persons to whom they apply, incorporate elements of this Regulation into their national law.
16 *See* Directive (EU) 2016/680, Art. 3 Definitions. For the purpose of this Directive: (7) 'competent authority' means: (a) any public authority competent for the prevention, investigation, detection or prosecution of criminal offences or the execution of criminal penalties, including the safeguarding against and the prevention of threats to public security; or (b) any other body or entity entrusted by Member State law to exercise public authority and public powers for the purposes of the prevention, investigation, detection or prosecution of criminal offences or the execution of criminal penalties, including the safeguarding against and the prevention of threats to public security. *See also* Art. 8 Lawfulness of processing.

factors specific to the physical, physiological, genetic, mental, economic, cultural or social identity of that natural person.[17]

The distinction between directly and indirectly identifiable data is as follows. Directly identifiable data is data relating to a person (data subject) whose identity can be unambiguously determined without detours, such as a name, possibly in combination with the address and date of birth. When data, such as a registration number, can be associated with a specific person as a result of further steps in the process, then there is indirectly identifiable data.

Data is not personal data if effective technical and organizational measures have been taken that reasonably exclude the actual identification of individual natural persons. The principles of data collection should therefore not apply to anonymous information, namely information that does not relate to an identified or identifiable natural person or to personal data rendered anonymous in such a manner that the data subject is not or no longer identifiable.

Through the use of cameras on drones, people can be seen or observed. That does not mean that personal data will be involved. This requires that the persons concerned are identifiable. This may be the case if a person's face is recognizable, although a striking piece of clothing can also lead to making someone recognizable. If the footage taken by a drone camera shows only the silhouette or outlines of a person, and that indefinite person cannot be identified without using sophisticated analytical means, it is not considered personal data.

Vehicle registration recorded with a drone camera is considered to be personal data if one is able to compare this data with data from the vehicle register. After all, these registration details can be traced back to an individual (the registrar). Other information, collected and processed by drones, such as biometric data, location data and traffic data, are in a general sense also to be considered as personal data if that information relates to an identified or identifiable person. Images and sound data related to an identified or identifiable person are considered personal data, even if they are not associated with a person's particulars, or if they do not concern individuals whose faces have been filmed, irrespective of the media used.

Whether recordings of houses can also be regarded as personal data depends on the circumstances. A house may be traceable to a person if the house number is also visible, or if an image or video of a house is made public along with other information. Recordings made by drones, equipped with GPS and surveillance cameras, of the

---

17 Directive (EU) 2016/680, Art. 3(1). *See also* Opinion 4/2007 (on the concept of personal data, Brussels, 20 June 2007) of the 29 Article Data Protection Working Party, replaced on 25 May 2018 by the European Data Protection Board (EDPB) under Regulation (EU) 2016/679. Art. 29 (Working Party on the Protection of Individuals with regard to the Processing of Personal Data) refers to Directive 95/46/EC of the European Parliament and of the Council of 24 October 1995.

livestock environment (e.g. meadows, stables, horse boxes) may, under certain conditions, also yield personal data.

If such recordings are made by an organization for the prevention of cruelty to animals aiming to spy on the treatment of farm animals in a bid to find abuse and disclose the recordings together with the personal details of the farmer, it is considered personal data and will have an impact on the farmer when this data is used as evidence before courts.[18]

If a camera on a drone digitally processes images of identified and identifiable persons, this is referred to as personal data. Digital processing is indeed a form of automated processing. This is also the case if after making such images the personal data on the images is made invisible at a later publishing or broadcasting time.

The controller is the person who, alone or together with others, determines the purpose and means of processing personal data. When using a drone for data processing, it is important to determine who is responsible. When using drones for this special activity, the controller may be, for example, an entrepreneur, a journalist or a public prosecutor. The controller does not have to be the pilot of the drone. After all, the pilot will not always determine the purpose and means of the processing. The pilot can also act on behalf of a customer or as an employee of a company. If the pilot carries out his work in accordance with the instructions and under the responsibility of the customer or the managing director of the company, the customer or the managing director is responsible for data processing. In that case, the pilot is the processor.[19]

In situations where different people are involved in the use of drones, it is important to determine in advance who has which role to play and who can ultimately be designated as being responsible. The focus is on the person who determines the manner in which and the purpose for which personal data is processed. Against this controller, a citizen, *in casu* the data subject, whose personal data is involved, can, if desired, exercise his or her rights, such as the right to inspect that data. The controller also has a number of obligations, such as informing a citizen that personal data about him or her is being processed.

A drone can be equipped with instruments or devices, constituting the payload, such as cameras, sensors for interception of telecommunication, microphones, radars, GPS and Wi-Fi routers. These sophisticated instruments are able, independently or in combination with each other, to collect information about persons in different ways

---

18 Finn R.L. *et al*, p. 275.
19 Regulation (EU) 2016/679, Art. 4 (7): 'controller' means the natural or legal person, public authority, agency or other body which, alone or jointly with others, determines the purposes and means of the processing of personal data; where the purposes and means of such processing are determined by Union or Member State law, the controller or the specific criteria for its nomination may be provided for by Union or Member State law. 'Processor' means a natural or legal person, public authority, agency or other body which processes personal data on behalf of the controller.

and to varying degrees, thereby affecting their privacy. Cameras are the most commonly used instruments on drones. For that reason, different types of cameras and their usage will be discussed in more detail:
- There are a variety of cameras: photo cameras, video cameras, night vision cameras, infrared cameras, high-resolution cameras, ultraviolet cameras, thermal imaging cameras, closed-circuit television (CCTV), etc. Depending on their technical capabilities, cameras can be used as a monitor, store images or send images to a ground station.
- Cameras may include zoom-in techniques to provide an ultra-detailed view of persons or objects on the ground or water.
- Cameras can be superintelligent so that they are able to recognize individuals, licence plates (automated number plate recognition), objects or situations or to identify certain behaviours as abnormal.
- A drone can be equipped with different cameras so that it is possible to create a 360° image.

The use of other sensors may also affect privacy but only if the data they provide are combined with other data. Such sensors are for detecting biological, chemical or nuclear spores. Such traces may be linked to people who left them behind. When using drone applications such as surveillance, maintaining public order, security of public and private objects, infrastructural inspections, border control, media and journalism and even recreational activities, it is very well possible that people or objects come into view that can be associated with certain people. One purpose is more likely than another. For example, the use of drones for investigative purposes will soon pose privacy concerns because investigation is aimed at finding perpetrators. On the other hand, it will be more or less a coincidence that a video inspection of a windmill also involves (innocent) people.

Owing to their generally small dimensions and relatively great height at which they operate, drones can often be hardly visible or audible. For these reasons, it is difficult for an ordinary person to discern whether an overhead drone is making recordings at random or, controversially, recording data about him or her. In these more common cases, it should be noted that drones are very well used to spy on someone, as when paparazzi continuously attempt to track celebrities concerning their whereabouts, or when private detectives do their daily work.

Drones can also be used in situations in which they are observed but not expected. People who live in a busy residential area on the ground floor may be aware that others are able to view the inside of their apartments. However, in that case they could have taken measures, if desired, to tackle the problem by using net curtains, blinds or shutters. People who live on the twentieth floor of an apartment building, for instance, do not have to take into account that they are being watched from outside. When a drone, equipped with a camera, appears in front of their windows, it must soon be assumed that their reasonable expectations regarding their privacy have been violated, or at least disturbed.

The fact that in some cases the operator of a camera-equipped drone is very well able to maintain a considerable distance from a person whom he or she is filming could lower the mental barrier to keep on filming. This is called the dehumanizing effect of drone use, which could involuntarily lead to an increase in this specific use of drones. Drones can be much more intrusive to privacy than other methods of data collection.

That is, drones can penetrate citizens' lives more drastically compared with other instruments or methods. For instance, the opportunities of cameras attached to a drone exceed those of cameras on the ground, because a drone can cross boundaries that define a private space, such as walls, windows and railings. For example, a drone camera can be used to film someone who is not or sparsely dressed, sunbathing in his or her walled backyard, while a ground-level camera would fail to get that image.

A drone can not only enter a space that is inaccessible to other methods, but can also be equipped with technology that enables it to collect information that could not easily be collected in another way with that same technology. This might include technology to collect information through walls, roofs or clouds, not only during daytime but also at night.[20]

Drones equipped with visual sensors allow their operators to film live and take footage of objects and individuals in private and public places, which in turn raises privacy issues that do not arise in the context of non-visual surveillance. Even if a drone is unequipped with an onboard camera or other sensors, flying a drone above people may violate someone's privacy expectations. People often cannot perceive whether a drone is equipped with those devices. This can lead to someone behaving differently under the influence of such a flying drone. This is called the chilling effect or panoptic syndrome of drones: one will behave less freely than one would otherwise. Depending on this situation, this may also relate to the protection of the human rights and fundamental freedoms, specifically the right to privacy, the freedom of opinion and expression and the freedom of peaceful assembly and association because individuals are discouraged from participating in social movements or public dissent activities for fear of being surveilled.[21]

The use of drones is in a way not yet absolutely transparent. While helicopters, particularly police- and rescue helicopters, often have typical stripes or livery, making them recognizable, drones usually have no distinguishing marks. If they already have

---

20 Night means the hours between the end of evening civil twilight and the beginning of morning civil twilight as defined in Commission Implementing Regulation (EU) No. 923/2012 of 26 September 2012 laying down the common rules of the air and operational provisions regarding services and procedures in air navigation and amending Implementing Regulation (EU) No. 1035/2011 and Regulations (EC) No. 1165/2007, (EC) No. 1794/2006, (EC) No. 730/2006, (EC) No. 1033/2006 and (EU) No. 255/2010, OJ L281, 13 October 2012, p. 1.
21 Universal Declaration of Human Rights (UDHR), Arts. 3, 19 and 20. European Convention on Human Rights (ECHR), Arts. 8, 10 and 11. *See also* Finn R.L. *et al*, p. 41.

external display registration numbers, which are conditionally required, it is highly questionable whether these marks would be visible from the surface given the size of the drone.[22]

In addition, it may also be difficult to observe the person operating the drone to identify the organization to which this person may belong, and to know what ends are being pursued using the drone or what data is being collected. However, the mandatory registration system is a way to connect drones to their owners, both to return drones that get lost and to ensure the operators are flying them responsibly.

In practice, the requirements of e-registration and identification marks or labels will contribute to more transparency. People on the ground or water are much more likely to be able to identify who is operating the drone and to directly raise questions or issues with the operator or team. Other flight and oversight requirements, such as safety risk assessment and VLOS obligations, can also assist in indirectly regulating the privacy, data protection and ethical issues associated with drone use, such as safety, public dissatisfaction, discrimination and illegal intrusions into wildlife. While this risk assessment likely focuses on safety and is silent about impacts on fundamental rights, it could easily be used as an existing framework through which issues related to privacy, data protection and ethics can be inserted.

The mobility of drones makes it possible to cover very large areas of several square kilometres to collect information, albeit by using the required BVLOS. For instance, a drone is capable of simultaneously storing data from many people over a wide area. Drones can collect a very wide range of diverse information using different sensors. A drone can not only receive or transmit video images or photos, but also, depending on the onboard technology, listen to communication signals, detect and identify individuals, record their movements, during day and night, or detect certain movements that are considered abnormal.

Drones are capable of collecting enormous amounts of information about individuals without distinguishing them. In other words, the collection of information will usually take place without any distinguishing criterion and without prior sorting of information relevant to the purposes for which the drone is being used. It is conceivable that a drone can eventually locate and track an individual for a longer period, without the disadvantages associated with other technical observation methods like a vehicle, a helicopter or just simple human visual observation.

Sensors attached to drones could lead to so-called function creep. This is the phenomenon that these special drones are purchased for specific, restricted operational uses but come to be used for more common, controversial reasons. This could include the case when a drone is purchased by the police for monitoring crowd gatherings but will also be used to detect people who have not paid for parking. In the private sector, this

---

22 Mandatory registration of drones with a total weight above a specified weight (250 g or 0.55 lbs) has been implemented in many states.

could include the situation where a real estate agent uses a drone to record houses on video that he wants to sell, but *en passant* films people, houses, gardens and cars in the immediate vicinity to get an idea of the prosperity of residents living in that particular neighbourhood. Working this way, the privacy of these people could be jeopardized.

Finally, the risk of data leaks is present. There is a potential risk that data, captured by onboard sensors, usually being transmitted via a wireless connection to a receiving ground station, will be intercepted. In that case, it could also pose a risk to the privacy of people whose data have been recorded. Thus, it should be kept in mind that the main problem with the drone technology from a privacy and data protection perspective is that the enforcement of data protection and privacy rules is difficult to accomplish.

Persons and organizations using drones are able to remove or reduce the risks in various ways. This may include the following methods:
- Implementation of a Privacy Impact Assessment (PIA);
- applying *privacy by design* and *privacy by default*;
- performing security measures;
- codes of conduct;
- certification;
- transparency; or
- performing privacy audits.

Each of these methods can be applied separately. However, some methods are in line with each other, and so it makes sense to apply them cumulatively. For example, the results of a PIA may indicate the direction to the application of *privacy by design*. A PIA is a systematic process for evaluating the potential effects on privacy and data protection of a project, initiative, proposed system or scheme and finding ways to mitigate or avoid any adverse effects. Or another definition:

> A PIA or Data Protection Impact Assessment (DPIA) is a method that can be used to provide a structured and transparent overview of the possible effects of drone use for the protection of personal data and what measures are to be taken to mitigate those effects.

A PIA has three elements:
1. A map of the information flows associated with the organization (or the integrated systems or the organization's activity), to be able to determine information decision points and privacy vulnerabilities.
2. A privacy analysis of the information flow, to determine whether:
    - Privacy principles are adhered to;
    - there is technical compliance with statutory and/or regulatory privacy;
    - these policies and laws afford the desired privacy protection.

3. An analysis of privacy issues raised by the system review, including a risk assessment and an evaluation of the options available for mitigating any identified risks.[23]

A combination of existing regulatory instruments and soft law measures such as PIA elements will certainly assist drone operators in developing innovative applications and services by combining harmonized regulations across Europe with a tailored impact assessment. In order to specify the open-ended wording of the law regarding the basic obligation to perform a PIA, the supervisory authorities are involved. The assessment must be carried out, especially if one of the rule examples set forth in Article 35(3) of Regulation (EU) 2016/679 is relevant. The implementation of a PIA is obligatory under this Regulation in cases where processing personal data using drones is likely to pose a high risk to the rights and freedoms of natural persons.[24]

Recital (75) of this Regulation states:

> The risk to the rights and freedoms of natural persons, of varying likelihood and severity, may result from personal data processing which could lead to physical, material or non-material damage, in particular: where the processing may give rise to discrimination, identity theft or fraud, financial loss, damage to the reputation, loss of confidentiality of personal data protected by professional secrecy, unauthorized reversal of pseudonymization, or any other significant economic or social disadvantage; where data subjects might be deprived of their rights and freedoms or prevented from exercising control over their personal data; where personal data are processed which reveal racial or ethnic origin, political opinions, religion or philosophical beliefs, trade union membership, and the processing of genetic data, data concerning health or data concerning sex life or criminal convictions and offences or related security measures; where personal aspects are evaluated, in particular analyzing or predicting aspects concerning performance at work, economic situation, health, personal preferences or interests, reliability or behaviour, location or movements, in order to create or use personal profiles; where personal data of vulnerable natural persons, in particular of children, are

---

23 *See* Cavoukian, A. (Information and Privacy Commissioner of Ontario, Canada), 'Privacy and Drones: Unmanned Aerial Vehicles', *Privacy by Design*, August 2012, pp. 16-17 (https://www.ipc.on.ca/wp-content/uploads/resources/pbd-drones.pdf).

24 Regulation (EU) 2016/679 (General Data Protection Regulation), Art. 35 Data protection impact assessment. Para. 3: A data protection impact assessment referred to in Para. 1 shall in particular be required in the case of: (a) a systematic and extensive evaluation of personal aspects relating to natural persons which is based on automated processing, including profiling, and on which decisions are based that produce legal effects concerning the natural person or similarly significantly affect the natural person; (b) processing on a large scale of special categories of data referred to in Art. 9(1), or of personal data relating to criminal convictions and offences referred to in Art. 10; or (c) a systematic monitoring of a publicly accessible area on a large scale.

processed; or where processing involves a large amount of personal data and affects a large number of data subjects.[25]

In addition to these general cases, a PIA should also be mandatory in the specific case of using drones, if:
- The drone operator risks to process inadvertently personal data;
- the processing activity is made by a visual payload and takes place in public places;
- the data processing activity is performed by state agencies in the framework of a covert surveillance investigation; or
- the personal data collected will be used, and the processing activity aims to build profiles or to perform direct marketing.[26]

With regard to the first two cases, a PIA may be recommended only if it concerns the professional use of drones. After all, making images for a purely personal or household activity falls outside the scope of the Regulation (Art. 2.2(c)).[27] The performance and publication of a PIA in data processing by drones can contribute to the transparency of this processing and thus to the public's understanding of the way in which and the reason for which this data is processed. Furthermore, a PIA can also contribute to public confidence in the use of drones. In addition, a PIA can assist in preventing the use of a payload on a drone that does not sufficiently meet the legal requirements for the protection of personal data. This reduces the risk that the payload will later need to be adjusted at great cost or replaced by another one.

As a matter of fact, privacy concerns relate not only to the drone as an aircraft, but also to the payload or software with which the drone is equipped. The level of impact of this technology on individual privacy is complex as it comprises several factors. The degree of impact depends on the purpose for which drones are used, as well as the extent and type of personal information that the drones may capture, the type of operator, the context and location of the drones, as well as the type of technology equipment they carry.

---

25 Directive (EU) 2016/680, Art. 3 Definitions. For the purpose of this Directive: (5) pseudonymization means the processing of personal data in such a manner that the personal data can no longer be attributed to a specific data subject without the use of additional information, provided that such additional information is kept separately and is subject to technical and organizational measures to ensure that the personal data are not attributed to an identified or identifiable natural person.
26 See Finn R.L. et al, pp. 337-338.
27 See also Regulation (EU) 2016/679, Recital (18). This Regulation does not apply to the processing of personal data by a natural person in the course of a purely personal or household activity and thus with no connection to a professional or commercial activity. Personal or household activities could include correspondence and the holding of addresses, or social networking and online activity undertaken within the context of such activities. However, this Regulation applies to controllers or processors which provide the means for processing personal data for such personal or household activities.

The *privacy by design* principle is an approach to protecting privacy by embedding it into the design specifications of technologies, business practices and physical infrastructures. Application of this principle means that the responsible person, the designated controller, must take appropriate technical and organizational measures. These measures are designed to implement data protection principles, such as minimization and pseudonymization of data, in an effective manner and to integrate the necessary safeguards into the processing in order to comply with this Regulation and to protect the rights of data subjects.

With due consideration for the state of the art, the cost of implementation and the nature, context, scope and purposes of data processing as well as the risks of varying likelihood and severity for rights and freedoms of natural persons, posed by the processing, the controller shall, both at the time of the determination of the means of processing and at the time of the processing itself, appropriately implement these technical and organizational measures.

Privacy by default means that the controller takes appropriate measures to ensure that in principle only personal data is processed that is necessary for each specific purpose of the processing. This applies to the data collected, the extent to which this data is processed, the period in which it is stored and its accessibility.[28]

In the case of drones, both principles imply that the privacy risks are already taken into account when designing the drone and the corresponding payload with which personal data is processed and, consequently, the need to take technical and organizational measures to mitigate these risks. This requires multidisciplinary cooperation between ICT experts and privacy lawyers from the initial phase of design. The ICT experts are capable of contributing privacy-protecting technologies.

Privacy by design can avoid the need to incur high costs, later, to adapt systems in such a way that they will still sufficiently meet the requirements regarding the protection of personal data. Consequently, software and process developers should adopt a paradigm shift to include privacy requirements in the early stages of design and associated design philosophy, to avoid laborious retrofitting of privacy elements into the systems or processes. The data protection by the design principle entails embedding privacy-protective technologies and policies, from design stage and deployment activities to use and final disposal, while data protection by default refers to the data minimization

---

28 *See also* Regulation (EU) 2016/679, Art. 25. Data protection by design and by default. Para. 2: The controller shall implement appropriate technical and organizational measures for ensuring that, by default, only personal data which are necessary for each specific purpose of the processing are processed. That obligation applies to the amount of personal data collected, the extent of their processing, the period of their storage and their accessibility. In particular, such measures shall ensure that by default personal data are not made accessible without the individual's intervention to an indefinite number of natural persons.

principle and requires companies to implement this latter through mechanisms inherent to the technology of its product.[29]

Privacy by design is based on seven principles that can be expressed in terms of the design and use of drones and their payloads as follows:

- The *privacy by design* approach is characterized by proactive measures rather than reactive measures. It does not wait for risks to materialize or offer remedies for resolving infringements once they have occurred; its aim is to anticipate and prevent them from occurring. In other words, it will help to prevent an unnecessary infringement of privacy. When using drones, this implies that the use, depending on its purpose, should be limited by place and time. Therefore, the purpose, location of use and those authorized to control the drone and have access to the payload must be specified in advance. Data collection, use, disclosure and retention should be kept to a minimum.
- Drone and payload should be set by default to protect privacy (*privacy by default*). This means that a camera on a drone, which is used for surveillance, must be set up in such a way that images can be taken only from those places where surveillance is required. The use of cameras adjustable by operators should be restricted, if possible, so that operators cannot adjust, zoom or manipulate the camera to monitor at places that are not intended to be covered by the video surveillance program.
- Cameras and other sensor modalities should not automatically start processing data and should be turned on only when necessary, in order to avoid unnecessary angling of data. Organizations should consider overwriting of recordings where there is potential for incidental collection of personally identifiable information.
- Any information obtained through the use of drones may be used only for the purposes of the stated rationale and objectives set out to protect public safety and to detect and assist in investigating criminal activity. Information should not be retained or used for any other purposes.
- Privacy must be embedded into the design principle. This implies that privacy protection is integrated into the core system, without diminishing its functionality. In fact, privacy becomes an essential component of the core functionality being delivered. For instance, when a drone is used for infrastructure inspection, the payload can be equipped with (digital) technology to remove or to blur images of faces, or use other graphical effects so as to prevent images of identifiable individuals from being collected whenever they are not necessary.
- If there is a strong possibility of collecting personally identifiable information, especially images of individuals or even their faces, organizations *casu quo* controllers, making use of video recording equipment, should consider the use of

---

[29] Shepherdson, K., Hioe, W., Boxall, L., *99 Privacy Breaches to Beware of: Practical Data Protection Tips from Real-Life Experiences*, Singapore: Marshall Cavendish Business, 2018, pp. 37-38.

anonymous video analytics. Anonymous video analytics software loaded on the detection device, processes the video feed to detect whether arrangements of pixels resemble the general pattern of human faces, using such factors as the pixel density and alignment around eyes.
- These so-called detection algorithms are based on the software having statistically learned face patterns, by being trained on an audience database of several thousands of face images. Depending on the purpose of using the drone, one can also choose to encrypt images immediately after they are collected and decrypt them only as necessary, provided that it is done only by authorized persons, being in possession of a secret key. If a camera on a drone is to be used only to control the craft, that particular camera should not be suitable for zooming in.
- Privacy and business interests as a positive sum. Privacy and business interests need not be a contradiction. The legitimate interests of both the organization using a drone and the public can be safeguarded by ensuring that personally identifiable data is stored securely in a locked receptacle located in a controlled-access area and is not to be kept longer than necessary.
- Access to the stored data must be technically secured and allowed only to authorized persons. Each storage device should be dated and labelled with a unique, sequential number or any other verifiable symbol. Access and processing must be logged for subsequent audit checks. Where records are maintained electronically, the logs should also be electronic.
- Full life cycle protection of data involved. Personal data should be protected throughout the data life cycle. This requires attention from the moment data is collected using drones to the moment data is destroyed. To ensure that personal data is adequately protected throughout the processing cycle, it is necessary to carry out a PIA beforehand. A PIA is a structured process that assists organizations in reviewing the impact that a new project may have on individual privacy.
- A key goal of the PIA is to effectively communicate privacy risks that are not addressed through other organizational mechanisms. The intention of a PIA is to contribute to senior management's ability to make fully informed policy, system design and acquisition decisions.
- Transparency. All relevant stakeholders involved in processing personal data using drone technology should be able to rely on the processing to be carried out according to its purpose and, if necessary, verify it. This requires that the processing cycle is sufficiently transparent. Organizations using drones should provide citizens with clear information about flight operations in their area, the purposes for which these flights take place, information regarding the possible processing of personal data during and after the flight, the policies and procedures that have been put in place, and the identity and contact details of the pilot and organization.

- All this information can be disseminated effectively via classic media such as the newspaper, a brochure or posters, but also via contemporary media such as websites, push notifications to people who have subscribed, social media or cell phone apps. Thus, these organizations can address many risks related to the privacy of citizens when using drones (chilling effect, function creep, exercise of the right of access by concerned citizens, etc.). Organizations that are using drones would also do well to have discussions with stakeholders about what may be acceptable and less acceptable uses. This can reduce the risk of dissatisfaction in regard to the use of drones.
- User-centric approach, which means respect for user privacy, but the focus is on the data subject. Designers and users of drones and payloads should focus on the interests of individuals whose data is being collected and processed. This should be reflected in the degree of transparency they practise, the codes of conduct they use, the selection menu in the processing system used, and the further organization of the procedure of data processing. In particular, the adoption of codes of conduct can help the various industry stakeholders and operators to prevent infringements and enhance the social acceptability of drones.
- Strong privacy defaults, appropriate notice and empowering user-friendly options are decidedly practical measures. While there is no privacy without security, security on its own is not sufficient for privacy. Privacy requires, in addition, systems and processes to provide individuals with notice, choice and consent. EU Member States have a legal duty in ensuring appropriate security and protection of personal data.[30]
- *Privacy by default* prescribes that privacy be built directly into the design and operation and requires that privacy be proactively intertwined with business practices in much the same way as other social norms and values such as fair play and transparency, necessitating the establishment of privacy at a much deeper level within system design, at the level of code, default settings and operational systems. The *privacy by default* approach would ensure protection is embedded from the outset. *Privacy by default* principles should be adopted into all aspects of drone operations in circumstances where personal information may be collected, processed, used, disclosed, retained, transferred and/or disposed. Obviously, drone operators need to ensure that any kind of personal data collection should be done on the basis of appropriate transparency.[31]

---

30 *See* Directive 2016/680, Art. 4 Principles relating to processing of personal data, Para. 1: Member States shall provide for personal data to be: (f) processed in a manner that ensures appropriate security of the personal data, including protection against unauthorized or unlawful processing and against accidental loss, destruction or damage, using appropriate technical and organizational measures. *See also* in this context Regulation (EU) 2016/679, Art. 5 Para. (f).

31 *See* Cavoukian, A., pp. 18-23.

Organizations flying drones can adopt codes of conduct that elaborate the legal requirements in regard to the protection of personal data concerning the specific processing of such data by their organizations. When it comes to the production and use of drones and payloads, it is conceivable that a code of conduct would be drawn up by an industry association for professional production and use of UAS. It is also possible to consider a deployment instruction for the police force.

Codes of conduct for the production and use of drones and payloads can convert legal regulations regarding the protection of personal data into customization for the technology used and provide practical examples. Consequently, a more practical and existential instrument can be created for the organizations concerned. Such a code of conduct for the manufacturers could, for example, prescribe that they enclose privacy instructions in the packaging of the drones and also place them on their websites. Establishing a code of conduct by companies that manufacture or operate drones can very well contribute to public confidence in the affiliated companies, thereby also representing a commercial interest.

Certification and use of quality marks will demonstrate that companies flying drones comply with legal requirements for personal data protection. Specialized accreditation-organizations can issue certificates and quality marks for drones to such companies. Issuing can be made dependent on the performance of a PIA. For companies that have such a certificate or quality mark, an additional advantage may be that they have a competitive dominance over companies that do not have such documents.

To reduce the risks regarding privacy in relation to the use of drones, privacy compliance audits may help. A privacy compliance audit is an instrument to systematically and independently verify whether the processing of personal data takes place in conformity with specific laws, standards and privacy policies. Such an audit differs from a PIA in that it presumes the existence of specific laws and/or standards and is an appropriate means whereby performance of an operational system can be evaluated.

A PIA adopts a much broader perspective than an audit. It considers the impacts of a proposed action and is not constrained by questions of whether the action is already authorized by law. Moreover, to the extent that relevant codes or standards exist, it does not merely accept them but considers whether they address the public's needs.

Privacy audits of organizations that fly drones can contribute to the transparency of the drone usage and, as a result, to the credibility of the relevant organization. The possibility of a privacy audit can also encourage an organization to act in accordance with the legal regulations governing the protection of personal data.[32]

Personal data must be collected for specific, explicit and legitimate purposes and not further processed in a way that is incompatible with those purposes. This means that the controller, who uses drones for security purposes, must predetermine the purpose for which personal data will be processed. This purpose should not be so vague or broad as to be unable to provide a framework during the processing activity to test whether the relevant personal data is necessary for that particular purpose. Moreover, the purpose must be justified. This means that the interest of the controller should reasonably give cause to process the relevant personal data for that purpose. Nor should the processing of personal data violate any law, public order or morality.

It follows from the foregoing that spying on third parties, illegal controls and violation of the intimacy of others are not acceptable purposes. That the processing may not violate any law whatsoever implies that, insofar as the use of drones in a specific case is contrary to aviation regulations, the collection of personal data during the flight in question can be considered unlawful.

In order to be lawful, the processing of personal data entailed by the civil application of drone technology should be based on one of the criteria for making data processing legitimate that are set forth in Regulation (EU) 2016/679, Article 6.[33]

The processing of personal data by means of a drone may take place only if there is an applicable principle, other than the existing specific legal principles for processing personal data, such as the legal principle for systematic observation by the police. In fact, there are six general principles:

a. Unambiguously given consent of the data subject;
b. performance of an agreement;
c. legal obligation;
d. safeguarding the vital interest of the data subject;
e. public-law task;

---

32 A privacy audit may be defined as follows: A systematic and independent examination to determine whether activities involving the processing of personal data are carried out in accordance with an organization's data protection policies and procedures, and whether this processing meets the requirements of applicable legislation. Audits may be voluntary or mandatory. Source: Clark, R., 'Privacy Impact Assessments', *Xamax Consultancy Pty Ltd.*, Canberra, February 1998. See also Regulation (EU) 2016/679, Art. 24 Responsibility of the controller.
33 Art. 6 Lawfulness of processing, Para. 1 Processing shall be lawful only if and to the extent that at least one of the following applies: [...] (c) processing is necessary for compliance with a legal obligation to which the controller is subject, [...] (e) processing is necessary for the performance of a task carried out in the public interest or in the exercise of official authority vested in the controller. Art. 6, Para. 3 The basis for the processing referred to in point (c) and (e) of Para. 1 shall be laid down by: (a) Union law; or (b) Member State law to which the controller is subject.

f. legitimate interest, unless the interest or the fundamental rights and freedoms of the data subject prevail.

A further explanation of these principles related to drones is set forth as follows:
Personal data may be processed only if:
a. The data subject has unambiguously given his or her consent to the processing of his or her personal data for one or more specific purposes. While consent is a common legal basis to be relied on, it seems that in this context it could be considered appropriate only in a few cases, especially as far as data is collected in public areas. Consent should be freely given, specific and informed. In most of the cases at issue, it would be very difficult to meet all these requirements since the consent, for example, would not be freely given whenever an individual is not free to enter or leave a surveyed area without being under surveillance. Consent will not be informed if that individual is not provided with all the necessary information on the processing, nor will it be specific if it is not possible for the individual to identify each purpose of the processing he or she is requested to consent to. Consent could be an appropriate legal basis for the processing of personal data carried out by means of a drone equipped with a camera, for instance in the case of a training session of a sports team;
b. data processing is necessary for the performance of an agreement to which the data subject is a party or for taking pre-contractual measures in response to a request from the data subject and that are necessary for the conclusion of an agreement. The processing of personal data is lawful on the basis of Article 6 of Regulation (EU) 2016/679 (formerly Art. 7b of Directive 95/46/EC). It should be considered that incidental processing of data of non-affected third parties is never covered by the fulfilment of obligations for the parties to a contract, and, therefore, the collection of personal data of third parties should be avoided or a different legal basis should be found to legitimize it;
c. data processing is necessary for compliance with a legal obligation that the controller is subject to. It is also necessary for the performance of a task carried out in the public interest or in the exercise of official authority vested in the controller or in a third party to whom the data is disclosed. This legal basis could be relied on in cases in which a legal obligation imposed by law is to be fulfilled by the controller, such as the surveillance of an archaeological site required by a specific provision or, for example, in some security-related issues, such as smuggling control, only where the use of drones is strictly necessary and proportionate;
d. the data processing is necessary to safeguard the vital interests of the data subject. This legal basis could be relevant in some cases of safety-related uses of a drone such as disaster relief, fire scene inspection, rescue of victims of snow and mountain accidents, etc;

e. the data processing is necessary for the proper performance of a public-law task by the relevant administrative body or the administrative body to which the data is provided; or
f. the data processing is necessary for the purposes of the legitimate interest. Personal data may also be processed if this is necessary for the purposes of the legitimate interests pursued by the controller or by the third party to whom the data is disclosed, except where the interests or fundamental rights and freedoms of the data subject, in particular the right to privacy, prevail if appropriate safeguards are implemented in the system.[34]

The most obvious processing principle for private individuals using drones for commercial or professional use has its basis in the legitimate interest to process personal data. At all times, it is necessary to weigh the interests between the legitimate interest of the controller and that of the person with regard to which personal data is processed. In this case, the nature and severity of the interests are relevant in the consideration. With a heavier interest, the balancing of interests can be more likely to favour the controller than with a minor interest, and vice versa.

For the security of a construction site or for the inspection of a building, there is, for example, an economic interest, in which it may be necessary to process personal data in the form of recordings of persons. This economic interest must be weighed against the data subject's right to privacy.

The issue of the processing principle may also arise at, for example, concerts and festivals. When filming at these events with a drone, the organizers cannot simply inform the people present. Then, that filming activity must also be included in the conditions at the time of purchasing an admission ticket for that particular concert or festival.

Personal data shall be processed lawfully, fairly and transparently in relation to the data subject and collected for specified, explicit and legitimate purposes and not further processed in a manner that is incompatible with those purposes.[35] In other words, the collector must undertake a compatibility assessment where personal data is collected for one purpose and a data controller wishes to utilize this data for another purpose. Nevertheless, the question of compatibility is assessed on the basis of the following factors:

- The context in which the personal data has been collected, specifically concerning the relationship between data subjects and the controller. Personal data shall be adequate,

---

34 *See also* Art. 29 Data Protection Working Party 01673/15/EN WP 231 Opinion 01/2015 on Privacy and Data Protection Issues relating to the Utilization of Drones, adopted on 16 June 2015.
35 Regulation (EU) 2016/679, Art. 5 Principles relating to processing of personal data, Para. 1 (a), (b).

relevant and limited to what is necessary in relation to the purposes for which it is processed;
- the nature of the personal data concerned, in particular whether special categories of personal data are processed, pursuant to Article 9, or whether personal data related to criminal convictions and offences are processed, pursuant to Article 10;[36]
- the possible consequences of the intended further processing for data subjects;
- any link between the purposes for which the personal data has been collected and the purposes of the intended further processing; and
- the existence of appropriate safeguards for those involved, which may include encryption or pseudonymization.

For example, when a drone is used at an open-air concert to film for promotional purposes, these images should, in principle, not be used to identify people later. The latter purpose is too distantly related to the first purpose. The public prosecutor will therefore only be able to obtain such images by applying the power to demand information provided to him by the national Code of Criminal Procedure.

Another example concerns the real estate agent who uses a drone to record the luxury homes of his clients. He may not make these recordings available to the municipality in order to enable them to monitor illegal buildings. The data processed must be adequate, relevant and not excessive. That means that the data, resulting from the processing, must be limited to what is strictly necessary to achieve the purpose of that processing.

Under this principle, drones equipped with different data collection technologies (cameras, GPS, altimeters, motion sensors) should collect only information that is necessary to achieve the purpose for which it is being done. For example, a camera on a drone that serves to take aerial images of landscapes should not be used to record faces or other personal data, such as the facades of houses or private gardens. If, in such a case, images of people have accidentally been taken, it may be necessary to blur the faces of these people. The argument that a camera with blur technology is more expensive than an ordinary camera is irrelevant: the absence of this technology may result in data processing not complying with the principle of proportionality.[37]

Personal data, which, because of its sensitive nature is considered special, includes data that reveals racial or ethnic origin, political opinions, religion or philosophical beliefs, trade union membership and the processing of genetic data, data concerning health or data concerning sex life or criminal convictions and offences or related security measures, including data about someone's unlawful or annoying behaviour, in connection with an imposed ban as a result of that behaviour.

---

36 Regulation (EU) 2016/679, Art. 9 Processing of special categories of personal data, Art. 10 Processing of personal data relating to criminal convictions and offences.
37 Finn R.L. et al, p. 286.

As a general rule, the processing of this special personal data is not permitted, but there are specific and general exemptions.[38]

For example, a private organization that is duly licensed to perform security work may break the prohibition on processing criminal data. If such an organization complies with the other privacy provisions and has the required exemption with regard to applicable aviation regulations such as a permit to fly within a restricted area, it could, for example, use a camera on a drone to monitor an industrial area for security reasons and make images containing criminal data.

Physical characteristics of people may be visible on camera images created by using a drone. For example, an image of someone wearing glasses could suggest something about the person's visual health or, in the case of a headscarf, could suggest something about his or her religious beliefs. A person's race, racial attributions and identity can also be derived from camera images.

In practice this would mean that camera images of people often contain special personal data. However, it seems realistic not to regard camera images as special personal data if:

- The purpose of the processing is not aimed at identification or distinction based on special personal data or additional information; and
- it is not reasonably foreseeable for the controller that the data processing will lead to a distinction.[39]

It should also be borne in mind that, on the basis of the foregoing criteria, personal data, resulting from camera surveillance using drones to protect people or property, must usually be classified as criminal data, since the purpose of the processing will also focus on the processing of criminal data. The prohibition on processing data does not apply, inter alia, if the controller applies camera surveillance for self-protection or when it concerns a private organization that carries out licensed security activities.

The controller is obliged to provide the data subjects the best possible information about the processing of personal data. When using drones, the controller will usually be the company or government agency or the relevant client. This obligation to provide information expresses the principle of transparency that must be applied when processing personal data.[40]

---

38 *See* Regulation (EU) 2016/679, Art. 9, Para. 1. *See also* Recital (34) Genetic data should be defined as personal data relating to the inherited or acquired genetic characteristics of a natural person which results from the analysis of a biological sample from the natural person in question, in particular chromosomal, deoxyribonucleic acid (DNA) or ribonucleic acid (RNA) analysis, or from the analysis of another element enabling equivalent information to be obtained.
39 *See also* Regulation (EU) 2016/679, Art. 11 Processing which does not require identification.
40 *See* Regulation (EU) 2016/679, Art. 12 Transparent information, communication and modalities for the exercise of the rights of the data subject.

When using drones, this transparency principle can be implemented by ensuring that the drones are sufficiently visible and identifiable during their usage. This can be achieved, for example, by colouring the drone so that it can be identified from afar; or by ensuring that the cameras are visible as far as possible; or by announcing the usage of the drone in advance through the press, internet or by an announcement at the location where the drone will fly its mission.

In addition, the data subjects must be able to identify the controller. This can be done as described previously to announce the presence of drones. Depending on the size and flight altitude of the drone, this can also be done through a visible identification of the drone or specific colour schemes that refer to a particular entrepreneur or a controller who is widely known to the general public.

The obligation to provide information, described previously, is not indisputable; there are exceptions to the rule, in particular, where the provision of information to data subjects proves to be impossible or will take disproportionate effort. In that case, the controller must determine the origin of the data. Whether there is a disproportionate effort or not will in part depend on the extent to which other methods are available in order to adequately inform data subjects and the medium that can be expected to be largely within the reach of those data subjects.

Suspension of the obligation to provide information is possible insofar as this is necessary in the interests of, among other things, the prevention, detection and prosecution of criminal offences, important economic and financial interests of the state and other public bodies, supervision of compliance with statutory regulations made for the benefit of the aforementioned interests, and the protection of the data subjects or the rights or freedoms of others.

In fact, the suspension of the obligation to provide information must be interpreted restrictively. For that reason, in principle it only offers room for incidental, non-structural forms of suspension. This could include the temporary granting of covert surveillance by drones.

Stored personal data, especially but not only for data processing using drones, must at all times be adequately secured by means of organizational and technical measures. Security risks can be intentional, such as hackers, as well as non-intentional, for example through accidental leakage.

Personal data can be protected against these methods by making data unusable for unauthorized persons using particular techniques. Typical techniques used are cryptographic operations such as encryption and hashing, which means converting data into a unique code. The keyed hash function with stored key, one of the pseudonymization techniques, corresponds to a particular hash function that uses a secret key as an additional input.

The application of such operations to identifying data will lead to pseudonymization, in that the identifying data is replaced by other identifying data.[41] Pseudonymization is therefore different from anonymization, in which data is converted into a form that no longer makes identification possible. In addition to such security risks regarding the outside world in the field of hacking and leakage of information, there are also security risks with regard to the inside world, that is to say, to unauthorized employees. Employees within an organization where information is collected using drones may want to look at information or data about others they are interested in, such as family members, neighbours and celebrities. Measures to counter this illicitness can be found in a good system of authorizations, access security and a system of logging and incidents monitoring.

The incorporation of storage and deletion schedules could be advisable. Hence, the devices carried by drones should be so designed as to allow the setting of a defined storage period of personal data collected and, as a result, the regular automatic deletion of personal data that is no longer necessary in accordance with deletion schedules. For data controllers it is important that:
- A limited number of authorized persons, to be specified, should be allowed to view or access the recorded images.
- Limited access should be granted to the aforementioned persons, on a need-to-know basis.
- Encrypted storage and transmission of information where necessary.
- Logs of all instances of access to and use of recorded material.
- Stringent data storage periods and automatic deletion and anonymization once the data storage period has expired.
- Personal data breach notification is reported to the supervisory authority, as far as legally mandatory.[42]

Security risks may arise from disrupting frequencies with which a drone or a payload is operated. Such a disruption could be an intentional action, for example through jamming. Jamming is the deliberate use of radio noise or signals in an attempt to disrupt communication, thus making a drone, being the target, uncontrollable.

---

41 See Art. 29 Data Protection Working Party 0829/14/EN WP 216 Opinion 05/2014 on Anonymization Techniques, adopted on 10 April 2014, Chapter 4, pp. 20-21.
42 Regulation (EU) 2016/679, Art. 4 Definitions. For the purposes of this Regulation: (12) personal data breach means a breach of security leading to the accidental or unlawful destruction, loss, alteration, unauthorized disclosure of, or access to, personal data transmitted, stored or otherwise processed. In Art. 29 Data Protection Working Party 01673/15/EN WP 231 Opinion 01/2015, the supervisory authority is called Data Protection Authority (DPA). The DPA is an independent public authority that supervises, through investigative and corrective powers, the application of the data protection law. It provides advice on data protection issues and handles complaints lodged against violations of the GDPR (Regulation (EU) 2016/679) and the relevant national laws. See also Recitals (117) to (123) of the GDPR.

Disrupting the active payload frequencies to freeze the transmission of data is another jamming method. These frequencies mainly concern the signals to send camera images, sound recordings or other sensory information to the ground station.

It is conceivable that a drone operator can take control of another drone with his signal. Taking over control of someone else's drone is referred to as spoofing, which makes it possible to hijack a drone. In this case, the information collected with the drone may fall into the wrong hands. In order to counteract this, it is desirable to not only take measures that ensure the security of the information itself, but also effectively consider a technical provision on the drone that ensures that the drone automatically returns to its starting point if the control connection to the drone pilot is interrupted (fail-safe element).

The controller shall report the data breach to the competent supervisory authority, because it can reasonably be assumed to have serious adverse consequences for the protection of the processed personal data. Additionally, in most cases a notification must be made to the data subject, if the breach will have negative consequences for his or her privacy.[43]

The reporting obligation rests on all controllers, both in the private and in the public sector. Failure to meet these obligations can be sanctioned by an administrative fine, imposed by the competent authorities. The purpose of the reporting obligation is to prevent data leaks due to breaches of security measures and, if they do occur, to limit as much as possible the consequences thereof for the data subjects.

Usually, personal data may not be stored longer than necessary for the realization of the purposes for which this data is processed. This implies that images made with a drone for security reasons, at a location where a festival is being held, may be kept only for as long as necessary to handle any complaints about the security associated with the festival. Where possible, automatic destruction or anonymization of the data should be provided for the retention period. Any data that is not linked to any complaint or issue should be deleted or anonymized immediately after the festival has ended. Retention periods may be prescribed for personal data that falls under specific regimes such as data collected by police drones.

Generally, any intended processing of personal data should be notified in advance to the competent supervisory authority. This also applies to the processing of personal data using drones. In many cases this may be omitted. This applies, inter alia, to the processing of personal data by means of camera surveillance, if such surveillance complies with the protection of persons and property entrusted to the care of the controller, the camera

---

[43] Regulation (EU) 2016/679, Art. 33 Notification of a personal data breach to the supervisory authority. Art. 34 Communication of a personal data breach to the data subject.

surveillance is clearly visible and the personal data is removed no later than four weeks after the video recordings have been made or after legal settlement of identified incidents.

Intended processing of personal data by covert camera surveillance must always be reported to the supervisory authority concerned. A preliminary examination must in any case be requested. This examination means that the supervisory authority, acting in complete independence in performing the tasks assigned to it, and exercising the powers conferred on it, in accordance with Regulation (EU) 2016/679, will examine the lawfulness of the intended processing. Processing should not begin until the supervisory authority has completed this examination or has decided not to initiate this procedure.

It may be assumed that the processing of personal data using a drone for activities with exclusively personal or household purposes may also be counted as taking images with a drone camera if those images are for private use alone. An example of this might be flying a drone for recreational purposes of which personal data are processed by using photo or video equipment. This exception does not apply in the event that images, which have been filmed with a drone for personal or household purposes, are subsequently provided towards an indefinite number of persons. This is the case, for example, if the images are placed on the internet and are accessible to everyone.[44]

The online social network user, who may be considered as the controller, can bring about serious privacy harms. Inadvertent disclosures, breaches of confidence and reputational damage are but a few examples that show the failing and quite pernicious side of social networking.[45] However, if a website or profile on social networking is accessible only to a limited circle of people, someone may post a photo or film taken with a drone without the permission of the persons featured on that photo or film.

The purpose for which one takes images with a camera attached to a drone is also important in determining the location where one may film. If someone makes images with a view to protecting his or her family or property and films only his or her own

---

44 See Case C-101/01 (Lindqvist-case) of 6 November 2003. *Bodil Lindqvist v. Åklagerkammeren i Jönköping* (2003). Decision by the European Court of Justice. The act of referring, on an internet page, to various persons and identifying them by name or by other means, for instance by giving their telephone number or information regarding their working conditions and hobbies, constitutes the processing of personal data wholly or partly by automatic means, within the meaning of Art. 3(1) of Directive 95/46/EC (Data Protection Directive). Such processing of personal data is not covered by any of the exceptions in Art. 3(2) of Directive 95/46/EC. Reply of the Court (46): As regard[s] the exception provided for in the second indent of Art. 3(2) of Directive 95/46/EC, the 12th recital in the preamble to that directive, which concerns that ex[c]eption, cites, as examples of the processing data carried out by a natural person in the exercise of activities which are exclusively personal or domestic, correspondence and the holding of records of addresses. (47) (*the so-called 'household exemption'*): That exception must therefore be interpreted as relating only to activities which are carried out in the course of private or family life of individuals, which is clearly not the case with the processing of personal data consisting in publication on the internet so that those data are made accessible to an indefinite number of people.

45 Van Alsenoy, B., 'The Evolving Role of the Individual Under EU Data Protection Law', KU Leuven Center for IT & IP Law, *ICRI Working Paper Series*, 10 August 2015, p. 22.

home and garden, this can be classified under activities with exclusively personal purposes. But as soon as the camera films part of the public road as well, the drone operator must comply with the stipulated restrictive provisions.[46]

A drone can very well be used in journalism. The same applies to audiovisual productions for artistic purposes. After all, a drone can easily record images or find locations for movie recordings in places that are rather difficult to access. In the case of the processing of personal data for such purposes, certain provisions do not apply. This rule particularly concerns the obligation to provide information to data subjects, to report the processing of personal data to the competent supervisory authority and the rights of data subjects, such as the right of access and rectification.

This exception therefore does not justify unlimited processing of personal data. The journalistic exception is delineated by requiring, among other things, that it should be a collection of objective information and regular activity. These requirements do not prevent the question of who may call him or herself a journalist from being interpreted broadly. This may also include relatively new types of journalists, such as bloggers,

---

46 See Case C-212/13 of 19 April 2013. Request for a preliminary ruling from the Nejvyšší správní soud (Czech Republic) – *Frăntisek Ryneš v. Úřad pro ochranu osobních údajů*. Question referred: Can the operation of a camera system installed on a family home for the purpose of the protection of the property, health and life of the owners of the home be classified as the processing of personal data by a natural person in the course of a purely personal or household activity within the meaning of Art. 3(2) of Directive 95/46/EC, even though such system monitors also a public space? Judgment of the European Court of Justice (Fourth Chamber) 11 December 2014. Consideration of the question referred.
Consideration no. 26: The referring court is uncertain whether such processing should nevertheless, in circumstances such as those of the case before it, escape the application of Directive 95/46/EC insofar as it is carried out 'in the course of a purely personal or household activity' for the purpose of the second indent of Art. 3(2) of the Directive.
Consideration no. 33: To the extent that video surveillance such as that at issue in the main procedures covers, even partially, a public space and as accordingly directed outwards from the private setting of the person processing the data in that manner, it cannot be regarded as an activity which is a purely 'personal or household' activity for the purposes of the second indent of Art. 3(2) of the Directive.
Consideration no. 35: Consequently, the answer to the question referred is that the second indent of Art. 3(2) of the Directive must be interpreted as meaning that the operation of a camera system, as a result of which a video recording of people is stored on a continuous recording device such as a hard disk drive, installed by an individual on his family home for the purposes of protecting the property, health and life of the home owners, but which also monitors a public space, does not amount to the processing of data in the course of a purely 'personal or household' activity, for the purposes of that provision.
Art. 3(2): This Directive shall not apply to the processing of personal data: – in the course of an activity which falls outside the scope of Community law, such as those provided for by Titles V and VI of the Treaty on European Union and in any case to processing operations concerning public security, defence, State security (including the economic well-being of the State when the processing operation relates to State security matters) and the activities of the State in areas of criminal law, – by a natural person in the course of a purely personal or household activity.

paparazzi, YouTubers and self-made journalists, as long as the purpose of the data processing is to disclose information, opinions or ideas to the public.[47]

Citizens whose personal data has been processed with the assistance of a drone have, apart from the aforementioned exceptional situations, different rights. In the first place, a citizen can turn to the controller with a request to inform him or her which personal data have actually been processed, for what purposes and to which third parties these data have been provided. The controller must answer the person concerned within four weeks. In the event that video images were taken with the drone and these images were stored in a digital archive without identifying data, it would seem reasonable to ask the person concerned for information that could assist in the execution of the access request.

A citizen about whom personal data has been processed, has, from a legal point of view, the right to request the controller for access, rectification, erasure or restriction with regard to personal data concerning him or her in respect of factual inaccuracies, in processing for incomplete or irrelevant purposes or in processing that violates a legal requirement. In certain cases, the data subject may object at any time to the controller with regard to the method of processing in connection with his or her special personal circumstances, as outlined in the aforementioned general principles.[48] When it comes to personal data collected by the police using drones, special regulations will apply with regard to access and rectification rights.

Special provisions also apply in regard to international transfer of personal data. Drones may collect personal data that the controller wants to pass on to persons or organizations in states outside the European Union. However, personal data may be transferred to such states only if those states ensure an adequate level of data protection. Under certain conditions, personal data may also be transferred to states that do not provide such safeguards. And even if the conditions are not met, a permit may be issued by the state for the transfer of personal data to a third state that does not provide guarantees of an adequate level of protection.

The protection of natural persons with regard to the processing of personal data by competent authorities for the purposes of prevention, investigation, detection or prosecution of criminal offences or the execution of criminal penalties, including the safeguarding against threats and the prevention of threats to public security and the free movement of such data, is the subject of a specific Legal Act of the European Union. Regulation (EU) 2016/679 should not, therefore, apply to processing activities for those purposes. However, personal data processed by public authorities under this

---

47 Gynnild, A., Uskali, T. (Eds.), *Responsible Drone Journalism*, Routledge Focus, Milton Park, Abingdon, Oxon: Routledge, 2018, pp. 15-19.
48 *See also* Regulation (EU) 2016/679, Arts. 13-19.

Regulation should, when used for those purposes, be governed by a more specific Legal Act of the European Union, namely Directive (EU) 2016/680.

There is no specific legal basis for the use of drones, equipped with cameras, to detect criminal offences. As regards the police's investigative powers, the condition is that the use of drones with cameras in a particular case may only infringe the fundamental rights of citizens to a limited extent and should not be very risky regarding the integrity and manageability of the investigation. If the camera use becomes more wide-ranging and, as a result, assumes the character of systematic observation, the applicable conditions of the Criminal Code of Procedure must be met. Systematic observation for the purpose of detection occurs if the use of camera-equipped drones, in view of aspects such as duration, intensity and frequency, is suitable to obtain a more or less appropriate picture of certain particularities of the individual's personal life.

Next to systematic observation of criminal offences, one could also think of the use of a drone for recording confidential communication with a technical device and to perform a judicial inquiry in a private place. Today, new-generation cameras on drones are able to portray persons recognizable in detecting criminal offences.

Except for investigative purposes, the police can also use drones with cameras to maintain public order in cases where there is a concrete disruption of public order or a substantial threat thereof. Furthermore, it is conceivable that the police will deploy drones to carry out its assistance task, for example, in the event of an emergency. The possible privacy breach that takes place in the context of assistance can quickly be considered proportional to the victims' interest in return.

Finally, it should be pointed out that the use of drones by the police must fit within the framework of aviation and privacy regulations. More specifically, given their intrusive nature, drones must not be used for arbitrary surveillance, bulk data processing, data linking and profiling. The condition is that the activities mentioned should be tested in advance against the necessity requirement and the requirements of proportionality and subsidiarity.

Drones may signal a fundamental transformation of law enforcement practices, in particular regarding the role of data in guiding law enforcement authority actions, ranging from monitoring an individual to determining targets from a review of the lifestyle and different activities of a specific population based on continuous surveillance. Surveillance by drones must not be used to identify subjects based on mere data analysis. In any case, the use of drones by the police will have to be limited according to place and time. In view of the chilling effect of the use of drones on the freedom of expression and the right of assembly and association, it is worth noting that, as far as possible, demonstrations do not involve surveillance using drones. As a result, the police and other law enforcement authorities using drones should make sure they have a solid and valid legal basis for processing personal data.[49]

Owing to the wider possibilities and the inherent privacy risks, the use of airborne cameras, such as cameras on drones, may be regarded as a heavier means than the deployment of fixed cameras. It is therefore obvious that the use of drone cameras is less permissible than the use of statically arranged cameras. The proposal to apply flexible camera surveillance does not necessarily aim to deploy cameras on drones but rather to make the rigid regime of fixed camera surveillance on the surface more flexible to adequately respond to fast-moving nuisances, such as drugs dealers, street robbers, pickpockets and vandals. An additional requirement regarding airborne cameras is that the controller must by all means clearly indicate that he or she is carrying out camera surveillances using drones. If this is not disclosed, the controller is punishable.

When law enforcement authorities process data collected by drones for enforcement of civil offences, they should comply with the requirement laid down by Directive 95/46/EC. In particular, such uses of drones should be restricted to cases where the processing is necessary in order to protect the vital interests of the data subject, or for the performance of a task carried out in the public interest, or in the exercise of official authority vested in the controller, or in a third party to whom the data is disclosed.

Citizens and companies can use camera surveillance with drones only if this is really necessary. This may be the case if theft occurs or property is vandalized in a specific area owned by a citizen or company. It should also be clear that other, less drastic measures, such as installing lighting or a fence, the introduction of extra surveillance by security staff or the use of security cameras on the ground or on water, have not adequately demonstrated effectiveness in fighting crime.

6.2 Privacy and Security

Drone technology is interesting in the cybersecurity field. However, the idea of having drones in airspace raises serious security and safety concerns for almost all strata of society ranging from law enforcement agencies, civil aviation authorities and drone operators to regular individuals. But more than that, the drone's eye view has obvious privacy implications. In addition, a drone is also a type of connected device, collecting and transmitting (personal) data for analysis, and this in turn creates implications for the safety and hackability of the device.

Drones are routinely used by governments all over the world for law enforcement and have proved to be indispensable tools for law enforcement agencies. However, concerns about the use of drone surveillance by government agencies are being raised by civil rights/civil liberties groups. These groups and other institutes are asking for tightened

---

49 *See* Art. 29 Data Protection Working Party 01673/15/EN WP 231Opinion 01/2015, pp. 10-11.

controls on the use of drones to uphold the right to privacy of the individual. Privacy is not the only thing at risk with drones. The wide use of drones in the military and law enforcement agencies has made their wide implementation in private or corporate security very imminent, considering that these entities are often unaware of restrictions and sometimes create hazardous situations.

In terms of security and safety, drones pose a series of considerable and serious risks. As reported by the media, drones have been spotted over civil aerodromes or close to them, disrupting and/or threatening civil aviation, including the tremendous risk of colliding with commercial aircraft, or where drones survey classified installations, such as strategic military objects or nuclear power plants, which can impact on security.

Furthermore, unspecified drones have crashed in densely populated areas, possibly by malicious takeover, severely impairing public safety, or have flown unauthorized over embassies, prisons and correctional facilities, critical infrastructures, tourist attraction sites and mass events, posing potential hazards and nightmarish scenarios. They are also spotted over private properties and can be subject to illicit, dangerous or criminal use.

States are facing the risks of these operations that can have serious consequences for safety and security. The remedy will be to enforce regulations that restrict airspace use for drones. However, states are practically unable to prevent unauthorized or illegal drone operations because of the open nature of the skies. Therefore, states are looking for other methods, such as geofencing or even unwanted drone defence systems, enforcing drone regulations in order to ensure safety, security and reliability as well as facilitating the integration in controlled airspace.

From a law enforcement viewpoint, compulsory identification of drones is an additional condition when it comes to safety and security. Regarding identification of drones, there is a trend for remote identification of drones through manufacturers or retrofitting airborne electronic identification devices, for example in Mainland China, the United Kingdom and the United States. Two options for identification are preferred. The first is for the manufacturer to stamp a serial number on the drone. This, preferably unique, serial number is included in the registration database, after the owner registers the drone. The second option is to use a serial number sticker, issued by the organization responsible for the registration database, and to attach this sticker to the drone and/or the controller unit. The serial number sticker could also include identification of pilots authorized by owners to operate the drone. Additionally, whatever identification method is used, either one or both options simultaneously, it has to be ensured that there is no potential for misuse.

Drones are at risk of being hijacked and used as weapons against other airspace users or targets on the surface. Terrorists could also use their own drones to crash into specific targets or jam or spoof GPS signals, Bluetooth or ADS-B signals of other drones, causing serious hazards to civil aviation safety. This could be achieved by physical attacks, for example, destruction of vital parts of remotely piloted aircraft system (RPAS) elements, in particular the RPS, including the remote pilot(s).

In addition, electronic attacks, such as jamming or spoofing of data links or satellite navigation systems, as well as cyberattacks, such as hacking through the internet Web, spoofing and cyberattacks on specific information networks, are certainly not inconceivable. The consequences of such cyberattacks could represent a major challenge for future large-scale RPAS operations. The security issues have been carefully addressed in both the regulatory system and R&D activities.[50]

Security and surveillance are one of the biggest growth areas in the ever-expanding drone sector, and, being smaller, discreet, flexible and more efficient than traditional manned aircraft such as helicopters, drones have even found their way into aerial security and surveillance. Depending on the application, drones can be dispatched rapidly to cover large areas of interest, scan confined perimeters or monitor objects that are impossible for regular fixed surveillance cameras, simply by using a variety of (digital) sensing and monitoring equipment.

Drones, in their capacity of aerial law enforcement surveillance vehicles, consequently imply the collection, processing, recording, organization, storing and use, as well as a combination of data allowing the identification of persons, directly or indirectly. The application of drones equipped with optical, zoom and thermal infrared cameras allows law enforcement agents to monitor unfolded crime scenes more accurately and at a much safer distance. A quickly deployable camera drone allows the police to have a better vantage point during times of chaotic situations, for example during mass rallies (protest movements), where deploying ground personnel is too risky.

Aerial vantage points also allow post-accident scenes or crime scenes to be fully documented and reconstructed to assist in understanding the timeline of events for each incident. The sole reliance on ground assets to respond to emergency events increases threats to the safety of the community, especially emergency response personnel, and decreases the efficiency and effectiveness of the emergency response. However, these activities may consequently imply an interference with the right to private and family life and data protection, regardless of the degree of validity of the data subjects.

The law enforcement Directive 2016/680, which complements Regulation (EU) 2016/679, aims to protect the rights of individuals to their personal data while guaranteeing a high level of public security by providing new rules, including standards. The aim of the new rules is to improve and facilitate the common work of police forces

---

50 Source: Altawy, R., Youssef, A.M., 'Security, Privacy, and Safety Aspects of Civilian Drones: A Survey', *ACM Transactions on Cyber-Physical Systems* 1(2), Art. No. 7, November 2016, Para. 4.1 Cyber-Physical Attacks.

and other law enforcement authorities in exchanging information and to help in fighting crime more effectively. The directive sets out standards for the processing of data of people who are under investigation or have been convicted, or when authorities exchange files, domestically or internationally, and contributes to building an area of freedom, security and justice with a high level of data protection, in accordance with the Charter of Fundamental Rights of the European Union.[51]

In relation to some aspects of personal data protection, as well as public acceptability of the technology, concerns have been raised about the use of drones for law enforcement purposes. Law enforcement applications remain outside the jurisdiction of European institutions, falling instead within the EU Member States' jurisdiction. As many police forces have started to use the technology, the European Council has expressed concern about the possibility of armed drones being used by law enforcement agencies. Concerns about the use of drones by the police often focus on privacy and surveillance aspects but can also stem from concerns about domestic militarism and the integrity of justifications for their use. The discussion regarding law enforcement aspects is based on recent research in Europe and third countries.

The law enforcement aspects of personal data protection in the context of civil drone development are principally focused on the norms, values and standards of police investigation and citizens' protection from government search, in particular the legal concept of reasonable expectations of privacy. There it was noted that as surveillance practices become known as standard practice, the reasonable expectation of privacy from such practices will be eroded. This aspect of civil drone usage for law enforcement is of particular relevance to the United States, where privacy is framed primarily as protection to government search, and its legal status is defined in terms of reasonable expectations of privacy. This had led to some local controversies. For example, in February 2013, Seattle police abandoned their US surveillance project after opponents raised concerns about the adequacy of civil protection from invasive state government surveillance. The following accounts show contrasting perspectives on the protest, balancing the need for protection of citizens by the police force against the need for protection of citizens from the police:

> Angry residents attending the community meeting in October chanted "No drones!" drowning out officers' attempts to explain how the unmanned aerial vehicles would support certain criminal investigations, help out during natural disasters, and assist in search-and-rescue operations. (Sorcher, 2013) [52]

---

51 Charter of Fundamental Rights of the European Union, *OJ* C 326/391, 26 October 2012. Art. 8 Protection of personal data: Para. 1. Everyone has the right to the protection of personal data concerning him or her.
52 Sorcher, S., 'The Backlash against Drones', *National Journal*, 2013.

> We are not opposed to the technology, but there needs to be examination of concerns about privacy [...]. We thought something stronger than internal police policies was needed, because those can be changed without the public being aware. (Cheng, Howard, & Meijer, 2013)[53]

A second concern raised about the use of civil drones for law enforcement is the rice of domestic militarism, including the integrity of procedures and justifications for their use. Research by Salter (2014) has exposed inconsistencies in the rhetoric and practical use of law enforcement drones, which he describes as being led by a 'weapons fetish', which obscures practical and ethical considerations with fantasies of control and domination.[54]

Through several examples, he raised three key points: first, that drones were likely to affect social groups in different ways, with disproportionate use in disadvantaged communities, and, second, that the justification regarding the cost of effectiveness of police drones was a myth, as they lead to higher life cycle costs for operations. His third point was that police use of drones until 2014 proved risky with a high incident rate, often involving frivolous use leading to crashes. He concludes that the rhetoric for law enforcement drones is characterized by "unrealized and unrealistic fantasies of total surveillance and swift intervention that are disrupted by an absence of supporting evidence and a tangle of technological legal and practical limitations". However, recently this aspect has become obsolete as the technology, procedures and handling has greatly improved.

Other research has highlighted the need to consider police use of drones in more detail. Instead of examining whether drones should or should not be used for law enforcement purposes, this work highlights the need to consider specific contexts in which police drones could be deployed and what level of force, if any, they could deploy (Straub, 2014).[55] This call for considering application areas at a higher resolution level is supported by research done by Bracken-Roche *et al* (2014) on Canadian citizens' level of support for the use of drones for a variety of possible law enforcement uses.[56]

They showed substantial differences between specific uses of drones within the broad application area. Specifically, they found that support was higher for finding missing persons (71%), disaster response (71%), and hostage situations (68%) than for speeding tickets (20%), identification at sporting events/political demonstrations (20/22%) and routine patrols (23%).

---

53   Cheng, A., Howard, A., Meyer, T., 'With Billions at Stake, States Lobby for Drone Test Sites', *National Security Zones,* 2013.
54   Salter, M., 'Toys for the Boys? Drones, Pleasure and Popular Culture in the Militarization of Policing', *Critical Criminology* 22(2), 2014, pp. 163-177.
55   Straub, J., 'Unmanned Aerial Systems: Consideration of the Use of Force for Law Enforcement Applications', *Technology in Society* 39, November 2014.
56   *See* https://www.ssqueens.org/sites/ssqueens.org/files/Surveillance_Drones_Report.pdf.

Support for the use of police drones in criminal investigation monitoring was between these levels (42%). The point here is that the use of drones for law enforcement purposes includes a wide range of possible operations for a variety of purposes. The specifics of operations, including their context and purpose, are crucial in understanding public support and congruence with ethical principles.

To conclude, the use of RPAS for law enforcement is potentially controversial in essence and must be managed carefully. Since the use of RPAS by police forces is regulated by the EU Member States, not at a European level, consultation and research are required at a national level. However, the success of a European civil drone sector rests on widespread public acceptance. Public responses will not be discreetly divided between those regulated at the national and European levels.

High-profile incidents of police abuse such as those recounted by Salter (2014) could be extremely damaging to the whole sector. To maximize the effectiveness of research and the readiness of the sector, actions should be coordinated and harmonized where possible. Until now, there has been no sophisticated understanding of European citizens' responses to police drones, and much of what is known has been derived from localized experiences, arising from specific use cases, and informed guesses about how citizens may react to what remains a little used technology.

The existing research and consultation on police use of RPAS are limited and call for more knowledge at a higher resolution, considering a wide range of specific applications, and in a diverse set of contexts; from search and rescue to crime intervention and from routine patrols to emergency procedures. While we can learn from the specific police applications of drones that are more acceptable to Canadian citizens, the results are likely to differ in Europe and across EU Member States. However, it would be prudent to expect a similar level of sophistication in European citizens' responses to police drones, with support depending on the specifics and context of the operation.

Finally, since insights on law enforcement to date have principally focused on personal data protection aspects of police drones, other societal and ethics issues associated with them, such as the militarization of domestic spaces, procedural integrity and justification for police operations, remain underexplored.[57]

Since the forecast economic and functional benefits of civil drone deployment are so positive, it is important to support their development and manage areas of uncertainty, controversy or concern. Drawing on the insights of responsible research and innovation (R&I), forms of technology push, including the provision of imbalanced information about the motivations for and predicted consequences of development, could be irresponsible and could increase the likelihood of public rejection of the technology.

---

57 Source: *See* Finn R.L. *et al*, p. 13. *See also* Bracken-Roche, C., Lyon, D., Mansour, M.J., Molnar, A., Saulnier, A., Thompson, S., 'Surveillance Drones: Privacy Implications of the Spread of Unmanned Aerial Vehicles (UAVs) in Canada', *A Report to the Office of the Privacy Commissioner of Canada, under the 2013-2014 Contributions Program*, Quebec, 30 April 2014, pp. 16-17.

Public engagement and consultation should be an opportunity for citizens to be empowered to inform civil drone development in a way that reflects their values and, in doing so, become co-producers of, and co-responsible for, the technology. Information and education actions remain important but must maximize transparency about all the motives and predicted consequences of development to provide the knowledge that is, according to responsible R&I, a prerequisite for responsibility.

This implies a shift from unidirectional information actions to bidirectional consultation and dialogic engagement. This, in turn, implies a shift in the positioning of citizens, from passive actors, whose acceptance of the technology is determined by information they received, to active agents, making an informed input to development and deployment. Such dialogue is particularly important in potentially controversial topics such as law enforcement, synergies with military drones, as well as personal data protection. Importantly, it would also allow the public to define key issues and priority areas in a bottom-up process.[58]

While the operation of surveillance and law enforcement using drones in the European Union must be done within the provisions of Directive 2016/680 and European aviation regulations, similar provisions apply in other states.

In the context of law enforcement, the jurisprudence dealing with aerial surveillance techniques, such as the use of unsophisticated forward-looking infrared (FLIR) cameras in drugs investigations, is limited, offering no concrete guidance regarding law enforcement's potentially wide use of evolving drone technologies. At present in the United States, there is no nationwide standard as far as drone utilization by law enforcement agencies is concerned. Connection must then be sought in corresponding forms of aerial law enforcement.

In 1989, the U.S. Supreme Court ruled that there is no right to privacy when it comes to police observation in public airspace (Florida v. Riley, 488 U.S. 445).[59]

The facts were as follows: Michael Riley lived in a mobile home situated on five acres of rural land in Florida. Riley owned a greenhouse located behind his home. From the ground, the contents of the greenhouse were shielded from view by its walls and the trees on his property.

In 1984, the Pasco County Sheriff's office received an anonymous tip that Riley was growing marijuana on his property. The investigation officer tried to look into the greenhouse from the ground but could not. A bit later he circled in a helicopter at 400 ft and saw what he believed to be marijuana growing inside Riley's greenhouse. Acting on

---

58 Source: Boucher, Ph., 'Civil Drones in Society: Societal and Ethics Aspects of Remotely Piloted Aircraft Systems', *Report EUR 26823 EN, JRC Science and Policy Reports*, European Commission Joint Research Center Institute for the Protection and Security of the Citizen, Luxembourg, 2014, pp. 28-39.

59 The U.S. Supreme Court or the Supreme Court of the United States (SCOTUS) is the highest court in the federal judiciary of the United States of America.

this information, the investigation officer obtained a search warrant, flew over the greenhouse and spotted marijuana through the openings in the roof, where two ceiling panels were missing. Consequently, Riley was charged with possession of marijuana under Florida law.

Subsequently, the trial court granted Riley's motion to suppress the evidence obtained in the search and held that viewing his property from the air violated his reasonable expectation of privacy and Fourth Amendment rights. However, the Florida Second District Court of Appeal disagreed, siding instead with the State of Florida, reversed the trial court's decision and denied Riley's motion to dismiss the evidence. Although reversing, the Court of Appeal certified the case to the Florida Supreme Court, which reinstated the trial court's order to suppress the evidence, thus overturning the Court of Appeal's decision.

The conclusion was the answer to the question whether the police officer violated the defendant's reasonable expectation of privacy by observing his property from a helicopter with the naked eye.

The Florida Supreme Court held that Riley had no reasonable expectation of privacy in this case because anyone could view Riley's property from a helicopter flying in navigable airspace and figure out what was inside. The police officer did not enter Riley's land or interfere with it in any way. Furthermore, the way in which he was flying the helicopter was well within the law, so he was within his right to view Riley's property from the air. The Florida Supreme Court determined that the police action in this case did not violate Riley's Fourth Amendment rights.[60]

The U.S. Supreme Court has never taken a position on whether the Fourth Amendment places limits on government use of drone surveillance. However, it allowed some warrantless aerial surveillance from manned aircraft. In this context, the U.S. Supreme Court has suggested that the pervasive or continuous use of a surveillance technology may heighten Fourth Amendment concerns. The American Civil Liberties Union (ACLU) has additionally argued that drones raise constitutional issues of a different order to manned aircraft.[61] The ACLU stated that:

Because of their potential for pervasive use in ordinary law enforcement operations and capacity for revealing far more than the naked eye, drones pose a more serious threat to

---

60 The Florida Supreme Court addressed the following question: Whether surveillance of the interior of a partially covered greenhouse in a residential backyard from the vantage point of a helicopter located 400 ft above the greenhouse constitutes a search for which a warrant is required under the Fourth Amendment and Art. 1, Section 12 – Searches and Seizures – of the Florida Constitution.
61 The American Civil Liberties Union is a non-profit organization founded in 1920. Its objective is to defend and preserve the individual rights and liberties guaranteed to every person in the United States by the Constitution and laws of the United States. In addition to representing persons and organizations in lawsuits, the ACLU lobbies for policy positions that have been established by its board of directors.

privacy than do manned flights. There are good reasons to believe that they may implicate Fourth Amendment rights in ways that manned flights do not.

Drones are potentially extremely powerful surveillance tools, and that power, like all government power, needs to be subject to checks and balances. Like any tool, drones have the potential to be used for good and ill. If we can set some good privacy ground rules, our society can enjoy the benefits of this technology without having to worry about its darker potentials. We impose regulations on what law enforcement can do all the time, for example allowing law enforcement to take a thermal image of someone's home only when they get a warrant. We need to impose rules, limits and regulations on drones, which means to recommend core measures to preserve the privacy Americans have always expected and enjoyed.[62]

These core measures include the following:
- Usage restrictions. Drones should be subject to strict regulation to ensure that their use does not eviscerate the privacy that Americans have traditionally enjoyed and rightly expect. Innocent Americans should not have to worry that their activities will be scrutinized by drones. To this end, the use of drones should be prohibited for indiscriminate mass surveillance, for example, or for spying based on First Amendment-protected activities. In general, drones should not be deployed except:
    o where there are specific and articulable grounds to believe that the drone will collect evidence relating to a specific instance of criminal wrongdoing or, if the drone will intrude upon reasonable expectations of privacy, where the government has obtained a warrant based on probable cause; or
    o where there is a geographically confined, time-limited emergency situation in which particular individuals' lives are at risk, such as a fire, hostage crisis, or person lost in the wilderness; or
    o for reasonable non-law enforcement purposes by non-law enforcement agencies, where privacy will not be substantially affected, such as geological inspections or environmental surveys, and where the surveillance will not be used for secondary law enforcement purposes.
- Image retention restrictions. Images of identifiable individuals captured by aerial surveillance technologies should not be retained or shared unless there is reasonable suspicion that the images contain evidence of criminal activity or are relevant to an ongoing investigation or pending criminal trial.
- Public notice. The policies and procedures for the use of aerial surveillance technologies should be explicit and written and should be made public. While it is legitimate for the police to keep the details of particular investigations confidential,

---

62 Stanley, J., Crump, C., 'Protecting Privacy from Aerial Surveillance: Recommendations for Government Use of Drone Aircraft', Report, New York: American Civil Liberties Union, December 2011, pp. 13-16. The Fourth Amendment restricts the use of drones. Recommendations.

policy decisions regarding overall deployment policies, including the privacy trade-offs they may entail, are public matters that should be openly discussed.
- Democratic control. Deployment and policy decisions regarding drones should be democratically decided based on open information, not made on the fly by police departments simply by virtue of federal grants (or other autonomous purchasing decisions or departmental policy fiats).
- Auditing and effectiveness tracking. Investments in drones should not be made without a clear, systematic examination of the costs and benefits involved. And if aerial surveillance technology is deployed, independent audits should be put in place to track the use of drones by government, so that citizens and other watchdogs can tell generally how, and how often, they are being used, whether the original rationale for their deployment is holding up, whether they represent a worthwhile public expenditure, and whether they are being used for improper or expanded purposes.[63]

Increasingly advanced drones capable of carrying sophisticated imaging equipment and significant payloads are readily available to the civilian market. These drones present the greatest risks because of their capabilities and widespread availability. Threat groups, consisting of non-state actors such as terrorists, cybercriminals and activists have already demonstrated the ability to take over control of civilian drones for illegal purposes such as attacks or to gain access to drones for gathering intelligence and other sensitive data.

For reasons of protection against external intervention into drone systems, the drone itself, the controller, ground control station (GCS) and communication data links must be provided with strict security features, encompassing defensive techniques and applications, in order to protect the confidentiality and integrity of its gathered and communicated information and to ensure its ability to adhere to its operational requirements, for example, in the field of law enforcement.

Securing information, including personal data, refers to protecting it from disclosure, disruption, modification and destruction. It is conceivable that innovations of design and certification may play a role in building in robust security functionality. For a secure drone operation, the following security requirements can be identified:

Authorized Access

The drone system must provide means to ensure that only authorized operators, such as controllers, are granted access to its resources. In the past, researchers, experts in hacking devices, were able to connect to a drone's camera feeds from any computer because its

---

63 Source: Cavoukian, A., pp. 13-14 (https://www.ipc.on.ca/wp-content/uploads/resources/pbd-drones.pdf).

CHAPTER 6   PRIVACY, DATA PROTECTION AND SECURITY

Wi-Fi access point was not password protected. In the event that someone is able to gain access to a drone's camera feed, actually that person could potentially access the system or network that operates the drone.

Like any device connected to the internet of things (IoT), a drone that is not properly secured is susceptible to criminal activity and has the potential to expose an entire network to cybercriminals. Authentication mechanisms and mandatory access control policies must be implemented to mitigate unauthorized personnel from accessing the GCS.

The mechanisms may also incorporate operation-specific distance bounding protocols to further authenticate the distance between the communicating entities. In addition, external malicious modification of multiple inputs from the external environment to the flight controller and sensors must be reduced to a bare minimum.

Availability

All the elements of the drone system should be guaranteed to perform their required functions under defined spatial and temporal circumstances such that the drone system sustains its availability without disruption during the operational period.

New ISO-approved drone standards, including protocols on quality, safety and security, seek to address public concerns surrounding privacy and data protection, demanding that drone operators must have appropriate systems to securely handle data alongside control and communications planning when flying.[64]

In addition, the hardware and software of all related operating equipment must also be kept up to date, and the utilization of alternative operational procedures such as using different sets of sensors to cross-check readings can allow the drone flight control system to tolerate specific components malfunctioning or alteration. It is of prime importance to manage the patching and updating processes in a manner that does not compromise the availability of the drone system during its operation.

Information Confidentiality

The drone system should employ mechanisms to mitigate unauthorized disclosure of the telemetric and control information. For encryption of the data link, different encryption

---

64   The International Organization for Standardization (ISO) is an independent, non-governmental international organization with a membership of 165 national standards bodies. ISO is located in Geneva, Switzerland. ISO Focus November-December 2020, pp. 6-13 Missions possible for UAS, Drones: one step closer to ATM, 'Through new developments in UTMs and UAS, and with the help of standards such as the ISO 21384 and 23629 series, UAS look set for a great lift-off'.

standards can be used. Encryption is the process through which data is encoded so that it remains hidden from or inaccessible to unauthorized users.

To encrypt data, an encryption key uses an encryption algorithm to translate (encode) plain text or readable data into unreadable data or ciphertext. Only the corresponding decryption key can decode the scrambled ciphertext into readable plain text. How the encryption is done and what type of encryption, symmetric or asymmetric, is used gets much more complex.[65] As for standard drone operations, encryption will help safeguard the communication between the drone and the GCS that communicates commands.

Information Integrity

The drone system should be able to ensure that the telemetric information and the GNSS as well as the control signals are genuine and have not been intentionally or unintentionally altered.[66] Authenticated encryption cryptographic primitives may be used to ensure both the integrity and the confidentiality of such information.

System Integrity

The drone system should be able to guarantee the authenticity of its software and hardware components. Coding standards should be in place to describe a high-level programming language subset that ensures the software is written as safely and securely as possible. Techniques from trusted computing such as memory curtaining, sealed storage and remote attestation can be used to ensure the authenticity of the system's firmware and sensitive data. The deployment of intrusion detection systems, anti-virus software, firewall and strict policies on the use of external storage media can aid in the detection and prevention of malware.

Accountability of Actions

The drone system should employ mechanisms that enforce non-repudiation to ensure that operators are held responsible for their actions. Digital signature algorithms may be used to both authenticate the operators and to bind them to an issued action. Moreover,

---

65 *See also* Daemen, J., Rijmen, V., *The Design of Rijndael: AES-The Advanced Encryption Standard*, Berlin, Heidelberg, New York: Springer-Verlag, 2013, pp. 30-56.
66 Global Navigation Satellite System. Examples of GNSS include U.S. NAVSTAR Global Positioning System (GPS), Europe's Galileo, Russia's Global'naya Navigatsionnaya Sputnikovaya Sistema (GLONASS), and China's BeiDou Navigation Satellite System.

CHAPTER 6   PRIVACY, DATA PROTECTION AND SECURITY

logging procedures, for post-flight analysis purposes, which are used to chronologically track the sequence of actions and changes in the system, should be implemented.

In a 2019 study focusing on the UK population, PwC found that 41% of citizens fear that drones might be misused, 27% fear they will be used by criminals and 26% are concerned about accident risks. The research also indicates that citizens' trust tends to increase for matters that are well regulated, emphasizing the importance of having rules and accountability for drone operators. In contrast, over 80% of the study's respondents were positive about the use of drones in search and rescue operations, natural emergencies and countering criminal activity.[67]

Ranked next to cyberthreats are physical threats to drone systems, to cope with which there are specific mitigation techniques. For theft and vandalism: authentication of data link and merchandize recipient and location-based drone electronic immobilizer, which means that such an immobilizer should allow the starting of the drone engine only when it is physically present at or near the GCS by relying on location-based information broadcasted by its GCS. For weather and civic challenges: situational awareness and strong AI approaches as well as sense (detect) and avoid features.

For friendly drone collision: dynamic inter-drone communication, sense and avoid capability and ADS-B (integrated). As TCAS uses secondary radar data, its performance could be improved with the greater positioning accuracies and sampling rates afforded by ADS-B, the satellite-based surveillance system that will be a key component of the NextGen air transportation system.[68]

While drones introduce a range of utilization cases, they also introduce a variety of new issues around privacy and surveillance. The growth of drones also represents a new physical threat that demands the attention of security and risk, especially from threat actors using their own drones or someone else's drone for malicious purposes. Indeed, drones are vulnerable to many types of threats.

It should be noted that continued demand for drones will significantly stimulate more drone innovation, leading to drones with increased payload capabilities with ultra-advanced sensors, greater endurance and the ability to unobtrusively survey large areas or privacy-sensitive objects and data. Furthermore, as the number of drones in operation increases, more drone-related incidents and disruptions are to be expected, accidentally

---

67   'Civil and Military Drones: Navigating a Disruptive and Dynamic Technological Ecosystem', *Briefing to the Members and Staff of the European Parliament*, European Union, 2019, p. 8. *See also* Study: 'Building Trust in Drones: The Importance of Education, Accountability and Reward', PwC, study was carried out by Opinium, 2019.

68   *See* Romli, F.I., King, J.D., Li, L., Clarke, J.P., 'Impact of ADS-B on TCAS Performance', *American Institute of Aeronautics and Astronautics*, 2008. *See also* Xu, Y., 'TCAS/ADS-B Integrated Surveillance and Collision Avoidance System', Aviation Engineering Institute Civil Aviation Flight University of China, Guanghan, Sichuan, China, Paris: Atlantis Press, 2013.

or intentionally. All this means that governments and international aviation organizations need to implement comprehensive drone regulatory procedures and standards to cope with the immense challenges in the field of drone screening and integration, risk, privacy, security and data protection.

Summary

Today, civil air transport is globally recognized as one of the most convenient, fastest and safest means of travel. Aviation has evolved from executive to mass transport and enables mankind to consider travelling across the world in a modern way, in terms of time rather than great distances. However, since the post-war modernization and globalization of civil aviation, the entire aerospace industry is currently at a major technological tipping point, represented by highly automated and autonomous unmanned aircraft or unmanned aerial vehicles (UAVs), colloquially known as drones, and their associated systems.

Often labelled as one of today's main disruptive technologies, drones have indeed earned this description by prompting a fundamental rethinking of traditional notions as business models, existing laws, safety and security standards, privacy, data protection, liability and the future of air transport. The use of drones, in any conceivable applications whatsoever, has the potential to dramatically alter multiple industries, and, in the ongoing process, change attitudes and behaviours of citizens with respect to the impact on everyday life.

Drones are extremely versatile and able to perform a huge variety of functions, especially the capacity to reduce risk to human life. On the other hand, there is also the potential for abuse of this evolving technology.

The earliest documented flight of unmanned balloons filled with explosives for aerial warfare is believed to have taken place in 1849 during the siege and fall of Venice as part of the First Italian Independence War. Aerial bombing by unmanned hot-air balloons continued during the American Civil War (1861-1865). In the early twentieth century, during World War I, unmanned or pilotless aerial vehicles were developed that have operated using revolutionary radio-controlled techniques, representing the most advanced drone technology of the time.

Elementary knowledge of electronic range finding, based on the principles of radar, developed by Professor Archibald Montgomery Lowe, was used in designing and developing this radio-guided pilotless aircraft by the Sopwith Company, well known for its fighter aircraft, and the Ruston Proctor & Co. Ltd, as well as the Havilland, which built the Queen Bee, an existing conventional aircraft converted to a special radio-controlled pilotless target aircraft.

In the United States, inventors such as Nikola Tesla, Peter Cooper Hewitt and Elmer Ambrose Sperry as well as Glenn Hammond Curtiss (Curtiss-Sperry Aerial Torpedo) were obsessed with remotely controlled unmanned aircraft. These engineers were pioneering in radio remote control, gyroscopes for naval use and automatic stabilization essential for effective radio control, resulting in gyro-based autopilots for (unmanned) aircraft.

The Hewitt-Sperry Automatic Airplane project was undertaken during World War I to develop an aerial torpedo, a pilotless aircraft capable of carrying explosives to its targets, preferably an enemy warship. In 1918, a more sophisticated properly functioning type of UAV, which eventually came to be known as the Kettering Bug, was developed under the management of Charles Franklin Kettering. Sperry and Kettering, as a professional electrical engineer, worked together to create a control system for this aerial torpedo. The Kettering Bug, regarded as the first practical example of a self-flying pilotless aircraft, was an autopilot-controlled unmanned aircraft that was computerized to drop a bomb on a pre-selected target.

Even before the outbreak of World War II, but much more intensively during the course of the war, Germany focused on developing missiles. While unmanned aircraft are intended to be recovered following the completion of an attack, a cruise missile, once it hits the target, completes its mission. Cruise missiles are fast, have a longer range and are much more accurate, not to mention more difficult to shoot out of the sky, than other types of unmanned autonomous aerial vehicles.

The secret Fi 103 V-1 weapon, a winged pilotless fuel-propelled flying bomb, manufactured by Fieseler, which actively participated in its development, was the first genuine military application of unmanned autonomous aircraft. The flying bomb was the result of technical and technological know-how extremely new for the time and was part of a comprehensive missile programme, the first of which was started in the 1930s.

Its first flight was successfully completed on 10 December 1942. The main production consisted of unmanned aircraft, while a limited number were equipped with a cockpit, the Fieseler Fi 103R Reichenberg IV's. During the last years of the war, the German armed forces launched the V-1 (Vergeltungswaffe I), also known as a 'buzz bomb' or 'doodlebug' owing to the pulse-jet noise, on a large scale from the western European German-occupied territories to destroy vital targets in Great Britain, including terror attacks on London, and the Antwerp harbour in Belgium, captured by the Allied forces in their effort to facilitate a supply line to liberate the Low Countries, as a last resort.

The V-1, which used a simple autopilot as a guidance system to just regulate altitude, airspeed and rudder control, was conceivable as the most 'famous' unmanned aircraft, but, above all, a terrifying German vengeance weapon.

During the Cold War, the two superpowers of the world, the United States and the Union of Soviet Socialist Republics (USSR), used UAVs to spy on each other, even though traditional manned aircraft, such as the American Lockheed U-2, were preferred at the time. The history of non-military unmanned aircraft or drones and their versatile usage started only just after the beginning of the third millennium. The fact that the same technological improvements in the military sector could be used in civil drones was a major reason for the immense production and proliferation of commercial and recreational drones. The popularity of civil drones is undeniably on the rise.

Drones have quickly become the most popular airborne devices for recreational, commercial and government uses. Microelectronics, nanotechnology, algorithms, artificial intelligence (AI) as well as computer power and programming are just beginning to accelerate the technological capabilities of drones, presenting exciting opportunities such as fully autonomous drone operations, extreme durability, new materials and innovative power sources.

Unmanned aircraft have many descriptions. The different expressions or terms do not always have exactly the same scope, and, in addition, the terms used vary according to the different stakeholders' divergent preferences. Today, drone, usually depicted as being fully autonomous, is the most popular name for a variety of unmanned military, civil utility and recreational aircraft. The term drone was originally used for military applications and still, for many people, has a military connotation, depending on the sector concerned.

This rather negative connotation, especially in relation to the remotely controlled killing potential of military drones in armed conflicts, seems to be slowly changing, and as a result drones are increasingly associated with civil applications, not least by the extraordinary global increase in civilian drones. However, both the rapidly developing drone technology and the continued expansion of the unmanned aircraft industry make it difficult to use a single descriptive term to serve as a consistent basic concept for a comprehensive regulatory framework.

The rather incomplete denomination of pilotless aircraft was replaced by remotely piloted vehicle, followed by the term unmanned aerial vehicle (UAV). Thereafter, the literally broad terms of unmanned aircraft (UA) and unmanned aircraft system (UAS), which stand for the complete system, were adopted. More recently, 'remotely piloted aircraft system' ('RPAS') was introduced. The designation remotely piloted rather than unmanned provides more clarity, in accordance with the remote elements. Remotely piloted aircraft (RPA) is used to indicate the flying part, also known as the platform, with or without a payload, while RPAS includes, among other things, the ground station that controls the platform. These more descriptive terms are used mainly in the United States and other English-speaking countries but are also known in quite a number of countries as an alternative to the predicate drone.

While there are some differences in designation and definitions of civil unmanned aircraft and their associated elements, such as the ground control station and data links, among international organizations such as the International Civil Aviation Organization (ICAO), supranational bodies such as European Aviation Safety Agency (EASA) and collaborative projects such as Single European Sky ATM Research (SESAR), in official (legal) instruments, including international treaties, protocols and national legislation, the terms UAV, UA, UAS, RPA and RPAS are mainly used. These different terms all have slightly deviating definitions that might generate different legal consequences.

At the European Union level, no uniform terminology is used to refer to what is commonly known as drones. The European Parliament uses the term civil drone to differentiate civilian drones from those intended for military purposes, while the European Commission uses the term RPAS. EASA, the EU body with the mandate to issue implementing rules and approve airworthiness standards, widely uses both the terms drone and unmanned aircraft.

EASA has considered several terms such as UAS, RPAS, as a subcategory of UAS, but eventually followed the common usage of the term drone, mainly in concepts of operations, reports, rule-making, in communications to the general public and EASA high-level conferences on drones. The European Commission has generally opted for the term unmanned aircraft, especially in formal documents.

In Regulation (EU) 2018/1139, the term unmanned aircraft has been used and defined as follows:

> Any aircraft operating or designed to operate autonomously or to be piloted remotely without a pilot on board.

A fully autonomous aircraft, other than an RPA, is defined as follows:

> An unmanned aircraft, the flight of which however is programmed in advance and does not allow pilot intervention in the management of the flight.

These aircraft are often equipped with autopilot and navigation technology, allowing them to fly autonomously without being manipulated by the remote pilot at all times. If the remote pilot can take over control of the aircraft at any time, such unmanned aircraft cannot be classified as fully autonomous.

In 2003, ICAO started discussions on UAS, followed by meetings to determine its potential role in providing a fundamental international regulatory framework as well as technical specifications and special Standards and Recommended Practices (SARPs) and supporting Procedures for Air Navigation Services (PANS) on UAS. In 2011, Circular 328 AN/190 was issued to apprise states of the emerging ICAO perspective on the integration of UAS into non-segregated airspace and at aerodromes, to consider the fundamental differences from manned aviation that such integration will involve, and to encourage states to help with the development of ICAO policy on UAS by providing information on their own experiences associated with these particular aircraft.

ICAO's non-binding Circular 328 AN/190 provides definitions related to unmanned aircraft:

Unmanned aircraft: an aircraft which is intended to operate with no pilot on board, and an unmanned aircraft system is an aircraft and its associated elements which are operated with no pilot on board.
Autonomous aircraft: an unmanned aircraft that does not allow pilot intervention in the management of the flight.

The U.S. Federal Aviation Administration (FAA), one of the world's leading governmental bodies with powers to regulate all aspects of civil aviation, has adopted the term unmanned aircraft to describe aircraft systems without a flight crew on board. The full definition is as follows: unmanned aircraft means an aircraft operated without the possibility of direct human intervention from within or on the aircraft.

Currently, regulators are putting their efforts mainly into the regulation of RPAS because only RPAS have the potential to be integrated into non-segregated airspace and at aerodromes operating alongside manned aircraft. However, throughout the text of this book, the term drone, as a generally well-known concept that covers all types of aircraft that are operated with no pilot on board, will mainly be used, although the other descriptions of unmanned aircraft (systems) will be stated when required by the context in the interest of explanation, clarity and origin.

Today's drones are part of a rapidly emerging cutting-edge technology that has gained considerable popularity and universality over the past few years. Ever since drones have been developed and researched, their applications have expanded to different social sectors. At present, drones or unmanned aircraft already offer a wide variety of possibilities for the benefit of global society, ranging from environmental control to civil security, as well as a fascinating variety of commercial services, which stand for a large number of applications.

Drones can perform any operations that traditional manned aviation in all forms struggle with, and their use results in evident economic savings and environmental benefits while reducing the risk to human life. In the foreseeable future, drones will become more and more disruptive, in the sense that this innovation will open up a new market that will disrupt the existing market in the medium term.

Because the possibilities and applications of drones are immense, the predictable disruptive effect on relevant markets will also be significant. With the exception of military applications, there are two other sectors in which the application of drones has become commonplace: the public and private sectors. Through the years, new technologies have turned drones into vital tools for life-saving actions, disaster relief and emergency response, firefighting, works at heights, safety and security in society, and harsh and hostile environments for humans.

A remarkable application in rather challenging times is virus control by drones. Between late 2019 and early 2020 the outbreak of the new coronavirus disease (Covid-

19) in Wuhan in the province of Hubei (People's Republic of China) was the first major epidemic, which even turned into a pandemic, in times of AI.

In many affected countries around the world, drones have demonstrated their ability to speed up the fight against the coronavirus disease, especially in the field of disinfection, detection, monitoring social distancing and crowd guidance, broadcasting and goods delivery.

Drones are used in the field of civil aviation safety, for example in investigating aircraft accidents. Within the public safety domain, the use of drones as observation and surveillance instruments, equipped with cameras and sensors, can generally provide background information about certain situations. Drones are used in agriculture, in particular precision farming and smart agriculture. In the environmental domain, drones can be equipped with sensors, so-called sniffers, to detect chemical particles in order to determine the intensity of emissions of certain substances.

Drones can be deployed around industrial infrastructure, especially for inspections and maintenance. On construction sites, they act mainly as workforce multipliers. Drones are used in law enforcement actions. Sophisticated drone technology is playing a rather effective role in criminal and administrative enforcement and detection and investigation of illegal practices, as well as in crowd and traffic control.

Drones, which are widely used in search and rescue operations and firefighting, have the ability to quickly reach a vantage point where humans cannot easily get access to. Firefighter drones are sent to fire locations as scouts, using cameras with thermal imaging technology to perceive in low light and dark conditions in order to be able to assist first responders in their rescue efforts.

Preparing for, and responding to, disasters is a major logistical challenge. Traditionally, search and rescue operations, often involving dangerous tasks, are performed by humans. In recent years, drone technology has successfully resulted in an increased capacity to take on effective early-stage search actions, enabling lives to be saved.

Drones play a role in wildlife conservation, which means animal detection and counting, accurate monitoring and the distribution and abundance of animal species as well as collecting data on possible threats to animals.

Drones are widely used in gathering and monitoring (extreme) weather data. They are able to cost-effectively collect weather data in severe or remote environments like the Arctic regions.

Drones are perfect tools for public and private safety and security and are mostly used as observation and surveillance instruments. However, the intrusive nature of data collection and processing by drones necessitates a strong regulatory framework for data protection serving wider public and private interests in an information society with ubiquitous data processing. Processing of personal data, such as imaging and privacy-sensitive recordings, collected by, often inconspicuous, drone cameras and sensors like microphones, is legally protected by Directive 2018/680 and Regulation (EU) 2018/679 in the European Union.

Drones are used in insurance and real estate, movie productions, news covering, applied sciences, sports coaching and broadcasting of games, in aviation such as the inspection of large commercial aircraft for the overall condition, but also for foreign object damage, bird strikes, flaws in paint quality, vertical stabilizers and tail fins, to name a few.

The growing interests of users of drones have developed new areas of application for this state-of-the-art technology, such as goods delivery and urban mobility. Unfortunately, there is a malicious, frightening dark side to the use of drones too: they are easy transporters to smuggle drugs into prisons or across borders. Even more staggering, drone technology could be deployed by terrorists seeking to attack random cities and innocent civilians anywhere in the world.

Regulatory and oversight challenges will always remain, particularly in the field of civil aviation safety. States and civil aviation organizations around the world, such as ICAO and EASA, are working to ensure a harmonized regulatory framework for safe drone operations. ICAO is a specialized agency that endeavours to bring together the best and brightest from government and industry to define how unmanned aircraft can be safely integrated into modern airspace and how their benefits can be optimized globally for the wide range of public and private sector operators. To ensure the free circulation of drones and a level playing field within the European Union, EASA has developed common European rules on drones. The latest piece of EU legislation has achieved the highest ever safety standards for drones.

In the ICAO regulatory scheme, no distinction is made between manned and unmanned aircraft, probably because the earlier regulatory structure under ICAO was inadequate to address the unique characteristics of unmanned aircraft. The 1944 Chicago Convention and its Annexes do not provide a clear definition of an unmanned aircraft. Only Article 8 provides some guidance and presumably recognized the potential hazards to persons and property on the surface as well as to other airspace users, possibly resulting in damage. Undeniably, this behaviour has an enormous impact on the sharing of airspace.

To merge unmanned aircraft safely into non-segregated airspace, for operations equal to traditional manned aviation, is considered an enormously challenging objective. Such a seamless, efficient and safe implementation will be achieved only through the application of innovative technologies and pioneering research along with the careful design of a tight and solid fundamental uniform international regulatory framework, based on appropriate principles, rules and guidelines. The principal objective of such a comprehensive regulatory framework is the safety of other airspace users and the safety of persons and property on the ground and water.

As safety is the predominant requirement in any modality of air transportation whatsoever, the safety of unmanned aircraft operations is just as important as that of manned aircraft. Automation and new technologies will continue to revolutionize safety standards, giving, in turn, an incredible boost to reliability.

The separation of all aircraft in flight will be managed by a comprehensive network of computers. Modified flight levels at much higher altitudes are introduced for NextGen aircraft, creating space for specific slower and lower air operations, such as unmanned all-cargo transport. Other (future) unmanned modes of air transport, in particular passenger aircraft, still face serious objections. In particular, lack of public confidence, despite the ultra-high level of automation and computerized decision-making, will ensure that passenger-carrying aircraft will continue to have pilot(s) on board, at least in the medium term and most probably for a considerable time thereafter.

The pilot still remains the pilot, whether he or she is at the remote console of the RPAS or on the aircraft flight deck. The skills must match. With the potential of unmanned aircraft, the standards for pilot training need to be set high to ensure that third parties on the surface and other airspace users are not jeopardized. A rather paradigmatic, but nonetheless professional statement comes from the side of IFALPA, which strongly opposes the use of UAS to supplant the role of pilots in any type of air transport system.

In another statement, IFALPA has asserted that the fact that the pilot is not on board the aircraft poses significant challenges in the way UAS may be utilized. New technical solutions should be developed to help compensate for the absence of a human on board. Contrary to this opinion, the European Commission High Level Group on Aviation and Aeronautics Research (December 2010) consistently proclaimed in its 2011 report on future aviation (Flightpath 2050 Europe's Vision for Aviation) that the European air transport system will operate uninterruptedly in 2050 through fully interoperable and networked systems allowing both manned and unmanned aircraft to safely operate in the same airspace, providing 90% of travellers within Europe a door-to-door journey within 4 hours by transferring seamlessly between transport modes to reach the final destination smoothly, predictably and on time.

As non-segregated airspace users, UAS have to meet, at least, not only the minimum international standards on personnel licensing and airworthiness established by ICAO Annex 1 and 8, but, additionally, the critical rules of the air as laid down in ICAO Annex 2.

With respect to the rules of the air for unmanned aviation, but also to other essential issues, such as flight operations, maintenance and licensing, the intention is to adhere as closely as possible to existing rules and standards. However, a prerequisite for the integration of unmanned aviation in non-segregated airspace is to possibly amend ICAO Annexes regarding these three essential domains, especially if specific characteristics and flight safety give cause for doing so.

SUMMARY

ICAO recognizes a variety of aircraft categories, including balloons, gliders, engine-powered fixed and rotary-wing aircraft. Aircraft can be land, sea or amphibious and whether it is manned or unmanned does not affect its status as an aircraft. Each category of aircraft will potentially have unmanned versions, today and in the future. This position is central to all further issues pertaining to unmanned aircraft and provides the foundation for addressing airworthiness, personnel licensing, rules of the air, airspace users, etc.

Until recently, ICAO had no specific SARPs pertaining to unmanned aircraft. ICAO Standards were established only when an agreement came into place between contracting states. In 2003, discussions began on this increasingly popular issue. In 2005, during the first meeting of the 169th Session of the Air Navigation Commission (ANC), ICAO's Secretary General was requested to consult selected states and international organizations with respect to current and future international activities of unmanned aircraft in civil airspace as well as procedures to avert danger to civil aircraft posed by unmanned aircraft operated as state aircraft, together with state's procedures that might be in place for the issuance of special operating authorizations for international civil unmanned aircraft operations.

In 2006, ICAO held its first exploratory meeting on unmanned aircraft, with the primary objective of exploring the current state of affairs regarding the development of regulatory material related to unmanned aircraft and determining the potential role of ICAO in the regulatory process.

The ICAO Unmanned Aircraft Systems Study Group, established by the ANC in 2007, served as the focal point for all UAS-related issues until it was superseded by the RPAS panel, composed of experts in the field of airworthiness, telecommunication for command and control and air traffic control, detect and avoid, personnel licensing, RPAS operations and ATM. Other panels of the ANC are involved in RPAS/UAS topics, such as aircraft accident investigation, communications, flight recorders, frequency spectrum, surveillance and safety management.

The ICAO's intention is that 18 of the 19 Annexes will be amended to accommodate RPAS/UAS requirements, with an emphasis on performance-based standards. The exploratory meeting agreed that although there would eventually be a wide range of technical and performance specifications and standards, only a portion of those would need to become ICAO SARPs. It was also determined that ICAO was not the most suitable institution to lead the effort in developing such specifications. However, it was agreed that there was a need for harmonization of terms, strategies and principles with respect to the regulatory framework and that ICAO should act as a focal point.

As a consequence, the main issue for ICAO at the time was to coordinate the development of a strategic guidance document that would guide the regulatory evolution to be used as the basis for the development of regulations by the different states and organizations, as these entities were facing regulatory challenges arising from the increased use of UAS for civilian applications. In 2011, ICAO issued the UAS Circular 328-AN/190. Its purpose was, and still is, inter alia, to inform states of the emerging ICAO perspective on the integration of UAS into non-segregated airspace and at aerodromes. The circular calls on states to provide comments in an effort to proceed with the development of the fundamental international regulatory framework through SARPs, amended and supplemented, supporting PANS and guidance material (GM).

Since 2012, ICAO has been actively involved in facilitating the development of a regulatory framework for unmanned aviation and in leading the discussion on RPAS and UAS through the organization of global symposia. These symposia provide opportunities to states, international organizations and stakeholders for a more detailed understanding of the functioning and responsibilities of RPAS and UAS operators, airspace management, training options, licensing authorities and requirements, regulators and the aerospace industry towards ensuring safe and secure operations.

EASA provides opinions and formulates technical rules relating to the construction, design and operational aspects of aircraft, including drones, and is also responsible for assisting the European Commission by providing technical, administrative and scientific support and by preparing draft regulations. EASA states that drones should be integrated in the existing aviation system in a safe and proportionate manner and that this integration should foster an innovative and competitive European drone industry, creating jobs and growth.

The European regulatory framework proposed by EASA should set a high level of safety and also environmental protection acceptable to the society and offer enough flexibility for the new industry to remain agile, to innovate, mature and continue to grow. Therefore, the exercise is not merely a matter of transposing the system put in place of traditional manned aviation but of creating one that is proportionate, progressive and risk based, and the new EU-wide drone rules must express objectives that will be complemented by industry standards. The further development of drones and their integration into non-segregated airspace will pose new challenges, necessitating a significant amount of further research to be performed.

Common rules for design, classification, certification, licensing, types of operation as well as demonstrating and validating the feasibility of technological drone services are all key elements of rule-making. Groundbreaking rules enable full and safe integration, with substantial functional and economic benefits predicted. The operation of drones, for example RPAS, should be regulated in a way that is proportionate to the risk of the specific operation. Since not all key technologies required for RPAS to operate in non-segregated airspace are mature and standardized yet, all aeronautical experts in the world agree that the integration of RPAS in airspace will be gradual, well substantiated and evolutionary.

Summary

The future RPAS transportation image, though technologically feasible, has not yet been resolved in regard to full integration into non-segregated airspace. This new air transport modality, including the associated elements, requires new classifications, qualifications, airworthiness specifications and licensing for remote pilots and observers.

Since 2003, EASA has been responsible for aviation safety within the European Union, especially with respect to traditional manned aviation and large drones. At that time, Regulation (EC) No. 216/2008 covered only drones with a maximum take-off mass (MTOM) of over 150 kg, which was merely a non-technically legal limit. This implied that EU Member States were responsible for all drones with an MTOM of up to 150 kg. This had led to a fragmented regulatory system hampering the development of a single EU market for drones and cross-border drone operations. The widespread introduction of drones and associated risks could cause some unease among the general public and existing airspace users with regard to the safety standards of such unmanned aircraft. Years later, however, through the formal adoption of Regulation (EU) 2018/1139, this issue has been solved by extending the competence of the European Union to cover the regulation of all drones, regardless of their MTOM.

In 2005, EASA launched a public consultation on the certification of drones weighing more than 150 kg. Certification was only a first step towards a more comprehensive regulation for safe drone operations. According to Advance Notice of Proposed Amendment (A-NPA) 16-2005, regulatory airworthiness standards should be set to be no less demanding than those currently applicable to comparable manned aircraft and, furthermore, should not penalize drones by requiring compliance with higher standards simply because technology permits.

NPA 2012-10 considered the alignment of the Standardized European Rules of the Air (SERA) with Amendment 43 of Annex 2 to the Chicago Convention concerning drones. The major aspects of this NPA were as follows: RPAS/RPA-related airworthiness and operator certifications, crew licensing and specialized operations. It also provided for alignment with ICAO regulations governing ICAO SARPs and harmonization of ICAO airspace classification to ensure the seamless provision of safe and efficient air traffic services within the Single European Sky (SES), while covering commercial air transport and specialized unmanned aircraft system operations. However, RPAS access to non-segregated airspace will be subject to authorization.

In 2015, EASA has been tasked by the European Commission, following the Riga Conference and its associated Declaration (RPAS: Framing the Future of Aviation), whose principles would be reflected in A-NPA 2015-10, to develop a regulatory framework for drone operations as well as concrete proposals for the regulation of low-risk drone operations. The objective of this A-NPA is to ensure safe, secure and environmentally friendly development and to respect citizens' legitimate concerns for privacy and data protection.

Following the publication of A-NPA 2015-10, EASA adopted a Technical Opinion containing proposals for an operation-centric, proportionate, and risk- and performance-based regulatory framework for all drones, establishing three categories of operations: Open category (low risk), Specific category (medium risk) and Certified category (higher risk). This regulatory framework will encompass European rules for all drones in all weight classes.

While, in the European Union, the rules for traditional manned aircraft are usually driven by an aircraft-centric approach, there has been a significant change in the regulation approach policy, which means moving away from the conventional approach (starting with factors associated with the aircraft itself such as airworthiness certification, etc.), usually in combination with a pure purpose-centric approach, towards a more comprehensive approach, being the operation-centric approach, initially focusing on risks as recognized by society and imposing certain restrictions on drone operations. The choice of an operation-centric approach is justified by the fact that there has been no human on board a drone up to now. Therefore, the consequences of a loss of control of a drone depend crucially on the operational environment. The operation-centric approach should be risk based and proportionate.

In 2016, EASA developed a road map, including information on rule-making, development of standards, research and cooperation with international organizations, to provide more clarity on what the plans will be to roll out the EU operation-centric approach, applicable only in the SES. However, this road map did not clarify all issues to be covered. Instead, the Agency decided to draft a prototype regulation, called the Prototype Commission Regulation on Unmanned Aircraft Operations, to assist in the upcoming rule-making process concerning the licensing and operational requirements for drone operations in the Open and Specific categories to accomplish clarity on relevant drone operational issues. The prototype regulation does not introduce changes to SERA.

To ensure the free circulation of drones and a level playing field within the European Union, EASA has developed common European rules, the EU regulatory drone regime, included in Regulation (EU) 2019/945 and Regulation (EU) 2019/947, replacing national rules of EU Member States. The overall regulatory intention is that the highest safety standards achieved in manned aviation should apply to drones as well. The rules are based on an assessment of the risk of a specific operation and to find a balance between the obligations of drone manufacturers and those of operators with regard to safety, respect for privacy, environmental issues, noise protection and security.

In 2019, both EASA and the European Commission developed a preliminary draft regulatory framework containing high-level safety requirements on the establishment of U-space to enable competent authorities to set performance requirements, including environmental objectives, needed to satisfy traffic density and complexity of operations, and high-level requirements for U-space services and service provider certifications, which will lay the foundation for innovative U-space services.

The growth of drones in the United States, as in other parts of the world, has surged tremendously, although this unprecedented increase will undeniably create operational challenges, including safe integration into the national airspace system (NAS). To ensure safe flights and safety for people and property on the surface, drones are subject to regulation by the FAA. Various local restrictions on drone operations were rather confusing and incompatible with federal air traffic rules, and, as a result, the FAA took certain measures to maintain stringent oversight over local laws to ensure consistency across the United States.

In 2015, the FAA published the first edition of its integration road map, describing the integration procedure in terms of three overlapping perspectives: accommodation, referring to granting drones limited access to the airspace on a case-by-case basis; integration, addressing medium-term aims such as enabling routine, regulated airspace access without the need for special authorization; and evolution, focusing on adaption to emerging needs and possibilities. The FAA organized test sites to focus on several aspects of the integration of civil drones into American airspace, including the training and certification of remote pilots.

The FAA collaborates internally and maintains extensive partnerships across government, industry and academia to develop integrated research plans that will support the development of regulations, policies, procedures, guidance and standards for drone operations and UAS traffic management (UTM). Research activities such as flight tests, modelling and simulation, technology evaluations, risk assessments and data gathering and analysis provide the FAA with critical information in areas such as detect and avoid, UAS communications, human factors, resource management, system safety and certification, all of which enable the FAA to make informed decisions on safe drone integration.

The future development of drones and their integration into non-segregated airspace will pose new challenges in the coming years. While today, flying a drone in non-segregated airspace with cooperative aircraft is possible with appropriate coordination and special procedures, operation of a large number of drones, possibly with non-cooperative aircraft, will be much more complicated and will require additional measures with a view to maintaining a high level of aviation safety.

ICAO predicts that by 2030 a large number of drones, in particular RPA, of any capacity, will share the airspace with traditional manned aviation, even flying under IFR conditions. While some RPA operations will be conducted in accordance with IFR, either for a portion of their flight or for the entire flight, others will operate only under VFR. Similarly, RPA will operate in and transit through national and international airspace as well as controlled or uncontrolled airspace and arbitrarily depart from and arrive at less congested or busy aerodromes. Particularly noteworthy is that the market for commercial drones is growing faster than anticipated potentially tripling until 2039, while the market for non-commercial drones appears to be slowing down in the United States, according to FAA's forecast.

ICAO stipulates that the scaling up of UAS air transport services such as humanitarian aid and urban mobility, particularly with the implementation of U-space/UTM, certainly faces a variety of challenges, including the varying legislative requirements worldwide and uncertainty surrounding applicable rules and responsibilities.

Over the past years, drones have become central to the functioning of a multiplicity of commercial activities, industries, governments and non-governmental organizations. A commercial drone is defined as any drone used commercially in connection with a business. The range of drones is nearly infinite with respect to design and performance. The potential of drones is based on their capability to reach the most remote and impassable areas with an extremely low or even no need for manpower and requiring the least effort, valuable time and energy. Moreover, they have the potential in commercial applications to dramatically alter a number of industries.

Globally, customized drones offer industries increasing work efficiency and balanced productivity, decreasing workload and production costs, improving accuracy, proportioning customer relations and services and resolving security issues on a large scale, to name just a few benefits. However, strict regulation of drone operations, in particular commercial drone operations, will be highly necessary given the hazards involved. The primary concern when commercial drones, with any assignment, are flying over public spaces or private properties is that the associated risk is not imaginary, in that crashes could occur, endangering the health and property of people. To properly regulate the use of commercial drones, so as to safeguard the individual property rights and safety, a number of stakeholders are involved, such as the national civil aviation authorities (CAAs) or regional aviation organizations, the industry and consumers, all of whom have their own motivations and responsibilities.

Generally, drones, privately or commercially operated, can be highly privacy intrusive. They should normally not be used to identify individuals without their unambiguous consent. Society is highly concerned about the privacy invasion issues that might be caused by commercial drone use. Currently, drone technology is far ahead of drone regulation, and for this reason commercial use of drones is still severely restricted, even for research and development (R&D) purposes.

One of the biggest hurdles to mass adoption of drones is the numerous regulations that restrict the use of privately and commercially owned drones. The most prevalent of these restrictions is the so-called visual line of sight (VLOS) rule, which mandates that drone operators keep the drone within eyesight at all times. This clearly removes any potential application of drones in the delivery space, as the need to keep a drone in VLOS defeats the purpose of sending a drone to deliver a product at a consumer's home, considered a remote location.

In any case, the regulations for commercial and recreational or private drone use differ; however, VLOS remains pivotal, at least as long as there are no reliable tests and adequate rules to prove otherwise. The problem is that drone users are often unaware of any rules for the correct use of drones. Therefore, information, harmonization and modification of regulations both at the national level and, especially, at the international level are extremely necessary to regulate and contain the risk to aviation safety and security, particularly near aerodromes and in controlled airspace.

There is no more striking example of the unbridled increase in the number of drone applications than the boom in drone air sports. Drone racing, in particular, is one of the fastest growing sports in the world. The drone sport, which is evolving to include new formats and larger drones, has a number of features that appeal to the younger generations: it is fast paced, comes across well online and has an element of gaming-style virtual reality thanks to the special goggles worn by the pilots. Drone racing is inextricably linked to electronics and technology, and, unsurprisingly, a great deal of cutting-edge technology is at work behind the scenes at drone racing events.

However, the airspace allocation for recreational and competitive air sports, such as drone sport, has already been adversely affected in recent years, prompting the FAI, also known as the World Air Sports Federation, a non-governmental, non-profit-making international organization, to publish, in 2018, an airspace manifesto calling on ICAO to ensure continued and fair airspace access for all air sports. The FAI was founded in 1905 with the basic aim of furthering aeronautical and astronautical activities worldwide, ratifying world and continental records and coordinating the organization of international competitions. It is recognized by the International Olympic Committee (IOC).

Airspace should not be designed as either purely civil or purely military airspace but should instead be considered as one continuum in which all users' requirements have to be maximally accommodated. There has always been a dispute about flight in international airspace. With respect to the issue of the status of airspace in public international law, there were two different standpoints: on the one hand, freedom of the air, by analogy with the freedom of the high seas, so that overflight is free for all airspace users; and on the other hand, the principle of sovereignty over national airspace, which means assimilating airspace to the national territory underlying the airspace. In that case, international flights might be subject to the authorization and conditions set by the sovereign state concerned.

The 1919 Paris Convention accepted that states do have sovereign rights over the airspace above their respective territories. Freedom of passage for foreign aircraft was set forth as a contractual right, followed by mostly bilateral international air service transit and transport agreements and permits. Prosperity, the demand for travel and the expansion of regulated international air services made it busier in the air.

The inevitable drawback of the significant growth of civil air traffic in its relatively brief history is that airspace has become overcrowded. Unfortunately, lower priority airspace users will have less airspace available, today and certainly tomorrow. Commercial and military air traffic is accorded priority, raising constraints for drones. This calls for a comprehensive global framework of regulations to be implemented to integrate these emerging airspace users in a way that ensures that safety of flight will not be impaired and that risk is minimized.

The current airspace structure and management still lacks a policy and procedures for flexible use of airspace, which hampers airspace design and management by not allowing the application of an optimum airspace infrastructure and the use of optimum flight paths.

Aviation experts anticipate that by 2050, many aircraft categories, diverse in size, performance and type, will be operating, some of which will still have a pilot on board, but most will be remotely controlled or fully automatic. Civil aviation will have achieved unprecedented levels of safety and will continue to improve. Advanced manned, unmanned and legacy aircraft as well as NextGen autonomous aircraft and types of rotorcraft operate simultaneously within the same airspace and in most weather conditions.

An extremely important condition is that the location of all drones in the airspace can be known and displayed. To mitigate the chances of conflict between drones and manned aviation, SESAR called for a project to merge existing technologies to build the core functions of an Unmanned Traffic Management System (UTMS).

Unlike manned aviation, drones use a different flight model by not operating point to point between fixed aerodromes but enabling a more dynamic use of airspace with a limited requirement of physical infrastructure. Regarding the concept of drone operations, the market is driven by new business opportunities, such as delivery and data services and, above all, urban air mobility, which put strong pressure on very low level (VLL) operations, quite contrary to the current rules of the air.

The European Commission introduced the U-space initiative to establish an efficient framework for all individuals and businesses to operate drones. It refers to the low-level airspace and covers the ecosystem of services and specific procedures necessary for reliable and safe drone operations.

Today, there are a wide array of RPA types. A large number of RPA manufacturers copy designs and flight characteristics of traditional manned aircraft. RPAS are themselves multisystems and involve a wide range of equipment and payloads. The potential for civil RPAS for mobility and transportation purposes in the near future has considerable implications for airspace management. The European RPAS Steering Group

Roadmap for the integration of civil RPAS into the total civil aviation system will not focus on fully autonomous aircraft because they lack the capability of a remote pilot in command and his or her associated responsibilities. However, continuously evolving technologies will lead to an ever-increasing role for aircraft full regime flight automation. At some point in the future, it is multidisciplinary technology, mechatronics and robotics that enable automation.

The objective of the Roadmap is to support the development of RPAS applications, while ensuring the safety, security and privacy of citizens as well as the safety of other airspace users. Successful safe operations of RPAS beyond visual line of sight (BVLOS) in either controlled or uncontrolled airspace will require the availability of a variety of technologies that are suggested to require worldwide support for an effective integration.

Practically all over the world, drones are a steadily growing business, technically capable of providing services in all environments, including congested urban areas. The challenge will be to create a regulatory framework that will facilitate this expanding market, while also being able to handle the increased drone traffic alongside manned aviation safely and efficiently.

The Warsaw High Level Conference, in 2016, building on the guiding principles set forth in the Riga Declaration on RPAS, called for the development of the concept of U-space on access to low-level airspace, especially in densely populated urban areas and all related aspects such as a regulatory framework, including the timely delivery of industry standards, the efficacy and funding of drone integration projects and the development of U-space.

U-space is described as a set of new services and specific procedures designed to support safe, efficient and secure access to airspace for many drones. These services rely on a high level of digitalization and automation of functions, whether they are on board the drone itself or part of the ground-based environment. As such, U-space is enabling a framework designed to facilitate any kind of routine mission, in all classes of airspace and all types of environment, even the most congested, while addressing an appropriate interface to manned aviation, air traffic management/air navigation service (ATM/ANS) providers and authorities.

The timing for U-space is critical given the rate of growth of the drone market. The different drone services projects, including demonstrations, are the first batch of drone-centric activities within the European setting, selected and funded by the SESAR Joint Undertaking to foster the development of the U-space system, which aims to enable complex drone operations with a high degree of automation in all types of operational environments. E-identification, e-registration and pre-tactical geofencing will be the first, while subsequent U-space services and their corresponding standards need to be developed in the foreseeable future.

A frequently raised question in this context is, who controls low-altitude airspace? Another more intriguing and controversial question, who is the owner of the low-altitude airspace? The latter question happens to be one of the most important issues of the commercial and recreational drone industry.

Normally, airspace should be used at or above 500 ft AGL (over ground and water), which is the minimum safe altitude for flights over non-congested areas. Below 500 ft, flight is allowed only for take-off and landing at airports or other authorized locations, military low-flying routes and areas, medical and rescue air services and areas to execute simulated forced landings, aerial crop spraying, firefighting, etc., permitted by regulation or ad hoc exemption. Technically, drones can take off and land at any location, but especially owing to the significant proliferation of drones, boundaries are required to define where private property rights end and navigable airspace begins. This borderline is extremely important for U-space operations.

Drones have to comply with aviation rules. As for manned aircraft, a uniform implementation of and compliance with rules and procedures should apply to drone operators and remote pilots. The applicable rules and procedures for drone operations should be proportionate to the nature and risk of the operation or activity and adapted to the operational characteristics of drones concerned.

Considering the specific characteristics of drones and the contrasting natures of the operational environments, such as the population density, the presence of constructions, other obstacles and surface conditions, they should be as safe as manned aircraft. A wide range of practicable drone operations is accomplished by cutting-edge technologies that make these complex operations fail-safe. Requirements related to the degree of airworthiness, organizations, operations and licensing of persons involved should be drawn up in order to ensure safety for third parties on the surface and in the air.

Even very small drones can quickly fly high enough, thus posing a severe risk to aviation safety. The challenge is to find the balance that ensures appropriate safety yet without hampering the market, considering that a zero-risk approach is not practical, let alone feasible. The classic assumption is that only the traditional certification and licensing processes would mitigate such hazards and keep the aviation system safe. The traditional manned aviation format is likely to produce too heavy an approach to drones, especially the small-drone market.

That does not alter the fact that setting of certification standards for drones presents rather specific challenges. Design concepts vary hugely, technologies develop rapidly. Therefore, EASA is taking a flexible approach by defining certification requirements that are objective and proportionate to the risk of the drone operation. Smaller drones, in particular, are increasingly being operated within the European Union, but until recently under a fragmented regulatory framework.

More uniformity, harmonization, risk-based categorization and an overarching structure are the main objectives of new EU legislation on drones in a manner that unmanned operations, performed by professionals and other users, will deploy safely, solid and fast with less paperwork.

Drones, equipped with cameras and sensors, are able to capture personal data. The applications of drone use in the service of society are versatile, ranging from subservient to, unfortunately, more obscure tasks. As soon as a drone is flown outdoors, any camera or sensor attached to the drone will generally be directed outwards from the private setting. Increasingly sophisticated cameras and sensors are some of the characteristics that make drones unique tools for flexible, effective and discreet video surveillance and monitoring of all kinds of activities.

However, the increased use of drones, resulting in their progressive integration into the airspace, may raise serious and unique privacy and data protection concerns within society and undermine the overall benefits of this innovative technology. The logical question is whether, and if so how, such a course of action will have a real adverse impact on the fundamental rights and freedoms of others, in particular the right to the protection of personal data, and therefore actually pose serious privacy concerns.

The following drone characteristics on this issue are mentioned: the almost invisible nature of this activity, the particular intrusive character compared with different data collection technologies, the ability to process data on very wide territories along with a massive amount of information, the ability to perform continuous surveillance and collect and store indiscriminately, and the evolving character of this cutting-edge technology.

The main regulatory cornerstone of personal data protection in the European Union was Directive 95/46/EC. On 4 November 2010, the European Commission adopted a Communication entitled 'A comprehensive approach on personal data protection in the European Union', followed by an Opinion on the subject adopted by the European Data Protection Supervisor (EDPS). The intention of the Communication was to lay down the Commission's approach for the review of the EU legal system for the protection of personal data in all areas of EU activities, particularly taking account of the challenges resulting from globalization and new disrupting technologies such as drones.

It represented an important step towards such a legislative change that in turn would be the most important development in the area of EU data protection since the adoption of the 1995 Data Protection Directive, which lacked uniformity of data subjects' rights in all EU Member States. The EDPS shared the Commission's view that a strong system of data protection would be needed, based on the notion that existing general principles of data protection will still be valid in a society that undergoes fundamental changes arising from rapid technological developments and globalization.

The resulting Regulation (EU) 2016/679 (General Data Protection Regulation, GDPR), which derived most provisions from the Directive, remedied the shortcomings of the Directive by extending its scope of application. It intensified existing requirements and introduced several new ones for legal entities, such as organizations in the world that become liable to the provisions of this Regulation when processing personal data of EU residents. Although it is directly binding and applicable, it provides flexibility for certain aspects of this Regulation to be adjusted by individual EU Member States.

During the rapid development of drones, more and more questions arise about the privacy aspects associated with their use in today's society. After all, the use of drones can infringe on privacy and will therefore have some far-reaching consequences. In fact, the question is not how but when the use of drones violates the right to privacy. Provided that there is an infringement of the right to privacy, this does not necessarily mean that the infringement is not permitted.

By its very nature, privacy legislation is rather abstract, as it is not possible to provide a specific rule for every situation where privacy is an issue. First of all, it is important to establish whether the use of drones affects the private sphere. The private sphere covers the intimate aspect of a human being's personality. The total private sphere is deliminated from the public sphere by physical boundaries, such as the walls of a house, personal relationships and by selected fields of information.

Reasonable expectation of privacy is quite different if one is dealing with a camera-equipped drone or a fixed camera on the surface. The requirement of foreseeability plays an emphatic role in technologies that are increasingly sophisticated and intrusive. Depending on the intensity of the violation of the right to privacy, more detailed regulations with restrictions on the use of drones may be appropriate. It should be emphasized that it must be obvious to citizens under what circumstances the use of drones is possible and how that use can infringe on privacy.

The question also arises as to whether differentiated limits that criminal law is placing on the use of cameras and sensors qualify as applied technical devices on drones. These devices also include telecommunication tapping and placement of eavesdropping instruments. Covert filming in a home and in locations that are not accessible to the public has been made a criminal offence. It is also a criminal offence to make secret images of persons with an applied technical device in publicly accessible places. Filming is a covert activity if the presence of a camera is not clearly disclosed. The next question is whether people being photographed or filmed from the sky, for example by a drone, are recognizable. It is widely believed that there is only an image if a person, photographed or filmed, is recognizable. However, it might have far-reaching consequences if the nature of this kind of observation can be qualified as wilful and repetitive. Voyeuristic behaviour, intimidation, (cyber)stalking and harassment have been criminalized in most jurisdictions.

Regulation (EU) 2016/679 does apply in case of processing of personal data by police and judicial authorities, while Directive (EU) 2016/680 applies to the protection of public safety by police and prosecution services when they perform their duties such as prevention, investigation, detection or prosecution of criminal offences or the execution of criminal penalties.

Personal data is data regarding an identified or identifiable natural person. The principle of data protection should apply to any information concerning such a person. With the use of cameras on drones, people can be seen or observed. That does not mean that personal data is involved. This requires that the persons concerned are identifiable.

Drones equipped with visual payload, cameras and sensors allow their operators to film live and take footage of objects and individuals in private and public places, and this raises privacy issues that do not arise in the context of non-visual surveillance. Even if a drone is not equipped with that kind of payload, flying the drone over people may violate someone's privacy expectations, potentially leading to the chilling effect or constrained behaviour than would otherwise be the case. Another drone-related phenomenon is called function creep, which means that drones are purchased for specific, restricted operational uses, but are actually used intentionally for more common, controversial reasons.

Privacy issues relate not only to the drone as an aircraft or platform, but also to the payload or software with which the drone is fitted. The level of impact of this technology on individual privacy is complex as it comprises several factors. The degree of impact depends on the purpose for which drones are used as well as the extent and type of personal information that the drone may capture, the type of drone operator, the context and location of the drones and the type of technical equipment they carry.

The *privacy by design* principle is an approach to protecting privacy by embedding it into the design specifications of technologies, business practices and physical infrastructures. The application of this principle means that the responsible person, the designated controller, must take appropriate technical and organizational measures, such as minimization and pseudonymization of data, in order to comply with the regulations governing the protection of personal data.

A different principle, *privacy by default*, means that the controller takes appropriate measures that are necessary for each specific purpose of the processing, ensuring that in principle only personal data is processed. This applies to the data collected, the extent to which the data is processed, the period for which the data is stored and its accessibility. In the case of drones, both principles imply that the privacy risks are already taken into account when designing the drone and the corresponding payload with which personal data is processed, and hence the need to take technical and organizational measures to mitigate these risks.

Indeed, the utilization of drones is growing at a fast pace worldwide and showing an extremely diversified pattern. Given the forecasted economical and functional benefits of civilian drone deployment, it is important to support their development and to manage areas of uncertainty, controversy, risk or concern. The further development of drones and their expected integration into non-segregated airspace, alongside traditional manned aviation, will undoubtedly pose new challenges, calling for a significant amount of research on the subject.

A globally applicable comprehensive uniform regulatory framework on drones must create a high level of safety, security and environmental protection acceptable to society. Furthermore, it must offer enough flexibility for the emerging drone industry to evolve, innovate and mature.

A comprehensive uniform regulatory framework on drones integrated into the legal order of civil aviation can be considered a synthesis of living documents, both consistent and subject to amendment and adjustment in accordance with future knowledge, experience, new insights or topical issues, completely dependent on how the drone technology in all its aspects will continue to develop.

The harmonization of rules and regulations and the availability of spectrum are fundamental to the success of drones. Finally, the development of the drone market, including applications, services and integration, needs to be carefully monitored to lead this disruptive drone technology in the right direction. After all, the development of this emerging market largely depends on the successful implementation of a comprehensive regulatory framework that will allow for safe, secure and environmentally friendly drone operations, while technologies need to be mature enough to ensure full integration into non-segregated airspace.

Bibliography

Books

Bensoussan, A., Gazagne, D., *Droit des Systèmes Autonomes: Véhicules Intelligents, Drones, Seabots*, Bruylant Éditions Juridiques, Bruxelles: Lefebvre Sarrut Belgium S.A., 2019.

Bestaoui Sebbana, Y., *Intelligent Autonomy of UAVs: Advanced Missions and Future Use*, Boca Raton: CRC Press Taylor & Francis Group, 2018.

Cureton, P., *Drone Futures: UAS in Landscape and Urban Design*, Milton Park, Abingdon, Oxon: Routledge, 2020.

Daemen, J., Rijmen, V., *The Design of Rijndael: AES-The Advanced Encryption Standard*, Berlin, Heidelberg, New York: Springer-Verlag, 2013.

De Florio, F., *Airworthiness: An Introduction to Aircraft Certification*, Second Edition, The Boulevard, Langford Lane, Oxford: Butterworth-Heinemann, 2011.

De Florio, F., *Airworthiness: An Introduction to Aircraft Certification and Operations*, Third Edition, The Boulevard, Langford Lane, Kidlington, Oxford: Butterworth-Heinemann, 2016.

Desmond, K., *Electric Airplanes and Drones: A History*, Jefferson, North Carolina: McFarland & Company Inc. Publishers, 2018.

Diederiks-Verschoor, I.H.Ph., Butler, M.A. (Legal advisor), *An Introduction to Air Law*, Eighth Revised Edition, Alphen aan den Rijn: Kluwer Law International, 2006.

Fukuyama, F., *After the Neocons: America at the Crossroads*, London: Profile Books, 2006.

Giemulla, E.M., Weber, L. (Eds.), *International and EU Aviation Law*, Selected Issues, Alphen aan den Rijn: Kluwer Law International, 2011.

Gynnild, A., Uskali, T. (Eds.), *Responsible Drone Journalism*, Routledge Focus, Milton Park, Abingdon, Oxon: Routledge, 2018.

Haanappel, P.P.C., *The Law and Policy of Airspace and Outer Space*, The Hague: Kluwer Law International, 2003.

Hodgekinson, D.I., Johnston, R., *Aviation Law and Drones: Unmanned Aircraft and the Future of Aviation*, Milton Park, Abingdon, Oxon: Routledge, 2018.

Kreuzer, M.P., *Drones and the Future of Warfare: The Evolution of Remotely Piloted Aircraft*, CASS Military Studies, Milton Park, Abingdon, Oxon: Routledge, 2016.

Masutti, A., Tomasello, F., *International Regulation of Non-Military Drones*, Cheltenham: Edward Elgar Publishing, 2018.

Milde, M., *International Air Law and ICAO*, Essential Air and Space Law Volume 4, Series Editor Benkö, M.E., Utrecht: Eleven International Publishing, 2008.

Mohanty, S., Vyas, S., *How to Compete in the Age of Artificial Intelligence: Implementing a Collaborative Human-Machine Strategy for your Business*, New York City: Apress, 2018.

Newell, C.R., Shrader, C.R., *Of Duty Well and Faithfully Done: A History of the Regular Army in the Civil War*, Lincoln: University of Nebraska Press, 2011.

Schnitker, R.M., van het Kaar, D., *Preserving Airspace Access for Air Sports: The International Regulation of Air Sports*, Amsterdam: Berghauser Pont Publishing, 2018, Foreword by Alvaro de Orléans-Borbón, FAI Executive Director.

Scott, B.I. (Ed.), *The Law of Unmanned Aircraft Systems: An Introduction to the Current and Future Regulation under National, Regional and International Law*, Aviation Law and Policy Series, Alphen aan den Rijn: Kluwer Law International, 2016, Foreword by Pablo Mendes de Leon, Director of the International Institute of Air and Space Law, Leiden University.

Shepherdson, K., Hioe, W., Boxall, L., *99 Privacy Breaches to Beware Of: Practical Data Protection Tips from Real-Life Experiences*, Singapore: Marshall Cavendish Business, 2018.

Stanley II, R.M. (Colonel Ret.), *V-Weapons Hunt: Defeating German Secret Weapons*, Barnsley, South Yorkshire: Pen & Sword Military, 2010.

Verzijl, J.H.W., *International Law in Historical Perspective*, Volume III, Leyden: Sijthoff, 1970.

Wallace, R.M.M., *International Law*, Third Edition, London: Sweet & Maxwell, 1997.

Articles and Reports

Altawy, R., Youssef, A.M., 'Security, Privacy, and Safety Aspects of Civilian Drones: A Survey', *ACM Transactions on Cyber-Physical-Systems* 1(2), Article No. 7, November 2016.

Baxter, William E., 'Samuel P. Langley: Aviation Pioneer' (Part I), *Smithonian Libraries*.

Boucher, Ph., 'Civil Drones in Society: Societal and Ethics Aspects of Remotely Piloted Aircraft Systems', *Report EUR 26823 EN, JRC Science and Policy Reports*, European Commission Joint Research Center Institute for the Protection and Security of the Citizen, Luxembourg, 2014.

Bracken-Roche, C., Lyon, D., Mansour, M.J., Molnar, A., Saulnier, A., Thompson, S., 'Surveillance Drones: Privacy Implications of the Spread of Unmanned Aerial Vehicles (UAVs) in Canada', *A Report to the Office of the Privacy Commissioner of Canada, under the 2013-2014 Contribution Program*, Quebec, 30 April 2014.

Brightmore, D., 'How Drone Technology is Influencing the Mining Industry', *Mining Global*, 13 November 2019.

Burger, R., '6 Ways Drones are Affecting the Construction Industry', *The Balance Small Business*, 15 August 2019.

Card, B. A., 'Terror from Above: How the Commercial UAV Revolution Threatens the US Threshold', *Air and Space Power Journal*, Vol. 32, no. 1, Spring 2018.

Cavoukian, A. (Information and Privacy Commissioner of Ontario, Canada), 'Privacy and Drones: Unmanned Aerial Vehicles', *Privacy by Design*, August 2012 (https://www.ipc.on.ca/wp-content/uploads/resources/pbd-drones.pdf).

Cheng, A., Howard, A., Meyer, T., 'With Billions at Stake, States Lobby for Drone Test Sites', *National Security Zones*, 2013.

Clark, R., 'Privacy Impact Assessments', *Xamax Consultancy Pty Ltd.*, Canberra, February 1998.

Connot, M.J., Zummo, J.J., 'United States: Navigable Airspace: Where Private Property Rights End and Navigable Airspace Begins', *Fox Rothschild LLP*, 2016.

'Convention Relating to the Regulation of Aerial Navigation', *Journal of Air Law and Commerce* 94, 1930.

Corrigan, J., 'FAA Predicts the Commercial Drone Market Will Triple by 2023', *Nextgov*, 3 May 2019.

De Jager, W., 'EU Droneregels: systeem van "drone zones" gaat kaart vervangen' (EU Drone rules: system of drone zones will replace the chart), *Dronewatch*, 17 April 2020.

Farner, M. (Manager Innovation and Advanced Technologies), 'SORA: Risk Assessment for Unmanned Airborne Mobility', *Federal Office of Civil Aviation FOCA*, Winterthur, 2017.

Finn, R.L., Wright, D., Donovan, A., Jacques, L., De Hert, P., 'Privacy, Data Protection and Ethical Risks in Civil Remotely Piloted Aircraft Systems Operations', Final Report, European Commission, Directorate-General Enterprise and Industries, Luxembourg: Publications Office of the European Union, November 2014.

Greenberg, Jared, 'Who Controls Low-Altitude Airspace?', *Los Angeles & San Francisco Daily Journal*, 4 May 2017.

Grief, N., 'The Legal Principles Governing the Control of National Airspace and Flight Information Regions and their Application to the Eastern Mediterranean', Report, Larnaca: European Rim Policy and Investment Council, 23 October 2009.

Guo, Y., 'Regulation of Drones from a Safety Perspective: With Special Focus on the EU Drone Regime', *Leiden University, Institute of Air and Space Law*, 26 August 2019.

Hawkins, S. (Senior Inspector of Air Accidents, UK AAIB), 'The Benefits of Using Drones at Aircraft Accident Sites', *ECACNews* # Spring 2017.

Hunter, S.K., Lt. Col. (Air Force Space Command), 'Safe Operations Above FL 600', *Space Traffic Management Conference*, Embry-Riddle Aeronautical University, 2015.

Keefe, P., Elmer, A., 'Sperry: Pioneer of Modern Naval Tech', *Marine Link*, 16 May 2014.

Khan, S., 'The Drone Market Could Triple in Size by 2023, Says the FAA', *The Science Times*, 24 May 2019.

Kikuchi, I., 'The Terrifying German "Revenge Weapons" of the Second World War', *Imperial War Museum* (GB), 18 July 2018.

Liptak, A., 'The FAA Says the Commercial Drone Market Could Triple in Size by 2023', *The Verge*, 4 May 2019.

Luckerson, V., 'Passenger Plane Barely Dodges Drone Above New York', *Time*, 29 May 2015.

Marr, B., 'Robots and Drones are Now Used to Fight COVID-19', *Forbs*, 18 March 2020.

Murphy, K., 'FAA Releases Final Rule on Remote ID and Operations Over People/Night Flights', *DPReview*, 29 December 2020.

National Academies of Sciences, Engineering, and Medicine, 'Assessing the Risks of Integrating Unmanned Aircraft Systems into the National Airspace System', Washington: The National Academies Press, 2018.

Niles, R., 'Drone Pilot Facing $ 182,000 In Fines', *AVweb*, 3 January 2021.

Osborn, K., 'Airforce Plans Recoverable Hypersonic Drones by 2040', *Defence Systems*, 23 March 2017.

Ostrower, J., 'Emergency Autoland puts Garmin on the Bleeding Edge of Autonomous Flying', *The Air Current*, 3 November 2019.

Pauner, C., Vigury, J., 'A Legal Approach to Civilian Use of Drones in Europe: Privacy and Personal Data Protection Concerns', Roma: Democracy Security Review Anno V, No. 3, 27 October 2015.

Polloczek, D., 'An Accident Waiting to Happen', European Cockpit Association Editorial of 21 September 2015.

Romli, F.I., King, J.D., Li, L. and Clarke, J.P., 'Impact of ADS-B on TCAS Performance', *American Institute of Aeronautics and Astronautics*, 2008.

Salter, M., 'Toys for the Boys? Drones Pleasure and Popular Culture in the Militarization of Policing', *Critical Criminology* 22(2), 2014.

Schilz, C.B., 'Terrorgefahr: EU warnt vor "feindseligen Akten" durch Drohnen', *Welt am Sonntag*, 3 August 2019.

Schubert, T., 'Drones: Work on the U-space Reegulation Advances', *Newsletter EAS*, July 2020.

Smith, D., 'Seventy Years On, Antwerp Remembers the V-bomb', *Flanders Today*, 27 September 2019.

Sorcher, S., 'The Backlash against Drones', *National Journal*, 2013.

Stamp, J., 'World War I: 100 Years Later – Unmanned Drones have been around since World War I', *Smithonian.com*, 2013.

Stanley, J., Crump, C., 'Protecting Privacy from Aerial Surveillance: Recommendations for Government Use of Drone Aircraft', Report, New York: American Civil Liberties Union, December 2011.

Straub, J., 'Unmanned Aerial Systems: Consideration of the Use of Force for Law Enforcement Applications', *Technology in Society* 39, November 2014.

Van Alsenoy, B., 'The Evolving Role of the Individual under EU Data Protection Law', KU Leuven Center for IT & IP Law, *ICRI Working Paper Series*, 10 August 2015.

Verstraete, D. (University of Sydney), 'Climate Explained: Why Don't We Have Electric Aircraft?', *The Conversation*, 20 September 2019.

Wallace, R.J., Loffi, J.M., 'Evolution of UAS Policy in the Wake of Taylor v. Huerta', *International Journal of Aviation, Aeronautics, and Aerospace* 4(3), 2017.

Ware, Jacob, 'Terrorist Groups, Artificial Intelligence, and Killer Drones', *War on the Rocks*, 24 September 2019.

Xu, Y., 'TCAS/ADS-B Integrated Surveillance and Collision Avoidance System', Aviation Engineering Institute Civil Aviation Flight University of China, Guanghan, Sichuan, China, Paris: Atlantis Press, 2013.

DOCUMENTS, CASES AND LEGISLATION

Article 29 Data Protection Working Party 0829/14/EN WP 216 Opinion 05/2014 on Anonymization Techniques, adopted on 10 April 2014.

Article 29 Data Protection Working Party 01673/15/EN WP 231 Opinion 01/2015 on Privacy and Data Protection Issues relating to the Utilization of Drones, adopted on 16 June 2015.

Case *United States v. Causby*, 328 U.S. 256(1946).

Case *Griggs v. Allegheny County*, 369 U.S. 84 (1963).

Case *Pierre Herbecq and the Association Ligue des droits de l'homme v. Belgium*. Decision of 14 January 1998 on the admissibility of the applications. Applications No. 32200/96 and No. 32201/96.

Case C-101/01(Lindqvist-case) of November 2003. *Bodil Lindqvist v. Åklagerkammaren i Jönköping* (2003).

Case *Boggs v. Merideth*, Civil Action No. 3: 16-CV-00006-TBR Document 20 (W.D. Ky. 2007).

Case C-212/13 of 19 April 2013. Request for a preliminary ruling from the nejvyšš správni soud (Czech Republic). *Frãntisek Ryneš v. Úřad pro ochranu osobních údasjů*.

Case *Taylor v. Huerta. John A. Taylor, Petitioner v. Michael P. Huerta*, as Administrator, Federal Aviation Administration, Respondent, on Petitions for Review of Orders of the FAA, No. 15-1302, U.S. Court of Appeals for the District of Columbia Circuit, decided May 19, 2017 (No. 15-1495).

Case *Singer v. City of Newton*, Massachusetts District Court Finds Portion of Local Drone Ordinance Preempted by FAA Regulation. Case No. CV 17-10071, 2017 WL 4176477 (D. Mass., 21 September 2017).

FAA Integration of Civil Unmanned Aircraft Systems (UAS) in the National Airspace System (NAS) Roadmap: A Five-year roadmap for the introduction of civil UAS into the NAS, Second Edition, July 2018.

Charter of Fundamental Rights of the European Union (2012/C 326/02) (CFREU), *OJ* C 326/391, 26 October 2012.

Convention on International Civil Aviation, Chicago 1944.

EASA A-NPA No. 16-2005 Policy for Unmanned Aerial Vehicle (UAV) Certification.

EASA Concept of Operations: A risk based approach to regulation of unmanned aircraft. Publication type: EASA Brochure, published on 01 May 2015.

EASA A-NPA No. 2015-10 Introduction of a regulatory framework for the operation of drones, 31 July 2015.

EASA NPA 2017-05 Introduction of a regulatory framework for the operation of drones – Unmanned aircraft system operations in the Open and Specific categories.

EASA Terms of Reference for rulemaking task RTM 0230, regulatory framework to accommodate unmanned aircraft systems in the European aviation system, Issue 2, 4 June 2018.

EASA Explanatory Note to Decision 2019/021/R, Introduction of a regulatory framework for the operation of unmanned aircraft systems in the Open and Specific categories.

EASA NPA 2019-07 Management of information security risks. RTM.0720.

Electronic Code of Federal Regulations (e-CFR): Title 14. Aeronautics and Space.

EUROCONTROL. UAS ATM Integration Operational Concept, European Organization for the Safety of the Air Navigation, Directorate of European Civil-Military Aviation (DECMA) and Aviation Cooperation and Strategies Division (ACS), Edition 1.0, 27 November 2018.

European Convention on Human Rights (ECHR), 3 September 1953.

FAA Integration of Unmanned Aircraft Systems (UAS) in the National Airspace System (NAS) Roadmap, First Edition 2013.

FAA Reauthorization Act of 2018 One Hundred Fifteenth Congress of the United States of America at the Second Session, 3 January 2018 (signed into law on 5 October 2018).

FAA NASA Unmanned Aircraft Systems (UAS) Traffic management (UTM) UTM Pilot Program (UPP) UPP Summary Report, October 2018.

FAA 49 U.S.C. 44809 Exception for limited recreational operations of unmanned aircraft (text contains those laws in effect on 7 September 2020), from Title 49 – Transportation, subtitle VII Aviation Programs, Part A Air Commerce and Safety, subpart iii safety, Chapter 448-UAS (New FAA Recreational Drone Laws, May 2019).

Final Report Mid-term evaluation of Regulation (EC) No. 785/2004 on insurance requirements of air carriers and aircraft operators, London: *Steer Davies Gleave*, July 2012.

BIBLIOGRAPHY

Global Air Traffic Management Operational Concept, First Edition 2005 (Doc 9854 AN/458).

Flightpath 2050 Europe's Vision for Aviation, Maintaining Global Leadership & Serving Society's Needs, Report of the High Level Group on Aviation Research, Luxembourg: Publication Office of the European Union, 2011.

ICAO Doc 9931 Continuous Descent Operations (CDO) Manual First Edition 2010.

ICAO Circular 328 AN/190 Unmanned Aircraft Systems (UAS), 2011.

ICAO Circular 330 AN/189 Civil/Military Cooperation in Air Traffic Management, 2011.

ICAO Doc 9993 Continuous Climb Operations (CCO) Manual First Edition 2013.

ICAO Doc 10039 AN/511 Manual on System Wide Information Management (SWIM) Concept, 2015.

ICAO Manual on Remotely Piloted Aircraft Systems (RPAS) Doc 10019 AN/507 First Edition 2015.

ICAO Safety Management Manual Doc 9859 AN/474, Fourth Edition 2017.

ICAO Remotely Piloted Aircraft System (RPAS) Concept of Operations (CONOPS) for International IFR Operations, March 2017.

JARUS UAS Operational Categorization, Document Identifier JAR-DEL-WG7-UASOC-D.04.

JARUS CS-UAS Recommendations for Certification Specification for Unmanned Aircraft Systems, Edition 1.0, 6 September 2019.

Pan-American (Inter-American) Convention on Commercial Aviation, Havana 1928.

Position Paper: Civil Drones, October 2016, Bundesverband der Deutschen Luftverkehrswirtschaft e.V. (BDL).

Roadmap for the Integration of Civil Remotely-Piloted Aircraft Systems into the European Aviation System, Final Report from the European RPAS Steering Group, June 2013.

SESAR European ATM Master Plan: Digitalizing Europe's Aviation Infrastructure, Executive View, 2020 Edition, December 2019.

SESAR European ATM Master Plan: The Roadmap for Delivering High Performing Aviation in Europe, Executive View, Edition 2015.

SESAR European Drones Outlook Study: Unlocking the Value for Europe, November 2016.

SESAR European ATM Master Plan: Roadmap for the Safe Integration of Drones in All Classes of Airspace, 2018.

SESAR JU Initial View on Principles for the U-space Architecture, Edition 01.04, 29 July 2019.

SESAR JU U-space: Supporting Safe and Secure Drone Operations in Europe: A Preliminary Summary of SESAR U-space Research and Innovation Results (2017-2019), SESAR JU 2020.

Small Remotely Piloted Aircraft Systems (drones) Mid-Air Collision Study, Military Aviation Authority (MAA), British Pilots' Association (BALPA), and the Department of Transport, 2016.

Universal Declaration of Human Rights (UDHR), 10 December 1948.

Study No. 404/2006 CDL-AD(2007)14 European Commission for Democracy through Law (Venice Commission), Opinion on Video Surveillance in Public Places by Public Authorities and the Protection of Human Rights Adopted by the Venice Commission at its 70th Planery Session (Venice, 16-17 March 2007), on the basis of comments by: van Dijk, P., Dimitrijevic, V. and Buttarelli, G., Strasbourg, 23 March 2007.

Council Regulation (EEC) No. 2407/92 of 23 July 1992 on licensing of air carriers, OJ L 240/1, 24 August 1992.

Regulation (EC) No. 45/2001 of the European parliament and of the Council of 18 December 2000 on the protection of individuals with regard to the processing of personal data by the Community institutions and bodies and on the free movement of such data, OJ L 8/1, 12 January 2001.

Regulation (EC) No. 549/2004 of the European Parliament and of the Council of 10 March 2004 laying down the framework for the creation of the single European sky (the framework Regulation), OJ L 96/1, 31 March 2004.

Regulation (EC) No. 550/2004 of the European Parliament and of the Council of 10 March 2004 on the provision of air navigation services in the single European sky (the service provision Regulation), OJ L 96/10, 31 March 2004.

Regulation (EC) No. 551/2004 of the European Parliament and of the Council of 10 March 2004 on the organization and use of the airspace in the single European Sky (the airspace Regulation), OJ L 96/20, 31 March 2004.

Regulation (EC) No. 552/2004 of the European Parliament and of the Council of 10 March 2004 on the interoperability of the European Air Traffic Management network (the interoperability Regulation), OJ L 96/26, 31 March 2004.

Regulation (EC) No. 785/2004 of the European parliament and of the Council of 21 April 2004 on insurance requirements for air carriers and aircraft operators, OJ L 138/1, 30 April 2004.

Commission Regulation (EC) No. 2150/2005 of 23 December 2005 laying down rules for flexible use of airspace, OJ L 342/20, 24 December 2005.

Council Regulation (EC) No. 219/2007 of 27 February 2007 on the establishment of a Joint Undertaking to develop the new generation European air traffic management system (Single European Sky ATM Research, SESAR), OJ L 64/1, 2 March 2007.

Regulation (EC) No. 216/2008 of the European Parliament and of the Council of 20 February 2008 on common rules in the field of civil aviation and establishing a European Aviation Safety Agency, and repealing Council Directive 91/670/EEC, Regulation (EC) No. 1592/2002 and Directive 2004/36/EC, OJ L 79/1, 19 March 2008.

Regulation (EC) No. 765/2008 of the European Parliament and of the Council of 9 July 2008 setting out the requirements for accreditation and market surveillance relating to the marketing of products and repealing Regulation (EEC) No. 339/93, *OJ* L 218/30, 13 August 2008.

Regulation (EC) 768/2008 of the European Parliament and of the Council of 9 July 2008 on a common framework for the marketing of products, and repealing Council Decision 93/465/EC, *OJ* L 218/82, 13 August 2008.

Regulation (EC) No. 1008/2008 of the European parliament and of the Council of 24 September 2008 on common rules for the operation of air services in the Community (Recast), *OJ* L 293/3, 31 October 2008.

Commission Implementing Regulation (EU) No. 1207/2011 of 22 November 2011 laying down requirements for the performance and the interoperability of surveillance for the single European sky, *OJ* L 305/35, 23 November 2011.

Commission Regulation (EU) No. 1332/2011 of 16 December 2011 laying down common airspace usage requirements and operating procedures for airborne collision avoidance, *OJ* L 336/20, 20 December 2011.

Commission Regulation (EU) No. 748/2012 of 3 August 2012 laying down implementing rules for the airworthiness and environmental certification of aircraft and related products, parts and appliances, as well as for the certification of design and product organizations, *OJ* L 224/1, 21 August 2012.

Commission Regulation (EU) No. 923/2012 of 26 September 2012 laying down the common rules of the air and operational provisions regarding services and procedures in air navigation and amending Implementing Regulation (EU) No. 1035/2011 and Regulations (EC) No.1265/2007, (EC) No. 1794/2006, (EC) No. 730/2006, (EC) No. 1033/2006 and (EU) No. 255/2010, *OJ* L 281/1, 13 October 2012.

Commission Regulation (EU) No. 965/2012 of 5 October 2012 laying down technical requirements and administrative procedures related to air operations pursuant to Regulation (EC) No. 216/2008 of the European Parliament and of the Council, *OJ* L 296/1, 25 October 2012.

Commission Regulation (EU) No. 1028/2014 of 26 September 2014 amending Commission Implementing Regulation (EU) No. 1207/2011, *OJ* L 284/7, 30 September 2014.

Regulation (EU) No. 2016/679 of the European Parliament and of the Council of 27 April 2016 on the protection of natural persons with regard to the processing of personal data and on the free movement of such data, and repealing Directive 95/46/EC (General Data Protection Regulation), *OJ* L 119/1, 4 May 2016.

Commission Implementing Regulation (EU) 2016/1185 of 20 July 2016 amending Implementing Regulation (EU) No. 923/2012 as regards the update and completion of the common rules of the air and operational provisions regarding services and procedures in air navigation (SERA Part C) and repealing Regulation (EC) No. 730/2006, *OJ* L196/3, 21 July 2016.

Commission Implementing Regulation (EU) 2017/386 of 6 March 2017 amending Implementing Regulation (EU) No. 1207/2011 laying down requirements for the performance and the interoperability of surveillance for the single European sky, *OJ* L 59/34, 7 March 2017.

Regulation (EU) 2018/1139 of the European Parliament and of the Council of 4 July 2018 on common rules in the field of civil aviation and establishing a European Union Aviation Agency, and amending Regulations (EC) No. 2111/2005, (EC) No. 1008/2008, (EU) No. 996/2010, (EU) No. 376/2014 and Directives 2014/30/EU and 2014/53/EU of the European Parliament and of the Council, and repealing Regulations (EC) No. 552/2004 and (EC) No. 216/2008 of the European Parliament and of the Council and Council Regulation (EEC) No. 3922/91, *OJ* L 212/1, 22 August 2018.

Regulation (EU) No. 2019/2 of the European Parliament and of the Council of 11 December 2018 amending Regulation (EC) No. 1008/2008 on common rules for the operation of air services in the Community, *OJ* L 11/1, 14 January 2019.

Commission Delegated Regulation (EU) 2019/945 of 12 March 2019 on unmanned aircraft systems and on third-country operators of unmanned aircraft systems, *OJ* L 152/1, 11 June 2019.

Commission Implementing Regulation (EU) 2019/947 of 24 May 2019 on the rules and procedures for the operation of unmanned aircraft, *OJ* L152/45, 11 June 2019.

Commission Implementing Regulation (EU) 2020/746 of 4 June 2020 amending Implementing Regulation (EU) 2019/947 as regards postponing dates of application of certain measures in the context of the COVID-19 pandemic, *OJ* L 176/13, 5 June 2020.

Commission Delegated Regulation (EU) 2020/1058 of 27 April 2020 amending Delegated Regulation (EU) 2019/945 as regards the introduction of two new unmanned aircraft systems classes, *OJ* L 232/1, 20 July 2020.

Commission Implementing Regulation (EU) 2020/639 of 12 May 2020 amending Implementing Regulation (EU) 2019/947 as regards standard scenarios for operations executed in or beyond the visual line of sight, *OJ* L 150/1, 13 May 2020.

Directive 95/46/EC of the European Parliament and of the Council of 24 October 1995 on the protection of individuals with regard to the processing of personal data and on the free movement of such data, *OJ* L 281/31, 23 November 1995 (Data Protection Directive).

Directive 2014/30/EU of the European Parliament and of the Council of 26 February 2014 on the harmonization of the laws of the Member States relating to electromagnetic compliance, *OJ* L 96/79, 29 March 2014.

Directive 2014/53/EU of the European Parliament and of the Council of 16 April 2014 on the harmonization of the laws of the Member States relating to the making available on the market of radio equipment and repealing Directive 1999/5/EC, *OJ* L 153/62, 22 May 2014.

Directive (EU) 2016/680 of the European Parliament and of the Council of 27 April 2016 on the protection of natural persons with regard to the processing of personal data by competent authorities for the purposes of the prevention, investigation, detection or prosecution of criminal offences or the execution of criminal penalties, and on the free movement of such data, and repealing Council Framework Decision 2008/977/JHA, *OJ* L 119/89, 4 May 2016.

COM(2012) 10 final, 2012/0010 (COD), Proposal for a Directive of the European Parliament and of the Council on the protection of individuals with regard to the processing of personal data by competent authorities for the purposes of prevention, investigation, detection or prosecution of criminal offences or the execution of criminal penalties, and the free movement of such data, Brussels, 25 January 2012.

COM(2012) 11 final, 2012/0011 (COD), Brussels, 25 January 2012, Proposal for a Regulation of the European Parliament and of the Council on the protection of individuals with regard to the processing of personal data and the free movement of such data (General Data Protection Regulation).

COM(2014) 207 final, (2015/C 012/14), Communication from the Commission to the European parliament and the Council. A new era for aviation. Opening the aviation market to the civil use of remotely piloted aircraft systems in a safe and sustainable manner, Brussels, 8 April 2014.

COM(2015) 613 final 2015/0277 (COD), Brussels, 7 December 2015 Proposal for a Regulation of the European Parliament and of the Council on common rules in the field of civil aviation and establishing a European Union Aviation Safety Agency, and repealing Regulation (EC) No. 216/2008 of the European Parliament and of the Council.

About the Authors

Dick van het Kaar, LL.M., has worked in the aviation industry for more than 40 years. He started his flying career as a Royal Netherlands Air Force helicopter and jet fighter pilot and flight instructor. In 1977 he joined the world of commercial aviation, logging over 23,000 flying hours. During his career as a senior captain B747 at KLM/Martinair between flights around the world, he studied International Law at the Open University of The Netherlands, where he earned his Master of Laws degree.

Dick van het Kaar was a member of the Appeal Council of the Dutch Airline Pilots Association and is author of a wide variety of aviation law-related essays, books and articles in a number of leading international air and space law journals. Following a six-year term as a board member at the Royal Netherlands Aeronautical Association, he now holds, within this organization, the positions of chairman of the Legal Committee and senior adviser on issues regarding rules of the air, airspace infrastructure and environmental affairs. Dick van het Kaar has for many years been associated, as an external examiner, with the Aviation Academy of the Amsterdam University of Applied Sciences.

Dr. *Ronald M. Schnitker* received a Master of Laws at the Open University of The Netherlands, and obtained his PhD at Tilburg University. As an judicial expert in the field of aviation law and aviation accident investigation, he has served as Head of Aviation Investigations of the Aviation Branch of the Dutch National Police Force, been Policy Officer at the Public Prosecutor's Office, and fulfilled the role of Head of Legal Affairs at Eindhoven Airport.

Alongside this, he has been a board member in several aviation organizations, President of the Royal Netherlands Aeronautical Association, and a member of the Fédération Aéronautique Internationale Statutes Working Group. He advocates the Rights of Recreational and Air Sports and conceived the FAI Manifesto: Preserving Airspace Access for Air Sports.

Ronald Schnitker is currently an aviation lawyer, specializing in the field of General Aviation. He is the author of many articles and (study) books in the field of aviation law and is examiner for Air Law & Operational Procedures (ATPL/PPL).

INDEX

1

1919 Paris Convention, xiii, 159, 333
1928 Havana Convention, xiv, 159
1944 Convention on International Civil Aviation, xiii
1952 Rome Convention, 130
1971 Montreal Convention, 130

2

2001 Cape Town Convention, 130

A

above ground level (AGL), 62
Acceptable Means of Compliance (AMC), 62
Advanced Flexible Use of Airspace (AFUA), 160
aerodrome traffic zone (ATZ), 140
Aerodrome Flight Information Service (AFIS), 140
Air Navigation Commission (ANC), 38, 327
air navigation service providers (ANSPs), 38, 162, 254
air traffic management/air navigation services (ATM/ANS), 56, 335
air transport pilot licence (ATPL), 36
Aircraft Certification, 100
aircraft-centric approach, 56, 89
airspace infringement, 134, 220
Airspace Management Cell (AMC), 225
Airworthiness Design Standard (ADS), 246
American Civil Liberties Union (ACLU), 312

anonymization, 299
Area Navigation (RNAV), 161
artificial intelligence (AI), 10, 17, 29-30, 74, 321
artificial neural network (ANN), 203
Automatic Dependent Surveillance-Broadcast (ADS-B), 161
autonomous aerial vehicles, 5, 320

B

basic regulation, 52, 56, 63, 86
bottom-up approach, 106

C

cargo air vehicles (CAVs), 27, 178
category
- certified, 56, 59, 62, 95, 252, 260, 267
- open, xvii, 56, 92, 142, 232, 234, 262, 330
- specific, xvii, 56, 66, 78, 92, 137, 234, 241, 260, 267, 330
- subcategory, 11, 81, 234, 238, 249, 260, 322

CBAs (Cross-Border Areas), 163
CE marking, 68, 92
Center, 101, 123
Central Flow Management Unit (CFMU), 225
certificate of airworthiness, 44, 46, 51, 53, 96, 130, 230, 240, 246, 254-255
certification specifications, 58, 76, 248, 252, 267
Circular 328 AN/190, xvi, 12, 34, 43, 139, 322

civil aviation authorities (CAAs), xiii, 52, 197, 305, 332
Clear Air Situation for UAS (CLASS), 165
closed-circuit television (CCTV), 282
command and control (C2) data link, 10
commercial air transport, 53, 173, 329
Commission Delegated Regulation (EU) 2019/945, 11
Commission Implementing Regulation (EU) No. 1207/2011, 161
Commission Implementing Regulation (EU) No. 2019/947, xvii, 147
Commission Implementing Regulation (EU) No. 923/2012, 266
communications, navigation and surveillance (CNS), 171, 255
concept of operations (CONOPS), xiv, 56, 179
Continuous Climb Operation (CCO), 163
Continuous Descent Operation (CDO), 163
control zone (CTR), 134
CORUS (Concept of Operation for European UTM Systems), 189
Covid-19, 17, 70, 137, 258, 268, 324
crew resource management (CRM), 37
cybersecurity, 49, 103, 188, 305

D

data protection, 177, 285
Data Protection Directive, 175, 337
data protection impact assessment, 239
Daylight Operations, 107
deep learning (DL), 75
delegated act, 67, 146, 254
Drone Helsinki Declaration, 72
drone no-fly zones, 92, 258
Drone Operator Safety Act of 2017, 106
dynamic inter-drone communication, 317

E

e-identification, 73, 116, 191, 206, 249, 335
emergency response plan (ERP), 242
Europe Air Sports (EAS), 152
European ATM Master Plan, 168, 175, 195
European Civil Aviation Conference (ECAC), 14
European Cockpit Association (ECA), 71
European Convention on Human Rights (ECHR), 272
European Data Protection Supervisor (EDPS), 270, 337
European Defence Agency (EDA), 127
European RPAS Steering Group (ERSG), 168, 334
exclusive economic zone (EEZ), 155
extended visual line of sight (EVLOS), 118, 139

F

FAA Joint Planning and Development Office (JPDO), 100
FAA Modernization and Reform Act, 99, 120
FAA Reauthorization Act of 2018, 109, 122, 143
FAI (Fédération Aéronautique), 148
Federal Aviation Regulations (FARs), 116, 231
Federal Register Notice (FRN), 111
First-Person View (FPV), 107
Flexible Use of Airspace (FUA), 160
Flight Information Management System (FIMS), 122
flight termination system (FTS), 242

G

General Air Traffic (GAT), 55
general aviation (GA), 173

general aviation rules, 233
General Data Protection Regulation (GDPR), 87, 337
geofencing, 30, 45, 60, 67, 118, 165, 191, 198, 213, 257, 306, 335
Global Air Navigation Plan (GANP), 174
Global UTM Association (GUTMA), 190
Ground and Airborne Sense & Avoid, 100
ground control station (GCS), 8, 314

H

High-Altitude Long Endurance (HALE), 25, 103
High-Altitude Pseudo Satellite (HAPS), 25
high-level flight rules (HFR), 227

I

ICAO Remotely Piloted Aircraft Systems Panel (RPASP), 247
ICAO Standards and Recommended Practices (SARPs), xv
Implementing Act, 67, 146
implementing rules, 76, 322
instrument flight rules (IFR), 43, 167, 229
International Civil Aviation Organization (ICAO), 10, 33, 321

J

Joint Authorities for Rulemaking on Unmanned Systems (JARUS), 176, 252
Joint Aviation Authorities (JAA), 37

K

Kettering Bug, 3, 320

L

launch and recovery equipment (LRE), 253
light aircraft pilot licence (LAPL), 36
Light UAS Operator Certificate, 61, 236, 239-240, 243
Low Altitude Authorization Notification Capability (LAANC), 111
low risk, 56, 79, 119, 262, 330
low-altitude airspace, 45, 124, 212, 219, 335
low-level flight rules (LFR), 227

M

maximum take-off mass, xvii, 329
model aircraft, xvi, 34, 60, 62, 67, 89, 111, 150, 234

N

National Aero Clubs, 151, 222
national airspace system (NAS), 96, 331
National Transportation Safety Board (NTSB), 115
non-segregated airspace, xii, 13, 34, 49, 94, 132, 214, 322, 328, 340
Notice of Proposed Rulemaking (NPRM), 108
Notice to Airmen (NOTAM), 225

O

Operation Authorization, 236, 239, 264
optionally piloted aircraft, 214, 253

P

Package Delivery by Drone, 113, 116
Performance-Based Navigation (PBN), 161
pilotless aircraft, xiii, xiv, 10, 33, 115, 319
Pre-Defined Risk Assessment (PDRA), 262
privacy
– by design, 285, 288, 291, 339

– by default, 285, 288, 339
Privacy Impact Assessment (PIA), 285
Procedures for Air Navigation Services (PANS), xv, 322
Prototype Regulation, 59, 65
pseudonymization, 286, 296, 298, 339

Q
Queen Bee, 4

R
Radio Control Multi-rotor FPV Racing, 150
regulatory framework, xvii, 34, 40, 67, 131, 186, 256, 321, 324
remote identification, 68, 122, 237, 306
remotely piloted aircraft, xii, xiv, 10, 15, 46, 54, 139, 321
remotely piloted aircraft system (RPAS), 38, 162, 307
Required Navigation Performance (RNP), 161
research and development, 135, 184, 332
restricted certificate of airworthiness (R-CofA), 240
Riga Declaration, 55, 335
RPAS Operator Certificate (ROC), 47, 137, 183
rules of the air, 13-14, 36, 44, 132, 156, 217, 230, 326-327

S
search and rescue, 21, 99, 197, 324
significant meteorological information (SIGMET), 225
Single European Sky (SES), 53, 55, 98, 169, 329
Single European Sky ATM Research (SESAR), 45, 165, 321

situational awareness, 19, 119, 182, 214, 317
Small Unmanned Aircraft Systems, 108
special conditions (SC), 267
Specific Assurance and Integrity Levels (SAIL), 80
Specific Operations Risk Assessment (SORA), 62
standard scenarios, 58, 78, 146, 262
Standardized European Rules of the Air (SERA), 52, 232, 329
State of Design, 47, 131, 246
State of Registry, 47, 132, 233, 245
State of the Operator, 47, 244
SWIM (System Wide Information Management), 223
synthetic vision systems (SVSs), 131, 181

T
third-country operators, 67, 148
transponder mandatory zone (TMZ), 153
Treaty establishing the European Community (TEC), 271
Treaty on the Functioning of the European Union (TFEU), 87, 271
Type Certificate, 131, 246, 248, 253
Type Certification, 96
Type Design, 47, 96, 183, 246
Type Rating, 233

U
U-space, xvii, 65, 77, 83, 126, 153, 166, 185-187, 198, 207, 259, 332
– airspace, xviii, 91
– service, 78, 196, 216
– services, 73-74, 192
U.S. Federal Aviation Administration (FAA), 9
UAS Integration Pilot Program (IPP), 113

UAS Service Suppliers (USS), 111
UAS test sites, 102, 118
UAS traffic management (UTM), 45, 119, 189, 331
UAS Type Certificate Holder, 246
UAS Type Design Holder, 247
unmanned aircraft systems (UAS), 12, 34, 229
Unmanned Traffic Management System (UTMS), 165, 334
urban air mobility, xviii, 15, 76, 126, 167, 186, 212, 217, 334
User-centric approach, 291
UTM Pilot Program (UPP), 119

V

V-1 (Vergeltungswaffe), 5
Vehicle to Infrastructure communication (V2I), 192
Vehicle to Vehicle communication (V2V), 192
Very Large Scale Demonstration (VLD), 190
very low-level airspace, 135
visual air risk mitigation (VARM), 78

Essential Air and Space Law (Series Editor: Marietta Benkö)

Volume 1: Natalino Ronzitti & Gabriella Venturini (eds.), The Law of Air Warfare – Contemporary Issues, ISBN 978-90-77596-14-2

Volume 2: Marietta Benkö & Kai-Uwe Schrogl (eds.), Space Law: Current Problems and Perspectives for Future Regulations, ISBN 978-90-77596-11-1

Volume 3: Tare Brisibe, Aeronautical Public Correspondence by Satellite, ISBN 978-90-77596-10-4

Volume 4: Michael Milde, International Air Law and ICAO, ISBN 978-90-77596-54-8

Volume 5: Markus Geisler & Marius Boewe, The German Civil Aviation Act, ISBN 978-90-77596-72-2

Volume 6: Ulrich Steppler & Angela Klingmüller, EU Emissions Trading Scheme and Aviation, ISBN 978-90-77596-79-1

Volume 7: Heiko van Schyndel (ed.), Aviation Code of the Russian Federation, ISBN 978-90-77596-80-7

Volume 8: Zang Hongliang & Meng Qingfen, Civil Aviation Law in the People's Republic of China, ISBN 978-90-77596-91-3

Volume 9: Ronald M. Schnitker & Dick van het Kaar, Aviation Accident and Incident Investigation. Concurrence of Technical, ISBN 978-94-90947-01-9

Volume 10: Michael Milde, International Air Law and ICAO, second edition, ISBN 978-90-90947-35-4

Volume 11: Ronald Schnitker & Dick van het Kaar, Safety Assessment of Foreign Aircraft Programme. A European Approach to Enhance Global Aviation Safety, ISBN 978-94-9094-793-4

Volume 12: Marietta Benkö & Engelbert Plescher, Space Law: Reconsidering the Definition/Delimitation Question and the Passage of Spacecraft through Foreign Airspace, ISBN 978-94-6236-076-1

Volume 13: Heiko van Schyndel (ed.), Aviation Code of the Russian Federation, second edition, ISBN 978-94-6236-433-2

Volume 14: Alejandro Piera Valdés, Greenhouse Gas Emissions from International Aviation: Legal and Policy Challenges, ISBN 978-94-6236-467-7

Volume 15: Peter Paul Fitzgerald, A Level Playing Field for "Open Skies": The Need for Consistent Aviation Regulation, ISBN 978-94-6236-625-1

Volume 16: Jae Woon Lee, Regional Liberalization in International Air Transport: Towards Northeast Asian Open Skies, ISBN 978-94-6236-688-6

Volume 17: Tanveer Ahmad, Climate Change Governance in International Civil Aviation: Toward Regulating Emissions Relevant to Climate Change and Global Warming, ISBN 978-94-6236-692-3

Volume 18: Michael Milde, International Air Law and ICAO, third edition, ISBN 978-94-6236-619-0

Volume 19: Nataliia Malysheva, Space Law and Policy in the Post-Soviet States, ISBN 978-94-6236-847-7

Volume 20: Philippe Clerc, Space Law in the European Context, ISBN 978-94-6236-797-5

Volume 21: Benjamyn Scott, Aviation Cybersecurity: Regulatory Approach in the European Union, ISBN 978-94-6236-961-0

Volume 22: Dick van het Kaar, International Civil Aviation: Treaties, Institutions and Programmes, ISBN 978-94-6236-972-6

Volume 23: Lasantha Hettiariachchi, International Air Transportation Association, ISBN 978-94-9094-758-3

Volume 24: Masataka Ogasawara & Joel Greer (eds.), Japan in Space, ISBN 978-94-6236-203-1

Volume 25: Ronald Schnitker & Dick van het Kaar, Drone Law and Policy, ISBN 978-94-6236-198-0